'Gifted Children' in Britain and the World

'Gifted Children' in Britain and the World

Elitism and Equality since 1945

JENNIFER CRANE

OXFORD
UNIVERSITY PRESS

OXFORD
UNIVERSITY PRESS

Great Clarendon Street, Oxford, OX2 6DP,
United Kingdom

Oxford University Press is a department of the University of Oxford.
It furthers the University's objective of excellence in research, scholarship,
and education by publishing worldwide. Oxford is a registered trade mark of
Oxford University Press in the UK and in certain other countries

© Jennifer Crane 2025

The moral rights of the author have been asserted

This is an open access publication, available online and distributed under the
terms of a Creative Commons Attribution-Non Commercial-No Derivatives 4.0
International licence (CC BY-NC-ND 4.0), a copy of which is available at
https://creativecommons.org/licenses/by-nc-nd/4.0/.
Subject to this licence, all rights are reserved.

Enquiries concerning reproduction outside the scope of this licence should be sent
to the Rights Department, Oxford University Press, at the address above.

Published in the United States of America by Oxford University Press
198 Madison Avenue, New York, NY 10016, United States of America

British Library Cataloguing in Publication Data

Data available

Library of Congress Control Number: 2024942666

ISBN 9780198928850

DOI: 10.1093/9780198928881.001.0001

Printed and bound by
CPI Group (UK) Ltd, Croydon, CR0 4YY

Links to third party websites are provided by Oxford in good faith and
for information only. Oxford disclaims any responsibility for the materials
contained in any third party website referenced in this work.

MIX
Paper | Supporting
responsible forestry
FSC® C013604

The manufacturer's authorised representative in the EU for product safety is
Oxford University Press España S.A. of El Parque Empresarial San Fernando
de Henares, Avenida de Castilla, 2 – 28830 Madrid (www.oup.es/en or product.safety@oup.com).
OUP España S.A. also acts as importer into Spain of products made by the manufacturer.

For ABC, EBC, and DBC

Contents

Introduction	1
Who was a 'gifted child' anyway?	5
Finding the 'gifted child'	9
Equal Elites?	13
Elites of 'the Future'	16
Voluntary Organisations	20
Family Activism	24
Children's Responses	27
Chapter Outline	31
Everyday Encounters with Stupidity and Intellect, 1944–1962	35
Post-war Breakdowns	36
(Some) Adults' Encounters with Intelligence and Stupidity	39
(Some) Children's Encounters with Intelligence and Stupidity	43
Contrast: America	46
Conclusion	54
Emergent Voluntary Action for Gifted Children, 1963–1969	56
Local Giftedness Experiments	57
Margaret Branch and Her National Association for Gifted Children	63
The National Association, Giftedness, and Disability	68
The House of Lords, Parliamentary Debates, and Further Limits of Equality	70
Conclusion	75
Young People's Engagement with Gifted Spaces, 1970–1987	79
Who Was Identified?	82
Why Did Parents Join?	85
New Opportunities?	92
Gifted Children	96
Rejecting Giftedness?	98
'She's a nice person but': Gifted Children on Their Teachers	103
Conclusion	106
Making Future Leaders: Psychology, Giftedness, and Legacies of Eugenics, 1970–1989	108
Psychology, Eugenics, and Giftedness	110
Tabloid Media and National Futures	114
The National Association for Gifted Children and Britain's Elites of the Future	121

Young People Engage with Leadership in 'the World'	126
Conclusion	130
Industrial and Industrious Future Elites, 1990–2010	**132**
Documenting 'Aspiration'	134
Identifying 'Gifted and Talented'	140
Experiencing the National Academy	146
Gifted Child Alumni	150
Conclusion	155
Gifted Children Saving 'Europe' and 'the World', 1975–2000	**157**
Founding the World Council	160
Gifted Children Save 'the World'!	165
Geographic Imaginaries	169
Gifted Children Can Save Europe!	175
What Did This Mean for the Gifted Young?	181
Conclusion	185
Conclusion	**189**
Think of the Children	193
Acknowledgements	199
Select Bibliography	203
Index	215

Introduction

In the Easter 1982 edition of the *Gallimaufry* magazine, designed for members of Britain's National Association for Gifted Children, an anonymous twelve-year-old told the story of Ogg, which unfurled rapidly over two hundred words in five rich paragraphs. Ogg, the child wrote, was very smart indeed, yet 'ugly and grotesque to look at'. This meant that he 'had trouble at school and at home'—his 'two normal brothers' wouldn't be seen with him, and teachers said he was 'too bright'. One day another boy came to live in the area. He was 'not as smart' as Ogg but 'nearly as ugly and grotesque to look at'. Ogg and this boy—Gil—spoke for some time and decided to 'overcome their problems of friends', engaging in the key tasks of life together; they would 'order everything from the shop and play and talk and work together'. The twelve-year-old closed their tale with a barely veiled moral lesson. Ogg, they stated, 'could have been a bank teller, an accountant, or even a politician. He did not waste his talents—the community wasted them for him.'[1]

In this story, a twelve-year-old reflected critically on the expectations put on gifted children and offered insight into the paths of resistance such children might have available to them. This book provides the first history and analysis of the construction of this group from the mid-twentieth century onwards.[2] *'Gifted Children' in Britain and the World* demonstrates that modern interest in the so-called 'gifted child' emerged in the late 1960s, due to concerted campaigning by voluntary organisations, who framed their work around embedding 'equality' in the post-war welfare state. Later, the distinct idea that gifted children would be 'elites of the future' was taken up powerfully in the 1970s and 1980s by the voluntary sector, as well as by clusters of policy-makers, journalists, psychologists, educationalists, and teachers, who posited that gifted children were critical to Britain's national and international successes. They were, as the National Association for Gifted Children and World Council for Gifted and Talented Children frequently

---

[1] National Association for Gifted Children Archives, Bletchley Park (hereafter NAGC Archives), *Gallimaufry*, Easter 1982, 'This is the story of Ogg', p. 2.
[2] For longer histories, see Sally Shuttleworth, *The Mind of the Child: Child Development in Literature, Science, and Medicine, 1840–1900* (Oxford: OUP, 2010); Claudia Nelson: *Precocious Children and Childish Adults: Age Inversion in Victorian Literature* (Baltimore, MD: John Hopkins University Press, 2012); Gillian Sutherland, *Ability, Merit and Measurement: Mental Testing and English Education, 1880–1940* (Oxford: OUP, 1984).

stated, both a 'national asset which we cannot afford to waste' and 'an invaluable global asset'.[3] Ideas of the gifted child as an elite of the future continued in subsequent decades, reflecting the changing anxieties and concerns of various periods. In the 1970s and 1980s, the gifted young could revive a flailing economy; in the late 1980s and 1990s, they could ameliorate the tensions of the Cold War; by the mid-to-late 1990s they would improve Britain's technological and scientific capacities and lead economic growth in the Global South. Indeed, these international hopes—constantly reiterated by groups discussed in this book—are the reason that it takes 'Britain and the world' in its title, to reflect these widely held, avid hopes that British children could restore not only national economic and social fortunes, but also global ones.[4]

From the late 1990s onwards, interest in the gifted young as elites of the future dissipated significantly, although rhetoric about 'the gifted child' remained. There was cultural, social, and political discomfort with the previous rhetoric of the gifted and their potential, particularly following the rise of educational sociology research demonstrating that children from minoritised ethnic backgrounds, poorer children, and girls were not being identified for gifted education programmes. Nonetheless, New Labour looked to celebrate all children's 'gifts' and 'talents' within broader programmes around 'equality' and 'inclusion', with cross-party support. While the framing of gifted child as symbol of equality continued, then, into the twenty-first century, many of the voluntary groups that initially drew this equivalence faded away. These voluntary groups, the book shows, had depended on the significant emotional labours of a few key individuals, often of the 'welfare state generation', who felt particularly invested in, and responsible for, civic action in this area.[5]

The book argues that this history matters. It is important—and hugely troubling—to recognise that ideas of 'the gifted child', 'elites', and 'leaders' were consistently primarily coded as white, male, and upper class. Affluent white boys were overidentified as 'gifted' in schools, by newspapers, by parents, and by

---

[3] NAGC, *Annual Report 1971–2*, p. 1; Bodleian Library, Joy Gibson and Prue Chennells (eds), *Gifted Children: Looking to their Future* (Essex: The Anchor Press, 1976), p. ii.

[4] Hugely useful discussion of the emergence, power, and limitations of this term in: Tehila Sasson, James Vernon, Miles Ogborn, Priya Satia, and Catherine Hall, 'Britain and the world: a new field?', *Journal of British Studies*, 57 (2018), pp. 677–708; this also references: Miles Ogborn, *Global Lives: Britain and the World* (Cambridge: CUP, 2008); *Britain and the World* journal. On the challenges of comparative history, see: Chris Lorenz, 'Comparative historiography: problems and perspectives,' *History and Theory*, 38 (1) (1999), pp. 25–39; Jurgen Kocka, 'Comparison and beyond', *History and Theory*, 42 (1) (2003), pp. 39–44; Michael Werner and Bénédicte Zimmermann. 'Beyond comparison: Histoire croisée and the challenge of reflexivity', *History and Theory*, 45 (1) (2006), pp. 30–50; Susanna Delfino, Marcus Graser, Hans Krabbendam, and Vincent Michelot, 'Europeans writing American history: the comparative trope', *American Historical Review*, 119 (3) (2014), pp. 791–799; Philippa Levine, 'Is comparative history possible?', *History and Theory*, 53 (2014), pp. 331–347.

[5] Eve Worth, *The Welfare State Generation: Women, Agency and Class in Britain since 1945* (London: Bloomsbury, 2021).

voluntary groups. This continued despite the significant efforts of the National Association and other voluntary organisations to insist that gifted children could come from 'any' background and to couch their work as part of constructing an 'equal' post-war society. This shows then the need to pay close attention to the invocations of 'equality' in modern history and contemporary society. Voluntary efforts to find gifted children from diverse populations could not always overcome the structural privilege entwined with and embedded in cultural and social assumptions around what 'high potential' and 'gifted' children might (or 'should') look like. The constant refrain that giftedness programmes of all forms could support 'equality' entailed a variety of interpretations: equality as ensuring all children, even those privileged in many ways, received special attention from the state; equality as allowing equal access to giftedness programmes; or equality as selecting a representative sample of young people for selective education. These ideas occurred again and again in the voluntary archives centred here, and yet also in such disparate source-bases as the Opie Archives and Mass Observation, archiving writings from the 1940s and 1950s, and online discussions of the 2010s and 2020s.

This story also matters because it helps to disrupt simple narratives of post-war British history as a shift from social democracy to neoliberalism. Analysing the rise and fall of concern about 'the gifted' from 1945 onwards shows there was no 'equal' or 'universal' welfare state. Even hugely privileged groups felt excluded by the late 1940s and in to the 1950s—gifted young people were elites of the future but, their own writings also show, also often profoundly unhappy. This led their families—typically their parents—to feel let down by a 'universal' welfare state that did not, they believed, cater for them. Yet these parents often responded relatively conservatively, by the 1960s: not by demanding significant change, but by providing extra resources themselves, collectively replacing state action. The rise of neoliberalism in the 1970s and 1980s, similarly, was not 'new'; interest in popular individualism, in this case encouraging young people to see themselves as 'elite', emerged out of the 1960s advent of leisure spaces for the gifted. By the 1990s and 2000s, children were increasingly measured, ranked, and compared as 'gifted', or not; and yet state measurement of the self was tempered by youth resistance. Analysis of international giftedness groups, likewise, shows that attempts to use children as global diplomats continued into the end of the twentieth century, in new form; these did not decline with the Cold War. Overarching—and simplistic—chronologies are then easily complicated by new histories of daily life, as mediated through national and international voluntary organisations.

This book encompasses analysis of the historical activities of the National Association for Gifted Children (its main case study), as well as the National Academy for Gifted and Talented Youth, the European Council for High Ability, the World Council for Gifted and Talented Children, Mensa's Foundation for Gifted Children, and the American Association for Gifted Children. These groups were all relatively small and yet were at times able to persuade significant clusters of policy-makers, press, and publics that they should all care about identifying the gifted young in order to address issues of economic decline, social relations, global competition, and humanitarianism. This finding speaks to a recent historiographical assumption that large, professionalised voluntary groups were significant in shaping opinion in the closing decades of the twentieth century. Rather, this book also contends that parents, families, and communities were also central to building the voluntary sector in the mid-to-late twentieth century, and thus in turn very powerful in shaping debates about the future, elitism, and equality. Parents were central members of the National Association for Gifted Children, and formed its work and demands through regional branches, campaigns, and the provision of weekend and holiday courses for the young. The activism of these families was specific to the late 1960s to late 1980s, mobilising the politics of experiential expertise growing in this period, and media interest in family life, but in a very different way to parallel social movements such as feminism and gay liberation. This kind of familial action has not been sufficiently examined or documented, yet it demonstrates the extent to which languages of emotion and experience reshaped activisms in the mid-to-late twentieth century.

Overall, a key argument of this book is that children and young people had highly engaged and critical responses to these largescale debates. Young people questioned the current educational system, metrics used to judge 'intelligence', the need for and structure of family life, and how voluntary groups and summer and afterschool clubs were run and organised. The critique of the young around these areas often preceded adult debate—young people, for example, immediately questioned definitions of 'intelligence' in early National Association newsletters, preceding significant debates in educational sociology and psychology of the 1980s and 1990s about the racism and sexism in psychological testing. The vignette of Ogg, with which this chapter opened, was by no means unusual. The lively critique of children, from when they could first write to voluntary groups or speak to interested press, is as important as the social history of any group.[6] Children's radicalism also illuminates the tactically neutral statements of parent-activists in these groups, who were careful to frame giftedness as separate from arguments about elitism and equality engulfing mainstream education. These arguments demonstrate the critical import of including young people in our social histories and geographies: despite recent scholarly critique of the history of childhood in particular, discussed below, their perspectives must be found and analysed.

[6] Hester Barron, Ewen Green Lecture from Hester Barron on 'Why schools matter to histories of interwar Britain', <https://www.youtube.com/watch?v=T6gl6kYmOOw> (22 February 2023). See also: Hester Barron, *The Social World of the School: Education and Community in Interwar London* (Manchester: MUP, 2022).

Who was a 'gifted child' anyway?

A central premise of this book is that the concept of 'the gifted child' was highly flexible. Indeed, this flexibility enabled voluntary groups to mobilise it effectively, interesting a range of policy-makers and press.

The National Association offered an expansive definition of giftedness. The group accepted referrals from 'heads of schools, teachers, educational psychologists, doctors, health visitors, social workers and others professionally interested' and also enabled parents to self-define their children before signing up—no formal testing was involved.[7] In a 1989 guide intended to advise parents, *Help with Bright Children*, the organisation stated that parents may recognise some—though not all—'sorts of behaviour' in their gifted young, including walking or talking 'early' or 'too much', asking questions, taking the lead, and quickly grasping new ideas.[8] The Association's list of signs was extensive: gifted children may pay 'extraordinary attention to detail' but they may also lose interest in tasks easily; they may have 'never needed much' but they may also be 'very demanding' with 'great physical and mental energy'.[9] These vague and somewhat contradictory definitions reflected the fact that the organisation hoped to support parents, whom they wrote, in 1978, were 'seldom wrong' in asking for further support, rather than to critique their systems of identification.[10]

The National Association was cautious about IQ testing, writing that such tests were perhaps 'the best *single* predictor of academic achievement that we have', yet also 'not particularly good predictors' nor 'very accurate measures of intellectual ability'.[11] While not central to the voluntary sector, psychological testing of intelligence was a significant framework for debate around giftedness in the mid-to-late twentieth century. Psychological testing underlay the 11+ test, determining, in many areas, which children would go to academically rigorous grammar schools and which would go to secondary moderns.[12] Some local education authorities screened even younger children in their area with verbal and non-verbal

---

[7] Institute of Education, London, SCC/1030/1037/1037/608, 'National Association of Gifted Children—Proposal to make a film', 1978–9, 'The film "Gifted Children" (1976)', 12 March 1978, p. 1.
[8] NAGC, *Help with Bright Children* (London: NAGC, 1989), p. 3.   [9] Ibid., p. 3.
[10] Institute of Education, London, SCC/1030/1037/1037/608, 'National Association of Gifted Children—Proposal to make a film', 1978–9, 'The film "Gifted Children" (1976)', 12 March 1978, p. 1.
[11] *Help with Bright Children*, p. 16.
[12] On intelligence testing in education, before and after the 1944 *Education Act*, see: Adrian Wooldridge, *Measuring the Mind: Education and Psychology in England, c. 1860–c. 1990* (Cambridge: CUP, 1994), pp. 251–252, 257–258 (pp. 257–258 states that: 'A National Union of Teachers survey of selection in 1947 revealed that, of the 106 LEAs who bothered to respond, seventy-eight used some kind of standardised intelligence test and nearly all used examinations in English and arithmetic. By 1952 almost all LEAs had incorporated an intelligence test into their selection exams'). On the 1944 Act, specifically, see: Peter Mandler, *The Crisis of the Meritocracy: Britain's Transition to Mass Education since the Second World War* (Oxford: OUP, 2020), ch. 3.

reasoning tests.[13] Some parents also took their children to private providers. Yet, at educational conferences of the 1970s, local education authority representatives were cautious about the fallibility of IQ testing and indeed about a precise definition of the term, 'gifted': one report stated that 'much time could be wasted' doing so, and also that children should not be 'singled out for a battery of tests' due to 'parental expectations' and 'pressure'.[14] Interest in IQ testing nonetheless circulated in contemporary media, with journalists in this period taking themselves or their children to be tested and reporting back, or using popular guides in the home, acting, as Mathew Thomson has described, as 'psychological subjects' in the spread of popular psychology.[15]

Critically, these background ideas about intelligence, which bolstered general interest in the voluntary groups in this book, were shaped by psychological testing that could be sexist and racist. IQ tests created in the early twentieth century and interwar period were normed around white boys, and contained cultural terms less appropriate for assessing Black and minoritised ethnic children.[16] For example, IQ tests asked about forms of cutlery more prominently used in white Western households.[17] This had profound and terrible effects, placing a disproportionate number of Black children into special needs education, which limited their opportunities across the life course. Rob Waters found that by 1967, African-Caribbean children represented 15 per cent of the Inner London Education Authority's primary and secondary school pupils, but 28 per cent of pupils in special needs schools.[18] Racist and sexist cultural assumptions pervaded school

---

[13] For example, writing for the journal of the National Association in 1979, Congdon described how all children in North Warwickshire were being screened for IQ between the ages of 8 and 9 (Peter J. Congdon, 'How North Warwickshire identifies gifted children', *Journal of the Gifted Child*, Autumn 1979, p. 68).

[14] Institute of Education, London, SCC/555/1152/049, Gifted Pupils—Identification and Provision—Policy and Finance, 1979–1983, Provision for Gifted Children, DES Invitation Conference N522, 19–23 November 1979, Conference Report, p. 2.

[15] Mathew Thomson, *Psychological Subjects: Identity, Culture, and Health in Twentieth-Century Britain* (Oxford: OUP, 2006).

[16] This is acknowledged in: Institute of Education, London, SCC/555/1152/049, Gifted Pupils—Identification and Provision—Policy and Finance, 1979–1983, Provision for Gifted Children, DES Invitation Conference N522, 19–23 November 1979, Conference Report, p. 8; Institute of Education, London, SCC/555/1152/049, Gifted Pupils—Identification and Provision—Policy and Finance, 1979–1983, Provision for Gifted Children, 'File Note: Note of a visit to Surrey LEA on 26 June 1980', p. 1.

[17] See for example Bodleian, Lewis M. Terman, *Test Material for The Measurement of Intelligence* (London: George G. Harrap & Company Ltd, 1919); L. M. Terman, E. L. Thorndike, G. M. Whipple and R. M. Yerkes, National Intelligence Tests, Scale A—Form 2, (London: George G Harrap & Co Ltd, 1921).

[18] Rob Waters, *Thinking Black: Britain, 1964–1985* (University of California Press, 2019), p. 130. Mathew Thomson also notes that the Inner London Education Authority had a disproportionate number of immigrant children in schools for the educationally subnormal: five had over 30% immigrant children in 1967, and by 1968, one had 60%; by 1970, 17% of children in ILEA schools were from immigrant backgrounds, compared to 34% in special needs schools—and 80% of these were West Indian (Mathew Thomson, *Lost Freedom: The Landscape of the Child and the British post-war Settlement* (Oxford: OUP, 2013), p. 199).

environments more broadly from the 1960s to the 1980s, which meant that minoritised ethnic and female children were far less likely to feel comfortable speaking in classrooms and far less likely to be brought forward for assessment as 'gifted'. Subsequent gaps in performance were often blamed on ideas of behaviour or social and emotional 'adjustment', or on language gaps, rather than on systematic failure of assessments. This is visible in analysis of contemporary teaching materials, and also contemporary critique from, for example, trade unions.[19] The lived impact of racism in British schools was also made visible, in the late 1950s to 1970s, by powerful autobiographical accounts, for example Dillibe Onyeama's *Black Boy at Eton* (1972) and Beryl Gilroy's *Black Teacher* (1976).[20] Demonstrative of the pervasiveness of racism of this period, one review of Gilroy's book, by another teacher, published in *Times Educational Supplement*, asked, 'Can the publishers seriously ask that the book should be taken to heart by educationists and parents?'[21]

It is important to acknowledge the ways in which these same ideas about intelligence and intelligence testing also had profound and damaging ramifications for children with learning disabilities or delays in the twentieth century. Rubahanna Amannah Choudhury has analysed the campaigning of The Association of Parents of Backward Children (later The National Association for Mentally Handicapped Children, then Mencap) in this regard. This group was founded in 1946 by Judy Fryd. Fryd had taken her two-year-old daughter to a Child Guidance Clinic for assessment, after some concerns that 'something was not quite right' with her language and communication. After a brief assessment, the test

---

[19] Sources discussing racism in classrooms in this period include: MRC, 937/3/14/1, Universities & Left Review, no.5, Autumn 1958. 'The habit of violence'; MRC, 601/R/24/49, Marina Maxwell, 'Violence in the toilets: The experience of a black teacher in Brent schools', [1969]; MRC, MSS.639/11/43/5, 'National Union of Teachers Memorandum of Evidence submitted to Commonwealth Immigrants Advisory Council', 1963; MRC, NUT/6/7/Ra/4, National Union of Teachers, The N. U. T. View on the Education of Immigrants, 1967. Sources discussing sexism in classrooms in this period include: MRC, NSH/5/5/80, National Association of Schoolmasters, Men teachers for junior schools, 1950, pp. 3, 5–6. This argument was reiterated by the Association in MRC, NSH/5/5/77, National Association of Schoolmasters, Sex as a fundamental factor in education, 1950. Co-education is also questioned by the Association of Assistant Headmistresses into the 1960s, see: MRC, AAM/P/3/20, Association of Assistant Headmistresses, 'Conference on women and girls in co-educational schools', 1968. Examples of attempts to combat these stereotypes are: MRC, EOC/2/7/9, Equal Opportunities Commission, 'Ending sex-stereotyping in schools: A sourcebook for school-based teacher workshops', 1981; MRC, EOC/2/7/19, 'Letters to a thirteen year old—from members of the YWCA girl apprentice courses 1983–84, 1985; MRC, NUT/6/7/G/9, 'Towards equality for girls and boys: guidelines on countering sexism in schools', [c1989]. See also: MRC, MSS.639/11/65/6, National Union of Teachers, 'An enquiry into the education of pupils between the ages of 13 and 16 of average or less than average ability', May 1962. See also Laura Tisdall, *A Progressive Education? How Childhood Changed in Mid-twentieth-century* (Manchester: MUP, 2020) on the able-bodied, white, male model of the 'ideal' school student.

[20] Dillibe Onyeama, *A Black Boy at Eton* (Reprinted edition, London: Penguin, 2022); Beryl Gilroy, *Black Teacher* (Reprinted edition, London: Faber, 2021).

[21] 'To Miss…with love', *Times Educational Supplement*, 27 August 1976, p. 16; see also 'Beryl Gilroy's *Black Teacher*', British Library: Windrush Stories, <https://www.bl.uk/windrush/articles/woman-version-beryl-gilroys-black-teacher> (25 October 2023).

supervisor, Fryd wrote, 'gave her [daughter] an IQ of 43 and wrote her off.'[22] Fryd subsequently established her organisation, and brought together parents whose children, as a result of labelling and intelligence testing, were receiving inadequate provision often, for example, as they were excluded from local education authority responsibility under the 1944 *Education Act*, and subsequently had to either be home schooled, placed in psychiatric institutions, or their parents had to find funds for special education.[23] Despite campaigning in this area, by Mencap and other organisations, it was not until the *Education (Handicapped Children) Act* of 1970 that education authorities would be responsible for educating *all* children, regardless of any disability.[24] In the intervening years, parents shared experiences with Fryd and her group of 'isolation, exclusion, and professional and social prejudice'.[25]

Building on broader discrimination in education and society, then, the label 'gifted' was entwined with ideas of a white, male, able, middle-class child. Clémentine Beauvais has demonstrated that this was also the case in popular culture, describing how the 1988 Roald Dahl novel, *Matilda*, presents giftedness as 'not just the property of an individual "lucky" child, but also a property of its rightful social category, the middle class'.[26] Voluntary groups mobilising around this issue were also often dominated by white, middle-class parents. Presenting the gifted child as a powerful future figure was then powerful partly because it built on a longer history of sexist and racist assumptions about who was fit for national leadership, and about healthy, productive children as not merely 'a precursor to a strong empire, but to international economic prosperity and political stability'.[27] These contexts fundamentally structured the campaigning of adults and children, even if many felt they were merely agitating for change in their own lives, without thinking about broader contexts, or barely interacting with this label beyond attending a few summer courses or afterschool clubs.

---

[22] D. Cohen, 'Judy Fryd: they told me my child had no mind', *The Telegraph* (23/08/1996), as cited in Rubahanna Amannah Choudhury, 'The forgotten children: The Association of Parents of Backward Children and the Legacy of Eugenics in Britain, 1946–1960', thesis submitted for the Degree of Doctor of Philosophy at Oxford Brookes University, December 2015, p. 21.

[23] On broader contexts, see Anne Borsay, 'Disabled children and special education, 1944–1981', *History & Policy*, 26 November 2012 <https://www.historyandpolicy.org/docs/dfe-anne-borsay-text.pdf> (26 March 2024); Anne Borsay and Pamela Dale (eds), *Disabled Children: Contested Caring, 1850–1979* (Milton: Routledge, 2016); David Kilgannon, 'Public attention for private concerns: intellectual disability parents' organisations in the Republic of Ireland, 1955–1970', *Medical Humanities*, 46 (2020), pp. 483–491.

[24] On other groups campaigning in this area, see, Choudhury, 'The forgotten children', pp. 29–31.

[25] Choudhury, 'The forgotten children', p. 23, 64.

[26] Clémentine Beauvais, 'Child giftedness as class weaponry: the case of Roald Dahl's Matilda', *Children's Literature Association Quarterly*, 40 (3) (2015), pp. 277–293. Beauvais argues that the Wormwoods are a 'materialistic petty bourgeois family', but that Matilda is positioned as 'somehow, always already middle class'; the reader is invited to criticise Matilda's family on this basis (pp. 282–283).

[27] Emily Baughan, 'History and humanitarianism: a conversation', *Past & Present*, 241 (1) (2018), p. e3.

Adults emphasised that they were merely providing additional resources for their own children, who were in distress, and also highlighted the import of identifying working-class, inner city, and Black and minoritised ethnic children as 'gifted'; these strategies can be seen as forms of indirect engagement with the legacies of biased ideas of 'giftedness'. Children often engaged more directly with the biases of this term: young people studied in this book, for example, questioned the accuracy of measurements and metrics around intelligence, and also, radically, whether adults should aim to make children 'happy' rather than 'intelligent'.

This case study then, reveals how labels have the power to both cause damage within broader systems of structural discrimination, and to collectively mobilise people through a new identity and articulation of their distinct experiences.[28] The biases ingrained in ideas of 'giftedness' structured the campaigning studied here, but this is also a history of children's activism, and of how the young—even when standing to benefit—may respond more critically to systems of power and privilege than adults. Studying how different groups examined have responded to, and acknowledged, their privilege, constitutes part of the critical academic project of interrogating our own position in systems of power.[29] In this case, young people often used the troubling label 'gifted', with its links to discriminatory historical systems, to 'destabilise privilege and re-imagine spatialised power relations'.[30]

Finding the 'gifted child'

Locating and listening to the voices of gifted children is central to this book's methodology. As Carolyn Steedman has demonstrated, most children were increasingly invited to grow through 'self-expression', and to create autobiographical outputs in general, from the post-war period onwards.[31] This text contends that such interest heightened in the 1970s and 1980s with regards to gifted children, in particular, and that voluntary organisations played a key role in asking gifted children to document and record their lives. Indeed, these organisations and others interested in giftedness claimed that this was significant work,

---

[28] On the responsibility to our research subjects, as found in the archives, and to reading and preserving their stories thoughtfully, see: Kate Boyer, 'Feminist geography in the archive: practice and method', WGSG, *Geography and Gender Reconsidered*, August 2004, p. 170; Sarah Mills, 'Cultural-historical geographies of the archive: fragments, objects and ghosts', *Geography Compass*, 7 (10) (2013), p. 708. For a fascinating case study of another educational label, see: Philip Kirby and Margaret J. Snowling, *Dyslexia: A History* (Montreal, Quebec: McGill-Queen's University Press, 2022).
[29] For important recent scholarship on this that also traces how calls for this reflection have been made, and not always heard, see: Janine Wiles, 'Health geographies 1: unlearning privilege', *Progress in Human Geography*, 46 (1) (2021), pp. 215–223.
[30] Ibid., p. 220.
[31] Carolyn Steedman, 'State-sponsored autobiography', in *Moments of Modernity? Reconstructing Britain, 1945–64*, ed. B. E. Conekin, F. Mort, and C. Waters (London, 1999), p. 52.

assuming that the gifted young were elites of the future. This was exemplified by a headteacher, quoted by the National Association for Gifted Children in 1979, who stated that the inner thoughts of gifted children represented a 'magic land', which one could access if one was 'patient'.[32] This headteacher reported encouraging gifted children to write, pushing them to produce poetry, and to obtain the 'muscular maturity' to enable them to 'put thoughts easily on to paper.'[33] Such life-writing diminished by the late 1990s onwards, as the somewhat chaotic, localised spaces of voluntary groups like the National Association were replaced by more formal programmes in schools. The 'success' of these groups, then, in bringing public attention to giftedness, also later led to the downfall of young people's ability to offer radical critique through writing.

The informal archives of the National Association for Gifted Children provide a key source for this investigation. These archives are kept uncatalogued in the office of the group's successor organisation, Potential Plus, and have never been fully analysed by researchers before.[34] Kate Boyer has written thoughtfully about the challenges of accessing non-public archives and warns that archives, which are 'non-public', have been filtered by organisational capacity and preferences; yet nonetheless they may also provide access to 'worlds otherwise unknown or lost'.[35] The National Association archives included a range of published newsletters edited by adults but written by children, and letters from parents, children's poetry, accounts of children's summer camps and leisure activities, and professional magazines and trade publications. Poetry, letters, drawings, and descriptions of playground games were also found in newsletters, publications, and archives from the American Association for Gifted Children, the World Council for Gifted Children, the Opie schools project, and in various contemporary newspapers. The National Association materials from the 1970s and 1980s are particularly rich and vibrant. This organisation catered to children from birth to eighteen, and enabled the young to define themselves as 'children', 'young', 'youth', or 'teenagers'; this book consciously follows this approach, looking to let young people in these sources define their own relationships with ideas of 'childlikeness'. Understanding of the contexts in which these voluntary groups operated, and their significance and networks, has been augmented through supplemental

---

[32] Bodleian Library, Per 264505 e. 4, National Association for Gifted Children, *Journal of the Gifted Child*, Autumn 1979, 'The highly gifted child', Phyllis Wallbank, p. 70.

[33] Ibid., p. 71.   [34] Boyer, 'Feminist geography', p. 172.

[35] Ibid, pp. 172–173. Fannin and MacLeavy remind us, also, that, in the same way, archives which have been catalogued—in their case writing about Feminist Archive South—have been entangled with 'forces of domination and oppression', Maria Fannin and Julie MacLeavy, 'Feminism, Resistance and the Archive', in Sarah M. Hughes (ed.) *Critical Geographies of Resistance* (Cheltenham: Edward Elgar, 2023),p. 31. See also: Andrew Flinn, 'Archival activism: independent and community-led archives, radical public history and the heritage professions', *Interactions: UCLA Journal of Education and Information Studies*, 7 (2) (2011); Tim Cresswell, 'Value, gleaning and the archive at Maxwell Street, Chicago', *Transactions of the Institute of British Geographers*, 37 (1) (2012), pp. 164–176; Mills, 'Cultural-historical geographies of the archive', pp. 709–710.

analysis of materials written by medical professionals, teachers, policy-makers, and journalists, stored across physical and digital archives.[36]

Looking to resist, as far as possible, 'the potential violence of speaking for others', sources written by children are read through reference to recent scholarly literature, particularly from historians and geographers around 'agency'.[37] Critically, such literature emphasises that scholars should not simply look to 'rescue' the agency of marginalised groups from our sources, desperately looking for any indication of voice as the endpoint of our study and then presenting ourselves as 'saviours'.[38] We must recognise that children and young people exercise influence in daily life—sometimes in public life but always also simply by living and existing within social structures in what Kathryn Gleadle has called the 'parochial' realm; young people contribute constantly to discussions and debate in 'the world of the neighbourhood, workplace, or acquaintance networks'.[39] As Harry Hendrick has similarly argued, children 'cannot but be active in history, if only in the sense of how they deal with their daily situations'.[40]

As Tatek Abebe has written, young people's agency must be seen in relation to the contexts in which they lived: their position in families, communities, and the world.[41] The agency of young people in these sources was exercised in relation to that of adults. Indeed, an adult curated these children's magazines, deciding which letters to publish and which to leave private, thus shaping what the

---

[36] Archives consulted included Cambridge University Archives, Cambridge; National Archives, London; Liverpool University Special Collections and Archives, Liverpool; Wellcome Collection Archives, London, Institute of Education Archives, London; Modern Records Centre, Coventry; Borthwick Institute for Archives, York; Mass Observation Archives, Brighton; Bodleian Library, Oxford; and the American Association for Gifted Children archives. Additional digital databases used included archives of *The Times, Guardian, Independent, Factiva, Times Educational Supplement*, British Newspaper Archives, Parliamentary Papers, Opie, and Race Today. Huge thanks to all archivists and technicians involved in setting up and maintaining these wonderful collections.

[37] Boyer, 'Feminist geography', p. 170.

[38] In influential examples from early women's history see, for example: Sheila Rowbotham, *Hidden from History* (London: Pluto Press, 1990); Gerda Lerner, 'Placing Women in history: a 1975 perspective', *Feminist Studies* 3 (1975), pp. 5–14; Chris Millard, 'Using personal experience in the academic medical humanities: a genealogy', *Social Theory & Health*, 18 (2019), pp. 184–198; Mona Gleason, 'Avoiding the agency trap: Caveats for historians of children, youth, and education', *History of Education*, 45 (4) (2016), pp. 446–459; Lynn M. Thomas, 'Historicising agency', *Gender & History*, 28 (2) (2016), pp. 324–339; Susan A. Miller, 'Assent as agency in the early years of the children of the American Revolution', *Journal of the History of Childhood and Youth*, 9 (1) (2016), pp. 48–65; Tatek Abebe, 'Reconceptualising children's agency as continuum and interdependence', *Social Sciences*, 8 (3) (2019), pp. 1–16; Sarah L. Holloway, Louise Holt, and Sarah Mills, 'Questions of agency: Capacity, subjectivity, spatiality and temporality', *Progress in Human Geography*, 43 (3) (2018), pp. 458–477; Craig Jeffrey, 'Geographies of children and youth II: global youth agency', *Progress in Human Geography*, 36 (2) (2011), pp. 245–253. See also the classic article: Walter Johnson, 'On agency', *Journal of Social History*, 37 (1) (2003), pp. 113–124.

[39] Kathryn Gleadle, *Borderline Citizens: Women, Gender and Political Culture in Britain, 1815–1867* (Oxford: OUP, 2009), p. 17.

[40] Harry Hendrick, 'The Child as a social actor in historical sources: Problems of identification and interpretation', in Pia Christensen and Allison James (eds) *Research with Children: Perspectives and Practices* (London, 2008), p. 46.

[41] Abebe, 'Reconceptualising children's agency', pp. 1–16.

children would encounter in each magazine issue. Children's very membership of the National Association and other voluntary groups, and their attendance at summer schools and afterschool clubs, depended on finance and logistical co-ordination from parents, providing space, time, and resources to write to the National Association, or to attend a summer course. Symbolically, indeed, to civil servants in November 1990, the National Association was a 'parents' organisation'.[42] This means, significantly, that the child-produced sources with which this book engages, as Siân Pooley has argued, can be used to substantiate *both* adult values and those of the young.[43] While recognising the critical role of adults in shaping these children's writings, they also represent young people's views: 'how boys and girls interpreted themselves when they thought they were children', and how young people 'composed their authorial selves in their writings.'[44]

Two critical messages emerge from analysing children's writings in this framework of agency. First, that many young people resisted the label 'gifted', while others ardently and passionately engaged with it. As Susan A. Miller has written, assent to prevailing social systems could represent agency, as much as dissent.[45] This is important because many scholarly accounts focus on children's agency as *dissent*: protests, lawsuits, skipping school, or engaging in crime.[46] This is particularly the case in accounts of youth culture from the 1960s, which frequently focus on juvenile delinquency, gangs, and sexual cultures.[47] Yet young people could also embrace the status quo—in this case, systems of education, family life, and a voluntary sector in which they were labelled as special.

---

[42] National Archives, Kew, ED 183/331, 'Provision for gifted children: correspondence with MENSA', 1990–1991, 'Meeting with officers of Mensa', 22 November 1990, p. 1.

[43] Siân Pooley, 'Children's writing and the popular press in England, 1876–1914', *History Workshop Journal*, 80 (1) (2015), pp. 75–98. See also: Christopher Hilliard, *To Exercise Our Talents: the Democratization of Writing in Britain* (Cambridge MA: HUP, 2006).

[44] Pooley, 'Children's writing', pp. 75–98.

[45] Miller, 'Assent as agency'. Harriet Cameron and Tom Billington have offered a case study of how young people exercise agency over psychological and educational labels, with reference to dyslexia. Analysing two focus groups, they found that students renegotiated this term, both looking to escape 'accusations of moral and intellectual inferiority' but also to police those who did not themselves cohere to their definitions of the category (Harriet Cameron and Tom Billington, 'The discursive construction of dyslexia by students in higher education as a moral and intellectual good', *Disability & Society*, 30 (8) (2015), pp. 1229–1237.)

[46] Michael Grossberg, 'Liberation and caretaking: fighting over children's rights in postwar America', in Paula Fass and Michael Grossberg (eds), *Reinventing Childhood After World War II* (Philadelphia, PA, 2012) p. 21; Stephen Humphries, *Hooligans or Rebels?: An Oral History of Working-Class Childhood and Youth 1889–1939* (2nd edition, Oxford, 1997), p. 1; Linda Mahood, *Policing Gender, Class and Family: Britain, 1850–1940* (London, 1995), pp. 112–115.

[47] See for example the following important and useful accounts of this terrain: Angela Bartie, 'Moral panics and Glasgow gangs: exploring "the new wave of Glasgow hooliganism", 1965–1970', *Contemporary British History*, 24 (2010), pp. 385–406; Bill Osgerby, 'The good, the bad and the ugly: postwar media representations of youth', in Adam Briggs and Paul Cobley, eds., *The media: An Introduction* (Harlow: Longman, 1997); discussions in Helena Mills, 'The experience and memory of youth in England c. 1960–c. 1969' (unpublished D.Phil. thesis, Oxford, 2016).

A second key message that emerges from this analysis of children's accounts, in relation to those of adults, is that young people identified as 'gifted' were expected to live a specific model of disruptive selfhood in the 1970s and 1980s. At this point, their critique of ideas of 'giftedness'—sought out in opportunities for writing—could be absorbed within a model of the gifted self as uniquely disruptive, in a playful, experimental, 'childlike' way.[48] Throughout, this book shows that critique made by gifted children themselves were shared in giftedness magazines and publications, but rarely fully absorbed into the policy of the voluntary organisations involved. Indeed, critique by young people was often presented by adults (particularly voluntary groups and interested press) as proof of their precociousness, rather than taken seriously. This is significant: as Laura Tisdall has argued, histories of childhood make clear that age can be 'a category of oppression in its own right'. Despite the fact that children labelled gifted in these groups were typically privileged in multiple ways—often from white, middle-class homes, and with parents invested in their education and development—conceptions of their age, as we see throughout this book, meant that they were often taken less seriously than adults.[49] Here, this work takes the voices of children seriously, and seeks to represent them in their own terms; it provides a social history 'from below' of gifted youth, and one which is attentive to how 'agency', as Craig Jeffrey argues, is always marked by distinct spatial and temporal variation.[50]

Equal Elites?

From close analysis of the gifted child, this book contends that gifted children were represented as symbols of both equality and elitism, with hugely different definitions attached, throughout the mid-to-late twentieth century. In the 1940s, policy-makers and teachers considering gifted provision feared that this threatened the 'equality' of the post-war school system. In the 1960s, voluntary organisations and parents, campaigning for more resources to be directed to gifted youth, framed their work as a matter of 'equality', insisting that this group was disadvantaged, unable to learn, and required further support and attention. Yet these organisations often also used the language of 'elite', and referred to gifted children as 'gold' or a 'top 2 per cent'. By the 1970s and 1980s, tabloid press argued that gifted youth were not provided for in the welfare state and that, therefore, broader aims of 'equality' in Britain had failed; a change of ideology, government, and focus was needed, they argued, as well as a reconsideration of broader

---

[48] On 'spirited mischief and irreverence' more broadly see: Craig Jeffrey, 'Geographies of children and youth II', *Progress in Human Geography*, 36 (2) (2012), pp. 250–251.

[49] Laura Tisdall, 'State of the field: The modern history of childhood', *History*, 107 (378) (2022), p. 957.

[50] Jeffrey, 'Geographies of children and youth II', p. 246.

'equalities' movements such as second-wave feminism. Otherwise, these 'elites', and their potential in reviving the national economy, would be "wasted"'. For a certain group of psychologists and media with eugenicist ties or echoes, meanwhile, such children must be identified as 'elites' with 'natural' capacities of leadership. By the 1990s and 2000s, gifted children were again intended to form part of New Labour's provision for an 'equal Britain', perhaps more through individual 'aspiration' to become elite leaders in industry and science.

The specific terms 'equality', 'elitism', 'equal', and 'elites' were echoed across my examination of multiple archives, by parents, children themselves, voluntary leaders, politicians, and press: so much so that this book's subtitle had to echo these insistent refrains (rather than related terms, less often found in my specific sources, such as 'meritocracy' or 'democracy').[51] Does this matter? Potentially, this observation merely echoes important arguments already made by Ruth Levitas: that words (in her case, 'inclusion') are used fuzzily and inconsistently by politicians and press.[52] Beyond this, however, the rhetorical emphasis on equality and elitism merits three further comments. First, that debates around 'elites' and 'equality' were somewhat distinct to Britain. This point is most powerfully made in Chapter Six, which analyses the twentieth-century work of two voluntary groups not situated in Britain: the European Council for High Ability and the World Council for Gifted and Talented Children. The World Council, when first founded and based in London with British leaders, framed its arguments strongly around 'elites' and 'equality'. In later years, however, and in the European group, these framings were notably less common; rather, these groups sought to conceptualise 'Europe' and 'the world', and how gifted young people could reshape these geographic imaginaries.

A second point is about the chronology of British history in the mid-to-late twentieth century. A classic analysis of Britain in the mid-to-late twentieth century would chart the rise of social democracy and the welfare state from the 1940s, and the challenge of these settlements and their decline with the election of Margaret Thatcher in 1979 and the emergence of neoliberalism. In recent years, historians have challenged such a smooth narrative.[53] This book contributes

---

[51] These terms have been the subject of useful scholarship in recent years, for example in Mandler's analysis of the changing definition of 'equal opportunity' from determined after a 'state-sanctioned test at age 11' to 'equal opportunity to acquire intelligence' in the longer term, Mandler, *The Crisis of the Meritocracy*, ch. 7.

[52] Ruth Levitas, *The Inclusive Society? Social Exclusion and New Labour* (Basingstoke: Palgrave, 2005), p. 2. See also Emily Robinson, *The Language of Progressive Politics in Modern Britain* (Basingstoke: Palgrave Macmillan, 2017).

[53] Emily Robinson, Camilla Schofield, Florence Sutcliffe-Braithwaite, and Natalie Thomlinson, 'Telling stories about post-war Britain: popular individualism and the "crisis" of the 1970s', *Twentieth Century British History*, 28 (2017), pp. 268–304; Jon Lawrence, *Me, Me, Me? The Search for Community in Post-war England* (Oxford: OUP, 2019); Roberta Bivins, *Contagious Communities: Medicine, Migration, and the NHS in Post-War Britain* (Oxford: OUP, 2015); Florence Sutcliffe-Braithwaite, *Class, Politics, and the Decline of Deference in England, 1968–2000* (Oxford: OUP, 2018);

further nuance, showing that there was dissatisfaction with social democratic education policy from the outset: this was seen as 'too equalising' and would not benefit those of high intellectual capacity. 'Popular individualism', once assumed as a development of the late 1970s and 1980s, reshaped daily life from the late 1960s onwards.[54] In these decades, gifted children were invited to see themselves as a significantly distinct social group that required distinct recreational and educational activities, not catered for by a declining welfare state. In later decades, also, ideas of equality continued to shape gifted provision in the 1970s and 1980s, amidst the rise of neoliberalism. Teachers, policy-makers, and voluntary groups remained concerned to acknowledge that anyone could be gifted, and invested in using giftedness provision to further social equality.[55] From the 1990s onwards, new histories have described how psychological and legal categories, from who was 'autistic' to who deserved a 'sick note', for example, extended state management of the self.[56] In part, this book further shows the extent of these processes: describing the ways in which the apparatus of giftedness spread to British schools and into children's leisure time. At the same time, the book also highlights resistance to these regimes by children, and thus the limitations of any strict assumption that governments' role in defining 'giftedness' extended clearly and without issues in the 1990s. Analysing international debates, also, the book finds that attempts to 'use children exclusively as pawns' in cultural exchanges did not entirely decline with the Cold War, but rather persisted, in this area, in to the 2000s.[57] The book suggests, then, that consideration of the interplay between

---

Gareth Millward, *Sick Note: A History of the British Welfare State* (Oxford: OUP, 2022); Amy Edwards, *Are We Rich Yet? The Rise of Mass Investment Culture in Contemporary Britain* (California: University of California Press, 2022); Caroline Rusterholz, *Responsible Pleasure: The Brook Advisory Centres and Youth Sexuality in Postwar Britain* (Oxford: OUP, 2024). See also: Alex Davies, Ben Jackson, Florence Sutcliffe-Braithwaite (eds), *The Neoliberal Age? Britain since the 1970s* (London: IHR Press, 2021). In this book, the editors reflect on chronology on p. 340: 'Many of the chapters in this volume move away from using "Thatcherism" as an exclusive frame to study the origins of British neoliberalism; instead, they trace the neoliberal project back to as early as the 1950s and still see it developing in the 1990s and 2000s.'

[54] Emphasising the party-political manifestations of popular individualism, see: Alex Davies, James Freeman, and Hugh Pemberton, '"Everyman a capitalist" or "free to choose"? Exploring the tensions within Thatcherite individualism', *Historical Journal*, 61 (2018), pp. 477–501; Sutcliffe-Braithwaite, *Class, Politics, and the Decline of Deference*, pp. 4–8. For new research calling for further interest in how popular individualism shaped daily life, see: Lawrence, *Me, Me, Me?*, p. 2; Robinson et al., 'Telling stories about post-war Britain', pp. 268–304.

[55] On complex definitions of 'neoliberalism', see: Alex Davies, Ben Jackson, and Florence Sutcliffe-Braithwaite, *The Neoliberal Age? Britain since the 1970s* (London: UCL Press, 2021).

[56] Bonnie Evans, *The Metamorphis of Autism: A History of Child Development in Britain* (Manchester: MUP, 2017), especially pp. 430–433; Gareth Millward, *Sick Note: A History of the British Welfare State* (Oxford: OUP, 2022), ch. 6. Forthcoming on this are outputs from a brilliant conference organised by David Geiringer and Helen McCarthy in 2021: see 'When Was the Nineties?', *Past & Present Blog* <https://pastandpresent.org.uk/when-was-the-nineties/> (20 September 2024).

[57] Quote is from: Paula S. Fass, 'Intersecting agendas: children in history and diplomacy', *Diplomatic History*, 38 (2) (2014), p. 298. Fascinating broader histories of earlier child diplomacy include: Mischa Honeck and Gabriel Rosenberg, 'Transnational generations: organizing youth in the Cold War', *Diplomatic History*, 38 (2) (2014), p. 234; Matthias Neumann, 'Children diplomacy during

'equality' and 'elitism' throughout this period may further complicate chronologies and established narratives.

A third, and final, argument is that, if considering the entwined nature and tensions of the concepts of 'elitism' and 'equality' in modern Britain, we must look to how these concepts were lived and felt by public groups. In part, this builds on Mandler's call to look at the 'demand side' of debates in education: away from the state education system and its markers in law, and instead towards new attitudes and their registers.[58] Yet, in this case, rather than examining the attitudes of parents to school and education, the book examines how families, communities, and children themselves, supported by networks of community organisers, teachers, and policy-makers, conceptualised what gifted children needed in terms of education, family life, careers, and friendships and socialisation. Overall, the book explores how children and the young thought of themselves as 'elites' and 'equals': many enjoyed the idea of being elite and incorporated it in to their interactions with peers and families, while others challenged the idea of elites based on intelligence in British society and, instead, were drawn to ideals of equality. Approaching huge concepts of 'equality' and 'elitism' can be bound by theoretical debates about the meanings and limitations of these terms, but equally generative, this book argues, is seeing how young people themselves defined and lived these concepts. Looking to experience and children's writings shows the lived tension between these concepts in daily life, and explains how both concepts coexisted in 'social democratic' and in 'neoliberal' societies: as individuals and families sought to configure and live with both concepts daily.

Elites of 'the Future'

This book demonstrates that gifted children were constantly presented not only as 'elites', but as 'elites of the future'. This is significant because ideas of children as 'the future' have been used to justify new spending priorities, and to mask divides in welfare states, as Laura King has shown.[59] The meaning of 'elites of the future'

---

the late Cold War: Samantha Smith's visit of the "Evil Empire"', *History*, 104 (360), (2019), pp. 277-278; Sara Fieldston, 'Little cold warriors: child sponsorship and international affairs', *Diplomatic History*, 38 (2) (2014), pp. 240-250; Christina Norwig, 'A first European generation? the myth of youth and European integration in the fifties', *Diplomatic History*, 38 (2) (2014), pp. 251-260; Marcia Chatelain, 'International sisterhood: Cold War Girl Scouts encounter the world', *Diplomatic History*, 38 (2) (2014), pp. 261-270; Sean Guillory, 'Culture clash in the socialist paradise: Soviet patronage and African students' urbanity in the Soviet Union, 1960-1965', *Diplomatic History*, 38 (2) (2014), pp. 271-281; Tamara Myers, 'Local action and global imagining: youth, international development, and the Walkathon Phenomenon in sixties' and seventies' Canada', *Diplomatic History*, 38 (2) (2014), pp. 282-293.

[58] Mandler, *Crisis of the Meritocracy?*, throughout, phrase is on p. 7.

[59] Laura King, 'Future citizens: cultural and political conceptions of children in Britain, 1930s-1950s', *Twentieth Century British History*, 27 (3) (2016), pp. 389-411. See also: Millward, *Sick Note*, ch. 4.

is also important, however, when considered from the perspective of young people themselves. The gifted young were frequently told that they would and should become leaders, winners, figureheads, and successes 'in the future', in various ways. The 'waithood' of these young people—their 'active anticipation of and engagement with the future'—was thus hugely privileged, but also laden with distinct forms of expectation and pressure.[60] While many young people excitedly prepared for a promised role as an elites of the future, others did not care for it, and thus responded neutrally or critically. Waithood, as Tatek Abebe and Alinda M. Honwana powerfully argue, can be transformative and creative; productive and anticipatory. To wait, for a young person, anticipating the future, has rarely been a passive act.[61]

This book posits that the concepts of 'elites' and 'leaders'—however phrased—are dynamically co-constructed, ingrained, and embedded from childhood and youth. These concepts are also made and remade by adults and children together. Thinking about the role of young people in constructing concepts of leadership is rare in existing literatures. A growing body of research from across disciplines has demonstrated that ideas of 'leadership' are not static, but cultural and historical, shifting over time and space.[62] Social scientists have looked to define and

---

[60] Hugely useful discussions of the concepts of waithood, and also of studies of waithood in contexts of precarity, can be found in Tatek Abebe, 'Lost futures? Educated youth precarity and protests in the Oromia region, Ethopia', *Children's Geographies*, 18 (6) (2020), pp. 584–600. Both that article and my own thinking about 'waithood' are also indebted to: Alinda M. Honwana, *The Time of Youth: Work, Social Change, and Politics in Africa* (London: Kumarian Press, 2012). The book focuses on Africa, and also conceptualises a global 'waithood generation' (p. 6).

[61] Ibid. Also relevant is Kyrre Kverndokk's argument, that young people are able to use the trope of 'the future' in debates around climate change to seize power in these debates; 'the child' becomes a 'privileged position of enunciation', Kyrre Kverndokk, 'Talking about your generation: "Our Children" as a trope in climate change discourse', *Ethnologia Europaea*, 50 (1) (2020), pp. 145–158.

[62] Biographies in this vein show different visions of 'leadership' that achieve success in different contexts (many written by and about politicians): Roy Jenkins, *Churchill: A Biography* (Macmillan, 2002); Michael Foot, *Aneurin Bevan: A Biography* (Davis-Poynter, 1973). There are also endless scholarly accounts of specific leaders and their lives, and of royal families (recent examples focusing on modern Britain include: Charles Moore, *Margaret Thatcher: The Authorised Biography Volume One* (London: Penguin, 2014); John Bew, *Citizen Clem* (Quercus, 2013); Ben Pimlott, *Harold Wilson* (London: Harper Collins, 1992); John Plunkett, *Queen Victoria: First Media Monarch* (Oxford: OUP, 2003)). For thorough discussions of some of the 'founding fathers' of Europe see, for example: Charles Williams, *Adenauer: The Father of the New Germany* (Oxford: Abacus, 2003); Daniela Preda, *Alcide De Gasperi: European Founding Father* (Bern: PIE-Peter Lang, 2018). Recently, historical accounts, for example by Laura Beers and Sarah Crook, have provided analysis of lesser known female politicians and their work in pushing social reform or liberal internationalism. Sarah Crook, 'The Labour Party, feminism and Maureen Colquhoun's scandals in 1970s Britain', *Contemporary British History*, 34 (1) (2020), pp. 71–94; Laura Beers, *Red Ellen: The Life of Ellen Wilkinson, Socialist, Feminist, Internationalist* (Cambridge, MA: Harvard University Press, 2016). Another body of historical literature has assessed the role of leaders during decolonisation, and highlighted the growing power of those representing the promises of 'science' and 'technology': see, for example: Gisela Mateos and Edna Suárez-Díaz, 'Development interventions: science, technology and technical assistance', *History and Technology*, 36 (3–4) (2020), pp. 293–309; John Krige and Jessica Wang, 'Nation, Knowledge, and imagined futures: science, technology, and nation-building, post-1945', *History and Technology*, 31 (3) (2015), pp. 171–179; Nick Cullather, *The Hungry World: America's Battle against Poverty in Asia* (Cambridge, MA: Harvard University Press, 2013); Jacob Darwin Hamblin, 'Let there be light…and bread: the United Nations, the developing world, and atomic energy's Green Revolution', *History and*

measure different attributes of leadership in comparative studies.[63] Political science, management theory, and psychological researchers have focused on interrogating the fixed ideas of *adults*, shaped by inequalities of gender, race, ethnicity, and class, about who political elites are and how they should look and behave.[64] These studies rarely interrogate the views of children, although recent surveys and analysis of children's magazines, from education, psychology, and policy, have started this endeavour, demonstrating that children are exposed to gender stereotypes from their early years, which shape their ambitions and expectations of political elites.[65] Recent work by Sam Friedman and Daniel

---

Technology, 25 (1) (2009), pp. 25–48. Recent work, for example, has illuminated the complex structures and mentalities of leadership within authoritarian states: see for example: Ian Kershaw, *The Hitler Myth: Image and Reality in the Third Reich* (Oxford: OUP, 1987); John Paxton, *Leaders of Russia and the Soviet Union: From the Romanov Dynasty to Vladmir Putin* (London: Routledge, 2004); Thomas Streissguth, *Soviet Leaders from Lenin to Gorbachev* (London: Oliver pr Inc, 1992). Looking at 'leadership' more broadly see, for example: Peter Grieder, *The East German Leadership 1946-1973: Conflict and Crisis* (Manchester and New York, MUP, 1999); Archie Brown, *Political Leadership in the Soviet Union* (London: Palgrave, 1989); Martin McCauley and Stephen Carter, *Leadership and Succession in the Soviet Union, Eastern Europe and China* (London: Palgrave, 1986); Graeme Gill, *Collective Leadership in Soviet Politics* (London: Palgrave, 2018); Michael R. Hayse, *Recasting West German Élites: Higher Civil Servants, Business Leaders and Physicians in Hesse between Nazism and Democracy, 1945–1955* (Oxford and New York: Berghahn Books, 2003); Kevin Morgan, *International Communism and the Cult of the Individual: Leaders, Tribunes and Martyrs under Lenin and Stalin* (Basingstoke: Palgrave, 2017).
[63] P. B. Smith, S. Dugan, and F. Trompenaars, 'National culture and the values of organizational employees', *Journal of Cross-Cultural Psychology*, 27 (1996), pp. 231–264; F. Trompenaars, *Riding the Waves of Culture* (London: Breatley, 1993); P. B. Smith, 'Leadership in Europe: Euro-management or the footprint of history?', *European Journal of Work and Organizational Psychology*, 6 (1997), pp. 375–386.
[64] See Nichole M. Bauer, 'Emotional, sensitive, and unfit for office? gender stereotype activation and support for female candidates', *Political Psychology*, 36 (6) (2014), pp. 691–708; Roosmarijn A. de Geus, John R. McAndrews, Peter John Loewen, et al., 'Do voters judge the performance of female and male politicians differently? experimental evidence from the United States and Australia', *Political Research Quarterly*, 74 (2) (2021), pp. 302–316. In management theory see: H. Astin and C. Leland, *Women of Influence, Women of Vision: A Cross Generational Study of Leaders and Social Change* (Wiley, 1999); Kari Pöllänen, 'Northern European leadership in transition–a survey of the insurance industry', *Journal of General Management*, 32 (1) (2006), pp. 43–63. Looking from management or business studies perspectives, with focus on efficacy, see, for example: Ingeborg Tömmel and Amy Verdun, 'Political leadership in the European Union: an introduction', *Journal of European Integration*, 39 (2) (2017), pp. 103–112; M. Arslan, 'A cross-cultural comparison of achievement and power orientation as leadership dimensions in three European countries: Britain, Ireland and Turkey', *Business Ethics: A European Review*, 10 (4) (2001), pp. 340–345; M. Arslan, 'A cross-cultural comparison of Turkish and British managers in terms of Protestant work ethic characteristics', *Business Ethics: A European Review*, 9 (1) (2000), pp. 13–19; S. Mukkamala and K. L. Suyemoto, 'Racialized sexism/sexualized racism: A multimethod study of intersectional experiences of discrimination for Asian American women', *Asian American Journal of Psychology*, 9 (1) (2018), pp. 32–46; Y. Cho, R. Ghosh, J. Y. Sun, and G. N. McLean (eds), *Current Perspectives on Asian Women in Leadership: A Cross-Cultural Analysis* (London: Palgrave, 2017); A. H. Eagly, C. Nater, D. I. Miller, M. Kaufmann, and S. Sczesny, 'Gender stereotypes have changed: A cross-temporal meta-analysis of U.S. public opinion polls from 1946 to 2018', *American Psychologist*, 75(3) (2020), pp. 301–315; Sam Friedman and Daniel Laurson, *The Class Ceiling: Why it Pays to be Privileged* (Bristol: Policy Press, 2020), pp. 39–40.
[65] A. Bos, M. Holman, J. Greenlee, Z. Oxley, and J. Lay, '100 years of suffrage and girls still struggle to find their "fit" in politics', *Political Science & Politics*, 53 (3) (2020), pp. 474–478; J. Lay, M. Holman, A. Bos, J. Greenlee, Z. Oxley, and A. Buffett, 'TIME for kids to learn gender stereotypes: analysis of gender and political leadership in a common social studies resource for children', *Politics & Gender*,

Laurson, likewise, has shown, from interviews and datasets about adults and life-courses, that 'those who start out ahead are the ones most likely to succeed'.[66] Nonetheless, these studies acknowledge that we still know 'relatively little' about how ideas of the elite are inculcated, and that researchers have paid 'little attention' to the decisive period of transition from childhood to young adulthood.[67]

This book offers a case study of how a certain group of children—primarily, as the book shows in Chapter Three, white, middle-class boys—were identified as elites of the future, and how they responded. In so doing, it uses the methodological insights of existing literature around 'leadership' and 'elites' and the flexibility of these concepts. It also advances such work, demonstrating that, at times, relatively small groups of people, mobilising via voluntary organisations, have had substantial power to determine the elites of the future, with significant lived consequences for groups of young people, their opportunities, and their experiences of school, voluntary society, and family life. The book demonstrates, also, as stated, that young people have been critical consumers of ideas about elites.

(2019), pp. 1–22; Hanns M. Trautner, 'The development of sex-typing in children: a longitudinal analysis', *German Journal of Psychology*, 16 (3) (1992), pp. 183–189; Ann Henshaw, Janette Kelly, and Caroline Gratton, 'Children's Perceptions of Gender Roles and Gender Preferences', *Educational Research*, 34 (3) (1992), pp. 229–235. Important work which demonstrates the lack of political ambition for adult female leaders includes: R. L. Fox and J. L. Lawless, 'Gendered perceptions and political candidacies: a central barrier to women's equality in electoral politics', *American Journal of Political Science*, 55 (1) (2011), pp. 59–73; R. L. Fox and J. L. Lawless, 'Uncovering the origins of the gender gap in political ambition', *American Political Science Review*, 108 (3) (2014), pp. 499–519; M. R. Holman and M. C. Schneider, 'Gender, race, and political ambition: how intersectionality and frames influence interest in political office', *Politics, Groups, and Identities*, 6 (2) (2018), pp. 264–280; M. R. Holman, J. L. Merolla, and E. J. Zechmeister, 'Terrorist threat, male stereotypes, and candidate evaluations', *Political Research Quarterly*, 69 (1) (2016), pp. 134–147; J. L. Lawless, 'Women, war, and winning elections: Gender stereotyping in the post-September 11th era', *Political Research Quarterly*, 57 (3) (2004), pp. 479–490.
[66] Friedman and Laurison, *The Class Ceiling*, p. 31.
[67] A. Bos, M. Holman, J. Greenlee, Z. Oxley, and J. Lay, '100 years of suffrage and girls still struggle to find their "fit" in politics', *Political Science & Politics*, 53 (3) (2020), pp. 474–478; J. Lay, M. Holman, A. Bos, J. Greenlee, Z. Oxley, and A. Buffett, 'TIME for kids to learn gender stereotypes: analysis of gender and political leadership in a common social studies resource for children', *Politics & Gender*, (2019), pp. 1–22; Hanns M. Trautner, 'The development of sex-typing in children: a longitudinal analysis', *German Journal of Psychology*, 16 (3) (1992), pp. 183–189; Ann Henshaw, Janette Kelly, and Caroline Gratton, 'Children's perceptions of gender roles and gender preferences', *Educational Research*, 34 (3) (1992), pp. 229–235. Useful studies, nonetheless, include those about how children and young people are trained into citizenship (rather than leadership): Alison Twells, *The Civilising Mission and the English Middle Class, 1792–1850: The 'Heathen' at Home and Overseas* (Basingstoke: Palgrave, 2009); Sarah Richardson, *The Political Worlds of Women: Gender and Politics in Nineteenth Century Britain* (New York: Routledge, 2013); Friedemann Pestel, 'Educating against Revolution: French émigré schools and the challenge of the next generation', *European History Quarterly*, 47 (2) (2017), pp. 229–256; Kathryn Gleadle, 'The Juvenile Enlightenment: British Children and youth during the French Revolution', *Past & Present*, 233 (1) (2016), pp. 143–184; Helen McCarthy, *The British People and the League of Nations: Democracy, Citizenship and Internationalism, c.1918–45* (Manchester: MUP, 2011); Stephen J. Hearthorn, *For Home, Country, and Race: Constructing Gender, Class, and Englishness in the Elementary School, 1880–1914* (De Gruyter, 2003); Jonathan Davies and Mark Freeman, 'Education for citizenship: the Joseph Rowntree Charitable Trust and the educational settlement movement', *History of Education*, 32 (3) (2003), pp. 303–318; Peter Yeandle, *Citizenship, Nation, Empire: The Politics of History Teaching in England, 1870–1930* (Manchester: MUP, 2015).

While young people have of course been influenced by adult ideas of leadership, which permeate their lives through family, school, and culture, even those studied here have questioned the validity of concepts of the elite and the value of being a leader. This positions 'elites' and 'leadership' alike as dynamic concepts, shaped across the life course, with children as powerful contributors. This then provides new insights to why concepts of leadership change; how they are made and remade across generations and time, with young people involved in constructing ideas that shape who they vote for or accept as elites, whether they see themselves as elites, and ultimately which models of leadership thrive. This is particularly visible in Chapter Five, which explores how adults recall and remember programmes from their childhood to 'raise their aspirations' or 'identify the gifted', notably the National Records of Achievement system. This analysis then demonstrates, also, that we must not only look at programmes for elites, or policy descriptions of their roles. Rather, we must analyse the complex and lived experiences of those so labelled, and at how these experiences shift across the life course. Sociologist Emma Uprichard argues that children are 'being and becoming'; they should be studied in terms of who they are, at present, as well as in terms of who they may become; we may also wish to analyse the adult's view of the child they had 'been'.[68]

Voluntary Organisations

The book demonstrates that voluntary organisations were a central landscape for the gifted child: bringing these children together, and building interest around this issue more broadly, in the 1960s, 1970s, and 1980s.[69] The central case study here, the National Association of Gifted Children, exercised significant influence despite its small size. The disordered nature of the group's uncatalogued archives means we do not have consistent figures for membership or staffing over time, but scattered snapshots make clear that it grew, although it was never huge. The organisation's first newsletter, published in May 1969, recorded only one part-time administrator, funded through an individual donation, and 1,100 members.[70] In 1974, the Association received its first government grant—£5,000 per year— which enabled its founder to work for it full-time. The Association continued to receive grants from the Department of Education and Science, Department for

---

[68] Emma Uprichard, 'Children as "Being and Becomings": children, childhood and temporality', *Children & Society*, 22 (4) (2008), pp. 303–313. Useful discussion of the 'Being' and 'Becoming' distinction in contemporary scholarship in: Sarah L. Holloway, Louise Holt, and Sarah Mills, 'Questions of agency: capacity, subjectivity, spatiality and temporality', *Progress in Human Geography*, 43 (3) (2018), pp. 467–470.

[69] The idea of 'landscapes' here is indebted to Thomson, *Lost Freedom*, pp. 4–10.

[70] NAGC, Bletchley, 'Appointment of an Administrator', *Newsletter*, May 1969, p. 1.

Health and Social Security, and Scottish Education Department in to the 1980s, the largest of which was £20,000 in 1989.[71]

Despite being relatively small, this organisation—and others explored throughout the book—powerfully drove and shaped interest in gifted children. The lobbying of National Association founder Margaret Branch alone galvanised a network of journalists to become interested in this area, as Chapter Two demonstrates. The National Association also had great success in keeping debates around giftedness separate from those about elitism in the educational system. The organisation was campaigning while tense and significant arguments raged about whether grammar schools should be abolished, and all schools become comprehensives.[72] Yet, despite this, media and policy interest in the gifted child, following National Association framing, emphasised that finding the gifted young was an issue of equality: gifted young people were, they argued, like disabled children in that they could be anyone, across class, gender, ethnicity, and race, and that they may at times need adjustments in family and educational life to thrive. Voluntary groups—from the National Association to the European Council for High Ability and World Council for Gifted and Talented Children— also played a critical role in associating interest in gifted children with a quest to identify and support the elites of the future, and in raising the stakes of what these children could do in terms of saving the economy or even 'the world'.

These findings are significant in the context of recent literature around voluntary organisations. In the early 2000s, Frank Prochaska made an influential argument that civic participation declined in Britain in the post-war period, in comparison to the 'golden age' of the Victorian era.[73] This thesis has been

---

[71] This grant came from the Department for Education and Science and was awarded until at least 1976, with discussion about 'the possibility of a renewed grant' made in August of that year. See: Hansard, House of Commons, Fifth Series, 18 July 1978, vol. 954, col.126. The same value grant was also awarded in 1979 (Hansard, House of Commons, Fifth Series, 28 June 1979, vol. 969, col. 326). In 1980, the organisation was awarded £4,509 (Hansard, House of Commons, Fifth Series, 22 July 1980, vol. 989, col. 192). In 1982, £800 (Hansard, House of Commons, Sixth Series, 31 March 1983, vol. 40, col. 229). In 1983, £5,000 (Hansard, House of Commons, Sixth Series, 22 July 1983, vol. 46, col. 245.) In 1984, £800 (Hansard, House of Commons, Sixth Series, 17 January 1984, vol. 52, col. 212). In 1985, £5,000 (Hansard, House of Commons, Sixth Series, 3 February 1986, vol. 91, col. 13). In 1988, £10,000 (Hansard, House of Commons, Sixth Series, 17 March 1988, vol. 129, col. 635). In 1989, £20,000 (Hansard, House of Commons, Sixth Series, 3 March 1989, vol. 148, col. 337). For evidence of these grants in NAGC materials, see: NAGC, Fifth Annual Report and Accounts of the National Association for Gifted Children, 1971–1972, p. 3; NAGC, Annual Report 1981, p. 7. From these reports we see that the Association's total income in the 1971–72 financial year was £8,587. By the 1980–81 financial year, it was £66,746. By the 1989–1990 financial year, it was £113, 653 (NAGC, The National Association for Gifted Children Report and Financial Statements, 30 April 1990).

[72] Mandler, *The Crisis of the Meritocracy?*, ch. 4.

[73] Frank Prochaska, *Christianity and Social Service in Modern Britain: The Disinherited Spirit* (Oxford: OUP, 2006), p. 97; Frank Prochaska, *The Voluntary Impulse: Philanthropy in Modern Britain* (London: Faber & Faber, 1988). A related argument is offered for the American context by Robert Putnam, who has influentially pinpointed a decline in political, civic, and community engagement since 1950. See Robert Putnam, *Bowling Alone: The Collapse and Revival of American Community* (New York, 2000).

contested by historians who have traced a history of non-governmental organisations (NGOs) acting increasingly 'professionally' over this period.[74] Tanya Evans describes how poverty NGOs professionalised between 1945 and 1995, employing increasing numbers of graduates with professional qualifications as paid staff in the 1970s, and thus becoming, in social work, fundraising, and policy work, 'much more effective'.[75] Matthew Hilton, James McKay, Nicholas Crowson, and Jean-François Mouhot argue that social and political activism became 'privatised' in the mid-to-late twentieth century. 'Active' participation in associational life and community-based groups, such as political parties, trade unions and churches, declined. This was broadly replaced by a more 'passive' set of relationships with large, professionalised NGOs led by 'technocratic elites'.[76]

The work of Alison Penn and Pat Thane has nuanced these findings, charting a longer history of technocratic knowledge and professionalisation in churches, schools, universities, friendly societies, social clubs, retail shops, public houses, and unpaid voluntary organisations, dating back to the eighteenth and nineteenth centuries.[77] Multiple historians and geographers have further honed the thesis of professionalisation in the mid-to-late twentieth century, showcasing a continuing strong strand of small-scale, informal activism that thrived in this period, for example through self-help organisations or informal education, shaping daily lives of families and also becoming influential in terms of policy.[78] The groups in

---

[74] James McKay and Matthew Hilton, 'Introduction', in Nick Crowson, Matthew Hilton, and James McKay (eds), *NGOs in Contemporary Britain: Non-state Actors in Society and Politics Since 1945* (Basingstoke: Palgrave Macmillan, 2009) p. 3.

[75] Tanya Evans, 'Stopping the poor getting poorer: the establishment and professionalisations of poverty NGOs, 1945–95', pp. 147–163.

[76] Matthew Hilton, James McKay, Nicholas Crowson, and Jean-François Mouhot, *The Politics of Expertise: How NGOs Shaped Modern Britain* (Oxford: OUP, 2013); Nick Crowson, Matthew Hilton, and James McKay (eds), *NGOs in Contemporary Britain: Non-state actors in Society and Politics Since 1945* (Basingstoke: Palgrave Macmillan, 2009); Matthew Hilton, 'Politics is ordinary: non-governmental organizations and political participation in contemporary Britain', *Twentieth Century British History*, 2 (2011), pp. 230–268.

[77] Alison Penn, 'Social history and organizational development: revisiting Beveridge's *Voluntary Action*', in Colin Rochester, George Campbell Gosling, Alison Penn, and Meta Zimmeck (eds), *Understanding the Roots of Voluntary Action: Historical Perspectives on Current Social Policy* (Brighton, 2011), p. 22; Pat Thane, 'Voluntary action in Britain since Beveridge', in Melanie Oppenheimer and Nicholas Deakin (eds), *Beveridge and Voluntary Action in Britain and the Wider British World* (Manchester, MUP, 2011), p. 123.

[78] See: Caitriona Beaumont, Eve Colpus, and Ruth Davidson (eds), *Histories of Welfare: Experiential Expertise, Action and Activism* (Basingstoke: Palgrave Macmillan, 2024); J. Barke, S. Cohen, T. Cole, L. Henry, J. Hutchen, V. Latinwo-Olajide, J. McLellan, E. Pridgeon, and B. Whitmore, 'A history of survival: preserving and working with an archive of single parent activism', *Women's History Review*, 33 (1) (2024), pp. 117–130; Alex Mold and Virginia Berridge, *Voluntary Action and Illegal Drugs: Health and Society in Britain since the 1960s* (Basingstoke: Palgrave Macmillan, 2010); Mold, Alex, *Making the patient-consumer: patient organisations and health consumerism in Britain* (Manchester: MUP, 2015); Sarah Crook and Charlie Jeffries (eds), *Resist, Organize, Build: Feminist and Queer Activism in Britain and the United States during the Long 1980s* (SUNY Press, 2022); Chris Moores, 'Opposition to the Greenham Women's Peace Camps in 1980s Britain: RAGE against the obscene', *History Workshop Journal*, 78 (1) (2014), pp. 204–227; Jennifer Crane, *Child Protection in England, 1960–2000: Expertise, Experience, and Emotion*

this book were most powerful in the 1970s and 1980s, both because of increasing media interest in capturing 'personal experience' and because of new responsibilities being placed on state organisations to consult with their publics.[79]

Following theoretical work by Jeremy Kendall, Martin Knapp, and Alex Mold, the voluntary sector here is conceptualised as a 'loose and baggy monster' that 'defies all simple labels'.[80] Beyond this, the book looks in detail at an area where many voluntary organisations did not aim to be 'professional', nor employ significant numbers of professional staff, nor hold particular strategies around PR, fundraising, or policy work. Rather, many groups in this book worked from a starting point of providing services and relief for families and, from this work, then agitating for political change (or not: for many groups and branches here, providing family services was sufficient). These groups represented a powerful form of voluntary action that continued to demand 'active' participation in community life, in contrast to the non-governmental organisations also active in this period. Indeed, involvement in these groups, the book shows, reshaped the leisure time of many families, and how they narrated and explored their own lives. The smallness of these groups meant that they had different formative influences from large non-governmental organisations: while NGOs were shaped by changes in government or policy, such as the election of Margaret Thatcher, these groups were more affected by the changing lives of their voluntary leaders—mothers returning to work, or families relocating. This story then shows the fine-grained nature of chronology in social histories, which are not always primarily driven by political histories of the same period. Looking in detail at specific voluntary

---

(Basingstoke: Palgrave, 2018); Angela Davis, *Pre-school Childcare in England, 1939–2010* (Manchester, MUP, 2015), ch. 4; Elizabeth, Hannah, 'Love Carefully and Without 'Over-bearing Fears': The Persuasive Power of Authenticity in Late 1980s British AIDS Education Material for Adolescents', *Social History of Medicine*, 34 (4) (2021), pp. 1317–1342; Sarah Mills, *Mapping the Moral Geographies of Education: Character, Citizenship and Values* (Milton Keynes: Routledge, 2022); Sarah Mills, '"An instruction in good citizenship": scouting and the historical geographies of citizenship education', *Transactions of the Institute of British Geographers*, 38 (1) (2013), pp. 120–134; Jacob Fairless Nicholson, 'From London to Grenada and back again: youth exchange geographies and the Grenadian Revolution, 1979–1983', *Antipode* (2020), pp. 708–728.

[79] See on this, Alex Mold, 'Making the patient-consumer in Margaret Thatcher's Britain', *The Historical Journal*, 54 (2011), pp. 509–528; Mold and Berridge, *Voluntary Action and Illegal Drugs*, pp. 147–149. With reference to effect on mental health services, see: Alison Faulkner, 'User involvement in 21st century mental health services: "This is our century"', in Charlie Brooker and Julie Repper (eds), *Mental Health: From Policy to Practice* (London, 2009), pp. 14–26; Lynda Tait and Helen Lester, 'Encouraging user involvement in mental health services', *Advances in Psychiatric Treatment*, 11 (2005), pp. 168–175; Michele Crossley and Nick Crossley, '"Patient" voices, social movements and the habitus; how psychiatric survivors "speak out"', *Social Science and Medicine*, 52 (2001), pp. 1477–1489.

[80] Jeremy Kendall and Martin Knapp, 'A loose and baggy monster: boundaries, definitions and typologies', in Justin Davis Smith, Colin Rochester, and Rodney Hedley (eds), *An Introduction to the Voluntary Sector* (London, Routledge, 1994), pp. 65–94; Alex Mold, 'The Changing Role of NGOs in Britain: Voluntary Action and Illegal Drugs', in Nicholas Crowson, James McKay, and Matthew Hilton (eds), *NGOs in Contemporary Britain: Non-state Actors in Society and Politics since 1945* (Basingstoke, Palgrave Macmillan, 2009), p. 166.

organisations matters, in itself *and* because it shows us the everyday motivations and stresses that ultimately channel 'upwards', to reshape culture and society.

Family Activism

Families were critical in building the voluntary organisations described in this book.[81] Families shaped the groups' central demands, through the regional branches, and also their key provision: weekend and holiday courses for young people. This book substantially strengthens our understanding of parents as activists in the 1970s and 1980s. It shows, in particular, how primarily white, middle-class parents, with relatively conservative demands—typically increased funding for giftedness programmes, rather than total educational or social reform—nonetheless adopted the politics of emotion and experience, more associated with contemporary liberationist movements, to make their case.[82]

The role of parents and families as activists has been somewhat neglected in scholarship, but some work has been done. Claire Sewell and Rubahanna Amannah Choudhury have written important accounts of the role of family carers and campaigners in challenging stigma and discrimination against children with disabilities.[83] Scholars have also examined the campaigning of often stigmatised or marginalised parents: Tanya Evans and Josie McLellan have explored how single mothers mobilised to provide self-help and mutual aid and to demand reform and support, within the progressive movements of the 1960s and 1970s.[84] Recently, Peter Mandler argued that parental pressure was the key factor behind bringing in grammar schools in England, although the parents themselves—their voices and their campaigning organisations—are not central to his narrative.[85] Indeed, Mandler argues that recent scholarship around family and gender often 'relegate[s] education to an afterthought'.[86] This book takes that path, consciously centring the writings of children and families around giftedness, not 'gifted education', and following children's and families' interests whether in family life, future occupations, play and hobbies, friendships, nuclear warfare, trains, and stargazing—their constellation of interests extended far beyond, and often only fleetingly crossed over with, seemingly parallel debates about

---

[81] They were another 'landscape' of the child: Thomson, *Lost Freedom*, pp. 4–10.

[82] I wrote about this in my first book, Crane, Jennifer, *Child Protection in England, 1960–2000: Expertise, Experience, and Emotion* (Basingstoke: Palgrave, 2018).

[83] Claire Sewell, '"If one member of the family is disabled the family as a whole is disabled": Thalidomide Children and the Emergency of the Family Carer in Britain, c. 1957–1978', *Family & Community History*, 18 (1) (2015), pp. 37–52; Choudhury, 'The forgotten children'.

[84] Evans, 'Stopping the poor getting poorer', pp. 154–155; 'Single Parent Action Network: a participatory history', UKRI <https://gtr.ukri.org/projects?ref=AH%2FS000542%2F1#/tabOverview> (4 January 2024).

[85] Mandler, *The Crisis of the Meritocracy?* [86] Ibid., p. 8.

education in policy or daily school life. Despite this choice of focus, the book does nonetheless make some contribution towards understanding 'the nitty-gritty of educational experience'—if 'education' may include informal and family life, as well as schooling—and thus in so doing contributes to responding to Mandler's call to 'revers[e] the usual top-down educational narrative'.[87]

The role of parents as campaigners has been comparatively neglected in scholarship, perhaps surprisingly. Historians have demonstrated that the 1970s and 1980s saw significant anxieties about family life from the conservative right. These anxieties, as Jennifer Somerville, Martin Durham, and Deborah Cohen have shown, were central to Thatcher's administrations, and also reflected in the later rise of reality television, for example, anxiously presenting the lives of single parents, unmarried parents, or those dealing with extramarital affairs and family conflict.[88] Historians have also shown that the post-war period, and the 1970s and 1980s, saw a significant expectation that campaigners and publics make their emotions visible, in various ways. Adrian Bingham has explored how newspapers published more accounts of experience in this period—building on interest from the immediate post-war period.[89] Martin Francis has traced a shift from a 'culture of self-discipline' to a 'culture of self-expression' for politicians, emanating from the late 1950s.[90] For Claire Langhamer, 'the claim to emotional authenticity could be used as a tool for subversion, resistance and personal transformation' in the twentieth century'.[91]

The parent campaigners in this book have not been studied before, and represent the combination of these two trends: growing conservative anxieties about family life and the expectation that publics make their emotions known if campaigning. This is significant, as much (likewise important) existing literature on the visibility of emotions examines liberationist movements in this period, and

[87] Ibid., p. 16.
[88] Deborah Cohen, *Family Secrets: The Things We Tried to Hide* (London: Penguin, 2014), p. 233; Andrew Gamble, *The Free Economy and the Strong State: The Politics of Thatcherism* (Basingstoke: Palgrave Macmillan, 1994), pp. 14, 136, 200; Martin Durham, *Sex and Politics: The Family and Morality in the Thatcher Years* (Basingstoke: Palgrave Macmillan, 1991), pp. 131–137; Martin Durham, 'The Thatcher Government and "The Moral Right"', *Parliamentary Affairs*, 41 (1989), pp. 58–71; Jennifer Somerville, 'The New Right and family politics', *Economy and Society*, 21 (1992), pp. 93–128; Pat Thane, 'Family life and "normality" in postwar British culture', in Richard Bessel and Dirk Schumann (eds), *Life After Death. Approaches to a Cultural and Social History of Europe during the 1940s and 1950s* (Cambridge: CUP, 2003), pp. 193–210; Pat Thane and Tanya Evans, *Sinners? Scroungers? Saints?: Unmarried Motherhood in Twentieth-Century England* (Oxford: OUP, 2012), pp. 170–177; John Welshman, *Underclass. A History of the Excluded, 1880–2000* (London: Bloomsbury, 2006), pp. 67, 81; John Welshman, '"Troubled Families": the lessons of history, 1880–2012', *History & Policy*, 1 October 2012 <http://www.historyandpolicy.org/policy-papers/papers/troubled-families-the-lessons-of-history-1880-2012> (20 July 2014).
[89] Ibid., pp. 75–76.
[90] Martin Francis, 'Tears, tantrums, and bared teeth: the emotional economy of three Conservative Prime Ministers, 1951–1963', *Journal of British Studies*, 41 (2002), pp. 354–387.
[91] Claire Langhamer, 'Everyday love and emotions in the 20th century', *The Many-Headed Monster Blog*, 28 August 2013 <https://manyheadedmonster.wordpress.com/2013/08/28/claire-langhamer-everyday-love-and-emotions-in-the-20th-century/#_ftn3> (4 July 2015).

the role of feminism or gay liberation in 'making the personal political'.[92] This book shows that small groups, led by middle-class families, with far more conservative aims, were likewise shaped by the emotional, experiential politics of this moment. Parents studied here were typically two-parent families in relatively traditional gender roles: the National Association, for example, stated in newsletters that, 'only one subscription is necessary for a husband and wife'.[93] Despite their relative positions of social and economic privilege, however, when speaking to the media, National Association families adopted the language of emotional struggle—discussing their personal pains, stress, and sadness in detail, and explicitly comparing the experiences of having a gifted child to those of having a disabled child, in terms of its impact on marriage, the constant struggle for assistance, and anxiety about letting their children down in a society that did not always care.

The emotional and experiential languages of these families was perhaps at odds with the limited nature of their demands. While liberationist movements of this period often used personal experiences to call for huge structural reform, these families typically requested very small changes. Primarily, they were happy to offer their own resources—family homes and time—to provide the gifted young with opportunities to learn. Notably, the families in this book rarely criticised the 'welfare state' explicitly and seldom positioned the educational system in Britain as a key issue, despite the clear relevance of schools to educating and identifying the gifted young. They normally accepted the school system as it was, seeking to offer alternate, extracurricular, provision for their children. Also, parents in this book rarely called for significant funding to be directed at giftedness. As such, these groups capitalised on the emotional politics of the 1970s and 1980s to make themselves visible, to connect to one another and build solidarities between families, but *not* to call for fundamental change. This approach, the book argues, was critical to the success of these voluntary groups, enabling them to gain attention and support particularly from Conservative politicians in the House of Lords, but also across parties, and from broadsheet left-wing

---

[92] For a small sample of significant works around gay and feminist liberation, see: Matt Cook, '"Gay Times": identity, locality, memory and the Brixton squats in 1970s London', *Twentieth Century British History*, 24 (1) (2013), pp. 84–109; Sarah Crook and Charlie Jeffries, *Resist, Organize, Build: Feminist and Queer Activism in Britain and the United States during the Long 1980s* (California: SUNY Press, 2022); Lucy Delap, 'Feminist bookshops, reading cultures and the Women's Liberation movement in Great Britain, c. 1974–2000', *History Workshop Journal*, 81 (1) (2016), pp. 171–196; George Severs, 'The Church of England's response to the HIV/AIDS epidemic, c. 1982–2000', MPhil thesis University of Cambridge (2017); Severs, George J., *Radical Acts: HIV/AIDS Activism in Late Twentieth-Century England* (London: Bloomsbury, 2024); Natalie Thomlinson, *Race, Ethnicity, and the Women's Movement in England, 1968–1993* (Basingstoke: Palgrave, 2016); Natalie Thomlinson, "Race and discomposure in oral histories with white feminist activists," *Oral History*, 42 (1) (2014), pp. 84–94; Jeffrey Weeks and Kevin Porter (eds), *Between the Acts: Lives of Homosexual Men, 1885–1967* (London: Rivers Oram Press, 1998).

[93] NAGC, Fifth Annual Report and Accounts of the National Association for Gifted Children, 1971–1972, p. 3.

newspapers and right-wing tabloid media alike. To study such activism is to recast 'resistance', in line with the writings of Maria Fannin and Julie MacLeavy, 'not as a constant, shared or even necessarily antagonistic activity, but as something achieved through inconsistent behaviours and actions: both collective and personal, inventive and also sustained by care, "outside" mainstream institutions and yet also deeply invested in the creation of new ones'.[94]

This book provides a specific snapshot of parental activism at a specific time, from the late 1960s to the late 1980s. By the 1990s, the voluntary groups discussed had typically crumbled, and indeed activism in this area was dominated by the National Academy for Gifted and Talented Youth; a huge professionalised organisation funded by New Labour, rather than by small groups of parents (studied in Chapter Five). In part, the collapse of parental activism around this issue may have reflected parents' feeling that their needs were met by state initiatives framed around 'giftedness', such as the National Academy. The National Association also suggested, by 1995, that the word 'gifted' may 'put people off becoming involved with us' and signal an 'intimidating or embarrassing organisation for ordinary families to join or admit belonging to'.[95] By this point, research in psychology and educational sociology about the biases in intelligence testing may have also damaged the group's cause. Finally, this book suggests that the parents of the late 1960s to late 1980s, studied here and also in Worth's work, may have been a cohort particularly willing to supplement the provisions of a welfare state they were born into or shortly in advance of, and who also had the leisure time, income, and sense of community to organise voluntary retreats.[96] This intimate analysis of family lives then, and of the motivations and efforts of families looking to provide new care for their 'gifted' children, signposts us towards an unexplored well of activist family life in modern Britain.

Children's Responses

Central here is the activism of children and the young, and the book demonstrates that young people had high critical engagement with voluntary groups mobilising around giftedness. By exploring the new spaces made available to young people—such as summer camps and afterschool clubs—in detail, and often from the perspective of children themselves, the book shows that the young

---

[94] Maria Fannin and Julie MacLeavy, 'Feminism, resistance and the archive', in Sarah M. Hughes (ed.), *Critical Geographies of Resistance* (Cheltenham: Edward Elgar, 2023), pp. 26–40; see also Paul Chatterton and Jenny Pickerill, 'Everyday activism and transitions towards post-capitalist worlds', *Transactions of the Institute of British Geographers*, 35 (4) (2010), pp. 475–490.
[95] NAGC, NAGC Newsletter, Summer 1995, 'A new name?', p. 7.
[96] Worth, *The Welfare State Generation*.

always remade the spaces available to them, beyond the intentions of adult organisers.

This is significant. Writing in 2017, Stuart C. Aitken stated that geographies of childhood and youth were 'once dismissed as naïve and of limited relevance': they were criticised as 'not objective', for having 'small sample sizes', or as holding 'little value for larger economic conditions'.[97] These criticisms continue to linger over the history of childhood at times, likewise. A critical review published as recently as 2020 maintained that 'age struggles to assert itself as a category of analysis beside class, gender, and ethnicity in historical study, and may continue to do so', because of a perceived lack of historical sources or because children are not 'an organized political constituency'.[98] Geographies of *youth*, in particular, were described in 2019 by Darren P. Smith and Sarah Mills as remaining somewhat 'dispersed and fragmented across different subdisciplinary outlets of Human Geography'.[99]

Despite such critiques and challenges, hugely sophisticated and innovative work is conducted around the distinct geographies and histories of childhood and youth. Such work challenges and troubles outdated ideals of 'objectivity', finds and generates rich sources in creative ways, and demonstrates that the young have exercised forms of 'power' which have been complex, nuanced, and meaningful.[100] This book follows and builds on such work, and it contends that

---

[97] Stuart C. Aitken, 'Children's geographies: tracing the evolution and involution of a concept', *Geographical Review*, 108 (1) (2017), pp. 4, 6. Other hugely useful discussions of the fields of geographies of youth and childhoods in: Sarah L. Holloway, 'Changing children's geographies', *Children's Geographies*, 12 (4) (2014), pp. 377–392; Darren P. Smith and Sarah Mills, 'The "youth-fullness" of youth geographies: "coming of age"?', *Children's Geographies*, 17 (1) (2019), pp. 1–8.

[98] Colin Heywood, 'On the margins or in the mainstream? The history of childhood in France', *Nottingham French Studies*, 59 (2) (2020), p. 135. Children do not gain much historical attention, perhaps because of their lack of political role, as argued by Harry Hendricks, interviewed in: Carmel Smith and Sheila Greene (eds), *Key Thinkers in Childhood Studies* (Bristol: Policy Press, 2015), p. 121, and the response to this article: Sarah Maza, 'The kids aren't all right: historians and the problem of childhood', *The American Historical Review*, 125 (4) (2020), pp. 1261–1285, and the responses to Maza's article: Steven Mintz, 'Children's history matters', *The American Historical Review*, 125 (4) (2020), pp. 1286–1292; Nara Milanich, 'Comment on Sarah Maza's "The kids aren't all right"', *The American Historical Review*, 125 (4) (2020), pp. 1293–1295; Robin P. Chapdelaine, 'Little voices: the importance and limitations of children's histories', *The American Historical Review*, 125 (4) (2020), pp. 1296–1299; Ishita Pande, 'Is the history of childhood ready for the world? a response to "the kids aren't all right"', *The American Historical Review*, 125 (4) (2020), pp. 1300–1305; Bengt Sandin, 'History of children and childhood—being and becoming, dependent and independent', *The American Historical Review*, 125 (4) (2020), pp. 1306–1316.

[99] Smith and Mills, 'The "youth-fullness" of youth geographies, p. 3.

[100] See, for example: Siân Pooley and J. Taylor (eds), *Children's Experiences of Welfare in Modern Britain* (London: IHR, 2021); Siân Pooley and Colin Pooley, '"Such a splendid tale": the late nineteenth-century world of a young female reader', *Cultural and Social History*, 2 (2005), pp. 329–351; Siân Pooley, 'Children's writing and the popular press in England, 1876–1914', *History Workshop Journal*, 80 (2015), pp. 75–98; Laura Tisdall, '"That was what life in Bridgeburn had made her": reading the autobiographies of children in institutional care in England, 1918–1946', *Twentieth Century British History*, 24 (2013), pp. 351–375; Catherine Sloan, '"Periodicals of an objectionable character": peers and periodicals at Croydon Friends' School, 1826–1875', *Victorian Periodicals Review*, 50 (2017), pp. 769–786; Sarah Kenny, '"Basically you were either a mainstream sort of person

the voices of children and the young must be made critical to understanding modern Britain. The book shows the particular complexities of the lives of those labelled as gifted. These children often enjoyed new voluntary spaces established for them in the 1970s and 1980s—although some resisted participation—and brought the identity of 'gifted' to schools and sibling relationships, often causing tension with children not so labelled. While historiographical attention at least has more typically focused on the 'radical' streams of youth culture—sex, drugs, and rock and roll—this case study shows how young people also gathered together on the basis of ideas of saving the world, leading a 'better' Britain, or engaging in intellectual puzzles and outdoor pursuits (disparate constellations of interests for 'the gifted' further explored in Chapter Three).[101] By the 1990s, as relevant voluntary groups declined, many young people became volunteers and several wrote to voluntary groups to bemoan the end of these spaces. Histories and geographies of young people, as Pooley and Tisdall have argued, are important in their own right, not merely in relation to who those children grow up to become.[102] The young people in this book engaged with the term 'gifted child' as young people, *and* it reshaped their lives for many years.[103]

---

or you went to the Leadmill and The Limit": understanding post-war British youth culture through oral history', in Kristine Moruzi, Nell Musgrove, and Carla Pascoe Leahy (eds), *Children's Voices from the Past: New Historical and Interdisciplinary Perspectives* (London, Palgrave Macmillan, 2019), pp. 233–259; Richard Ivan Jobs, *Backpack Ambassadors: How Youth Travel Integrated Europe* (Chicago: University of Chicago Press, 2017); Mischa Honeck and Gabriel Rosenberg, 'Transnational generations: organizing youth in the Cold War', *Diplomatic History*, 38 (2) (2014); Sarah L. Holloway and Gill Valentine (eds), *Children's Geographies: Playing, Living, Learning* (Milton Keynes: Routledge, 2000); Jacob Fairless Nicholson, 'From London to Grenada and back again: youth exchange geographies and the Grenadian Revolution, 1979-1983', *Antipode*, pp. 708–728; Sarah Mills, *Mapping the Moral Geographies of Education: Character, Citizenship and Values* (Milton Keynes: Routledge, 2022); Karen Wells, *Childhood in a Global Perspective* (Third edition, Cambridge: Polity, 2021).

[101] For discussions of the lives of radical youth, see Celia Hughes, 'Young socialist men in 1960s Britain: subjectivity and sociability', *History Workshop Journal*, 73 (2012), pp. 170–92; Celia Hughes, *Young Lives on the Left: Sixties Activism and the Liberation of the Self* (Manchester: MUP, 2015). A classic account of moral panic around youth can be found in: Stanley Cohen, *Folk Devils and Moral Panics: The Creation of the Mods and Rockers* (London, Paladin, 1972). See also: Bill Osgerby, 'The good, the bad and the ugly: postwar media representations of youth', in Adam Briggs and Paul Cobley (eds), *The Media: An Introduction* (Harlow, 1997); Angela Bartie, 'Moral panics and Glasgow gangs: exploring "the new wave of Glasgow hooliganism", 1965-1970', *Contemporary British History*, 24 (2010), pp. 385–406; Louise Jackson and Angela Bartie, *Policing Youth: Britain, 1945-1970* (Manchester: MUP, 2014). For contemporary and historiographical accounts that acknowledge that youth lives were varied—and indeed often mundane rather than radical, see Michael Schofield, *The Sexual Behaviour of Young People* (London: Longmans, 1965); Michael Schofield, *The Sexual Behaviour of Young Adults* (London: Allen Lane, 1973); Pearl Jephcott, *Time of One's Own: Leisure and Young People* (Edinburgh: EUP, 1967); Jim Gledhill, 'White heat, guide blue: the Girl Guide movement in the 1960s', *Contemporary British History*, 27 (2013), pp. 65–84; Helena Mills, 'The experience and memory of youth in England c. 1960–c. 1969' (D.Phil. thesis, Oxford, 2016), <https://ora.ox.ac.uk/objects/uuid:f0bdc321-b580-414d-a7ff-35d2c92e3ad4> (4 June 2021), pp. 2, 6.

[102] Siân Pooley, 'Children's writing and the popular press in England 1876–1914', *History Workshop Journal*, 80 (1) (2015), p. 75; Laura Tisdall, 'State of the Field: the modern history of childhood', p. 7.

[103] Worth's *The Welfare State Generation* wonderfully traces how school experiences, more generally, and the experience of being streamed at an early age, shaped how women thought about themselves across their lives, see for example interviews on pp. 27–28.

Significantly, this book contends that the experience of being 'a gifted child' was distinct between the 1960s and 1990s. As Celia Hughes writes with reference to young left-wing radicals in the earlier part of this period, 'the experience of social and political maturation intersected with a specific social and political moment'.[104] In the case of gifted young people, their experiences intersected, shaped, and were shaped by, a moment in which policy-makers, press, and the voluntary sector were enamoured of ideas of 'crisis' and 'decline', in the 1970s and 1980s.[105] These ideas were culturally significant, and drove New Right concerns about family life, as well as the shutting down of many landscapes of the child, such as playing outdoors, as Mathew Thomson has shown.[106] These anxieties about crisis and change impacted the children in this book, motivating families to set up alternate retreats where their middle-class children could 'safely' experience rural life, in the company of other 'special', gifted youth, for example. Such anxieties were also critical in enabling families to successfully bid for funding, and to gain media attention; they also contributed to the idea that these children could be elites of the future, solving various social and economic problems. Examining how some children relished these hopes, and others resented them shows, as Nicholas Stargardt discusses, the 'emotional impact, the human meaning, of historical change'; in this case the lived impact—the excitement and the stresses—of being labelled as 'an elite' who must rescue the world.[107]

Gifted children then have their own social history, which is worthy of study, partly because they played a role in shaping modern Britain and indeed also constructions of 'Europe' and 'the world'. Siân Pooley and Jonathan Taylor argue that 'the young were integral to the making, interpretation, delivery and impact of welfare services, and that their involvement has left a distinctive imprint on the shape of welfare in modern Britain'.[108] Richard Ivan Jobs has demonstrated the transnational significance of youth, and his innovative study of backpacking shows that young people and their travel was 'central' to the social and cultural aspects of European integration in the late twentieth century.[109] Mischa Honeck and Gabriel Rosenberg, likewise, conclude that young people left 'footprints' in the 'dynamic, interconnected, and volatile world of the Cold War—both as individuals and as members of adult-led organisations'.[110]

---

[104] Celia Hughes, 'Young socialist men in 1960s Britain: subjectivity and sociability', *History Workshop Journal*, 73 (2012), p. 171.

[105] David Edgerton, *The Rise and Fall of the British Nation: A Twentieth Century History* (London: Allen Lane, 2018). See also: David Edgerton, *England and the Aeroplane: Militarism, Modernity and Machines* (London: Penguin, 2013); David Edgerton, *Warfare State: Britain, 1920–1970* (Cambridge: CUP, 2005).

[106] Thomson, *Lost Freedom*.

[107] Nicholas Stargardt, 'German childhoods: the making of a historiography', *German History*, 16 (1) (1998), , p. 15.

[108] Pooley and Taylor, 'Introduction', in *Children's Experiences of Welfare*, p. 1.

[109] Jobs, *Backpack Ambassadors*, p. 1.

[110] Honeck and Rosenberg, 'Transnational generations', p. 234.

The critique of young people regarding giftedness in education eventually manifested in reducing programmes that aimed to find elites of the future; the happiness agenda that young people called for did eventually filter into policy. Yet, there were also significant limits to the influence of the young. For Jobs and Honeck and Rosenberg, young people influenced global debate through their behaviours, while in this case study, analysis of the European Council for High Ability and World Council for Gifted and Talented Children (Chapter Six) shows that young people's voices rarely cut through in historic debates, and it was more typically the invocation of 'the child' and their interests that became powerful. In part, this reflected the challenges of organising voluntary groups across countries and with limited funds—few countries had national programmes for identifying gifted youth, let alone international ones. At the same time, this history highlights the level of structural challenges that young people faced in making a visible policy contribution to the world: when international organisations struggled to fund initiatives and meetings around giftedness, children themselves were the first to be excluded. Again, using a framework of 'Britain in the world', and putting the international organisations in this area—the European Council for High Ability and the World Council for Gifted and Talented Children—alongside the national ones were critical to reveal this disjuncture. Children themselves are, therefore, central to this work.

This book demonstrates that children's voices can and must be placed alongside those of adults in our social histories and geographies—the experiences of the young are fascinating and powerful on their own account, and also contribute to debate in family lives and beyond. Examination of the group 'the gifted young' enables us to view the privileges afforded to those labelled 'gifted' and, simultaneously, the structural challenges faced by those considered 'young'; the push and pull between these factors and competing identities is at the core of this book.

Chapter Outline

Gifted Children in Britain and the World has a chronological structure, to further detail the broad terrain of this topic, which has not been written about before, and to underscore and emphasise how the phenomenon of the gifted youth as a future elite was distinct from, and definitive of, mid-to-late twentieth-century Britain. Chapter One traces a prehistory of interest in giftedness from which the central narratives of this book later emerge. Notably, it explores accounts by adults (as provided to Mass Observation) and by children (to the Opie project) that showed how interest in intellect was present in daily life. Furthermore, it shows that 'everyday' debates constantly positioned intellect in relation to themes of elitism and equality—echoing higher-level educational debates and setting the stage for the challenges voluntary groups subsequently faced.

Chapter Two explores how ideas of giftedness began to take root in Britain in the 1960s, in disparate ways. The Brentwood Experiment in Essex, which started in 1963, looked to find the gifted young in local schools to ensure that they were educationally fulfilled. The National Association was founded in 1966, and emphasised that providing resources for gifted children was an equalities measure, remedying significant deficits in the welfare state. Conservative Members of the House of Lords, meanwhile, typically from prestigious educational backgrounds, asked whether the educational system was missing elites of the future, and whether it should be more 'elitist'. This disparate band of groups, then, had reasons for finding 'the gifted young', although also looked to recognise intellect as a key form of difference, and also provided critique—from various angles—of the post-war settlement.

The next two chapters of this book consider the 1970s and the 1980s, years in which the National Association flourished across more than fifty regional branches. Chapter Three discusses how young people themselves engaged with National Association spaces. It shows that many embraced the idea that they had distinct needs because they were 'gifted'—and indeed that this type of difference showed their superiority in society and their promise as elites of the future. The chapter also traces those who resented this label. It examines, finally, how young people's engagement with families and schools were changed by this label—and in doing so demonstrates that the label 'gifted' significantly changed young people's self-perceptions, beyond, for example, simply entering a grammar school: being singled out as 'gifted' truly forged a unique sense of self for many young people.

Chapter Four examines the relationships between giftedness, popular eugenics, and elites of the future in the 1970s and 1980s. It first critically interrogates the work of Cyril Burt, in demanding that gifted children be identified as elites of the future—and traces the critique of such work. The chapter also shows how assumptions that the gifted child would be white, middle-class, and male entered tabloid newspapers—where journalists often expressed shock and fascination when this was not the case. Finally, the chapter shows how many children involved in the National Association themselves engaged with ideas of elites of the future—some feeling great responsibility for the world, and others echoing broader critiques of racial pseudoscience and intelligence testing.

Chapter Five analyses how the gifted child entered national policy, for the first time, in the 1990s and 2000s, moving beyond local experiments and voluntary action to assume a place in both John Major's Conservative and Tony Blair's New Labour administrations. The chapter closely examines the National Academy for Gifted and Talented Youth, showing how this organisation fostered a new vision of the gifted young as future corporate and industrial leaders. The chapter reads against the grain of National Academy publications to show how young people remade the summer camps available, often adapting them as social spaces, rather than to develop careers—while nonetheless also still living with the idea that intelligence conferred significant social difference.[111] It shows, also, how adults remember childhood debates about giftedness—for example, analysing the sensationalist coverage of 'gifted child alumni' in American press, as well as Britain-centred discussions of giftedness, and memories of the National Records of Achievement folders.

Chapter Six considers the work of the European Council for High Ability and the World Council for Gifted and Talented Children in the late twentieth century. It shows that British psychologists and those involved in the National Association played a key role in the foundation and organisation of these groups. It demonstrates how these organisations from the 1970s until the 2000s held perhaps the clearest and more explicit range of hopes that the gifted young, if identified, could use their special talents to forge global connections across borders, preventing warfare, developing cultural and social ties, and fuelling international development. This was highly ambitious given that the organisations faced significant logistical challenges such as language barriers and lack of funding. The chapter also reads against the grain of these groups' newsletters to discuss how children themselves engaged in such international networks, and how these contributed to their sense of uniqueness and difference.

The Conclusion explores the moral and political questions raised by this history of giftedness. As discussed, the voluntary sector made huge efforts to recruit gifted children from minoritised ethnic and poorer areas, and also to recruit girls and boys equally. Yet these efforts were rarely successful in the voluntary sector and, more broadly, media and policy continued to frame elites of the future as white, male, and affluent. Voluntary sector efforts to compare gifted children to disabled ones, through reference to parents' emotional struggles, were also problematic. This chapter argues that this history then demonstrates another mechanism through which privilege prevails: campaigning with the best intentions around equality can, nonetheless, further ingrain existing structural hierarchies.

Gifted children then have social histories on local, national, and international levels, and which have not been explored until now. This book explores that social history at multiple scales, and makes the voices of the gifted young themselves central. Those labelled 'gifted' sometimes loved this label, and felt special in

---

[111] There is a rich range of literatures around archives and reading 'against the grain'. In this book, my thinking is particularly indebted to the following: on the 'light and shade an archive can project on the documents it safeguards', Mela Dávila-Freire, 'Reading the archive against the grain: Power relations, affective affinities and subjectivity in the documenta Archive', *Art Libraries Journal*, 45 (3) (2020), (quote p. 99); Merle Patchett, 'Archiving', *Transactions of the Institute of British Geographers*, 44 (2019), pp. 650–653; Kate Boyer, 'Feminist geography in the archive: practice and method', WGSG, *Geography and Gender Reconsidered*, August 2004, p. 170; Sarah Mills, 'Cultural-historical geographies of the archive: fragments, objects and ghosts', *Geography Compass*, 7 (10) (2013), p. 701–713; Maria Fannin and Julie MacLeavy, 'Feminism, resistance and the archive', Sarah M. Hughes (ed.), *Critical Geographies of Resistance* (Cheltenham: Edward Elgar, 2023), pp. 26–40.

comparison to peers at school and siblings at home. For others, 'gifted' was a silly or embarrassing label, and many questioned the idea of separating off young people in terms of intelligence, as well as the specific forms of testing being used. Ideas of the gifted child also reshaped family lives—parents dedicated time to providing special clubs for those thought of as gifted, running them in their own homes and taking their children significant distances to spend time with others that were also 'gifted'. Voluntary organisations were critical here, as the medium through which young people and adults encountered the term, 'gifted', and lived and created it relationally, through interactions with one another. Voluntary organisations, looking to gain attention and visibility, also critically shaped the idea that the gifted young were elites of the future, central to answering challenges of economic decline, global warfare, or humanitarian aid. The hopes placed on gifted children between the 1960s and the 1990s were sky high—yet many gifted young, such as the twelve-year-old who opened this chapter, still felt that the community 'wasted' their talents, and did not support them.[112] This, then, is a story of optimism, hope, disappointment, and criticism, in which young people themselves play a central role.

'Gifted Children' in Britain and the World: Elitism and Equality since 1945. Jennifer Crane, Oxford University Press.
© Jennifer Crane 2025. DOI: 10.1093/9780198928881.003.0001

[112] NAGC, *Gallimaufry*, Easter 1982, 'This is the story of Ogg', p. 2.

Everyday Encounters with Stupidity and Intellect, 1944–1962

> 'a sap is a stupid person, a mug, High School Mugs.'
> *Opie Archive, Bodleian Libraries, University of Oxford (hereafter Opie Archive), OP/A/1/3/8/32/1, MS. Opie 3 fol. 381r, Kirkcaldy High School, Kirkcaldy, Fife, Scotland, c. 1952.*

The testimony above was written by a girl, whose age was not provided, attending the Kirkcaldy High School in Fife around 1952. On a single sheet of paper, she explained eleven different games and expressions important to her peer groups. As this brief description suggests, children in the 1950s were interested in ideas of 'stupidity', seeing them as a way to make sense of the world. This testimony is central to understanding the key challenge unpicked by this chapter: what cultural ecosystems and understandings laid the groundwork for the establishment of voluntary groups interested in giftedness in the 1960s and 1970s? What precedents shaped these groups' framing of 'equality' and 'elitism', which persisted in subsequent decades?

First, this chapter describes a near immediate breakdown in any post-war 'settlement' around the provision for the gifted young, primarily through local media discussion between parents, teachers, and journalists. Second, the chapter analyses adult and child discussions of intellect, in their everyday lives in the mid-twentieth century, through study of Mass Observation diaries, bulletins, and surveys, and Opie archives of children's play. Overall, this discussion then sets the scene for subsequent discussions of the 1960s and 1970s onwards, the focus of the book. The chapter shows that the post-war settlement did not fully satisfy earlier concerns about the education of the particularly intelligent young. By the 1960s and 1970s, Parliamentarians, parents, and campaigners sought to address this terrain, and to frame support for the gifted as a critical issue of *both* 'equality' and 'elitism', presenting gifted children variously as unfortunate, neglected, ignored by the welfare state *and* as a critical resource for a supply of elites of the future. These framings were not so explicit in the 1940s and 1950s, but built on earlier assumptions and everyday beliefs, in particular that to be particularly intelligent was a gift and a challenge, a virtue and a peculiarity.

Post-war Breakdowns

Interest in childhood intelligence, in culture and education, was far from new to the mid-to-late twentieth century. Nor were tensions between the broad ideas of equality and elitism, manifested in various forms.[1] Nonetheless, educational policy was reformed once more in the post-war welfare state. The 1944 *Education Act* was proposed by the wartime cabinet led by Winston Churchill, and mandated that local education authorities in England and Wales provide free separate secondary education for all young people. Local education authorities would determine how education was arranged, but were mandated to ensure it suited students' 'ability and aptitude', which in practice often meant that students were allocated to modern, technical, or grammar schools.[2] The subsequent *Education (Scotland) Act* of 1945 extended '[s]imilar obligations' to Scottish local authorities—although less changed here, subsequently, because of Scotland's existing 'lead in expanding secondary education since 1918'.[3] Scholarly debate around the 1944 Act, in England and Wales, recognises that it reflected both a post-war moment of consensus around expanding a 'universal' welfare state, and 'key Conservative beliefs', such as the 'desirability of preserving educational privileges and the belief in hierarchy'.[4] For Peter Mandler, the 1944 Act represented

---

[1] In terms of scientific and cultural interest in the precocious child, in the nineteenth century, see: Sally Shuttleworth, *The Mind of the Child: Child Development in Literature, Science, and Medicine, 1840–1900* (Oxford: OUP, 2010); Claudia Nelson: *Precocious Children and Childish Adults: Age Inversion in Victorian Literature* (Baltimore, MD: John Hopkins University Press, 2012). For discussions of earlier educational interest in ability, from the nineteenth century, see: Peter Mandler, *The Crisis of the Meritocracy: Britain's Transition to Mass Education since the Second World War* (Oxford: OUP, 2020), pp. 18–28.

[2] Mandler, *Crisis of the Meritocracy*, ch. 3. There has been considerable scholarly debate about this Act (see for example R. G. Wallace, 'The aims and authorship of the 1944 Education Act', *History of Education*, 4 (1981), pp. 283–290; 'Briefing paper: Secondary modern schools', *Secondary Education and Social Change Project (hereafter SESC)*, October 2017 <https://sesc.hist.cam.ac.uk/wp-content/uploads/2018/02/Briefing-paper-Secondary-modern-schools.pdf> (13 September 2021), p. 2. This briefing note highlights that: in Wales many rural areas had multilateral (comprehensive) schools, providing for all young people, due to a lack of concentrated staff members and resources. On the responsibility held by Local Educational Authorities, see: 'Local Educational Authorities', *SESC*, December 2018 <https://sesc.hist.cam.ac.uk/wp-content/uploads/2020/09/Briefing-Paper-LEAs.pdf> (13 September 2021).

[3] Mandler, *Crisis of the Meritocracy*, p. 32; Scotland briefing note <https://sesc.hist.cam.ac.uk/wp-content/uploads/2018/08/Briefing-paper-Scotland.pdf>. The difference in the Scottish context was recognised as the Earl of Roseberry (briefly the Secretary of State for Scotland in Churchill's caretaker Ministry, May–July 1945) presented the Bill to the House of Lords. He stated that, while, 'the educational history and traditions of Scotland are different from those of England', he felt that 'the adaptions made' would 'present no difficulty to your Lordships' (Hansard, House of Lords, Education (Scotland) Bill, 6 June 1945, vol. 136, col. 435).

[4] 'Hartmut Kopsch, "The approach of the Conservative Party to social policy during World War Two", unpublished University of London Ph.D. thesis (1970), 385–386', as cited in, Brian Simon, 'The 1944 Education Act: A Conservative measure?', *History of Education*, 15 (1) (1986), p. 31; Kevin Jeffreys, 'R. A. Butler, the Board of Education, and the 1944 Education Act', *History*, 69 (227) (1984), pp. 415–431; Wallace, 'The aims and authorship of the 1944 Education Act', pp. 283–290. An influential account about the effect of wartime on post-war social policy can be found in: R.M. Titmuss, *Problems of Social Policy* (London: Ministry of Health, 1950); Mandler, *Crisis of the Meritocracy*, ch. 3.

'the triumph of the meritocratic ideal of "equal opportunity" in popular and academic imagination'.[5] However, it did not guarantee equality in practice: educational systems remained 'fragmented, under local control, and driven essentially by changes at the local level', while maintaining selection at age 11 in many places, on the basis of an exam, maintained privilege, 'rather than disrupting it'.[6] Notably, indeed, certain children were deemed 'ineducable' under this Act, and subsequently placed under care of the National Health Service, rather than local authorities.[7]

Clearly, interest in intellectual ability and aptitude was present in these policies and debates, and ideas about the post-war settlement, as well as the legislation itself, shaped discussion for years to come. In particular, these Acts, and how they were realised differently at local levels, permitted endless further debates about equality and elitism. For example, the notion that children could be categorised and framed by 'ability and aptitude', as well as by age, begged the question of what children of 'higher' and 'lower' aptitudes needed and deserved, and what they would receive. This was variously positioned as 'elitist'—categorising and labelling children by ability—or as embedding 'equality'—recognising different views of ability and kinds of intelligence.

This book argues that satisfaction with any post-war settlement, vis-à-vis provision for gifted children, conclusively broke down in the 1960s and 1970s, some time before our typical narratives around the rise of neoliberalism and individualism in the late 1970s and 1980s. Nonetheless, in the 1940s and 1950s, huge criticism about provision for exceptionally gifted children, or the lack thereof, was already being made by teachers, parents, and journalists. In 1945, teachers wrote to the *Surrey Advertiser* to ask whether, in their area, 'with junior classes containing the most backward as well as the brightest, progress will inevitably be conditioned by the former, and irreparable damage will be done to the more gifted children, whose opportunities of advancement will be gravely jeopardised'.[8] These ideas were reiterated by the Director of Education for Derbyshire, speaking to the *Stapleford & Sandiacre News* in 1955, and by an editorial in the *Coventry Evening Telegraph*, in the same year.[9] For these teachers and commentators,

---

[5] Mandler, *Crisis of the Meritocracy*, p. 33.   [6] Ibid., pp. 33–34.
[7] It was not until 1970 that the *Education (Handicapped Children) Act* changed this, making education authorities responsible for the education of all children. See on this: Rubahanna Amannah Choudhury, 'The forgotten children: The Association of Parents of Backward Children and the legacy of eugenics in Britain, 1946–1960', thesis submitted for the Degree of Doctor of Philosophy at Oxford Brookes University, December 2015, pp. 5, 32–33; Anne Borsay and Pamela Dale (eds), *Disabled Children: Contested Caring, 1850–1979* (Milton: Routledge, 2016).
[8] 'Education in Surrey', *Surrey Advertiser* (27 October 1945).
[9] 'Education's greatest problem', *Stapleford & Sandiacre News* (9 April 1955), p. 6; 'Shall it be parents' choice or "factory" schools?', *Coventry Evening Telegraph* (17 May 1955), p. 12. We cannot fully trace the views of these early proponents of gifted education, due to the limited space afforded to this issue in local newspaper coverage. However, such views were particularly prevalent in areas where the local education authorities had unusual plans—in Coventry, for example, the Labour-controlled

grammar schools did not challenge the most intellectually gifted nearly enough. Notably, grammar schools educated between 24.6 per cent and 37.8 per cent of the secondary school-aged population between the late 1940s and early 1960s, a relatively large proportion (although reducing over this period as the baby boomers came of school age).[10]

Local newspaper coverage, as above, typically called for increased provision for 'the gifted', because teachers felt that these young people were struggling; they felt socially and emotionally isolated, and alone in the classroom and beyond. Nonetheless, local and national newspapers also, at times, suggested that the country needed elites of the future. In 1950, the *Manchester Guardian* asked whether the grammar school system could prevent 'wastage' in Britain by identifying gifted youth.[11] In 1965, the *Birmingham Daily Post* likewise questioned whether grammar schools, provided for children with significant variation in their educational abilities, were able to 'develop the full talents of the nation's gifted children', not just those who qualified to attend.[12] Anxious parents shared these concerns. One, writing to centre-right broadsheet *The Times* in 1948, characterised post-war educational policy in terms of a push towards uniformity, with children all taking exams at the same time. For this parent, this policy marked an 'inevitable degradation from democracy to tyranny', and acted as 'preventive measures against the emergence' of intelligent citizens.[13] Another letter to *The Times* in 1953 argued that the intelligent should be made leaders, lest the nation be 'lost'—and that this leadership was not promoted by the current educational system.[14] For this author, gifted young people must 'mix sufficiently in their formative years' to be 'recognized by the potentially led', but must also become elites

---

authority had 'adopted long-term plans for comprehensive reorganization early on' ('Briefing paper: Comprehensives', *SESC*, October 2017 <https://sesc.hist.cam.ac.uk/wp-content/uploads/2018/02/Briefing-paper-Comprehensives.pdf>, p. 1).

[10] 'Briefing paper: Grammar Schools', *SESC*, January 2018 <https://sesc.hist.cam.ac.uk/wp-content/uploads/2018/01/Briefing-paper-Grammar-Schools.pdf> (13 September 2021), p. 1. This figure continued to fall sharply to 9.8 per cent in 1975 and down to 5.2 per cent by 2015, due to the comprehensivation process (see 'Briefing paper: Comprehensives', *SESC*, October 2017 <https://sesc.hist.cam.ac.uk/wp-content/uploads/2018/02/Briefing-paper-Comprehensives.pdf>, p. 3).

[11] 'School Entrance', *The Manchester Guardian* (7 June 1950), p. 6.

[12] 'Education changes must "aid gifted"', *Birmingham Daily Post* (8 April 1965), p. 7. Derbyshire's Director of Education referred to ideas of national futures, stating that 'it was necessary in the national interest to ensure that the naturally gifted children were given the fullest opportunity to develop their talents' ('Education's greatest problem', *Stapleford & Sandiacre News* (9 April 1955), p. 6). This point was reiterated in local coverage around Coventry also: 'One headteacher told the *Coventry Evening Telegraph* in 1950, for example, that, "it is of the greatest importance to the country, to its trade and industry, that the gifted children shall receive the education that will fit them for their life work"' ('Selecting Pupils for Coventry's "11-Plus" Schools', *Coventry Evening Telegraph* (6 February 1950), p. 8).

[13] T. P. Creed, 'New certificate examination', *The Times*, 16 October 1948, p. 5.

[14] G. V. King, 'Brilliance at school', *The Times*, 13 April 1953, p. 7.

of the future.[15] These letters, and other editorials, were pervaded by the idea that 'democracy to-day needs natural leaders as never before'.[16]

There was then huge local variety within the post-war welfare systems, visible as a new educational policy was implemented and realised in local contexts. The introduction of the welfare state was not a pure moment of equality or universalism. New settlements in education, as in welfare more broadly, were complex and criticised from their outset.[17] Calls to foster gifted young people as critical to national futures escalated in the 1960s and 1970s. This activism is worthy of our attention, as are the ways in which policy changes, debates, and tensions reshaped everyday life for young people and their families.

(Some) Adults' Encounters with Intelligence and Stupidity

Evidently, adults and children alike discussed intelligence in the 1940s and 1950s, before the rise of giftedness-related organisations in the 1960s and 1970s—but how were these debates framed? Adult discussions are traced here through analysis of Mass Observation, a social research organisation operative from 1937 until the 1950s and well known to researchers, because of its rich archives of diaries, surveys, and snapshot directive replies, all looking to create an 'anthropology of ourselves' from volunteers.[18] While mining Mass Observation materials

---

[15] Ibid. [16] 'Cradle of genius?', *The Times*, 29 April 1957, p. 13.
[17] Daisy Payling, '"The people who write to us are the people who don't like us:" Public responses to the Government Social Survey's Survey of Sickness, 1943–1952', *Journal of British Studies* 59 (2020), pp. 315–342; Gareth Millward, *Sick Note: A History of the British Welfare State* (Oxford: OUP, 2022), ch. 2; see Jane Lewis, 'Gender and the development of welfare regimes', *Journal of European Social Policy*, 2 (2) (1992), pp. 159–173; Helen McCarthy, *Double Lives: A History of Working Motherhood in Modern Britain* (London: Bloomsbury, 2020); Jeroen van Der Waal, Willem de Koster, and Wim van Oorschot, 'Three worlds of welfare chauvinism? how welfare regimes affect support for distributing welfare to immigrants in Europe', *Journal of Comparative Policy Analysis: Research and Practice*, 15 (2) (2013), pp. 164–181.
[18] 'History of Mass Observation', Mass Observation <http://www.massobs.org.uk/about/history-of-mo> (14 September 2021). Powerful contemporary scholarship drawing on Mass Observation materials includes: Penny Summerfield, 'Mass-observation: social research or social movement?', *Journal of Contemporary History*, 20, 1985, pp. 439–452; Claire Langhamer, 'Mass observing the atom bomb: the emotional politics of August 1945', *Contemporary British History*, 33 (2) (2019), pp. 208–225; Claire Langhamer, 'An archive of feeling? mass observation and the mid-century moment', *Insights*, 9 (4) (2016), pp. 1–15; Claire Langhamer, *The English in Love: The Intimate Story of an Emotional Revolution* (Oxford: OUP, 2013); Ian Gazeley and Claire Langhamer, 'The meanings of happiness in mass observation's Bolton', *History Workshop Journal*, 75 (1) (2013), pp. 159–189; James Hinton, *Nine Wartime Lives: Mass Observation and the Making of the Modern Self* (Oxford: OUP, 2010); Andrew Burchell, 'Mass observing general practice', *People's History of the NHS project*, <https://peopleshistorynhs.org/mass-observing-general-practice/> (14 September 2021); Nick Clarke and Clive Barnett, 'Archiving the COVID-19 pandemic in Mass Observation and Middletown', *History of the Human Sciences*, 36 (2) (2023), pp. 3–25; Nick Clarke and Jonathan Moss, 'Popular imaginative geographies and Brexit: Evidence from Mass Observation', *Transactions of the Institute of British Geographers*, 46 (3) (2021), pp. 732–746.

is a well-worn path, it is worth reading these archives once more in terms of intelligence and stupidity, which has never been a key focus of analysis (perhaps, in part, because of the assumption that Mass Observation looked to study everyday or 'ordinary' life and, in doing so, draw focus from the 'men of genius' ruling British society).[19] Despite democratic framing, however, Mass Observation structuring materials, such as the *Resistance to Advertising* report (1944), assumed that its volunteers would be 'for the most part of people above the average of intelligence', 'with an interest in observing things, and particularly inclined to observe themselves objectively'.[20]

Mass Observers themselves were, perhaps, disproportionately likely to self-identify as *particularly intelligent*, in addition to being disproportionately likely to be female, middle-class, and older.[21] This shaped how they wrote their directives: Dorothy Sheridan has described the observers' complex relationship with Mass Observation, as they wrote with the awareness—and indeed hopes—that their thoughts would be archived, stored, and used in an imagined future.[22] Beyond this, volunteers also often framed their participation in this project as uniquely intellectual work. Various observers noted casually that they needed, 'my brain sufficiently alive to write these observations', for example, or that they had taken 'much trouble' to compile 'authentic data' for Mass Observation.[23] Observers casually mentioned, for example, that: '[m]y brain must have food for thought every minute I'm awake', and emphasised remarkable patterns of reading and thinking, 'to keep me going'.[24] They were concerned that a demeaning job could have a 'deadening effect' on my intelligence, or believed that doing different tasks with both hands would 'develop the brain immensely'.[25] One Mass Observer even

---

[19] Charles Madge and Tom Harrisson, *Mass Observation* (London, 1937), p. 10, as cited in, Alexander Campsie, 'Mass-observation, left intellectuals and the politics of everyday life', *English Historical Review*, CXXXI, 548 (2016), p. 98. Ian Gazeley and Claire Langhamer quote from the same publication, making a related point, that Mass Observation must look beyond London to, 'ensure against a predominance at the centre of intellectuals living in academic isolation' (Gazeley and Langhamer, 'The Meanings of Happiness in Mass Observation's Bolton', p. 163). Relatedly, Alexander Campsie has argued that this organisation played a specific role in shaping the thought of 'unaligned left intellectuals' from the 1930s to the 1950s and, in so doing, British progressive thought more broadly: Campsie, 'Mass-observation, left intellectuals and the politics of everyday life', pp. 96, 100.

[20] Mass Observation, Resistance to Advertising, January 1944, p. 3.

[21] See: Annebella Pollen, 'Research methodology in mass observation past and present: 'scientifically, about as valuable as a chimpanzee's tea party at the zoo?', *History Workshop Journal*, 75 (1) (2013), pp. 214–216, 218–222; Peter Gurney, '"Intersex" and "Dirty Girls": mass-observation and working-class sexuality in England in the 1930s', *Journal of the History of Sexuality*, 8 (2) (1997), pp. 261–262, 288; James Hinton, 'The "class" complex: mass-observation and cultural distinction in pre-war Britain', *Past & Present*, 199 (2008), p. 210.

[22] Dorothy Sheridan, 'Writing to the archive: mass observation as autobiography', *Sociology*, 27 (1) (1993), pp. 27–40.

[23] Mass Observation, Day Survey, Respondent 539, June 1937–July 1937; Mass Observation, Day Survey, Respondent 564, July 1937–September 1937.

[24] Mass Observation, Diarist 5399, August 1939–March 1947.

[25] Mass Observation, Day Survey, Respondent 293, August 1937–September 1938; Mass Observation, Diarist 5399, August 1939–March 1947.

wrote of becoming a parent member of the National Association for Gifted Children—providing an unsolicited account about this to Mass Observation in 1984.[26] Analysis of Mass Observation, then, can provide one way to trace how those who regarded themselves as 'intelligent', and were perhaps also more likely to join campaign groups around giftedness, connected ideas of intelligence and social worth from the 1940s onwards.

Observers were hugely interested in analysing the intelligence of others—at times to further bolster ideas of their own intellect. Writing in 1937, one woman described her maid as 'most decidedly above [average] intelligence', while another author mentioned a man with 'plenty of intelligence which he does not use'.[27] Distinguishing herself as a distinct member of society, with distinct talents, one 1937 observer wrote that, 'I live in a typical suburb [sic], where the houses are middle-class and all alike, where the women are mainly without any suggestion of brain, but full of animal cunning'.[28] Observers also critiqued the lack of intellectual fuel provided by popular culture. One radio programme was described, for example, as 'an insult to the intelligence of the listening public'.[29] Advertisers, likewise, were condemned for 'an appalling poor idea of their readers' intelligence'.[30] Books were described in terms of presenting 'people of exceptional honesty and intelligence' or depicting children who were 'all very clever'.[31]

Observers were interested, also, in the perceived intelligence of young people. One, for example, asked in 1937 to describe everyone they had encountered recently, first described several adults as variously 'intelligent' or 'ignorant' (or as disliking 'superior intelligence in others').[32] Describing a seventeen-year-old who worked at their company, this observer wrote that he had, '[p]recocious intellect, and [he] has already evolved [a] philosophy of life (which is a faulty one, however!)'[33] The author felt responsible for fuelling the young person's discerning mind, lending them 'all kinds of books to read', 'trying to guide his tastes and views while at the same time being careful not to hamper his own individuality'.[34] Speaking to the observer's own talents of observation, the description closed with, '[I c]onsider him a bit of a find.'[35]

The idea that adult observers could, and wished to, 'discover' or 'recognise' the special and unique intelligence of young people they encountered was prominent. Contributors wrote confidently about the objectivity or failures of

---

[26] The Keep Archives, SxMOA2/2/13/34, Special Report number 794: Membership of the National Association for Gifted Children by Mass Observer, 18 September 1984.
[27] Mass Observation, Day Survey, Respondent 099, December 1937; Mass Observation, Day Survey, Respondent 019, May 1937–November 1937.
[28] Mass Observation, Day Survey, Respondent 160, June 1937–April 1938.
[29] Mass Observation, Day Survey, Respondent 495, June 1937–November 1937.
[30] Mass Observation, Day Survey, Respondent 369, June 1937–July 1937.
[31] Mass Observation, Day Survey, Respondent 147, July 1937–January 1938; Mass Observation, Day Survey, Respondent 148, July 1937–November 1937, p. 14.
[32] Mass Observation, Day Survey, Respondent 471, July 1937–January 1938, p. 10.
[33] Ibid.   [34] Ibid.   [35] Ibid.

scholarship exam systems for private schools, which categorised the young through formalised testing, and equally confidently about their own abilities to recognise children who were 'exceptionally undisciplined but quite intelligent'.[36] Acting on this instinct, a female observer from London spontaneously provided a 'Report on conversation with small boy'. The child had asked for permission to gather conkers that had fallen at the back of the observer's house. Encountering this boy subsequently at a bus stop, the woman asked whether he got all he had needed and whether there had been fewer conkers than in previous years. The woman reported that the boy's face had lit up as he joked that the trees were instead giving marbles, and that marble season was early this year. From this, she concluded, he was 'probably of superior intelligence'.[37] Again, observers presented themselves as able to identify the gifted young.

These discussions were referring to children who were later thought of as 'gifted', though observers used a range of language, such as 'precocious', 'intelligent', 'clever', and they made reference to children's 'brains'.[38] Nonetheless, these writings—from a self-selected group of intelligent commentators—also foreshadowed later tensions that the following chapters of this book trace, around ideas of equality and elitism in the gifted movement. Notably, the idea that intelligence should determine a 'social elite', and serve a structuring role in society, was emergent within Mass Observer accounts. Individuals were described as unsuitable for work in the civil service or banks due to lacking 'any signs of intelligence'.[39] These judgements about workplace suitability were at times made purely on appearance, speaking of someone who 'doesn't look' as if he was intelligent'.[40] Judgements were also made on hierarchical lines, with criticism, for example, of one of the 'most junior of the juniors' at the Health and Cleanliness Council, who must be 'mentally defective' since she 'can't even hold a plate of biscuits without dropping half of them': a point the observer overheard and argued against, stating the need for a confirmatory intelligence test.[41] For many observers, intelligence should shape all workplace hierarchies and, in particular, the selection of national leaders. Politicians in Britain and internationally (including Adolf Hitler), were described by observers as 'clever', with 'intellectual brilliance', or a 'brain that could govern!'.[42] Observers expressed concern about the

---

[36] Mass Observation, Diarist 5376, August 1939–September 1945.
[37] Mass Observation, Day Survey, Respondent 160, June 1937–April 1938.
[38] Mass Observation, The British Sense of Humour, August 1948, p. 11; Mass Observation, Evacuation 1939–1944, January 1939–December 1944, p. 789; Mass Observation, Children and Education, 1937–1952, January 1937–December 1952, p. 1591; Mass Observation, Jokes 1939–1947, January 1939–December 1947, p. 180; Mass Observation, Religion 1937–50, January 1937–December 1950, p. 1544. Mass Observation, Man and His Cigarette, December 1949, p. 105; Mass Observation, First Weekly Morale Report, June 1940, p. 27; Mass Observation, Juvenile Drinking, June 1943, p. 68.
[39] Mass Observation, Day Survey, Respondent 101, April 1937.
[40] Mass Observation, Day Survey, Respondent 564, September 1937.
[41] Mass Observation, Day Survey, Respondent 020, July 1937–December 1937.
[42] Mass Observation, Day Survey Respondent 839, August 1938, p. 1; Mass Observation, Day Survey, Respondent 434, June 1937–August 1938, p. 17; Mass Observation, Day Survey, Respondent

'intelligence of the human race' and the 'tremendous lack of intelligence' in 'our civilisation', and emphasising the need for powerful, intellectual leaders.[43]

Ideas of intelligence and elites were also tied to ideas of whiteness and breeding. One observer, for example, described a discussion with a friend about human nature and development. The observer wrote that one could see 'the most primitive stages' of development in 'children and to a certain extent in "savage" races'. They considered, also, 'whether it will one day be possible to get an idea of the psychology of embryos, and remember that a child at birth has 6% of the intelligence it will have as an adult'.[44] In what was then an unusual account, this observer was interested in the identification and fostering of childhood intelligence, even before birth. They also suggested that intelligence was less likely to be developed in the 'savage' or 'primitive'.[45] Another diarist mentioned in passing, eugenicist comment, how 'terrible inbreeding' in their village, with one 'particular family' that was 'connected with so many', had led to 'a low general standard of intelligence in the [local] school'.[46] Ideas of 'good stock' were present more broadly in observers' accounts.[47]

By the 1970s and 1980s, this book argues, the gifted child was a significant feature of public, political, and culture debate, and merited analysis in family homes, schools, and voluntary life. Many of those who contributed to Mass Observation were interested in ideas of intelligence, decades before the rhetoric about the gifted child became so hugely significant. This shows one space from which later interest started to grow, as well as the longer historical roots of tensions between equality and elitism in relation to giftedness. Chapter Four, also, further interrogates connections between eugenic thinking and giftedness, which were visible from the 1940s and 1950s and which became yet more prominent by the 1970s and 1980s.

(Some) Children's Encounters with Intelligence and Stupidity

Interest in intellect, and in categorising young people by intellect, continued into the 1950s and was visible in the writings of young people themselves. This is made

---

315, June 1937–September 1938, p. 19; The General Election 1945, July 1945, p. 17a; Sir Stafford Cripps, December 1942, p. 10; Morale in April, May 1942, p. 10.

[43] Mass Observation, Day Survey, Respondent 596, Harrow, Middlesex, August 1938; Mass Observation, Day Survey, Respondent 160, June 1937–April 1938.

[44] Mass Observation, Day Survey, Respondent 143, July 1937–September 1938.

[45] Notably, this framing of 'savage', in opposition to 'civilisation' was used playfully—but also revealingly—by Tom Harrisson himself in published work (see Gurney,' "Intersex" and "Dirty Girls"', pp. 261–262, 8).

[46] Mass Observation, Diarist 5376, August 1939–September 1945.

[47] Hinton, 'The "class" complex', p. 210. See also the observer who describes his wife as having a 'very clever brain, but emotional rather than intellectual' and being from 'Celtic stock' (Mass Observation, Day Survey, Respondent 467, February 1937–August 1937).

clear through study of the Opie Archive of children's play in the twentieth century. Collated by Iona and Peter Opie, this archive provides an unprecedented survey of writing from school children, describing the games they played, the customs they lived by, and the understandings they had of the world.[48] Games were in part constructed by the children themselves—'not intended for adult ears'—and indeed were part of children constructing their own independent social worlds.[49] At the same time, children's games and discussions are also formed in dialogue with adults—families, teachers, community members,— and with cultural representations. These sources suggest a level to which children frequently used the language of 'intelligence', as well as describing themselves and others as 'smart' and 'clever' in the 1950s—though, as with the Mass Observation sources, the specific language of 'giftedness' was rare at this point. Notably, further, the Opie materials sample children from a range of schools and areas, not predominantly the self-identified upper-middle classes primarily captured by Mass Observation. These sources are then significant in revealing a cultural ecosystem whereby 'intelligence' was significant in the 1950s, foregrounding what was often enthusiastic acceptance from (some) young people of the label 'gifted' in subsequent decades.

The ways in which ideas of intelligence were embedded in children's social lives are visible, for example, in thirteen poems written by a boy in Cheshire in the 1950s. This boy was at Sale County Grammar School for Boys, and thus identified as academically able. His poems described the diverse topics of seafaring, a teacher, schools, weddings, the zoo, reading, and talent. The poem on schools stated that his school was, '[a] school for a swot, / Not a school for a careless lot'.[50] Another declared that while 'A Boy is gallant / When he has talent', such children may at times need 'to be taken upon the knee'.[51] Another notes that a book was 'a friend / For those in need'. And another poem, still, stated playfully that his form master, while a 'generous sort', while 'not inclined for any sport' and held the nickname 'Basher'.[52] Written above this poem was a line from the teacher, stating, 'Save me!'[53] In all of this poetry, the boy presented intellect as a key marker of

---

[48] The Opie Archive is available from the Bodleian Libraries, University of Oxford, and also much is digitised and available under CC BY-NC 4.0 license, see: 'The Iona and Peter Opie Archive', <https://www.opiearchive.org/> (18 December 2020). See also interesting reflections in: Kenneth Kidd, 'The child, the scholar, and the children's literature archive', *The Lion and the Unicorn*, 35 (1) (2011), pp. 1–23; Michael Eades, 'Documenting disappearance: a day in the "research laboratory" of Iona and Peter Opie', *Performance Research: A Journal of the Performing Arts* (24) (7) (2019), pp. 99–102; Laura Jopson, Andrew Burn, and Jonathan Robinson, 'The Opie recordings: what's left to be heard?', in Andrew Burn and Chris Richards (eds), *Children's Games in the New Media Age* (Basingstoke: Taylor Francis, 2014).

[49] Marina Warner, 'Introductory', in Iona and Peter Opie (eds), *The Lore and Language of Schoolchildren* (New York: New York Review of Books, 2001), p. 1.

[50] Opie Archive, OP/A/1/1/3/13/13, MS. Opie 1 fol. 112v, Sale County Grammar School for Boys, Cheshire, c. 1951–1953 and 1959.

[51] Ibid.   [52] Ibid.   [53] Ibid.

social difference. While he was at a 'school for a swot' and therefore 'gallant', and while he enjoyed reading and playful discussions with his teachers, those outside his school were 'a careless lot'. His own intelligence shaped his self-perception, even as he ostentatiously discussed a broad range of other topics. Another poem, from the same student, further evidenced how this school environment permitted a teasing relationship between students and teachers. This poem suggested that his headteacher was 'edified', and also mockingly referred to him as the schools' 'EAD', suggesting that others were 'jealous of his brain'.[54] Chapter Three, focusing on specialist spaces created for those labelled as 'gifted' in the 1970s and 1980s, argues that children labelled as gifted were often encouraged to speak in particularly critical ways, that disrupted presumed hierarchies between adult and child. Encouragement of a disruptive gifted self may also have been present in elite grammar and private schools, in earlier periods, and particularly in elite, all-male institutions.[55]

Other material from the Opie archives show that ideas of intelligence and ability did sometimes structure children's collaborative play also. This was the case in all schools, not merely all-male grammar schools. A girl writing in 1952 at a school in Kirkcaldy, Fife, for example, wrote that 'a sap is a stupid person, a mug, High School Mugs'—the quote that opened this chapter.[56] Games also revealed children's interest in intelligence. Another girl who recorded her age as '11 yrs 2 months', writing from a non-selective school in Acocks Green Junior School in the West Midlands, discussed childhood games with friends in which, '[w]e say which team we are in and they say a rhyme'. Looking at the teams of green, red, yellow, and blue, she reported that while the opposition might chant, 'Reds Reds wet the beds', the team themselves would declare 'Reds Reds clever heads'.[57] Another girl from this same school, aged '11 years, 2 ½ months', discussed a playground game in which you asked a partner 'Are you strong?', while holding out a thumb. If the person said 'yes', then the child said 'Pull my finger then'. If the

---

[54] Ibid.
[55] See: Catherine Sloan. 'Family, community, and sociability', in Heather Ellis (ed.), *A Cultural History of Education in the Age of Empire (1800–1920)* (London: Bloomsbury, forthcoming); Catherine Sloan, '"Periodicals of an objectionable character": peers and periodicals at Croydon Friends' School, 1826–1875', *Victorian Periodicals Review*, 50 (4) (2017), pp. 769–786. On how young people's 'spirited mischief and irreverence' is mobilised as agency, see: Craig Jeffrey, 'Geographies of children and youth II', *Progress in Human Geography*, 36 (2) (2012), pp. 245–253.
[56] Opie Archive, OP/A/1/3/8/32/1, MS. Opie 3 fol. 381r, Kirkcaldy High School, Kirkcaldy, Fife, c. 1952. There is some more detail about the specific nature of this school, as 'not a truly multilateral school since it contains only half the senior but all the grammar school children', in 'The Nation's Schools', *Times Educational Supplement*, 26 May 1945, p. 247.
[57] Opie Archive, OP/A/1/9/8/44/5, MS. Opie 9 fol. 499r, Acocks Green Junior Mixed School, Birmingham, Warwickshire, 1952-3. Presumed non-selective: lack of mention of scholarships on local / national newspaper databases, and letters framing Opie contribution, on deposit, were written on notepaper from the 'City of Birmingham Education Committee' (Opie Archive, OP/A/1/9/8/2, 'Letter to Opies from Acocks Green Junior Mixed School', Birmingham, 17th December, 1952).

person pulled their thumb, you said 'Your [sic] not very clever that was my thumb.'[58] These games could diffuse across areas at great speed, and become significant in multiple settings when children moved or socialised across regions.[59]

Children in selective and non-selective schools alike were, then, interested in categorising and considering their own intelligence, and in using intelligence as a cultural framework to govern childhood play. Such play could be highly imaginative, embedding ideas of intelligence as an assumed structuring tool. Demonstrating this, another poem by a child in a Church of England primary school in Northamptonshire, written in 1952, discussed an imaginary figure, Dick, 'Silly Dick had no brains / soon he didn't have no vains [sic]'.[60] In this poem, the child conceptualised a significant relationship between 'brains', presumably a proxy for intelligence, and the ability to live, suggesting that Dick's lack of brains lead to his untimely, unspecified end—a narrative trick with a sinister undertone.

Overall, then, engagement with the Opie collection suggests that ideas of intelligence permeated peer cultures in a range of school environments in the mid-twentieth century. This has also been identified in Jonathan Taylor's analysis of a set of twenty-eight essays submitted to Mass Observation, written by teenagers aged 14–16 in 1942 from East London. Taylor argues that these essays show 'that enthusiasm for changes to the educational system predated the government's plans for educational reform in 1944'.[61] Taylor highlights concern from a student that, 'some…children who are in elementary school are very brainy but their parents have not the money to give them secondary school education', meaning that 'promising pupils' were unable to fully develop.[62] Taylor's analysis further supports a critical argument of this book; that children were often more radical critics of state policy than adults in modern Britain.

Contrast: America

Contrasting to the British post-war moment, in the same period in America, national policy, media, voluntary sector and culture were highly invested in ideas of the gifted child, and specifically used that term. Drawing a comparison

---

[58] Opie Archive, OP/A/1/9/8/40/2, MS. Opie 9 fol. 495r, Acocks Green Junior Mixed School, Birmingham, Warwickshire, 1952–3.
[59] Warner, 'Introductory', p. 8.
[60] Opie Archive, OP/A/1/9/5/37/8, MS. Opie 9 fol. 282r, Oundle Church of England School, Northamptonshire, 1952.
[61] Taylor, '"The Borough Council have done a great deal,…I hope they continue to do so in the future": children, community and the welfare state, 1941—55', in Sian Pooley and Jonathan Taylor (eds), *Children's Experiences of Welfare in Modern Britain* (London: University of London Press, 2021), p. 161.
[62] Ibid., pp. 161–162.

illustrates the distinctive nature of debates around giftedness in Britain in this period—despite significant transatlantic connections between researchers in the early-to-mid twentieth century.[63] Tellingly, British debates in newspapers and the voluntary sector, as we see throughout this book, frequently used American programmes as a key point of comparison.[64]

American debates around 'giftedness', and this terminology, had roots in the 1920s and 1930s and in eugenicist psychology. Building on the 'psychologization of society' in America from the 1910s, and increasing interest in categorising all children by intellect, in 1921, the controversial psychologist Lewis Terman began the largest ever longitudinal study of gifted children.[65] His project *Genetic Study of Genius* continued over several decades, analysing 1,528 young people who scored over 140 on an IQ test devised in part by Terman himself, with recruitment particularly focused in California.[66] The young people were tested frequently by project staff, who collected case histories from parents and teachers; conducted medical examinations and took anthropometric measurements; and analysed various tests pertaining to character, intellect, maturity, masculinity, play, and the home environment.[67]

The size and length of this study was remarkable, and it has remained influential in public discourse and psychology. However it remains controversial, premised as it was around ideas of the 'essential nature of great man' and intellectual precocity as 'pathological' and biological.[68] Its research design included a

---

[63] On the challenges of comparative history, see: Chris Lorenz, 'Comparative historiography: problems and perspectives', *History and Theory*, 38 (1) (1999), pp. 25–39; Jurgen Kocka, 'Comparison and beyond', *History and Theory*, 42 (1) (2003), pp. 39–44; Michael Werner and Bénédicte Zimmermann. 'Beyond comparison: Histoire croisée and the challenge of reflexivity', *History and Theory*, 45 (1) (2006), pp. 30–50; Susanna Delfino, Marcus Graser, Hans Krabbendam, and Vincent Michelot, 'Europeans writing American history: the comparative trope', *American Historical Review*, 119 (3) (2014), pp. 791–799; Philippa Levine, 'Is comparative history possible?', *History and Theory*, 53 (2014), pp. 331–347.

[64] 'New body aims to get help for the gifted child', *The Times*, 18 June 1966, p. 10; John Izbicki, 'Teaching the gifted child', *Daily Telegraph*, 17 August 1981.

[65] Lewis Terman, *Mental and Physical Traits of a Thousand Gifted Children* (1925); Lewis Terman, Barbara Burks, and Dortha Jensen, *The Promise of Youth: Follow-up Studies of a Thousand Gifted Children* (1930); Lewis Terman and Melita Oden, *The Gifted Child Grows up: Twenty-five Years Follow-up of a Superior Group* (1947); Lewis Terman and Melita Oden, *The Gifted Group at Mid-Life: Thirty-Five Years' Follow-up of the Superior Group* (1959). Another longitudinal study in a similar period is discussed in: Leta Hollingworth, *Children above 180 IQ; Stanford-Binet: Origin and Development* (1942). The Terman papers can be consulted at the University Archives of Stanford University <https://oac.cdlib.org/findaid/ark:/13030/kt3p303833/>. On the role of Terman in developing earlier forms of intelligence testing, and measuring the IQs of soldiers, as well as children, see: Jon Agar, *Science in the Twentieth Century and Beyond* (London: Polity Press, 2013), pp. 73, 105.

[66] Lewis M. Terman and Melita H. Oden, 'The Stanford studies of the gifted', in Paul Witty (ed.), *The American Association for Gifted Children* (Boston: DC Heath and Company, 1951), p. 21. Original criteria for inclusion was IQ of 140, though some participants were included with IQ 135–139 if siblings of other participants or if their 'scores were deemed to be spuriously low' (Terman and Oden, *The Gifted Group at Mid-Life*, p. 2).

[67] Ibid., p. 22.

[68] Lewis Terman, *Genetic Studies of Genius: Volume 1*, Preface. Terman's interest in eugenics was demonstrated by his memberships of the Human Betterment Foundation, the American Eugenics

disproportionate number of white boys, and Terman became very involved in the lives of his subjects. The study was framed in terms of identifying elites of the future, and around concerns that the, 'vigorous growth' of 'democratic sentiment' in Western Europe and North America over 'the last few hundred years' had discouraged interest in human endowment and difference.[69] These kinds of ideas—that the promotion of giftedness related to the curation of 'the nation's success' and avoidance of 'waste'—were echoed in parts of the American contemporary national press.[70] Terman's work received some attention in the British press of the 1920s and 1930s, but his work was not seriously covered by these newspapers until it was reassessed amidst the controversies around popular eugenics in the 1970s and 1980s (as traced in Chapter Four).[71]

By the mid-twentieth-century, ideas about giftedness had become even more broadly popularised in America, despite these eugenicist connections. Several national newspapers offered sympathetic discussion of the need for special provision for the gifted. At times, this was described in terms of ensuring that the gifted young could achieve happiness and live normal lives. In 1940, for example, the *New York Times* described the 'miseries' that 'child geniuses' could face without sufficient support.[72] Yet, interest in using gifted children to promote a vision of national progress remained. Indeed, this same *New York Times* article discussed a conference at Columbia University's Teachers College, at which Dr Nicholas Murray Butler, president of the University, stated that educating the gifted was '[t]he main test of democracy.'[73]

Society, and the Eugenics Research Association. This is a legacy with which members of the University of Stanford continue to grapple. See: Ben Maldonado, 'Eugenics on the farm: Lewis Terman', *The Stanford Daily*, 6 November 2019 <https://www.stanforddaily.com/2019/11/06/eugenics-on-the-farm-lewis-terman/> (14 September 2021); 'The vexing legacy of Lewis Terman', *Stanford Magazine*, July/August 2000 <https://stanfordmag.org/contents/the-vexing-legacy-of-lewis-terman> (14 September 2021). See also: Alexandra Minna Stern, *Eugenic Nation: Faults and Frontiers of Better Breeding in Modern America* (California: University of California Press, 2015).

[69] Terman, *Genetic Studies of Genius*. Terman was vigorously critiqued by the American Progressive Labor Party, which arose from the Communist Party. See for example contemporary pamphlets: Michigan State University Library, Progressive Labor Party: *Education, Capitalism, Racism, and Schools* (Progressive Labor Party, 1974), p. 4; Michigan State University Library, Progressive Labor Party, *Committee Against Racism* (Progressive Labor Party, 1976), p. 143.

[70] 'Miscellaneous brief reviews of recent non-fiction', *New York Times*, 27 June 1937, p. 95; 'Flexner urges a school for gifted pupils', *New York Times*, 19 March 1933, p. 1.

[71] The limited contemporary reporting around Terman's work in British press included: E. M. Goodman, 'Testing brains', *Daily Telegraph*, 9 August 1919; 'The Intelligence Quotient: measuring brain power', *The Manchester Guardian*, 10 April 1931, p. 6. In the 1970s and 1980s, it was controversial. See for example: Alan Ryan, 'The psychometric disaster', *The Sunday Times*, 6 June 1982; By the 1990s and 2000s, his work was considered interesting, with the concerns about eugenics no longer a strong feature of news coverage. See: James Le Fanu, 'Honesty is the best policy for a long life', *Sunday Telegraph*, 16 April 1995; George Gordon, 'Earning a long life', *Daily Mail*, 31 August 1995; Victoria McKee, 'Rich gifts with a high price', *The Times*, 18 April 1990; Sarah Vine, 'Today's little darlings...or tomorrow's little monsters?', *The Times*, 25 November 2008.

[72] 'Miseries of a child genius's life bared by 20 of them, now adults...', *New York Times*, 14 December 1940, p. 1.

[73] Ibid.

The American Association for Gifted Children was founded in 1946 by Ann Isaacs, an educator and child psychologist. Isaacs's interest in this area, subsequent accounts recall, was driven by experience of working with young people and concern, from having organised a preschool, that bright children were underachieving.[74] Ideas about national progress were significant in the early days of the Association, to justify the organisation's value, but also reflect the prevalence of such ideas. In 1951, a study funded by the Association was published, which aimed to summarise the existing knowledge in this area. It was edited by Paul Witty (1898–1976), later described as 'one of the leading spokespersons of gifted education', and a professor of education at Northwestern University from 1930 until 1966.[75] Many contributors throughout Witty's edited volume presented the gifted child as a critical national resource. The book's foreword, for example, by the groups' President and Secretary, Harold F. Clark and Pauline Williamson, stated that:

> Much of the vision necessary for the promotion of human welfare must come from our gifted boys and girls educated for worthwhile leadership and productivity in a democracy.[76]

In his own chapter, 'Progress in the Education of the Gifted', Witty directly quoted Terman's idea that such research was discouraged by 'democratic sentiment in Western Europe and America'.[77] Terman also contributed to the collection and the interwar foundations of interest in 'the gifted child' thus remained present in post-war America.

Framing the gifted child in relation to 'national progress', and as potentially oppositional to 'democracy', featured elsewhere in American popular culture. Gifted children who were also cruel appeared in short stories, novels, and films, for instance *The Veldt* (1950), *The Bad Seed* (1954), *It's a Good Life* (1953), and *The Gamma People* (1956), and in contemporary comics.[78] In *The Gamma People*,

---

[74] 'A Finding Aid to the Ann Fabe Isaacs Papers', American Jewish Archives <http://collections.americanjewisharchives.org/ms/ms0723/ms0723.html> (11 July 2019); 'Ann Fabe Isaacs: She made our garden grow (1920–2001)', in Ann Robinson and Jennifer Jolly (eds), *A Century of Contributions to Gifted Education: Illuminating Lives* (New York: Routledge, 2013), p. 21.

[75] Jennifer L. Jolly and J. H. Robins, 'Paul Witty: A gentleman scholar (1898–1976)', in Robinson and Jolly (eds.), *A Century of Contributions to Gifted Education*, pp. 118–129; 'Dr Paul A. Witty, Educator, 77, Dies', *New York Times*, 14 February 1976.

[76] Paul Witty (ed.), *The Gifted Child* (Boston: DC Heath and Company, 1951), p. v.

[77] Paul Witty, 'Progress in the education of the gifted', in Witty, *The Gifted Child*, p. 2. Citing, Lewis Terman, *Genetic Studies of Genius*.

[78] Kirsten Gregory, 'Exceptional and destructive: the dangerous child and the atom bomb in post-war science fiction', in Monica Flegel and Christopher Parkes (eds), *Cruel Children in Popular Texts and Cultures* (London: Palgrave Macmillan, 2018), pp. 153–172; Hans Staats, '"Tag…you're it": Cold War comics and the performance of boyhood and criminality', in Monica Flegel and Christopher Parkes (eds), *Cruel Children in Popular Texts and Cultures* (London: Palgrave Macmillan, 2018), pp. 173–191.

journalists find themselves in 'Gudavia', a land where children are divided into 'future leaders of the world' and 'mindless goons' by a disgraced scientist. These children, all of whom are blonde with German accents, 'recall Hitler's Youth', a point further emphasised as they dress in collared shirts, shorts, and knee socks.[79]

From October 1957, interest in the gifted child expanded greatly in America, as the Soviet Union launched the satellite Sputnik into space, where it orbited Earth in ninety-eight minutes.[80] Following Soviet testing of new nuclear weapons in the early 1950s, this launch further motivated media, cultural, and political analyses of America's technical and scientific capacity. In 1958, Congress passed the *National Defense Education Act*, which provided $1 billion over four years for loans, scholarships, and graduate fellowships to students without the financial means to pursue degrees, particularly those in science, technology, engineering, and medicine.[81] To encourage local initiatives, the Act matched funding for states to strengthen equipment, materials, and teachers' professional development in maths, sciences, and, significantly, languages.[82] Matthew Smith has written that this period 'provided clear evidence for something that they [American policy-makers] had suspected for quite some time, namely, that American schools were not producing students capable of competing with their Soviet counterparts in the fields of science, engineering, and technology.'[83] Specifically, this moment pushed gifted education 'into relevancy' and marked 'one of its most productive research periods', although, as in Britain, there were significant regional variations.[84] Speaking in 1975, Professor James J. Gallagher, a child development expert at the University of North Carolina, informally told the World Conference on Gifted Children that the 1950s was a decade in which, 'gifted artists were being pushed

---

[79] Gregory, 'Exceptional and destructive', pp. 164–165.

[80] On the American reaction to this context, see: Ryan Boyle, 'A red moon over the Mall: The Sputnik panic and domestic America,' *The Journal of American Culture*, 31 (4) (2008), pp. 373–382; Michael Brzezinski, *Red Moon Rising: Sputnik and the Rivalries that Ignited the Space Age* (London: Bloomsbury, 2007); Deborah Cadbury, *Space Race: The Battle to Rule the Heavens* (London: Harper, 2005); Paul Dickson, *Sputnik: The Shock of the Century* (New York: Berkley Books, 2001). On the media reaction in Britain, see: Nicholas Barnett, *Britain's Cold War: Culture, Modernity and the Soviet Threat* (London: Bloomsbury, 2018); Nicholas Barnett, '"Russia wins space race: the British press and the Sputnik Moment, 1957,' *Media History*, 19 (2) (2013), pp. 182–195.

[81] Jennifer L. Jolly, 'The National Defense Education Act, Current STEMP Initiative, and the Gifted', *Gifted Child Today*, 32 (2) (2009), p. 50.

[82] Ibid., p. 51.

[83] Matthew Smith, 'The hyperactive state: ADHD in historical perspective', in Ewen Speed, Joanna Moncrieff, and Mark Rapley (eds), *De-Medicalizing Misery II: Society, Politics and the Mental Health Industry* (Basingstoke: Palgrave Macmillan, 2014), pp. 89–104.

[84] Jolly, 'National defense', p. 51; Charles J. Russo, 'Unequal educational opportunities for gifted students: robbing Peter to pay Paul?,' *Fordham Urban Law Journal*, 29(2) (2001), p. 734. Details of the programmes provided by the 1970s can be found in: Bodleian Library, Joy Gibson and Prue Chennells (eds), *Gifted Children: Looking to their Future* (Essex: The Anchor Press, 1976), pp. 20–34. On regional variation, see: Mary Waddington, 'Able children from ancient times till now', *Looking to their Future: The News Letter of the National Association for Gifted Children*, May 1977, p. 2. Regional variations was one of the chief complaints of, and motivating forces behind the foundation of, the American Association for Gifted Children (see for example: 'Dear NAGC', *Gifted Child Quarterly*, 10 (4) (Winter 1966), p. 195.

into engineering and into physics on the grounds that it was patriotic to catch the Russians in space'.[85]

Further demonstrating the power of this moment in cultural and daily life, as well as in policy, in 1959 Fred M. Hechinger, an educational correspondent for the *New York Times*, reported that, '[e]ver since the cold war moved into outer space, the American people have been concerned about education'. In this 'futuristic contest', the paper reported, 'classrooms are the launching platforms'.[86] Hechinger continued this analysis in *The Big Red Schoolhouse* (1959), which compared American and Russian schools. Hechinger argued that Russian schools were more demanding, specialised, and rigorous, while American schools were hindered by the idea that it was 'undemocratic to have serious differentiations between the type and quality of education offered'.[87]

From the 1950s, the American Association grew in size and strength. It established a new journal, *Gifted Child Quarterly*, in 1957, with the slogan: 'For a brighter future tomorrow, identify the gifted child today'. Adding to this vision in 1964, the group's founder, Isaacs, wrote that: '[i]t is suggested that many of the world's problems could be solved were the gifted more regularly motivated and inspired to attempt solutions'.[88] Isaacs suggested that teachers and parents should be 'better informed of the attributes of the gifted and their cultivation'; that the 'general public must realize it is they who reap the benefits of the contributions of the gifted'; and that the children themselves 'must not be made to feel guilty and rejected'.[89] Only in these circumstances, in which all members of the public and local communities were involved in children's care and nurture, would 'our worlds…come ever closer to the ideals of diminished accents on poverty, illness, and war', with 'peace and plenty' resulting.[90] The mechanisms through which gifted education would realise these utopian visions were not fully laid out, yet the idea remained that gifted children would be instrumental and significant in national futures.[91]

Multiple arenas of policy, press, and voluntary sector were thus emphasising the significance of the gifted child in America from the 1920s until the 1960s, at a time when this debate was less prominent in Britain. The archives of *Gifted Child Quarterly* provide occasional intriguing insights into how American

---

[85] Bodleian Library, Gibson and Chennells (eds), *Gifted Children*, p. 222.
[86] Fred M. Hechinger, 'Five basic problems of education', *New York Times*, 25 January 1959, p. 11.
[87] Fred M. Hechinger, *The Big Red Schoolhouse* (New York: Doubleday, 1959), p. 106. In *What Ivan Knows that Johnny Doesn't* (1961), likewise, American educator Arther Trace compared the school textbooks used in the Soviet Union and America as a way to critique American public education, particularly in the arts and humanities, as unchallenging and limited.
[88] Ann F. Isaacs, 'Role expectancy and its effect on performance and achievement among gifted students', *The High School Journal*, 48 (2) (1964), pp. 112–113.
[89] Ibid., p. 115.   [90] Ibid.
[91] David Edgerton, 'The "White Heat" revisited: the British Government and technology in the 1960s', *Twentieth Century British History*, 7 (1) (1996), pp. 53–82.

commentators saw the British context.[92] Overall, and looking to promote further action in America, Isaacs wrote in 1957 that 'some colleagues' had been abroad and had observed that 'in England interest is in the average child, in America, interest is in the dull or slow learners, and in France the people attend to their gifted'.[93] Belief that the French system was best was reiterated in the journal, where another article in the same year stated that France provided every child, including the gifted, with 'the kind of education by which he may best profit'.[94] French campaigners in this area did not entirely agree, and established their own National Association for Gifted Children (ANPES) in November 1971, looking to, 'wake up the French Ministry of Education to the problems of gifted children'.[95] *Gifted Child Quarterly* focused on American case studies, despite some transatlantic contact—notably for example, a British member of Mensa wrote to this American organisation in 1959, confident that members would be keen to 'sponsor an Association in Britain similar to your own'.[96]

As noted, the early giftedness movement in America had some links to eugenicist thought. This was challenged by the Civil Rights Movement, which radically reshaped education across in America in the 1960s and 1970s.[97] Speaking in 1975, to the World Conference on Gifted Children, James J. Gallagher, working at the Frank Porter Graham Child Development Center, University of North Carolina, argued that in America, the 'spirit of egalitarianism has caused us to devote a great deal of attention, in the last decade, to finding gifted children from culturally different backgrounds'; devising specialist tests and looking more broadly for 'talents'.[98] In 1999, three articles in *Gifted Child Today* argued that the Civil Rights movement: led to 'a rethinking of "access" and to policies that opened doors to

---

[92] Robert Cardew, 'The gifted child in France', *Gifted Child Quarterly*, 1 (2) (April 1957), p. 1; 'The most academically talented students in the world', *Gifted Child Quarterly*, 19 (3) (September 1975), pp. 185–188.

[93] Ann F. Isaacs, 'Presidents' message', *Gifted Child Quarterly*, Vol. 1 No. 2, April 1957, p. 8.

[94] Cardew, 'The gifted child in France', pp. 2–3. Emphasising his expertise, the article's byline stated that while Cardew was an Associate Professor at the University of Cincinnati, he had also been to France '[m]ore than once', and had been 'honored with a medal by the French Government'. William Bagley observed that the French elementary schools operated to produce a 'stable, law-abiding, literate population' and, in secondary schools, 'an intellectual elite from which the leadership of the nation may be recruited' (William C. Bagley, 'Getting the Pupil's Best: Aims that Govern Schools in Handling the Gifted and Slow Children Weighed', *New York Times*, 26 March 1933, p. 5).

[95] Bodleian Library, Gibson and Chennells (eds), *Gifted Children*, pp. 304–305.

[96] Basil Mager, 'Mensa', *Gifted Child Quarterly*, 3 (3) (Autumn 1959), p. 59. Notably by 1966 this focus had shifted somewhat, acknowledging that, '[s]ome of the advocates of special provisions for the education of gifted children in the United States have cited the methods and procedures of the English school system as a model to be emulated' (E. Paul Torrance and Richard T. Johnson, 'Gifted thirteen-year-olds in two cultures: Greater London and greater twin cities', *Gifted Child Quarterly*, 10 (3) (Autumn 1966), pp. 125–131. The kind of programmes inspiring this new confidence are traced in Chapter Two of this book.

[97] See: Michael J. Klarman, *Brown v. Board of Education and the Civil Rights Movement* (Oxford: OUP, 2007); James T. Patterson, *Brown v. Board of Education: A Civil Rights Milestone and Its Troubled Legacy* (New York: OUP, 2001); Anders Walker, *The Ghost of Jim Crow: How Southern Moderates used Brown v. Board of Education to Stall the Civil Rights Movement* (Oxford: OUP, 2009).

[98] Bodleian Library, Gibson and Chennells (eds), *Gifted Children*, p. 59.

equalizing opportunities for children from all cultural and economic backgrounds'; 'encouraged us to appreciate the multifaceted nature of gifts and talents'; and was 'tremendously important to gifted education'.[99] These articles also acknowledged that progress had been slow and, despite the best efforts of the Civil Rights movement, only 'begun to come to fruition' in 1999, remaining 'one of the most significant challenges for us to carry into the next century'.[100] There are few archival traces of attempts to bring the Civil Rights agenda into gifted education in the mid-to-late twentieth century. Nonetheless, the Movement invited giftedness campaigners to reflect (a little) on how they recruited and identified 'the gifted'.

Overall, interest in 'the gifted child' emerged more prominently in mid-century America than it did in Britain. America continued to be seen as a 'world leader in gifted/talented education', by educators and campaigners across the world, in subsequent decades.[101] Mid-twentieth-century American interest was driven by several factors, analysis of which shed light on the distinctiveness of British debates. In particular, the role of individual campaigners is clear, and remains so throughout this book. In the mid-twentieth century, both America and Britain had underlying cultural and popular interest in intelligence. In America, prominent individuals (such as Lewis Terman and Ann Isaacs) lobbied effectively to bring public attention to the gifted as early as the 1930s. In Britain, by contrast, the next chapter of this book shows that interest in giftedness did not emerge as a public issue until the lobbying of Margaret Branch, the founder of the National Association for Gifted Children, in the 1960s. The policy contexts which these activists worked in were also different. Sputnik fuelled American debate around and funding of giftedness, but not so much in Britain, where post-war policymakers fixated on ideas of equality. By contrast, in America, gifted education was more immediately seen as a way to bolster equality.[102] This comparison demonstrates the significance of contingency. Developing interest in giftedness was

---

[99] Mary Ruth Coleman, 'Back to the future: the top 10 events that have shaped gifted education in the last century', *Gifted Child Today*, 22 (6) (1999), p. 17; Susan Johnsen, 'The top 10 events in gifted education', *Gifted Child Today*, 22 (6) (1999), p. 7; Marcia B. Imbeau, 'A century of gifted education: a reflection of who and what made a difference', *Gifted Child Today*, 22 (6) (1999), p. 40. Ideas of 'model minorities' further marginalised African Americans in education, see on this: Madeline Y. Hsu, *The Good Immigrants: How the Yellow Peril Became the Model Minority* (Princeton: Princeton University Press, 2015).

[100] Ibid. This analysis is supported by sociological studies finding that Black students are less likely to be referred to gifted programs, particularly when taught by non-Black teachers: Jason A. Grissom and Christopher Reading, 'Discretion and disproportionality: explaining the underrepresentation of high-achieving students of color in gifted programs', *AERA Open*, 2 (1) (2016), pp. 1–25.

[101] Bruce M. Mitchell and William G. Williams, 'Education of the Gifted and Talented in the World Community', *The Phi Delta Kappan*, 68 (10) (1987), p. 532.

[102] For example James J. Gallagher, a press obituary of whom is available at: 'James J. Gallager Dies at 87; Educator Focused on Disabled and Gifted', *New York Times*, 4 February 2014 <https://www.nytimes.com/2014/02/04/us/james-j-gallagher-child-development-expert-is-dead-at-87.html> (6 October 2021).

never guaranteed in Britain, but represented a shifting coalition of activists and cultural understandings.

Conclusion

This chapter traces a significant prehistory to voluntary campaigning around gifted children in the late twentieth century, the key focus of this book. This history stretches back to the nineteenth century, and through educational reforms of the early twentieth century, although the chapter focuses on cultural understandings visible in writings by adults and children, from the mid-twentieth century, describing the judgements they formed of one another on the basis of intellect.

Interest in gifted children in the 1970s and 1980s then did not emerge from nowhere, of course. Nonetheless, these earlier interests did not immediately result in voluntary action and campaigning. Indeed, Mathew Thomson describes how Mensa, founded in October 1946, failed to gain much popularity in this period. He argues that its

> 'real constituency' was 'both frustrated by the apparent levelling tendencies of the day, and looking for a new way to advance eugenic concerns in an ideological climate that had sidelined the prevalent interwar strategies of segregating or sexually sterilising the less able.'[103]

Into the mid-1950s, Thomson argues, Mensa was 'in a state of poor health and lacked clear direction'; membership 'had struggled to reach 280 by 1952, and now fell to just 100 by 1956'.[104] Yet, by the 1960s, Thomson charts, this had shifted dramatically. With lowered entrance qualifications and discarded limits on membership, Mensa attracted some 10,000 applications a year; by 1966, membership had risen to 110,000.[105] In this case, an adult organisation focusing on intelligence was not popularised in the 1940s and 1950s—despite a level of concurrent interest in intellect in the educational system, letters to newspapers, and daily life alike.

By contrast, in America, voluntary action around giftedness was thriving in the 1940s and 1950s. The next chapter of this book shows when and why interest in giftedness emerged in Britain, building on the cultures analysed in this chapter. It pinpoints this in the mid-1960s, and argues that interest was significantly pushed by local educational experiments, particularly in Brentwood, Essex; the passionate voluntary campaigning of the National Association for Gifted Children, particularly under its intriguing leader, Margaret Branch; and the lobbying of

---

[103] Mathew Thomson, *Psychological Subjects: Identity, Culture, and Health in Twentieth-Century Britain* (Oxford: OUP, 2007), p. 264.
[104] Ibid.   [105] Ibid.

members of the House of Lords. The voluntary leaders in these debates, notably Branch, sought to avoid a vision of the 'gifted child' as a symbol of nation-building and national progress. Instead, they emphasised that providing for gifted children was merely a necessary extension of a post-war welfare state, and part of its mandate for catering for 'ability' and 'for all'. Yet, involvement from House of Lords supporters, and the framing by certain local experiments, meant that ideas of the gifted child as 'an elite of the future' remained present and powerful.

This matters as a history, first, in terms of showing how satisfaction within the post-war settlement broke down in subsequent decades. As this chapter shows, there was concern from the outset, in local and national papers, that this system could not both be 'equal', in terms of providing the same services for all, and also 'equal' in terms of offering hope and progression for gifted, non-privileged children. This book traces how parents and children themselves sought to create voluntary spaces in which their apparently distinct needs could be catered for. This story matters, second, because it shows how debates around giftedness became a vocal point—for parents, media, politicians, and children themselves—for broader and hugely malleable debates about 'equality' and 'elitism' in modern Britain; and the book shows, finally, how this felt for young people involved and affected.

'Gifted Children' in Britain and the World: Elitism and Equality since 1945. Jennifer Crane, Oxford University Press.
© Jennifer Crane 2025. DOI: 10.1093/9780198928881.003.0002

Emergent Voluntary Action for Gifted Children, 1963–1969

> 'They are the country's gold and nothing is being done for them. All we ask is for the same amount of money to be spent on the top 2 per cent as is being spent on the bottom.'
>
> *'If your child seems dull, he may be much brighter than you think…', The Times, 25 August 1966.*

In an article in *The Times* in August 1966, Margaret Branch, the dynamic founder of the new voluntary group, the National Association for Gifted Children, passionately called for more money to be spent on educating the nation's intellectually high-achieving young. Her statement above encapsulated the ways in which this debate quickly came to public and policy attention in the 1960s—notably via interest from broadsheet media. It shows, also, how the National Association sought to frame its work around ideas of equality. The group argued that, in identifying gifted children, they were not aiming to forge a new elite, but rather a fairer Britain. Nonetheless, ideas of elitism crept into debates about giftedness from their inception: Branch used the language of 'gold' and 'top 2 per cent', proposing a hierarchy with gifted children at 'the top'.

This chapter explores how interest in the gifted child substantively emerged in mid-to-late twentieth-century Britain, building on the ecosystems and cultural understandings traced in Chapter One. Interest came first from disparate local experiments and then, more strongly, from the passionate campaigning of the National Association. In its first section, the chapter discusses early and localised educational experiments explicitly focused on the 'gifted' for the first time in Britain, notably the Brentwood Experiment in Essex, which started in 1963. These experiments made a significant difference to the lives of young people, but were highly localised and did not receive much broader attention. Second, the chapter discusses the life of Margaret Branch and her work in establishing the National Association in 1966. It demonstrates that Branch had significant success in driving broadsheet interest around her new organisation, and in framing ideas of giftedness around equality. The chapter then reflects on the multiple ways in which the early Association sought to position giftedness in relation to disability; arguing that giftedness *was* a disability, generated the familial stresses of a disability, and was less funded than disabilities, at various points—these arguments became controversial in subsequent years. Third, the chapter explores how members of the House of Lords became significant policy advocates for the National Association in the late 1960s. These were typically Conservative members from prestigious educational backgrounds, further adding to a perception of this as an 'elite' issue. There was less interest more broadly from the House of Commons and contemporary policy reports.

In the 1960s, more broadly, Mathew Thomson has described how Mensa—the adult society for the 'intellectually advanced'—sought to advance itself 'on the basis that the future of world peace depended on creating a dialogue of the intelligent—a "self-conscious world-wide cadre of the able"—who alone might overcome the irrationality at the heart of the Cold War.'[1] Mensa feared in this decade that '[r]ational thinking was being swamped by the nihilistic and anarchistic tendencies of the emerging beat generation on the one hand, and the domination of market values of the other'.[2] While the National Association was described once in very early press coverage as 'a juvenile Mensa', this chapter shows that the idea of the gifted child as an elite of the future was not central to early campaigning around this issue.[3] The idea of who the 'gifted child' was, and why anyone should care, was constantly in flux: in the 1960s, the gifted child was presented as a vulnerable individual, struggling in education and family life and in need of assistance. By the 1970s and 1980s, as subsequent chapters show, the gifted child was more consistently represented as a powerful elite of the future—able to solve a range of economic and diplomatic issues.

Local Giftedness Experiments

In the early 1960s, growing interest in gifted children emerged from local experiments looking to provide educational support. At first, only the musically gifted were of particular interest, but later all gifted youth were included. To an extent, locally varied provision was embedded in the 1944 *Education Act*. A Ministry of Education pamphlet of 1945, on *The nation's schools*, emphasised that '[l]ocal initiative and experiment will be more than ever necessary if the Act is to fructify fully in all the different parts, with their varying conditions, of England and Wales'. In this pamphlet, local variation was presented as generating new 'ideas and experience' that could later be used 'for assistance of the whole service'.[4] By 1962, the National Union of Teachers conceded that the system had extreme 'disparity of provision', arguing that policies varied 'sometimes for purely

---

[1] Mathew Thomson, *Psychological Subjects: Identity, Culture, and Health in Twentieth-Century Britain* (Oxford: OUP, 2007), p. 265.
[2] Ibid., p. 264.   [3] 'Deep talk in the tents of the talented', *Guardian*, 20 August 1966, p. 3.
[4] MRC, MSS.126/TG/RES/X/1011A2/1/18, Ministry of Education pamphlet no.1.' The nation's schools: Their plan and purpose', 1945, p. 4.

educational reasons, sometimes for economic reasons and sometimes, regrettably, for political reasons'.[5]

In 1964, the National Union of Teachers wrote that many authorities in London, Coventry, Sheffield, and Wolverhampton operated some 'only partly comprehensive' schools, in which some 'more able children' went to selective schools, while other areas such as Manchester were considering a 'two-tier system of comprehensive education' in which a 'modified 11+ examination' would select 5 per cent of children for upper schools.[6] A few authorities looked to separate out education even further. In 1965 the *Aberdeen Press and Journal* described how a musically gifted ten-year-old received a £300 scholarship from the Glasgow Corporation education committee to be taught by a world-famous violinist at a school in London. The education committee was empowered to allocate these funds in exceptional circumstances under the *Education (Scotland) Act* of 1962.[7] In the same year the Oxfordshire education committee announced that it was sponsoring a scheme to help musically gifted children, and also starting a Junior Music School.[8] The Yehudi Menuhin School was founded in 1963, in Surrey, by a violinist and conductor, Yehudi Menuhin—himself a former 'child prodigy' who reflected on his own childhood experiences.[9]

Brentwood, in Essex, was at the forefront of these local efforts. In 1964, the educator Sydney A. Bridges led a project working with the Essex local authorities, Brentwood College of Education, and several local schools. While there is a little biographical information available about Bridges in his books, the press, or Parliamentary archives, he was clearly recognised as an expert on giftedness. Bridges held positions on a Working Party on Gifted Children established by the Schools Council (in charge of examinations in England and Wales).[10] In this

---

[5] MRC, MSS.639/11/65/6, National Union of Teachers, 'An enquiry into the education of pupils between the ages of 13 and 16 of average or less than average ability', May 1962.

[6] As cited in MRC, MSS.639/11/65/49, National Union of Teachers, 'The reorganisation of secondary education', 3rd edition, June 1964, p. 8. See also, Peter Mandler, *Crisis of the Meritocracy: Britain's Transition to Mass Education since the Second World War* (Oxford: OUP, 2020), pp. 50–55.

[7] 'Little musician gets her chance', *Aberdeen Press and Journal*, 9 September 1965, p. 7.

[8] 'Public notices', *Reading Evening Post*, 28 September 1965, p. 9.

[9] 'More than 20 things you'll need to know about...Yehudi Menuhin', *Guardian*, 26 July 1992, p. 9. Lengthy description of the foundation, environment, and experiences of this school in: Bodleian Library, Joy Gibson, and Prue Chennells (eds), *Gifted Children: Looking to their Future* (Essex: The Anchor Press, 1976), pp. 73–87.

[10] Discussions of this committee are available at the National Archives, London (hereafter NA), EJ 1/279, 'Working Party on Gifted Children: meetings 1–7; meeting 4 missing at transfer', 20 May 1969–1 May 1972. It is unclear whether the committee continued beyond this point. However, they do have a publication on one of their inquiries: Eric Ogilvie, *Gifted Children in Primary Schools* (London: Macmillan, 1973). This inquiry is discussed in NA, EJ 1/279, 'Working Party on Gifted Children: meetings 1–7; meeting 4 missing at transfer', 20 May 1969–1 May 1972, Minutes of the Fifth Meeting held on 8 October, 1971 at 160 Great Portland Street, London, 'Study into the Teaching of Gifted Children in the Primary School: Draft Report', p. 2. For context on the Schools Council, see: Institute of Education, London (hereafter IoE), ME/R/5/1, Various DES reports, July 1963–July 1977, Reports on Education, 'The Schools Council', February 1966, No. 29.

committee, which operated from at least May 1969 until May 1972, Bridges served alongside representatives from the Schools Council, Department of Education and Science, Colleges of Education in Dorset and Essex, Schools of Education at Universities of Leeds and Liverpool, and the National Foundation for Educational Research.[11] Suggesting that Bridges' work had some global influence, his death in 1980 was acknowledged by the World Council for Gifted and Talented Children: their newsletter described Bridges as an 'innovator, experimenter and protragonist [sic] of gifted education'.[12]

Under Bridges's guidance, in 1964 members of the Educational Department of Brentwood College—a teacher training college—started working with twelve boys and eight girls who had scored highly in a reasoning test used for secondary school selection.[13] This collaboration aimed to provide trainee teachers with experience of intellectually gifted young people, and the pilot study provided involved children with two hours of extra tuition per week, in Nature Study, Physics, Chemistry, Mathematics, or Art and Craft.[14] Bridges's project later expanded to work with 24 boys and 14 girls with an average IQ of over 155. Writing about this project, Bridges reflected briefly that the children involved all came from 'homes of fairly high socio-economic status'. While the study looked to recruit from 'less economically favoured homes', it was unsuccessful.[15] This occurred time and time again in the voluntary efforts and organisations traced in this book: groups insisted that they had 'tried' to recruit gifted students from working-class or minoritised ethnic backgrounds, but had been unable to do so. While such groups may well have tried, the fact that their work went ahead, catering primarily to affluent, white children, supported hugely problematic connections between ideas of 'giftedness', whiteness, affluence, and, later, elites of the future.

The Brentwood Experiment was filmed by the documentary series *Horizon*, which aired a programme, *The Gifted Child*, on 30 January 1969. The primary content of this show was interviews with teachers, voluntary sector experts, and educational psychologists, including those working at Brentwood, the Yehudi Menuhin School, the National Foundation for Educational Research, and the prestigious private sector Westminster School.[16] A teacher was pictured putting a jar over a candle and filling it with water to teach the children about vacuums. Children were also shown using film equipment, presenting mock television

---

[11] NA, EJ 1/279, 'Working Party on Gifted Children: meetings 1–7; meeting 4 missing at transfer', 20 May 1969–1 May 1972, 'Schools Council: Working Party on Gifted Children', 1969, p. 1.

[12] 'In Memoriam: Sidney Bridges', *World Gifted: Newsletter of the World Council for Gifted and Talented Children*, March 1981, Vol. 2, No. 1, p. 3.

[13] S. A. Bridges, 'The pilot scheme', in S. A. Bridges (ed.), *Gifted Children and the Brentwood Experiment* (London: Sir Isaac Pitman & Sons Ltd, 1969), p. 1.

[14] Ibid., p. 3.   [15] Ibid., p. 8.

[16] British Film Institute, 79570, *Horizon: The Gifted Child*, 30 January 1969.

shows, and experimenting with origami.[17] An article in *The Times* of June 1966 suggested that this 'unique' experiment could 'claim some success...as several of the children who have been coming to them are far more interested in their normal work and have become more integrated in their ordinary classes'.[18] By working with 'their equals', the article reported, 'they become less arrogant and less lonely'.[19] There are no published accounts available from the participating young people to further interrogate this idea. Nonetheless, it is significant that early coverage of these small experiments immediately began to present gifted young people as a unique social community, who needed to spend time together. Initial accounts suggested that this social activity helped the gifted young feel more fulfilled, but by the 1970s and 1980s, voluntary groups and press argued that social activity fostered a generation of elites of the future.

The Brentwood Experiment challenged some existing understandings for the adults participating, and reinforced others. Later writings suggested that the experiment challenged adult ideas of gender, for example. A subsequent book about this experiment, edited by Bridges, called for the 'right and proper treatment of the different sexes in the school situation' to be 'radically revised'. The experiment had found that boys had interests in 'dressmaking, cooking, dolls' houses, etc', and girls in 'mechanical problems, etc'.[20] Adults participating in this experiment also began to rethink assumed hierarchies between students and pupils. In the *Horizon* documentary, an anonymous presenter stated that participation gave teachers the opportunity to work with children 'who are maybe cleverer than they are', as well as to see 'what makes them tick' and 'to what extent their needs differ to [those of] the average child'.[21]

While involved adults then reflected on norms of gender and hierarchy, many continued to hold specific ideas about 'childlikeness' and childhood. Subsequent writings from Bridges suggested that one lesson that 'constantly obtruded itself upon us, and which seems of paramount importance, so that we are tempted to repeat it at frequent intervals' was that 'despite the high intelligence possessed by most of our children, and despite the high level of achievement of which the majority proved themselves capable, they were all still small boys and girls'.[22] This was 'made abundantly apparent as soon as they were released from the classroom for a break', where football or 'more feminine games' would see a 'maximum expenditure of energy'.[23] The idea that these children must be understood through the lens of childlikeness was reiterated by the headteacher of the Yehudi Menuhin

---

[17] Ibid.   [18] 'New body aims to get help for the gifted child', *The Times*, 18 June 1966.
[19] Ibid.
[20] Anthony Kinsey, 'The importance of creativity as an area of study', in Bridges (ed.), *Gifted Children*, p. 51.
[21] British Film Institute, 79570, *Horizon: The Gifted Child*, 30 January 1969.
[22] S. A. Bridges, 'Lessons from the first two groups', in Bridges (ed.), *Gifted Children*, p. 32.
[23] Ibid.

School, who, in the *Horizon* documentary, stated that he was 'very anxious' that these children should be given plenty of time 'to be children'.[24]

Overall, Bridges argued that this small localised project had identified 'genuine problems connected with the education of children who could score highly in I.Q. tests': problems that had not been fully recognised by teachers.[25] Bridges advocated an expansive new view of education in his subsequent work, reproducing a quote from an American publication arguing that 'schools of the future' should be 'designed not only for learning but for thinking', but to:

> produce men and women who can think, who can make new scientific discoveries, who can find more adequate solutions to impelling world problems, who cannot be brainwashed, men and women who can adapt to change and maintain sanity in this age of acceleration'.[26]

The project was thus tied to ideas of future national excellence and progress.

The experiment reflected and led changes on a local level. Essex authorities subsequently were seen by voluntary leaders as 'extremely sympathetic' to gifted youth, henceforth taking a 'flexible approach' to the age at which children should enter primary and secondary school.[27] In 1969, the local authority established an 'Essex Curriculum Extension Project', which formed a working party of teachers to be trained in gifted education, produced materials for classroom use, and ran residential courses for gifted children, employing an advisor throughout.[28] Bridges's work also influenced other specific projects in this area. When the Schools Council developed a £3,500 grant in late 1969, for example, to encourage a 'study of the teaching of gifted children in primary schools', internal papers noted that Bridges's book 'contained some very revealing comments'.[29]

Yet, looking more broadly, there was minimal media coverage of the Brentwood project. It was briefly featured in the *Horizon* documentary and *The Times* coverage mentioned, as well as in a House of Lords debate of 1969 (described later in this chapter), but these were isolated and brief representations.[30] Slightly more media interest—although not a great deal—came later, in the 1970s, offering

---

[24] British Film Institute, 79570, *Horizon: The Gifted Child*, 30 January 1969. These ideas were also visible in educational discussions of the period—notably by Her Majesty's Chief of Inspectors: NAGC, Newsletters, May 1969, p. 4; NAGC, Department of Education and Science, Reports on Education, July 1968, Number 48, 'Educating Gifted Children', p. 1.

[25] S. A. Bridges, 'Lessons from the First Two Groups', in Bridges (ed.), *Gifted Children*, p. 22.

[26] Ibid. On fears of 'brainwashing': Daniel Pick, *Brainwashed: A New History of Thought Control* (London: Wellcome Collection, 2022).

[27] NAGC, Newsletters, May 1969, 'Essex', p. 5.

[28] Julian Whybra, 'News around the world', *Gifted Education International*, 2001, 15, p. 310.

[29] NA, EJ 1/279, 'Working Party on Gifted Children: meetings 1–7; meeting 4 missing at transfer', 20 May 1969–1 May 1972, 'A study of the teaching of gifted children in primary schools', p. 1.

[30] Hansard, House of Lords, fifth series, 14 May 1969, vol. 302, cc. 155; BFI, *Horizon*, 1969; 'New body aims to get help for the gifted child', *The Times*, 18 June 1966, p. 10.

mixed views of this endeavour compared to other local schemes, particularly in Devon.[31] The project was also of continuing interest to educational researchers—although many were cynical about its potential. In 1972, for example, academic Phillip Williams—looking to develop teacher-training resources about giftedness—wrote to the Schools Council that it would be very difficult to make the Brentwood approach available nationwide, because of 'the demands for talented manpower which it involves'.[32]

Local schemes and schools were highly important in the lives of children identified as gifted and their families, significantly changing the provision available to them. These schemes were not unique—limited archival evidence also mentions, briefly, the existence of related schemes around screening, curriculum development, or provision of extra-curricular activities also in, for example, Devon, Oxford, Liverpool, and Swansea, all also starting in the late 1960s or early 1970s.[33] More broadly, however, such schemes were relatively isolated, particularly in the early-to-mid 1960s. And no school fully dedicated itself to the education of gifted children in particular—as confirmed by the Secretary of the Independent Schools Association in a 1967 letter.[34] These schemes hence demonstrate growing interest in the gifted child, from various quarters and professions, but also that this issue had not yet become prominent on national scales. Notably, also, these schemes were not explicitly framed around elitism or equality. Nor were the schemes explicitly connected, in discussions, to the concurrent shifts to comprehensive education underway in the 1950s and 1960s—despite the likely connections between those concerned about the reduced grammar school provision and those interested in supporting 'the gifted'.[35] Instead of linking to elitism, equality, or educational debates, the schemes charted in this section were typically presented as interesting experiments, to the benefit of teachers and psychologists. The framing of giftedness as an issue of equality was to develop slightly later in the 1960s, and then to flourish in the 1970s and 1980s, as arguments for gifted education as supporting elites of the future also magnified.

---

[31] 'Is a Super School a big mistake?', *Daily Mail*, 15 June 1977, p. 27.

[32] IoE, SCC/1030/1037/079, Working party on gifted children—proposal to create individualised learning packages (the Open University), 1971–1972, Individualised Learning Materials in Primary Schools: A Proposal for a Schools Council Project, Phillip Williams, p. 2.

[33] Swansea scheme mentioned in: NA, EJ 1/279, 'Working Party on Gifted Children: meetings 1–7; meeting 4 missing at transfer', 20 May 1969–1 May 1972, 'Minutes of the Second Meeting held on Tuesday 23rd September, 1969 at 160 Great Portland Street, London, W.1.', p. 2. See also: Bod, Oxfordshire Education Committee, *Exceptionally Gifted Children* (Oxford: Oxfordshire Education Committee, 1956?), p. 1; N. R. Tempest, *Teaching Clever Children, 7–11* (London: Routledge and Kegan Paul, 1974); IoE, SCC/555/1152/049, Gifted Pupils—Identification and Provision—Policy and Finance, 1979–1983, Provision for Gifted Children, DES Invitation Conference N522, 19–23 November 1979, Conference Report.

[34] IoE, WEF/B/1/2/24, Gifted Children—correspondence relating to, Letter from Secretary of Independent Schools Association, 6 February 1967.

[35] Mandler, *Crisis of the Meritocracy*, ch. 4: The transition to comprehensive education.

Margaret Branch and Her National Association for Gifted Children

The National Association for Gifted Children was founded in 1966 by Margaret Branch and recognised by the Charity Commission in May 1967.[36] This organisation marked a significant development in interest around gifted children. It was the first formal group lobbying in this area, and it operated on a national level, garnering significant interest from broadsheet newspapers. Significantly, the Association sought to present giftedness as an issue of equality, and this framing became prevalent. Branch in particular emphasised frequently that providing for the gifted young was necessary in a 'fair' and 'equal' society.

Branch is a fascinating and influential—yet little known—figure in modern British history. Few traces of her life story (beyond her campaigning and activism) can be found in archives. The primary sources available to form any biography are limited: a local newspaper report, from 2016 in the *Southwark News*, describing a proposed book about Branch; and a Gender Variance Who's Who website.[37] According to these fragmentary sources, Branch was born Margaret Johnston in 1912. In 1936, she worked as 'an ambulance driver during the Spanish Civil War' and then in 1938 'helped smuggle Jews out of occupied Prague'.[38] During World War Two, she joined the Women's Auxiliary Air Force and then the French Resistance, before—news reports claim—being 'jailed and tortured' by Nazis then 'smuggled out after a friend bribed a guard with gold'.[39] By 1941, she worked as an Assistant Labour Manager at the Royal Ordinance Factory near Newcastle-under-Lyme.[40] She married a man and took his surname (Branch), although the marriage quickly broke down.[41]

After a brief spell as a journalist in London, these sources state that Branch travelled to West Germany in 1945 to work with the UN's Relief and Rehabilitation Administration.[42] Here, she met her future life partner, Camilla Ruegg. Branch also studied with the influential psychiatrist and psychoanalyst Carl Jung.[43] In the 1950s, she became a psychiatric social worker at St Guy's Hospital London, where

---

[36] 'The National Association for Gifted Children', *Charity Commission for England and Wales*, <https://register-of-charities.charitycommission.gov.uk/charity-search/-/charity-details/313182/governing-document> (18 August 2021).
[37] Callum Burroughs, 'New book will explore life of Guy's Hospital Psychotherapist Margaret Branch who was former WW2 secret agent', *Southwark News*, 17 March 2016 <https://www.southwarknews.co.uk/news/new-book-will-explore-life-of/> (16 August 2021); 'Margaret Branch (1912–1997) social worker', *Gender Variance Who's Who*, 17 September 2020 <https://zagria.blogspot.com/2020/09/margaret-branch-1912-1997-social-worker.html#.YRpl-4hKjIV> (16 August 2021).
[38] Ibid.
[39] Burroughs, 'New book will explore life of Guy's Hospital Psychotherapist Margaret Branch'.
[40] 'Margaret Branch (1912–1997) social worker', *Gender Variance Who's Who*.   [41] Ibid.
[42] Burroughs, 'New book will explore life of Guy's Hospital Psychotherapist Margaret Branch'; 'Margaret Branch (1912–1997) social worker', *Gender Variance Who's Who*.
[43] 'Margaret Branch (1912–1997) social worker', *Gender Variance Who's Who*, 17 September 2020.

Ruegg also worked.[44] From here on, Branch begins to feature in newspaper reports and we have more sources that tell us about her life. We know that Branch initially worked in children's therapy. A later *Guardian* article claimed that, in 1952, she met 'a disturbed and epileptic boy with an IQ of 150' who 'put her on the track of the lonely ones who are so much more gifted than their contemporaries, their parents, or their teachers'.[45] Later, Branch went on to work more with trans and intersex people.[46] She conducted research in this area, and later volunteered for the Albany Trust, and Gay & Lesbian Bereavement Project helpline.[47]

While few sources remain about this remarkable life history, we know much more about Branch's establishment of the National Association, while working at St Guy's, due to her sophisticated engagement with newspapers. Branch garnered substantial broadsheet press interest around the establishment of her organisation—much more than coverage of the local schemes mentioned above. On 20 March 1966, the *Guardian* published a five-paragraph article about an exploratory meeting to plan the formation of the National Association.[48] The article reported that '[a]bout 70 educationalists and proud but anxious parents attended' at Caxton Hall, London.[49] A draft constitution was presented, to be 'put forward in two weeks so the association could achieve charity status', becoming 'a centre for collecting and disseminating information' and giving 'opportunities for parents of gifted children to meet and consult specialists'.[50] Branch was quoted at length in the piece, stating first that, 'bringing up a gifted child is as difficult as bringing up a retarded one'. She argued also that, '[t]he government is giving £500,000 to retarded children. Now let's have a little pressure for the other end'.[51] Finally, and with a flair suggestive of her media savvy, and perhaps her former experiences as a journalist, the article closed with Branch's statement that, '[t]hey've got better brains than we have—let's face it.'[52] A second article about this meeting was published by the *Guardian* the following day, where Branch, again displaying her rhetorical flair, stated that: '[t]he train robbers obviously had an IQ of over 140.'[53]

The Times also published a piece about the launch of the National Association, placing Branch centrally, three months later—on 18 June 1966. Entitled, 'New Body Aims to Get Help for the Gifted Child', it was the lengthiest piece yet:

---

[44] Burroughs, 'New book will explore life of Guy's Hospital Psychotherapist Margaret Branch'; 'Margaret Branch (1912–1997) social worker', *Gender Variance Who's Who*.
[45] Mary Stott, 'In April', *Guardian*, 6 April 1967, p. 6.
[46] Including Peter Stirling, see: 'Peter Stirling (1936–2000) shoe retailer', *Gender Variance Who's Who*, 23 November 2015 <https://zagria.blogspot.com/2015/11/peter-stirling-1936-shoe-retailer.html#.YRpoSYhKjIU> (16 August 2021).
[47] Burroughs, 'New book will explore life of Guy's Hospital Psychotherapist Margaret Branch'.
[48] Oliver Pritchett, 'The loneliness of the too-gifted child', *Guardian*, 20 March 1966.
[49] Ibid.   [50] Ibid.   [51] Ibid.   [52] Ibid.
[53] 'Serious lack of facilities for creative children', *Guardian*, 21 March 1966, p. 2.

twenty-four paragraphs long.[54] Notably, the article itself, written by a 'staff reporter', started by framing this Association in the context of the potential 'waste' of 'genius' in schools.[55] These young people may be unnoticed by parents and teachers, The Times reported, and 'stop learning', failing to get in to grammar schools, even appearing 'educationally subnormal'.[56] The article suggested that the Association had been established to take up the cause of these young people. Interviewed for this, Branch again reiterated her key messages:

> We are spending hundreds of thousands of pounds a year on the retarded child—quite rightly. All I want to do is to spend the same on the gifted... these children need help just as badly. They are handicapped by their brilliance unless they get the right treatment.[57]

Failing to identify the gifted, this article argued, could lead to children 'becoming rebels or delinquents' or 'slipping through apathy into backwardness'.[58] Making some connection to contemporary educational debates, case studies emphasised that children who were 'gifted' were not often catered for in the state system and that this must be urgently addressed. George Robb—involved with the Brentwood Experiment as an educational psychologist for Essex County Council—was also quoted stating that, '[w]hen you want to do something about gifted kids, people say it clashes with the comprehensive ethos that is around at the moment. It seems to be selecting children for special treatment.'[59] From the mid-1960s, then, Branch promoted the idea that giftedness was an equalities issue—but other sympathetic professionals recognised that this was a controversial framing. Most likely, this shaped later reticence, by campaigners, to connect gifted children with debates about school provision, preferring to emphasise the vulnerability of gifted children in life, or to call for gifted provision within comprehensive schools, rather than demanding the expansion of grammar schooling or the establishment of even more specialised educational establishments.

In August 1966—two months later, The Times reported that the National Association had about 200 members, the majority of which were parents, but also with 'some educationists and psychologists' involved.[60] The organisation held an 'experimental residential weekend' in Surrey, for twenty children and thirty adults, which again was reported in mainstream national press. This type of weekend became highly significant in their later provision (see Chapter Three) and brought together such niche pursuits as 'watching badgers and foxes at

---

[54] 'New body aims to get help for the gifted child', The Times, 18 June 1966.
[55] Ibid. [56] Ibid. [57] Ibid. [58] Ibid.
[59] 'New body aims to get help for the gifted child', The Times, 18 June 1966.
[60] 'If your child seems dull, he may be much brighter than you think...', The Times, 25 August 1966.

4 a.m., swopping views on Karl Marx and Kant, and discussing chess and games, in between listening to lectures from child specialists on one's problems'.[61]

As the organisation grew in the late 1960s, Branch continued to emphasise to the press that giftedness was itself a special need, and that therefore providing for gifted children was an equalities issue, not an elitist pursuit. Following an interview with Branch for *The Times* in November 1966, as it reported on another conference held by the Association, the newspaper repeated this message, stating supportively that: '[f]ar from demanding privileged treatment for gifted children, N.A.G.C. sought mere equality...The 1944 Education Act said that every child should be educated as best suited him, and at present the highly intelligent child was not receiving his statutory right.'[62] Branch was quoted in further articles in the *Guardian* and *The Times*, for example, stating that there should be special courses for teaching the gifted, 'as in teaching the sub-normal'; and that while 'help was available for those who might never learn, nothing was being done for the children at the other end of the scale—although they need just as much help and stimulation'.[63] This idea of a 'scale' of ability, with gifted young people at 'the top', recurred in her statements: Branch argued also that the same amount of money should be spent on 'the top 2 per cent as is being spent on the bottom'—as an issue of fairness.[64] While wishing for special provision, Branch was against the idea of special schools for the gifted—a policy the National Association maintained throughout its lifespan. Instead Branch, and the Association, argued that classes within a comprehensive system were best for the social and emotional development of the gifted, and the academic advancement of their peers.[65] The Association then was not calling for an end to comprehensivisation, underway from the 1950s and 1960s; rather, they constructed interest in 'the gifted child' as compatible with broader shifts.

In addition to discussing educational policy, media coverage around the National Association also often emphasised the emotions of parents involved with the Association. This interest was in part driven by a more intrusive and family-focused style of media developing at this time.[66] Such coverage also reflected the early insistence of the Association that its campaigning was responding to family needs and distress. The *Guardian* reported in 1967 that Branch was 'not, as an outsider might have guessed, the bedazzled mother of a putative

---

[61] 'Deep talk in the tents of the talented', *Guardian*, 20 August 1966, p. 3.

[62] 'Classes for the elite suggested', *The Times*, 21 November 1966.

[63] 'If your child seems dull, he may be much brighter than you think...', *The Times*, 25 August 1966; Paula James, 'The loneliness of a bright child', *Daily Mirror*, 11 April 1972, p. 9.

[64] 'If your child seems dull, he may be much brighter than you think...', *The Times*, 25 August 1966; Pritchett. 'The loneliness of the too-gifted child'.

[65] Stott, 'In April', p. 6.

[66] Pat Thane, *Unequal Britain: Equalities in Britain since 1954* (London: Continuum, 2010), p. 5; Deborah Cohen, *Family Secrets: Shame and Privacy in Modern Britain* (Oxford: OUP, 2017); Adrian Bingham, *Family Newspapers? Sex, Private Life, and the British Popular Press, 1918–1978* (Oxford: OUP, 2009).

genius'.[67] Indeed, the article stated that, 'there are, she has found, remarkably few parents claiming their little geese are swans'.[68] Rather, as an article in *The Times* of 1966 reported, mothers with gifted young people took the 'bitterest pill of all': they could not 'talk about your child or compare notes with other mothers', for example, due to jealously and resentment from peers.[69] These ideas were echoed by parents in the *Horizon* documentary. Here, a mother stated that, when her child was 'a couple of months old', she had told someone that, 'oh well he's getting on fine he's well, he stands up holding a chair'. Other children, an anonymous narrator commented, were still lying down and potentially just about able to hold a bottle at this age. The mother reported that her friend had 'never spoken to me since' this conversation—both out of envy and concern that the mother was boasting. As a result, the mother stated, 'I think one becomes then very aware of who one talks to and of what one says'.[70] Giftedness, then, was constantly framed from these early representations as a huge challenge for families. As a consequence, newspapers and the Association, together, emphasised that providing for gifted children was addressing a negative life experience, not seeking to identify elites.

Yet ideas of elitism did creep in to this early reporting, setting the scene for later 1970s and 1980s debates (see Chapter Four), whereby the conservative press sought to argue that the gifted *should* rule British society. Even in sympathetic early coverage of the Association, such as by *The Times*, articles were titled, for example, 'Classes for the elite suggested'.[71] Branch also had the habit, reported in multiple newspapers, of referring to the gifted young as 'Children of Gold'; a reference to Plato's Republic in which children said to be born with certain metals within them would assume particular social positions.[72] This framing, Chapter Four shows, continued in factions of psychology and tabloid media fixated on genetics. Foreshadowing a later 1970s emphasis of broader conservative press, the *Daily Telegraph* stated in the 1960s that these were 'children whose gifts we urgently need, both socially and materially, in the future' and that 'the country cannot afford to lose the asset which they represent'.[73]

Margaret Branch was then a hugely significant figure in this field, doing impressive work to bring gifted children to national attention. Before her work, focused local experiments made a significant difference in the lives of individual families; after it, the issue was presented by national press, charting in remarkable detail the foundation meetings and early encounters of the National Association.

---

[67] Stott, 'In April', p. 6.   [68] Ibid., p. 6.

[69] 'If your child seems dull, he may be much brighter than you think…', *The Times*, 25 August 1966.

[70] British Film Institute, 79570, *Horizon: The Gifted Child*, 30 January 1969.

[71] 'Classes for the elite suggested', *The Times*, 21 November 1966.

[72] Margaret Branch, 'Readers' letters', *The Times*, 30 October 1972.

[73] 'The neglected ones…', *Daily Telegraph*, 6 May 1966; 'Saving the brainy', *Daily Telegraph*, 30 April 1968.

As news coverage acknowledged, Branch was 'the moving spirit of the association' in its earliest days, using personal charisma, a knack for a catchy quote, and her professional authority and networks, to bring this cause to public attention.[74] On Branch's resignation from the National Association, in June 1976, the groups' newsletters reflected on her remarkable dedication. She had frequently 'worked late into the night preparing for each new day' and woken 'up at 3AM to lead' children's excursions, 'while mere parents slept'.[75] Biographies also alluded to her strong personality, describing her as 'very straight to the point and outspoken'.[76] Branch's framing of giftedness as an issue of equality remained significant after her resignation and in to the 1970s and 1980s, although the early rush of media interest in the Association and the minutiae of its early events waned.

The National Association, Giftedness, and Disability

The ways in which the National Association compared giftedness and disability, in the group's earliest years, merits further reflection. Notably, at least three competing conceptions of the relationships between 'giftedness' and 'disability' were at play, as visible in the discussions above. First, some of the National Association's statements implied a constructed hierarchy, with gifted children at 'the top' ('elites'?) and disabled children at the bottom. Second, at times early Association spokespeople claimed, as above, that disabled children were in some ways *more* privileged by or in the welfare state than gifted ones. Third, and finally, the Association also often sought to present the experiences of parents of gifted and disabled children as similar—as equally prone to stress, uncertainty, and challenges.

These parallels were drawn as disability emerged as 'a more prominent public issue' in Britain, from the 1940s and in particular from the 1960s.[77] In this context,

---

[74] 'Bright but deprived', *Daily Telegraph*, 22 March 1972.

[75] National Association for Gifted Children archives, Bletchley, *Looking to their Future magazine*, June 1976, 'Margaret Branch' by Denis W. Ockleton, p. 1. The significant 'time and dedication' required to organise such a voluntary group was also commented on by the partner of Ann Isaacs, who established the American Association for Gifted Children, after her death in 2001: 'Ann Fabe Isaacs: She Made Our Garden Grow (1920–2001)', in Ann Robinson and Jennifer Jolly (eds), *A Century of Contributions to Gifted Education: Illuminating Lives* (New York: Routledge, 2013), p. 21.

[76] Burroughs, 'New book will explore life of Guy's Hospital Psychotherapist Margaret Branch'.

[77] Pat Thane, *Unequal Britain: Equalities in Britain since 1954* (London: Continuum, 2010), p. 167. See also: Bonnie Evans, *The Metamorphosis of Autism: A History of Child Development in Britain* (Manchester: Manchester University Press, 2017); Gareth Millward, 'Social security policy and the early disability movement—expertise, disability, and the Government, 1965–77', *Twentieth Century British History*, 26 (2) (2015), pp. 274–297; Rubahanna Amannah Choudhury, 'The forgotten children: The Association of Parents of Backward Children and the Legacy of Eugenics in Britain, 1946–1960', thesis submitted for the Degree of Doctor of Philosophy at Oxford Brookes University, December 2015 <https://radar.brookes.ac.uk/radar/file/26b8d017-0527-4006-8029-0426ea259b75/1/choudhury2015forgottenRADAR.pdf> (26 March 2024).

the National Association perhaps looked to capitalise on growing social and media concern about disability. Perhaps, the Association was also looking to build solidarity with disability campaign groups. Certainly, before the 1950s, media coverage had occasionally connected disability with giftedness, in terms of, for example, printing stories about physically disabled children with particular artistic, musical, or intellectual talents.[78] Certainly also, parents of giftedness groups and parents of disability groups—as we see throughout this book—both did narrate their lived experiences, in mid-to-late twentieth-century voluntary groups and media alike, in terms of 'isolation, exclusion, and professional and social prejudice'.[79]

This contemporary comparison drawn between disability and giftedness campaigners, by the National Association, was not a simple one. Notably, disability campaigners rarely—if ever—made parallel comparisons: leaders of disability campaign groups were not typically looking to compare their work to that of the giftedness movement, nor to seek out connections with these voluntary organisations. It is unlikely that disability campaigners recognised the idea, from the National Association above, that the welfare state privileged disabled children over gifted ones (as disability groups were agitating against the treatment of disabled children in institutions and the educational ramifications of the term, 'ineducable').[80]

The idea of gifted children being as hard to parent as disabled ones, likewise, was likely not welcomed by parents mobilised in disability campaign groups. There is little archival material to understand this; however, there is one fleeting example from the archives of the Association of Parents of Backward Children, as explored by Rubahanna Amannah Choudhury. Writing to this organisation's newsletters, in 1949, a parent member, 'Mrs T', described how a doctor had labelled one of her children 'ineducable'. 'Mrs T' reported questioning this diagnosis, and recounted that the doctor had told her, '[do] not spend any money on J…keep it for the other two as they looked brainy children!'[81] This fleeting archival trace then troubles the equivalences being drawn, in the 1960s and beyond, between parenting gifted and disabled children. The National Association continued to draw these equivalences in to the 1970s and 1980s, as Chapter Three

---

[78] 'Work by Handicapped Children: A Record of Courage', *Guardian*, 22 September 1950; Stuart Murray, 'Autism and the contemporary sentimental: fiction and the narrative fascination of the present', *Literature and Medicine*, 25 (1) (2006), p. 27. For Tisdall, *both* gifted and disabled children were 'marginalised by a school system focused on the education of the "normal" working-class child'. Laura Tisdall, *A Progressive Education? How Childhood Changed in mid-twentieth-century* (Manchester: MUP, 2020), p. 199.
[79] Choudhury, 'The forgotten children', pp. 23, 64.
[80] Ibid. On broader context, see Anne Borsay, 'Disabled children and special education, 1944-1981', *History & Policy*, 26 November 2012 <https://www.historyandpolicy.org/docs/dfe-anne-borsay-text.pdf> (26 March 2024); Anne Borsay and Pamela Dale (eds), *Disabled Children: Contested Caring, 1850-1979* (Milton, Abingdon: Routledge, 2016).
[81] 'APBC', *Newsletter*, 2 (5) (October 1949), as cited in Choudhury, 'The Forgotten Children', p. 65.

shows. However, Chapter Three also suggests that these connections came under increasing critique: for example as some journalists and local education authority representatives asked, explicitly, whether 'the handicap of brightness seems an easier handicap to live with than most'.[82]

The House of Lords, Parliamentary Debates, and Further Limits of Equality

While the National Association garnered newspaper attention from its outset, its messages were not taken up quickly in policy circles. To be more specific: the organisation gained support in the House of Lords, but not in the House of Commons. Whether the support of the Lords helped the Association or not is open to debate: the Lords who supported the group often argued that it would and should identify some kind of social elite, and were often themselves conservatives from wealthy backgrounds. Fewer Labour politicians were sympathetic, if paying attention at all to this group, in the 1960s.

Many members of the House of Lords were sympathetic to the cause of gifted education—and more interested in this area than those in the House of Commons—from the early 1960s, before the National Association was established. This is visible in Lords' response to the Plowden Report, commissioned by a Conservative politician, then also the Minister of Education, Edward Boyle, in 1963. In this year, Boyle directed the Central Advisory Council for Education to 'consider primary education in all its aspects and the transition to secondary education'. The Plowden Report did not focus on gifted education. When presented to the Secretary of State for Education and Science, Anthony Crosland, in 1966, the report included a statement that members had not 'undertaken, or commissioned, any special study of the education of gifted children'.[83] The report however 'briefly' described 'some impressions' formed of this area, suggesting members' growing interest.[84] Notably, it stated that there was 'an egalitarian suspicion of the whole concept of giftedness' due to 'dislike of privilege, doubts about intelligence tests and defensiveness about comprehensive schools', and it also discussed problems of identification as 'giftedness' as a broad and mixed category.[85] The report conceded that gifted children were 'bound to have particular needs' that were not always met, and that there were various potential models—including

---

[82] Caroline Moorehead, 'A gifted child can be a problem child', *The Times*, 9 May 1974, p. 9; Institute of Education, London, SCC/555/1152/049, Gifted Pupils—Identification and Provision—Policy and Finance, 1979–1983, Provision for Gifted Children, DES Invitation Conference N522, 19–23 November 1979, Conference Report, p. 1.

[83] Central Advisory Council for Education (England), *Children and their Primary Schools* (London: HMSO, 1967), 'Chapter 22: The Education of Gifted Children', p. 305.

[84] Ibid.   [85] Ibid.

the Brentwood special lessons—alongside special schools or acceleration.[86] Overall, it stated, '[l]ong term studies' should be made in this area, and there was 'much still to be discovered'.[87]

Several members of the House of Lords, discussing this report, were dissatisfied by the lack of space given to giftedness. Lord James of Rusholme told the Lords in March 1967 that he was 'sorry to see that the single chapter' in this report about giftedness 'is the shortest' and, 'as is so frequent nowadays, lends colour to the view that it is only outstanding abilities in the arts, in music and the ballet that need bother us much at all', although broadly he supported Plowden's recommendations.[88] Rusholme was made a life peer in 1959. He had been educated at two state grammar schools, attended Queens College, Oxford, and then taught at the prestigious schools of Winchester and Manchester Grammar.[89] During this debate, Rusholme served as the Vice-Chancellor of the University of York, newly formed in 1963. James himself, biographies and his own speeches suggest, strongly believed that special education should be targeted to intelligent children, regardless of social background.[90] His interest in giftedness continued in to the 1970s, and he gave a speech on this topic to the University of York, arguing that 'one of the most important duties of an educational system was to foster the gifted individual'.[91]

Boyle echoed the critique that giftedness was not discussed enough. Boyle had attended Eton and then Christ Church, Oxford. Echoing James, Boyle told the House that 'the chapter on gifted children [was] just a shade weak'.[92] In 1967, Boyle would become a sponsor for the National Association. Charles Morrison,

---

[86] Ibid.

[87] Ibid., pp. 307–308. Parallel debates in higher education are aptly discussed in: Josh Patel, 'Imagining the role of the student in society: ideas of British higher education policy and pedagogy 1957–1972', PhD thesis, University of Warwick (2021); Josh Patel, 'The Puzzle of Lionel Robbins: how a neoliberal economist expanded public university education in 1960s Britain', *Twentieth Century British History*, 34 (2) (2023), pp. 220–245.

[88] Hansard, House of Lords, Fifth series, 14 March 1967, vol. 281, cols. 230–231.

[89] Borthwick Institute for Archives, York, JAM/2/1/1, Scripts, Speeches and Lectures, 'The Education of the Gifted Child', Lord James of Rusholme, 1970s, p. 2; Roger Young, 'James, Eric John Francis, Baron James of Rusholme', *Oxford Dictionary of National Biography*, 8 October 2009 <https://www.oxforddnb.com/view/10.1093/ref:odnb/9780198614128.001.0001/odnb-9780198614128-e-51145> (2 October 2019). Notably also, James was asked by Secretary of State for Education and Science, Margaret Thatcher, to chair a government inquiry into teacher training: the subsequent report is available here: Department of Education and Science, *Teacher Education and Training: Report by a Committee of Inquiry appointed by the Secretary of State for Education and Science, under the Chairmanship of Lord James of Rusholme* (London: Her Majesty's Stationery Office, 1972) <http://www.educationengland.org.uk/documents/james/james1972.html> (10 December 2021).

[90] Borthwick Institute for Archives, York, JAM/2/1/1, Scripts, Speeches and Lectures, 'The Education of the Gifted Child', Lord James of Rusholme, 1970s, p. 3; Young, 'James, Eric John Francis, Baron James of Rusholme'. For more on the details of Rusholme's views, see Gary McCulloch, *Philosophers and Kings: Education for Leadership in Modern England* (Cambridge: CUP, 1991), pp. 70–74.

[91] Borthwick Institute for Archives, York, JAM/2/1/1, Scripts, Speeches and Lectures, 'The Education of the Gifted Child', Lord James of Rusholme, 1970s, pp. 1–18.

[92] Hansard, House of Lords, Fifth Series, 16 March 1967, vol. 743, col. 747.

meanwhile, a Conservative politician who had also attended Eton and then Cambridge, emphasised that:

> There is no section of children, from whatever background they come, who are of more overriding importance than these gifted children. It is from their numbers that the leaders of the community should emerge, but they will emerge only if their gifts and their ability are encouraged to the full. And if they do not emerge it will be less to their own disadvantage than to the nations.[93]

Morrison believed that the report was correct to identify 'egalitarian suspicion' of gifted children. However, he argued that, '[i]rrational obstacles and suspicion must be removed, and more knowledge and more research is needed.'[94] Overall, Morrison argued that, '[o]nly by providing the right opportunity for gifted children can the pace of advance towards the ever receding goal of the pursuit of excellence be hastened.'[95] This overall idea of gifted children as central to national 'excellence' was not without contemporary critique: indeed, in the Chamber, John Pardoe, a Liberal MP, stated that: '[a]lthough the talent of the gifted child is important, it is the happiness of the average child that is essential.'[96]

In early debates then, Conservative Members of the Commons and Lords argued that gifted children were neglected in Britain. Some Lords took this argument further, claiming that gifted young people should be identified as elites of the future—critical for some vision of British 'success'. The idea that any child could be gifted was occasionally mentioned in these debates, but relatively little attention was paid to issues of gender, race, ethnicity, or class. Little attention, also, was paid to the kinds of family experiences and dynamics emphasised by the National Association, as discussed above.

The first full Parliamentary debate specifically about gifted children was also hosted in the House of Lords, on 14 May 1969, and entitled, 'Needs of Gifted Children'. By this time, the National Association had been established for nearly three years, and many of the Lords with an early interest in this area supported it. Opening the floor at 2.57PM, Lord Carrington 'rose to call attention to the needs of gifted children and the necessity for Government action.'[97] Carrington's particular motivation for discussing this area was unclear. In Parliament, he had not previously shown significant interest in education: he had served in the Lords since 1945, following military service in the Grenadier Guards, and held positions in the Ministry of Defence, the Foreign Office, and as High Commissioner to Australia, working under Winston Churchill, Harold Macmillan, Alec Douglas-Home, Edward Heath, and Margaret Thatcher.[98] Carrington himself, opening the

---

[93] Ibid., col. 825.   [94] Ibid, col. 826.   [95] Ibid.   [96] Ibid, col. 818.
[97] 'Needs of Gifted Children', House of Lords, Hansard, Fifth Series, 14 May 1969, vol. 302, col. 123.
[98] 'Death of a Member: Lord Carrington—Tributes', House of Lords, 10 July 2018 <https://www.theyworkforyou.com/lords/?id=2018-07-10b.851.2> (17 August 2021).

debate, stated that he was 'conscious' that 'many of your Lordships...know very much more about this subject than I do'.[99] While he was not 'intimately concerned with' this issue in 'everyday life', he sought 'to ventilate the problem' and to 'express my own personal concern'.[100] He would later become a supporter of the National Association.

Carrington made clear, from the outset, that his motion was 'not concerned in any way with the current discussion about comprehensive or grammar schools, [or] about streaming or about the 11-plus', but rather revolved around 'a much narrower field'.[101] He wished to discuss gifted children specifically, and indeed to make the case that they required separate schools, beyond grammar schools.[102] Revealing the tight networks in which early knowledge in this area was constructed, Carrington's testimony drew on examples from the Yehudi Menuhin School ('an extremely successful experiment'), and the local authority in Essex (which had done 'a certain amount of work in this field').[103] The subsequent debate continued over approximately three hours, with two interruptions for other discussions, and fourteen other Lords commented. The Yehudi Menuhin School was mentioned favourably twice more—and its namesake one more time, while the Brentwood Experiment was mentioned three more times. The National Association featured in this debate also, mentioned by three Lords. Lord Aberdare (1919–2005), who later became one of the National Association's patrons, advocated strongly for this group. Like Carrington, Aberdare was born in 1919, served in the British Army during World War Two, and then in various positions in Conservative Cabinets. Underscoring the parallels between their lives, Aberdare attended the Sandroyd School, an independent school for primary school pupils, with Carrington. Aberdare opened his contribution to the Lords debate referencing this, remarking that: 'I cannot help thinking that he [Carrington] put the Motion down from personal experience as one whose great gifts were not early recognised but have been fully demonstrated later—and I say this because many years ago I was at school with my noble friend.'[104]

Aberdare stated that the Association 'has been founded for that very purpose of advising parents what action they can take in the event of their having a particularly gifted child, as well as drawing attention to the problems of gifted children'.[105] Aberdare repeated directly a story he claimed was told to him by the Association, 'of one small girl who was luckier than some'.[106] This girl, 'the daughter of a dustman' was given a piano by her father—he had been paid £5 to remove it.[107] She subsequently 'spent all day long banging away on the piano' and 'is now at the Yehudi Menuhin School, where obviously her talents are rightly used'.[108] This social progress, Aberdare stated, was facilitated by the work of the National

---

[99] 'Needs of Gifted Children', House of Lords, Hansard, Fifth Series, 14 May 1969, vol. 302, col. 122.
[100] Ibid, col. 123.   [101] Ibid.   [102] Ibid., cols. 126–127.   [103] Ibid.
[104] Ibid., col. 154.   [105] Ibid., col. 155.   [106] Ibid.   [107] Ibid.   [108] Ibid.

Association, who 'got this little girl her chance'.[109] As in previous debates, the idea that all children could be gifted was alluded to, but the precise mechanisms through which gifted education and advocacy could alleviate or entrench inequalities were rarely explicitly discussed.

Lord Kennet, a Labour Minister who later joined the Social Democratic Party, responded that he was 'particularly grateful to the noble Lord, Lord Aberdare, for mentioning—for the first time, incidentally, in this debate…the National Association for Gifted Children'.[110] While feeling that this was a 'rather new Association' which 'has not yet got a very definite platform', Kennet stated that, 'I hope I carry the House with me in wishing the Association wisdom in developing its programme, and success in achieving it, to the measure that it is wise when it is developed'.[111] Lord Carrington, closing this debate as he had opened it, stated that: 'this is a young organisation and it is one in which I am interested'.[112] He hoped that the organisation would 'read this debate…with great care', 'benefit from this debate', and also 'be a little more widely known as a result of it'.[113] Carrington hoped, furthermore, that the 'Department of Education will read' the debate text, adding also that: '[s]ometimes I wonder whether they do read the debates in your Lordships' House.'[114]

So the National Association garnered supportive interest in the House of Lords from the late 1960s. Lords also later supported the organisation in various ways: several members became patrons. Lord Edward Boyle spoke in 1972 at the Association's conference, stating that, 'everywhere in the western world, the stimulation of intelligence was discouraged in favour of special attention to the handicapped'.[115] Lord Rusholme spoke at the World Conference on Gifted Children, which the National Association organised in 1975 (see Chapter Six) and stated that 'many of my views are in some important ways in direct opposition to those that are the official policy of this association'.[116] In particular, while the Association called for all children to be educated in the same schools, citing the benefits of peer interaction, Rusholme believed that selective education should be 'a vital part of our education system'.[117] For Rusholme, selective schools '*reflected* rather than created class divisions in society', but were key to 'a more equal society, meaning by that not a society in which all men have the same tasks and the same ambitions, but one in which all men have opportunities for their own individual development, united by a common culture'.[118]

While many Lords supported the National Association, their support was not as strong, frequent, nor vocal as the discussion in broadsheet newspapers. The broader discussions of the Lords also demonstrated the challenges the Association

---

[109] Ibid. [110] Ibid., col. 193. [111] Ibid.
[112] Ibid., col. 198. [113] Ibid. [114] Ibid.
[115] 'Handicapped children: mental and social—Letters to the Editor', *Guardian*, 20 April 1972, p. 12.
[116] Bodleian Library, Gibson, and Chennells (eds), *Gifted Children*, p. 11.
[117] Ibid., p. 18. [118] Ibid., p. 19.

faced in drawing connections between giftedness and equality, and in avoiding associations with ideas of elitism. Notably, the vast majority of Lords supporting these measures were conservatives with elite educational backgrounds. They often argued that gifted children must be taught in specialist schools, completely contradicting campaigners' focus on supporting broader shifts to comprehensivisation. Further, many Lords also positioned gifted children as elites of the future, even in these early debates, again not aligning with the framing the National Association sought to push around gifted provision as easing familial stress and tension, similarly to provision for disabled young people. The idea that the gifted were 'children of gold', likewise, was reiterated frequently. Even opening the debate, Carrington stated that:

> as a nation we cannot afford to neglect that very small section of the community who are the originals—those who are going to make the greatest contribution to our society, whether it be in the field of arts, science or technology. There are not very many of them. We cannot afford to waste them.[119]

Lord Rusholme, in a 1970s speech, likewise, mobilised Plato to critique the 'strong psychological opposition, particularly from parents' to selection.[120] He also echoed the framing of the National Association that giftedness was a 'special need' and thus needed special treatment, although he also contrasted the needs of 'naturally clever children' to 'the stupid ones'; a framing the Association avoided.[121]

These examples are somewhat disparate, yet also demonstrate the significant challenges the Association faced in raising awareness of giftedness, and in constructing it in relation to equality; challenges that remained and grew in decades to come. It is also notable that the Lords were unsure if their support for this organisation would be heard in the Commons, or whether the Association itself was well-known, even after a flurry of newspaper coverage. The Lords' concerns in 1969 were, in part, duly founded, and the National Association was not mentioned in a Commons debate until 1978.

Conclusion

This chapter has traced ways in which the idea of the gifted child began to come to significant public attention in 1960s Britain, shaped by cultural ecologies of interest in intelligence from adults and children discussed in Chapter One.

---

[119] 'Needs of Gifted Children', House of Lords, Hansard, Fifth Series, 14 May 1969, vol. 302, cols. 128–129.
[120] Borthwick Institute for Archives, York, JAM/2/1/1, Scripts, Speeches and Lectures, 'The Education of the Gifted Child', Lord James of Rusholme, 1970s, p. 5.
[121] Ibid., pp. 1–2, 11.

Emergent interest in the early 1960s was localised and delivered through localised educational initiatives. In 1975, a former Headmaster of the Yehudi Menuhin School, Antony Brackenbury, remarked that it was interesting that his school was founded at the same time as other initiatives, for example 'a year or two before the NAGC [National Association] itself was launched': this was, he claimed, 'an example of the commonly observed phenomenon that when the time is ripe people begin to take similar initiatives quite independently of each other'.[122] The 'ripeness' of this time, of course, was shaped by a 1950s and 1960s context in which, broadly, there were increasing shifts in secondary education towards comprehensive provision, where all children would be educated together.[123] Support for 'the gifted' could be viewed as one form of resistance to this shift. Yet, support for the gifted was also broader than that: for voluntary groups, in particular, supporting the gifted was rarely solely about redesigning education, but rather necessary to address unmet familial needs in an equal welfare state.

Small, localised experiments in supporting and identifying the gifted young did not initially forge a national network, nor gain widespread interest. The Brentwood Experiment ran a small-scale pilot in this area, which received some national media attention that suggested that it led participating teachers and local educational authority staff to rethink educational provision. Yet the experiment was small-scale and we have no evidence with which to trace the impact of involved young people. Lively local experiments continued, struggling to join up with one another, in to the 1970s and 1980s. A conference organised by the Department of Education and Skills in 1972, for local education authorities, for instance, reported 'a trend for promising experiments in provision for the gifted to be curtailed for lack of money'.[124] The work of the National Association drove national interest in this area, particularly from broadsheet newspapers. This was in large part due to the lively and charismatic advocacy of Margaret Branch, who worked in sophisticated ways to drive media attention, even in minor meetings of the Association, with punchy statements and hard work. Members of the House of Lords took a special interest in this area throughout the 1960s also, supporting the National Association's work and becoming patrons. Yet Lords also recognised that this organisation was not yet prominent—and indeed hoped that their discussions would influence the Association, rather than the other way round.

---

[122] Bodleian Library, Gibson, and Chennells (eds), *Gifted Children*, p. 73.

[123] Peter Mandler has analysed the long roots of this shift and writes that, by the end of 1963, 'no fewer than 92 of 129 English LEAs had initiated plans to end selection at 11'. Nonetheless still significant—and hugely symbolic in debate since—*Circular 10/65* (1965) instructed local education authorities to 'prepare development plans ending selection at 11+', Peter Mandler, *Crisis of the Meritocracy: Britain's Transition to Mass Education since the Second World War* (Oxford: OUP, 2020), pp. 50, 55.

[124] See: IoE, SCC/555/1152/049, Gifted Pupils—Identification and Provision—Policy and Finance, 1979-1983, Provision for Gifted Children, DES Invitation Conference N522, 19-23 November 1979, Conference Report, pp. 1-3.

The Association was not yet central in policy circles more broadly—within educational reports or in the Commons—in the 1960s.

The early National Association under Branch sought to emphasise that supporting gifted children—particularly through enrichment classes—was part of constructing an equal Britain. The Association's campaigning drew on contemporary public concerns about the provision for disabled children, and Branch argued that gifted children had, by comparison, been neglected by the post-war welfare state. Yet ideas of an 'elite' also framed the National Association's early work. Notably, Branch at times presented giftedness as a binary with disability, with gifted children as the 'top 2 per cent' and disabled children at 'the bottom'. Newspaper coverage reiterated this premise, describing gifted children as elites of the future, made 'of gold', and critical for national progress. Thus, specific visions of 'the future' and troubling hierarchies were built into early campaigning around giftedness. The work of the National Association continued to be framed by claims about equality and the post-war settlement in years to come: into the 1980s, the organisation was still at times aping the language of the 1944 *Education Act*, emphasising that, 'all children whose natural gifts enable them to learn quickly should receive an education according to their ability, aptitude and needs.'[125] Claims that the gifted were, or should be, elites of 'the future' likewise continued from these early debates to develop substantively by 1980s, shaping media and policy rhetoric.

Subsequent chapters in this book each open with a quote from a young person, and contain significant archival material enabling us to think about how young people received later giftedness schemes, and interpreted debates about elitism and equality. This chapter was not able to uncover young people's views. They were not yet documented by the National Association in its earliest days, nor by the experiments mentioned above, nor were they sought out by Lords discussing this issue. Indeed, what instead became apparent in these debates was an emphasis on the childlikeness of the gifted young. This changed in later years, for several reasons. By the 1970s and 1980s, the practices of asking young people to write down their experiences, and to reflect on them, became more common. The National Association played a critical role here, and volunteers were particularly interested, as we will see, in understanding how gifted children thought and wrote. At times the testimonies of the young were still framed around adult-led notions of precociousness and subversion, rather than taken seriously on their own terms. Nonetheless, this moment in which the testimonies of involved young were unclear, and unseen, was to pass quickly.

---

[125] Bodleian Library, National Association for Gifted Children, *Teaching Able and Gifted Children: A Study of Initial and In-Service Teacher Training in England, Scotland and Wales 1981/82* (London: NAGC, 1982), p. 1.

Debates about gifted children demonstrate that there was no simple shift from the 'equal' moment of the post-war welfare state and permissive legislation of the 1960s to the neoliberal divided society of the 1980s, building on the rise of popular individualism in the 1970s. Rather, these two worlds co-existed and conflicted throughout these decades. Even in the 1960s, as the gap between richest and poorest narrowed, hopes of identifying elites of the future were embedded.[126] They become highly visible in these debates and, as subsequent chapters go on to show, had significant influence on the lives of young people—whose leisure time, education, peer cultures, and family lives were significantly reshaped as consequence.

'Gifted Children' in Britain and the World: Elitism and Equality since 1945. Jennifer Crane, Oxford University Press.
© Jennifer Crane 2025. DOI: 10.1093/9780198928881.003.0003

---

[126] Pat Thane, *Unequal Britain: Equalities in Britain since 1954* (London: Continuum, 2010), p. 4.

Young People's Engagement with Gifted Spaces, 1970–1987

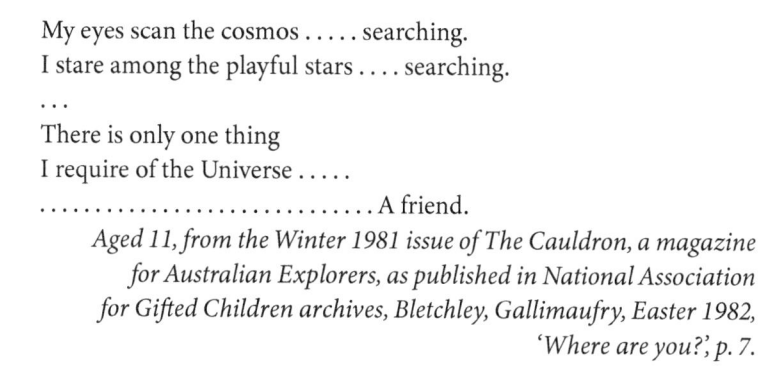

> My eyes scan the cosmos . . . . . searching.
> I stare among the playful stars . . . . searching.
> . . .
> There is only one thing
> I require of the Universe . . . . .
> . . . . A friend.
>
> *Aged 11, from the Winter 1981 issue of The Cauldron, a magazine for Australian Explorers, as published in National Association for Gifted Children archives, Bletchley, Gallimaufry, Easter 1982, 'Where are you?', p. 7.*

The above poem appeared in the Easter 1982 edition of *Gallimaufry*, a magazine for children aged seven to twelve, co-ordinated by the Explorers Club of the National Association for Gifted Children. Here, an eleven-year-old boy, writing from a similar Australian group, expressed a sense of loneliness, despite recognising his place within an extended universe and enjoying looking at stars. Similar longing for friendship was reiterated across magazines of the National Association, for example in requests for penpals with which to 'exchange ideas and thoughts on anything (except pot-pourri).'[1] This demonstrates an idea that gifted young people may wish to socialise together, in distinctive spaces, with the shared identity of 'giftedness'. It also suggests that gifted young people were able to make critique of the idea of giftedness, and its limitations, questioning, for example, if this label in fact left them lonely.

This chapter further explores the lived experiences of being 'gifted', for children and their families, in the 1970s and 1980s, and it analyses how participation in voluntary organisations helped families to manage their social and intellectual lives.[2] In the 1970s and 1980s, the National Association for Gifted Children

---

[1] National Association for Gifted Children archives, Bletchley (hereafter NAGC), Dialogue, Easter 1982, 'Is anybody else breathing?', p. 4.
[2] Earlier experiments with the ideas in this chapter were published in: Jennifer Crane, 'Gifted Children, Youth Culture, and Popular Individualism in 1970s and 1980s Britain', *The Historical Journal*, 65 (2022), pp. 1418–1441 (under CC BY 4.0 license, permitting unrestricted re-use, distribution, reproduction, with proper citation and link to the license <https://creativecommons.org/licenses/by/4.0/>).

flourished. In 1974, for example, it received its first government grant (£5,000 per year) enabling its lead, Margaret Branch, to work full-time for the Association. The Association continued to receive grants from the Department of Education and Science into the 1980s, receiving £20,000 in 1989.[3] More broadly, educational and cultural interest in giftedness also grew over these decades. One of Her Majesty's Chief Inspectors of Education took 'a special interest in gifted children' from 1973, running new training courses in this area, and publishing *Gifted Children in Middle and Comprehensive Secondary Schools* (1977).[4] Local initiatives, supported by local education authorities, also continued and thrived in Birmingham, Cleveland, Essex, Devon, Nottingham, and Somerset.[5] By the mid-1970s, Henry Collis, then the Director of the National Association, reflected that the term 'gifted children' was 'no longer an emotive phrase' and that 'at last people are beginning to realise that a minority of these children can be handicapped because they are so bright'.[6]

While 'giftedness' was explicitly incorporated in educational discussions of the 1970s and 1980s, particularly in certain local areas, this idea was not fully integrated to national policy. Many parents still felt unsupported by mainstream state education, and those advocating for further gifted provision still argued that the gifted young had been 'relatively ignored'.[7] Parents, as a consequence, joined the

---

[3] The grant came from the Department for Education and Science and was given until at least 1976, with discussion of 'the possibility of a renewed grant' in August of that year: Hansard, House of Commons, Fifth Series, 18 July 1978, vol. 954, col. 126. The same value grant was also awarded in 1979 (Hansard, House of Commons, Fifth Series, 28 June 1979, vol. 969, col. 326). In 1980, the organisation was awarded £4,509 (Hansard, House of Commons, Fifth Series, 22 July 1980, vol. 989, col. 192). In 1982, £800 (Hansard, House of Commons, Sixth Series, 31 March 1983, vol. 40, col. 229). In 1983, £5,000 (Hansard, House of Commons, Sixth Series, 22 July 1983, vol. 46, col. 245.) In 1984, £800 (Hansard, House of Commons, Sixth Series, 17 January 1984, vol. 52, col. 212. In 1985, £5,000 (Hansard, House of Commons, Sixth Series, 3 February 1986, vol. 91, col. 13). In 1988, £10,000 (Hansard, House of Commons, Sixth Series, 17 March 1988, vol. 129, col. 635). In 1989, £20,000 (Hansard, House of Commons, Sixth Series, 3 March 1989, vol. 148, col. 337). These grants were a significant part of the National Association's income, although they raised more from donations and subscriptions (around £51,000 and £15,000 respectively, in 1981, for example: NAGC, Annual Report 1981, Income and Expenditure Account, p. 14).

[4] Janet Watts, 'The plight of the children of gold'. See: Her Majesty's Inspectorate, *Gifted Children in Middle and Comprehensive Secondary Schools* (London: HMSO, 1977); Institute of Education, London, SCC/555/1152/049, Gifted Pupils—Identification and Provision—Policy and Finance, 1979-1983, Provision for Gifted Children, DES Invitation Conference N522, 19-23 November 1979, Conference Report, p. 1.

[5] Ibid. The University of London Institute of Education also started a special Diploma in Education with special reference to Gifted Children, in the 1970s, for past exam papers see: Institute of Education, London, IE/EXN/4/40, Examination papers for the diploma in education with special reference to gifted children.

[6] Paula Davies, 'Why bright children can be so "Handicapped"', *The Daily Telegraph*, 5 September 1975, p. 13. Notably however in the same article Branch still contended that progress remained slow because 'people [still] assume the bright children will do well anyway'. Notably other forms of support for the gifted young declined in this period: in 1980 the Secretary of State for Education and Science agreed to reduce the number of assisted places—which were designed to include gifted children places in independent schools—by about half in an effort to reduce government spending (A. Crawford, 'Housing to bear brunt of new cuts', *The Guardian* (3 February 1980), p. 1.).

[7] Institute of Education archives, London, SCC/1030/1037/079, Working party on gifted children—proposal to create individualised learning packages (the Open University), 1971-1972,

Association as never before, looking for support. This chapter first explores who joined the National Association as it grew, demonstrating that the organisation made significant attempts to recruit a diverse membership. Second, the chapter examines parents' stated motivations for joining: emotional support and solidarity, and typically looking to supplement existing educational provision, rather than replace it. Third, the chapter explores what opportunities being labelled as 'gifted', through the National Association, gave to young people. The Association organised children's activities nationwide under the label 'Explorers Unlimited'. These weekend clubs and holiday retreats facilitated a range of pursuits such as creative arts, intellectual debate, drama, computer science, mineralogy, and chess.[8] Exploring the new voluntary spaces that the gifted young entered, and their engagement with these, demonstrates that ideas of 'childlikeness' pervaded these spaces, and hierarchies between adults and children remained. Fourth, the chapter traces how young people rejected the label of 'gifted' and the system of intelligence testing often behind it; even if accepting giftedness spaces, they often found the term problematic. Fifth and finally, the chapter explores how young people of the National Association rethought their relationships with teachers and peers, having been labelled gifted.

Overall, this chapter follows Craig Jeffrey's imperative, summarising contemporary literature in geographies of global youth agency, to value a 'grounded approach to the analysis of young people's practices, one sensitive to the importance of space not as an static container for action but as actively entangled in the drama of youth in practice'.[9] As such, the chapter looks closely from the perspective of children's writings about youth-created spaces, notably voluntary organisations for giftedness and schools. The chapter argues, subsequently, that 'in practice' the specific label 'gifted' held power to affect everything about children and family's lives.[10] Many young people felt that they benefited from participating

---

Individualised Learning Materials in Primary Schools: A Proposal for a Schools Council Project, Phillip Williams. Nonetheless, interested local education authorities were carrying out experiments in this area and, looking to co-ordinate these nationally, the Schools Council conducted a project from September 1980–August 1982, 'to coordinate the work of local authority groups in the development and evaluation of resources for able children'. The Councils hired a co-ordinator for this post, a senior lecturer at Edge Hill College of Higher Education. The project ended with the closure of the Schools Council in 1984: Institute of Education, London, SCC/555/1152/049, Gifted Pupils—Identification and Provision—Policy and Finance, 1979-1983, Provision for Gifted Children, 'Resources for Gifted Pupils' advert; Institute of Education, London, SCC/555/1152/049, Gifted Pupils—Identification and Provision—Policy and Finance, 1979-1983, Provision for Gifted Children, 'Publicity for programme', 14 July 1980; Institute of Education, London, SCC/555/1152/049, Gifted Pupils—Identification and Provision—Policy and Finance, 1979-1983, 'Resource Centre for teachers of Able Children', January 1983, p. 1.

[8] Activities reported in: June Tarlin, 'Brain power just going to waste!', *Daily Mail*, 16 March 1976, p. 11; Barbara Jefery, 'These children have a problem—they're too intelligent!' *Daily Mail*, 31 January 1977, p. 10; Bodleian Library, Per 264505 e. 4, NAGC, *Journal of the Gifted Child*, Autumn 1979, inside leaf.

[9] Craig Jeffrey, 'Geographies of children and youth II: Global youth agency', *Progress in Human Geography*, 36 (2) (2011), p. 249.

[10] Ibid.

in gifted spaces, and also that this label enabled them to feel 'equal' to their peers and teachers, now understanding themselves as having distinct needs. At the same time, other young people felt that this label marked them out as 'others'. These beliefs were often held by the same individuals, over time, and 'entangled'.[11] When labelled 'gifted', young people's opportunities were still restricted by ideas of their 'youthful' and 'childlike' nature.

Who Was Identified?

The National Association did not require a specific IQ score or other such accreditation for entry. Parents could simply identify their children and pay a membership fee.[12] Fees were, the Association stated in 1972, 'kept deliberately low so that the Association can be accessible to the widest number of people': £2 per year 'for a husband and wife', 50p for students who were training, and £4 for 'schools and other educational establishments'.[13] This covered 'all the services of the Association and four copies per issue of the newsletter'.[14]

From the early days of giftedness voluntary groups, organisers were aware that their recruitment would be shaped by assumptions about who, precisely, was 'gifted'. At first, the National Association focused primarily on issues of class, without remarking so much on gender, race, or ethnicity. Some media discussions of class tended to assume that working-class families hindered their children: they may 'miss out' on spotting their potential and then not know how to support them. In 1970, for example, a National Association spokesperson told *The Times* that there were probably more gifted children in Britain than the figure of 2 per cent often quoted in press. Many of these children were, he suggested, 'suppressed' by their 'poor home backgrounds'.[15] Echoing this assumption that working-class career paths were inadequate, in some way, in 1971, the *Daily Express* reported that 30,000 working class boys left school every year to start 'dead end' manual jobs, when they could have been lawyers, doctors, or school teachers.[16] Statements from the National Association described gifted children who were 'rescued' through being identified.[17] Association leaders, speaking to press, rarely discussed what working-class families themselves said about giftedness

---

[11] Ibid.

[12] Association publications emphasised that intelligence tests 'can be useful' but were 'not particularly good predictors' nor 'very accurate measures of intellectual ability' (The Education Committee of the NAGX, *Help with Bright Children* (London: National Association for Gifted Children, 1989), p. 16).

[13] NAGC, *Annual Report and Accounts of the National Association for Gifted Children, 1971–2*, p. 3. Inflation calculators available online would suggest that this was around £22 equivalent in 2021.

[14] Ibid.   [15] '"Miracle" view of gifted children criticized', *The Times*, 9 November 1970, p. 2.

[16] Bruce Kemble, 'Talent spotting begins at home', *Daily Express*, 24 March 1971, p. 6.

[17] Linton Mitchell, 'Where are all the missing Children of Gold?', *Reading Evening Post*, 21 July 1975, p. 6.

groups. One fragment of evidence around this is from the *Evening Post* in 1975, where an Association spokesperson stated that letters from working class parents, whose children had participated in giftedness schemes, expressed that, 'my husband and I feel we have brought a stigma on the family'.[18] Clearly, then, the Association did not fully engage with issues of privilege and giftedness in its early years. We should be highly cautious about blithe statements such as from the new branch chairman of a Lichfield branch, in 1975, that the National Association was a 'classless organisation, and a non-political one'.[19]

By the late 1970s, Association leaders began to think more about how to recruit children from more diverse backgrounds. Alongside interest from local education authorities, the Association started to organise groups in inner city areas in particular, assuming that this would enable them to work with children from minoritised ethnic and working-class families.[20] Association staff recognised in 1979 that this focus on inner cities, and race and ethnicity, represented a 'change in direction' and a new 'social priority' for the group.[21] Key places identified in which to work with 'underprivileged children in Inner City areas' were in the North East of England, Liverpool, the East End of London, Brixton, and Greater Manchester.[22] Rather than directing efforts to parents, the Association more typically brought their own Regional Officers for these areas together with local education authorities and schools, seeking out children by approaching headteachers to identify disadvantaged but gifted children.[23]

A 1984 Association newsletter described the work of the Merseyside and Wirral branch as a particular 'success', with 350 families involved and, in addition, nearly 60 children given free places at Saturday morning enrichment classes.[24] In 1980

---

[18] 'Crime risk warning on gifted kids', *Evening Post*, 6 September 1975, p. 3.

[19] Sue Fisher, 'Children with a special gift...', *The Mercury*, 25 April 1975, p. 11.

[20] The broader interest of local education authorities also working in this area, and in particular the leading work of Tom Marjoram, from Her Majesty's Inspectorate, is reported in: 'Third UK-DES Invitational Conference', *World Gifted: Newsletter of the World Council for Gifted and Talented Children*, October 1982, vol. 3, 2, p. 3.

[21] NAGC, 'Chairman's Report', *Twelfth Annual General Meeting Held at the Royal Institution of Saturday, 3 November 1979*, p. 3. On the early branches and foundation see: NAGC, 'Margaret Branch', *Looking to their Future*, June 1976, p. 1.

[22] NAGC, Twelfth Annual General Meeting held at the Royal Institute, 3 November 1979, Directors Report, p. 2; NAGC archives, Bletchley, Twelfth Annual General Meeting held at the Royal Institute, 3 November 1979, Chairman's Report, p. 1; NAGC archives, Bletchley, *Looking to their Future*, March 1979, 'Gifted Children and Inner City Areas', p. 1. On the history of Liverpool in this period, see: Brian Marren, *We Shall Not Be Moved: How Liverpool's Working Class Fought Redundancies, Closures and Cuts in the Age of Thatcher* (Manchester: MUP, 2016); Aaron Andrews, 'Dereliction, Decay and the Problem of De-industrialization in Britain, c. 1968–1977', *Urban History* 47 (2) (2019), pp. 236–256. The Brixton project started slightly later than the others, on this see: Institute of Education, London, SA/5/1, Articles about Handwriting, 1983–1989, *Looking to their Future: The Newsletter of the National Association for Gifted Children*, Spring 1985, 'The NAGC Brixton Project', p. 1.

[23] NAGC, Newsletter, Undated but inner material says 1984, 'Recipe for Success: Merseyside & Wirral', p. 11.

[24] Ibid.

Agnes Crawford, a psychology lecturer at the University of Liverpool, wrote a supportive letter about this scheme to the *Guardian*. She emphasised that these children 'have been able to join in on equal terms with children from "posher" areas of the city and the Wirral', and that this was part of 'fighting... the damaging assumption that inner city children are less able than the children in other parts of the city'.[25] This defence of Liverpool's children was made as the city faced incredibly high unemployment, particularly among its youth and Black populations, and a year before prominent members of Thatcher's Cabinet secretly proposed a 'managed decline' and 'tactical retreat' in this city.[26]

This work showed that the Association recognised the challenges in separating 'giftedness' from privilege. Yet such outreach work did not fundamentally reshape the membership of the National Association, because children primarily joined through their parents—typically middle-class—identifying them as 'gifted'. We do not have precise demographic data about the Association, and its publications wrote very little about the race, ethnicity, and class of the membership. One small survey by a charity in 1987, looking at a sample of just 125 member families, suggested that, despite outreach, membership remained disproportionately middle-class and well-educated, with only 6 per cent of their sample parents working in manual professions.[27] What this meant, precisely, is complex: an increasing number of people defined as 'middle-class' from 1945 until 2010, in part due to rising affluence and also cultural factors.[28] Nonetheless, the survey's authors acknowledged, this did not mean that 'most gifted children are in the middle classes— rather that the NAGC has not yet succeeded in attracting as many members from the working classes'.[29] Echoing earlier rhetoric, researchers suggested that this was due to the reluctance of working-class families: 'in an age which is so against elitism', they wrote, many people did not identify their children, for 'fear of doing anything which might single them out or make them appear different'.[30]

The organisation's membership then was dominated by more affluent parents. Parents who became leading volunteers in local branches or ran weekend and holiday retreats were also typically affluent. The holiday camps, for example, were hosted by parent members with large rural estates: the South Wales holidays were described in 1977 as organised by parents within their 'eight acres of rough

---

[25] Anne Crawford, 'Waiting for action on mergers', *The Guardian*, 17 June 1980, p. 13.

[26] Alan Travis, 'Thatcher government toyed with evacuating Liverpool after 1981 riots', *Guardian*, 30 December 2011 <https://www.theguardian.com/uk/2011/dec/30/thatcher-government-liverpool-riots-1981> (15 September 2021). See also: Simon Parker and Rowland Atkinson, 'Disorderly cities and the policy-making field: the 1981 English riots and the management of urban decline', *British Politics*, 15 (2020), pp. 160–177.

[27] Patricia Mason and Juliet Essen, *The Social, Educational, and Emotional Needs of Gifted Children* (Ciceley Northcote Trust, July 1987), p. 6.

[28] Pat Thane, *Unequal Britain: Equalities in Britain since 1954* (London: Continuum, 2010), p. 4.

[29] Mason and Essen, *The Social, Educational, and Emotional Needs of Gifted Children*, p. 3.

[30] Ibid., p. 6.

pasture...and [with] an assortment of domestic and farm animals'.[31] Other camps were held 'on a large estate on the borders of Surrey and Hampshire'.[32] Despite significant work in inner city areas, the Association's activities did not fundamentally challenge existing ideas that children with great potential or gifts were most likely to be from the white, middle classes. It is not the 'fault' of voluntary organisers that their groups were typically dominated by middle-class children; but this illustrates that, when initiatives around 'giftedness' were left in the voluntary domain, assumptions around the demographics of 'gifted children' and 'elites of the future' were not fully challenged. Should involved children then gain power and influence, these assumptions about 'elites of the future' as white, male, and affluent were further embedded.

Why Did Parents Join?

The majority of parents who joined the National Association framed their participation along two lines. First, they joined because they felt that the welfare state did not provide adequately for gifted children in this period. Second, they joined because they felt lonely and isolated, as parents of gifted young people. In response to these two problems, parents joining the Association did not typically call for huge reform of Britain's educational or welfare systems. Rather, they looked to use local and national systems of the Association to mitigate these issues themselves; hoping that they could organise weekend and holiday activities, and penpal schemes, through which children and parents would be intellectually and socially fulfilled. Parents joining the Association were in part aligned with those taking part in a range of progressive social movements in the 1960s and 1970s, particularly in their insistence that personal experience *mattered* and should be shared. However, the Association parents were far less radical than those involved, for example, in second-wave feminism; they typically simply called for minimal change that they could construct themselves, through volunteer work, rather than for a huge restructuring of any social settlement.

Parents discussing National Association membership typically framed their accounts around emotional struggle. One powerful unsolicited account was written by a mother to Mass Observation in September 1984. This mother had been an active participant of the Mass Observation project. She had answered 1980s directives 14–22 on such eclectic topics as 'Christmas cards and Buying British', 'Social Well-Being', 'Electronic Banking', 'Attitudes To USA', and 'Morality &

---

[31] NAGC, 'Country Holidays for Young Explorers', *Looking to their Future: The News Letter of the National Association for Gifted Children*, May 1977, p. 5.

[32] NAGC, *Explorers Unlimited*, March 1981, 'Young Adventurers' Camp, Summer 1981', p. 5.

religion'.[33] In addition to these requested responses, the mother also sent in an unsolicited contribution, along with her Summer Directive of 1984, which she titled, 'Membership of the National Association for Gifted Children'.[34] The opening sentence, which continued in tight text over three pages, stated simply that, '[t]here were many reasons why we joined the N.A.G.C but the main reason was to find support to allay our fears for our sons future happiness.'[35] The letter described in emotional terms the huge challenges of raising a gifted child. Her first child was, from a baby, 'at times quite difficult to cope with': he 'rarely smiled' and 'watched everything around him', even when very young.[36] Because of his intelligence, the mother wrote, this child was hugely difficult to parent: he would be 'frustrated' if he couldn't see everything happening around him, and also 'when his body could not obey his mind'.[37] The parents joined the Association, when the child was three years old, 'for some advice and to meet other children like him', as well as out of concern about how he might cope at school.[38] Initially, the mother wrote, they found that activities were for older children, and she had 'little chance to do what I most needed…just to talk to someone who understood and who realised that I was not trying to boast.'[39] But when the child reached school age, she found membership helpful. For her child, membership put his 'mind at rest to know that he wasn't just a freak'.[40] For herself, meetings were a space to discuss her challenges and struggles with a friendly and supportive 'informal' group.[41] Littered through this description were mentions of those who this mother found hostile: those who thought she was 'imagining' her child's gifts as 'few people' believed her, in particular.[42] The Association, by contrast, was described as providing a safe space of solidarity and support. For this mother, having a gifted child was a source of stress and difficulty—there was no mention in this account of the idea that this child should or must be an 'elite of the future', merely a sharing of this experience in emotional terms. By sharing this with Mass Observation, choosing to write on this topic, even though no Directive directly requested it, the mother consciously documented her explanation for future years.

This kind of representation of the reasons for joining the National Association was common, echoed by other parents speaking to the press. As mentioned in Chapter Two, one of the earliest press features about the National Association, the Horizon documentary *The Gifted Child* (1969), showed a mother likewise stating that she felt isolated and socially stigmatised due to having a gifted

---

[33] 'Search the Mass Observation Archive Writers Database', *Mass Observation Project (MOP) Database 1981+* <http://database.massobs.org.uk/projects_database/mass_observation/> (7 December 2021).
[34] The Keep, Mass Observation archives, G848, 'Membership of the National Association for Gifted Children', 18 September 1984.
[35] Ibid. [36] Ibid. [37] Ibid. [38] Ibid.
[39] Ibid. [40] Ibid. [41] Ibid. [42] Ibid.

child.⁴³ Such ideas were reiterated in the tabloid press the *Daily Express*, *Daily Mirror*, and *Daily Mail* throughout the 1970s and early 1980s, as expositions of giftedness quoted parents who discussed how their gifted child put a 'strain' on their marriage, 'upsets the rest of the family', and left them 'embarrassed', and 'bewildered'.⁴⁴ The 1978 documentary, *In with a Head Start*, produced by the Northern Ireland branch of the National Association in partnership with the Community Programme Unit at the BBC, made parents' testimonies central, and again echoed these narratives.⁴⁵ The Chairperson of the Northern Irish Branch stated, 'such a child often needs an exceptionally talented mother and father', and featured parents describing their children as 'exhausting' and 'a problem child'.⁴⁶ So in available accounts, parents framed their explanations for joining the National Association around ideas of emotional struggle, isolation, and desperation; having a gifted children was not 'a source of unalloyed joy' but, rather, often 'agonizing and heart searching'.⁴⁷

Association spokespeople, journalists, researchers, and parents also often compared the experiences of raising a gifted child to the experiences of raising a disabled child, or referred to 'the handicap of brilliance'—a comparison made from the inception of the National Association, and further discussed and problematised in Chapter Two.⁴⁸ National Association parents speaking to journalists stated that a 'young genius' could be as hard to raise as 'any handicapped child', and that it was 'outrageous' that there were 'special schools for handicapped

---

[43] British Film Institute, 79570, *Horizon: The Gifted Child*, 30 January 1969. Similar points are made in: Institute of Education, London, SA/5/1, Articles about Handwriting, 1983-1989, *Looking to their Future: The Newsletter of the National Association for Gifted Children*, Spring 1985, 'A Pushy Mother?', p. 8.

[44] Paula James, 'The loneliness of a bright child', *Daily Mirror*, 11 April 1972, p. 9; 'The bright, the backward', *Daily Express*, 3 September 1974, p. 8; Stanley Bonnett, 'Is there a genius in your family?', *Daily Mirror*, 11 September 1975, p. 7; Ian Smith, 'Treated like a freak for being clever', *Daily Mail*, 28 November 1978, pp. 6-7; Geoffrey Levy, 'Watch out, genius at work—and one's born every week', *Daily Express*, 20 August 1981, p. 9; Mrs Grey, 'Family Affair', *Daily Express*, 23 June 1981, p. 24.

[45] Patricia Holland and Ieuan Franklin, 'Editorial Introduction: Opening Doors: the BBC's Community Programme Unit 1973-2002', *History Workshop Journal*, 82 (1) (2016), pp. 213-234; Giles Oakley with Peter Lee-Wright, 'Opening Doors: the BBC's Community Programme Unit 1973-2002', *History Workshop Journal*, 82 (1) (2016), pp. 213-234; British Film Institute, *Open Door: In with a Head Start?*, 7 December 1978. See for National Association thoughts on this partnership: NAGC, 'Goings on in Northern Ireland', *Looking to their Future*, November 1980, p. 13.

[46] British Film Institute, *Open Door: In with a Head Start?*, 7 December 1978.

[47] Quote from: Institute of Education, London, WEF/B/1/2/24, Gifted Children—correspondence relating to, Leaflet entitled 'The National Association for Gifted Children', undated, p. 2. Mirroring this concern, the National Foundation for Educational Research also looked to establish a research project about the emotional problems of gifted children, from the 1970s, on this see: Institute of Education, London, SCC/1030/1037/118, 'NFER proposal—A study of the emotional problems of children of high academic potential' (Working party on gifted children), 1972.

[48] Institute of Education, London, SCC/1030/1037/608, 'National Association of Gifted Children—Proposal to Make a Film', 1978-1979, 'Profile: The National Association for Gifted Children', 12 March 1978, p. 1.

children, but nothing really' for the gifted.[49] Association leaders, also, remained committed to this framing: Collis told press that parents were 'more reluctant to make a fuss' about gifted children than 'subnormal' ones, for example, and the chairman of the Lichfield branch, founded in 1975, stated that 'giftedness can in itself be a handicap'.[50] Writing for the *Daily Telegraph* in 1973, Collis suggested that this comparison was about social acceptance of labels: it was 'high time', he argued, that 'we' accepted the term gifted 'as we have done with "brain damaged" and "spastic"'.[51] Besides this, however, lines of argument traced in Chapter Two, from the 1960s, remained—particularly the idea that the welfare state provided less for the gifted than for disabled children, and that parenting both disabled and gifted children was 'just as difficult'.[52]

More broadly, some in education, media, and policy supported the comparisons made by the National Association between disability and giftedness. Professor Phillip Williams, for example,—developing teaching-training projects about giftedness from the Open University—wrote to the Schools Council that, the gifted was 'one very important group of handicapped children'.[53] Yet, from the 1970s, as disability and giftedness groups became more embedded in public life, this linkage, made by giftedness groups, also became more subject to critique. Caroline Moorehead, for example, wrote for *The Times* in May 1974 that, 'the handicap of brightness seems an easier handicap to live with than most'.[54] Representatives from a number of local education authorities, likewise, meeting at a conference in 1979, reported encountering on the ground 'resistance to of [sic] making special provision for a group of children who were seen as privileged rather than disadvantaged by their natural gifts'.[55]

Positioning membership of the National Association as a response to struggle may have reflected many parents' lived experiences, but this was also a powerful

---

[49] 'The bright, the backward', *Daily Express*, 3 September 1974, p. 8; Stanley Bonnett, 'Is there a Genius in your Family?', *Daily Mirror*, 11 September 1975, p. 7.

[50] Sally Holloway, 'Gifted, but for these children life is more a problem than plain-sailing', *Daily Telegraph*, 7 April 1972, p. 15; Sue Fisher, 'Children with a special gift…', *The Mercury*, 25 April 1975, p. 11.

[51] Henry Collis, 'Group system for gifted children', *Daily Telegraph*, 2 April 1973.

[52] NAGC, *Fifth Annual Report and Accounts of the National Association for Gifted Children, 1971–1972*, p. 11; NAGC, *Newsletters*, May 1969, p. 3; Sally Holloway, 'Gifted, but for these children life is more a problem than plain-sailing', *Daily Telegraph*, 7 April 1972, p. 15; Philippa Pigache, 'Heads and tail-enders', *Guardian*, 27 February 1973, p. 15; Janet Watts, 'The plight of the children of gold', *Guardian*, 10 January 1974, p. 11; 'Talented Underdogs', *Daily Telegraph*, 9 September 1975, p. 14.

[53] Institute of Education archives, London, SCC/1030/1037/079, Working party on gifted children—proposal to create individualised learning packages (the Open University), 1971–1972, Individualised Learning Materials in Primary Schools: A Proposal for a Schools Council Project, Phillip Williams.

[54] Caroline Moorehead, 'A gifted child can be a problem child', *The Times*, 9 May 1974, p. 9.

[55] Institute of Education, London, SCC/555/1152/049, Gifted Pupils—Identification and Provision—Policy and Finance, 1979-1983, Provision for Gifted Children, DES Invitation Conference N522, 19–23 November 1979, Conference Report, p. 1.

strategy in a media context which expected campaigners' emotions and experiences to be made visible. While fewer traces of this exist in the archives, it is possible also that other parents joined the Association to secure better educational provision—and to seek its support in navigating complex local legal systems around where their children would be educated. Certainly, there was also, in the 1980s, occasional media coverage of parents who did look to use contemporary legislation to challenge and change their children's educational provision (though typically independently, rather than with or through the National Association). One such case was that of a five year old girl: in 1989, her mother felt that the Estate school provision in part of London was inadequate, and that this girl was 'picked on' by a teacher at the school.[56] Her mother applied for a grant from her local education authority, using the 1981 *Education Act*, which stated that local authorities must make provision for schoolchildren with 'special needs', to claim that her daughter had the right to go to a private school.[57] The council stated that her needs could be adequately met by her existing provision, and that this Act did not apply to high ability young people—it had typically been interpreted around disability, not giftedness and, Department of Education and Science representatives wrote in 1991, 'current legislation' more broadly 'does not place specific duties upon LEAs to identify and make special provision for gifted children in the same way as for children with special educational needs.'[58] The council also argued that, while some local authorities could award grants for pupils to attend private special needs schools, it was not their policy.[59]

The girl was then taken out of her school and taught at home, with the help of a tutor. She briefly attended a private school funded by an executive recruitment firm, whose leaders read about her case in newspapers, but this company

---

[56] Julie Cohen, 'The prodigal daughter', *The Sunday Times*, 6 March 1994. This case was also discussed on the Thames Television programme 'A Class of their Own', aired in 1992 (discussed in 'Mensa, modesty and the missing link: Television', *Guardian*, 2 September 1992, p. 33.

[57] Education Act 1981, ch. 60.

[58] Cohen, 'The prodigal daughter'; 'Local authority schools unable to accommodate "gifted" children', *The Times*, 20 August 1990; National Archives, Kew (hereafter NA), ED 183/331, 'Provision for gifted children: correspondence with MENSA', 1990–1991, 'Gifted Children: Mensa Accreditation and Establishment of Mensa Foundation Schools', p. 1—written by a Department of Education and Science representative—states that the *Education Act* of 1981 would exclude gifted children without special educational needs, and rather focused on those with learning difficulties, as defined if he (a) 'has a significantly greater difficulty in learning than the majority of children his age'; (b) 'has a disability which either prevents or hinders him from making use of educational facilities of a kind generally provided in schools'; or (c) 'is under the age of five years and is, or would be if special educational provision were not made for him, likely to fall within paragraphs (a) or (b) when over that age.' Interestingly, Department of Education and Science officials discussed omitting the phrase 'unlike children with special educational needs', from their later correspondence with the Mensa Foundation for Gifted Children, suggestive of their awareness that this comparison was in the terrain of campaigners: NA, ED 183/331, 'Provision for gifted children: correspondence with MENSA', 1990–1991, 'Gifted children: Mensa accreditation and establishment of Mensa Foundation Schools', 15 March 1991, p. 1; 'Letter from Department of Education and Science Representative to Education Director of the MENSA Foundation for Gifted Children', 5 March 1991, p. 2.

[59] 'Local authority schools unable to accommodate "gifted" children', *The Times*, 20 August 1990.

'foundered after the collapse of the Bank of Credit and Commerce International'.[60] Her mother continued the legal battle. In 1993, the Education Department stated that its Secretary of State, John Patten, was satisfied a state school could meet her needs.[61] By 1994, a High Court judge urged Patten to reconsider this issue 'with all due expedition'.[62] This was in part a battle over definitions of ability of one young child. In 1993, the statement from the education department's appeals team, released to press, stated that the child's 'attainments are by no means exceptional'.[63] Her mother, however, cited independent assessment that she had the vocabulary of a thirteen-year-old, the visual memory of a sixteen-year-old, and required education with older pupils.[64] Yet, this was not only a case about one student. It was also presented in press—by *The Sunday Times*, for example—as a 'test case which could force schools across the country to pay as much attention to gifted pupils as they do to children who perform badly in the country'.[65] This case exemplified the ongoing tensions, as traced throughout this book, between ideas of gifted children as in dire need of help and assistance, and as privileged, lucky, key to future national success.

This case could be read as an entirely separate story from that of the National Association. The National Association did not have the resources to support legal cases and, while the organisation often provided an index of private schools to interested parents, it typically did not have capacity to advise on individual school choices either.[66] Accounts from parents speak more about joining the Association to participate in extra-curricula activities, and to combat isolation, rather than to navigate or change mainstream education. Instead, such test cases were more often pursued by the Mensa Foundation for Gifted Children, which made this area more of a priority—files from the Department for Education and Science show this group writing to local and national policy-makers to criticise the restriction on early admission for individual children, and the lack of 'flexibility for the exceptional case', for example.[67] The Mensa Foundation also offered to

---

[60] Alexandra Frean, 'Bright pupil sues for right to top teaching', *The Sunday Times*, 25 November 1990; John O'Leary, 'Minister refuses to help Mensa girl', *The Times*, 7 October 1993.

[61] John O'Leary, 'Minister refuses to help Mensa girl', *The Times*, 7 October 1993.

[62] 'Judge in school fees plea', *Independent*, 26 February 1994, p. 2.

[63] O'Leary, 'Minister refuses to help Mensa girl'.   [64] Ibid.

[65] Alexandra Frean, 'Bright pupil sues for right to top teaching', *The Sunday Times*, 25 November 1990.

[66] There is one piece of archival evidence, however, of representatives of the NAGC writing to the Home Office to share concerns about the educational provision for one specific child, who had been bored in a comprehensive school, disruptive, and then placed at a boarding school where the children were 'delinquent or very disturbed' (NA, DPC 261/410, 'Letter from National Association for Gifted Children', 1976, p. 1).

[67] NA, ED 183/331, 'Provision for gifted children: correspondence with MENSA', 1990–1991, Letter from Deputy Chairman of Mensa Foundation for Gifted Children to Assistant Director of Education, West Sussex, undated but between 1990 and 1991; 'Provision for gifted children: correspondence with MENSA', 1990–1991, Letter from Deputy Chairman of Mensa Foundation for Gifted Children to DES, London', 4 February 1992.

suggest alternative schools for children who needed it, helped parents to navigate the government Assisted Places scheme, and proposed, in 1990, the establishment of an independent primary day school in the Greater London Area for 'about 200 outstandingly studious and promising children aged between three and thirteen'.[68] The organisation even drew up plans for their own 'Mensa Foundation Schools', to work in every local education authority, which they would accredit once their 'independent consultants' ensured 'that the agreed standards, objectives, and principles' were maintained, and which would be 'highly selective for well-motivated pupils of exceptional ability'.[69] The National Association was, by contrast, Department of Education and Science officials wrote in 1990, while 'professionally managed', a 'parents' organisation'—less focused on education.[70]

The story of the five year old girl from London and other such children, nonetheless, tells us important things about the context of the National Association and the motivations of its parent-members for joining. First, notably, these legal test cases, when covered in the press, were, like those of the Association, framed around emotion. The girl's mother, for example, told *The Sunday Times* in 1994 that, during the case, her daughter 'became a behaviourally and emotionally disturbed child'.[71] Again, this shows how these decades were a time in which parents felt they could and should use new languages to articulate their experiences and emotions, particularly to the popular press. A second key overlap is that the National Association was itself offering an alternative to state services that parents felt were missing. The Association booklet, *Help with Bright Children*, for example, stated in 1989 that funds to send children to private school were 'increasingly difficult to obtain' from local education authorities.[72] Parents may not have joined the Association explicitly to seek out educational advantage in schooling, but they did, in joining leisure clubs for weekends and holidays, use this group to supplement a school system that many felt was in crisis.

---

[68] NA, ED 183/311, Mensa Foundation for Gifted Children leaflet, undated, backpage; 'Provision for gifted children: correspondence with MENSA', 1990–1991, Letter from Chairman of Mensa Foundation for Gifted Children to Junior Under Secretary of State for Education, undated but 1990–1991.

[69] NA, ED 183/331, 'Provision for gifted children: correspondence with MENSA', 1990–1991, 'Mensa Foundation Schools Model Charter', pp. 1–5; 'Provision for gifted children: correspondence with MENSA', 1990–1991, 'Mensa Accreditation of Independent Schools', p. 1.

[70] NA, ED 183/331, 'Provision for gifted children: correspondence with MENSA', 1990–1991, 'Meeting with officers of Mensa', 22 November 1990, p. 1; 'Provision for gifted children: correspondence with MENSA', 1990–1991, Letter from Department of Education and Science officer to Junior Undersecretary of State for Education on 'Mensa—Foundation for Gifted Children—Request for Advice and Meeting', 13 June 1990, p. 1.

[71] Cohen, 'The prodigal daughter'.

[72] NAGC, *Help with Bright Children* (London: NAGC, 1989), p. 15.

New Opportunities?

But what were these 'new opportunities'? Being labelled as gifted through the National Association gave young people access to a range of new arenas, particularly to participate in voluntary activity clubs at weekends and in school holidays. These kinds of club ranged across the UK. By November 1980, the National Association had established forty-eight clubs, with two more in formation. The majority were in the south-east of England, with one club in Northern Ireland (in Belfast), two in Scotland (in Strathclyde and the Lothians), and two in Wales (labelled 'North Wales' and 'South Wales'), as well as some clubs ranging in to the north and south-west of England and one in the Isle of Wight.[73] Their specific provisions varied because they were typically organised by parent volunteers, who thought '[i]f I felt the need, I reasoned, others did too, so if no-one else was prepared to fill the gap why not do it myself?'[74] Fathers are mentioned in newsletters as actively organising holiday courses and weekend clubs, but mothers seem to have shouldered most of the burden of this logistical and emotional labour. For one London-based Saturday club, the mother organising was said in 1976 to be 'temporarily running' this group until her three children were 'old enough for her to go back to primary school teaching'.[75] Association accounts frequently emphasised the precarity of these groups, and their reliance on members' labour and donations.

We have most information from the archives about the activities and reception of one particularly longstanding National Association and local authority partnership: the Moberly Saturday Club for gifted children.[76] The club developed in 1971, when two parents established the London Explorers' Club in their home; typical of the informal manner in which these groups often opened. In 1976, after partnership with the Inner London Educational Authority (ILEA) was established, the group's activities moved to the Moberly Centre, and the ILEA also provided additional teaching staff to work with the young people. This fostered significant expansion and by November 1978, the National Association newsletter reported that the group served up to 150 Explorers each Saturday afternoon in term-time.[77] The newsletter stated also that, unusually, the group had employed a

---

[73] NAGC, *Looking to their Future: The News Letter of the National Association for Gifted Children*, November 1980, 'National Association for Gifted Children: Location of Branches', p. 12. For description of how much activities from these clubs varied, see: Institute of Education, London, SCC/1030/1037/1037/608, 'National Association of Gifted Children—Proposal to Make a Film', 1978–1979, 'Profile: The National Association for Gifted Children', 12 March 1978, p. 2.

[74] 'Country Holidays for Young Explorers', *Looking to their Future: The News Letter of the National Association for Gifted Children*, May 1977, p. 5.

[75] NAGC, 'Practical Support from the Inner Location Education Authority', *Looking to their Future: The News Letter of the National Association for Gifted Children*, June 1976, p. 1.

[76] Bodleian Library, Per 264505 e. 4, NAGC, *Journal of the Gifted Child*, Autumn 1979, inside leaf.

[77] 'The Annual General Meeting', *Looking to their Future: The News Letter of the National Association for Gifted Children*, November 1978, p. 20.

part-time professional Director, and that its initial founder was available to advise on similar projects; showing how the Association encouraged and supported localised and familial voluntary work.[78]

The Moberly group provided special training in specific subjects thought to be of particular use to the gifted child. Initially, when the Club was run from a domestic house, these activities were dispersed across the home, with one National Association newsletter describing 'woodwork in the basement, photography in the airing cupboard—in the hall, cooking, all kinds of games, maths, logic, chess and the more mundane kinds in the dining room'.[79] This vision of messiness, informality, and controlled intellectual chaos was reiterated in newsletters and supported a vision of gifted children as particularly physically and intellectually active. Discussions also reflected a common trope in voluntary action of this moment, serving to underscore the friendliness of a voluntary group alongside its reliance on members' labour and donations.[80] The idea that gifted children required this range of pursuits, physical, creative, intellectual, on disparate fields, went beyond this one club: the Association's Annual Report of 1971–1972, likewise, stated that Association children could enjoy 'a wide range of creative and intellectual subjects—atomic power, creative writing, woodwork, electronics, ecology, drama, fossil-hunting, music and philosophy'.[81]

From 1976, in the Moberly Centre, the group's activities were more managed and formalised, and the young people involved had to book and choose activities in advance, rather than using whatever household items they came across to fuel imaginative play. One Association report stated that a 'few' of the 'original' members did not like 'the new regime', and that it had lost 'intimacy' and an 'easy and free choice of things to do'.[82] Nonetheless, other young Explorers very much enjoyed the new space, and the activities made available to them. Two relevant testimonies were offered in a 1979 edition of the journal of the National Association, from a ten-year-old and a thirteen-year-old. These testimonies—while selected by adults invested in this organisation to be disseminated among interested and supportive audiences—nonetheless suggested that, for both of these children, being identified as 'gifted' had meant that they were able to access activities and conversations that they found intellectually stimulating. The ten-year-old boy stated that typically he joined in with school games played by his friends, but that 'what I would really like to do also would be to talk about the world with them

---

[78] Ibid.

[79] NAGC, 'Practical Support from the Inner Location Education Authority', *Looking to their Future: The News Letter of the National Association for Gifted Children*, June 1976, p. 1.

[80] See also: Jennifer Crane, *Child Protection in England: Expertise, Experience, and Emotion* (Basingstoke: Palgrave, 2018), p. 117.

[81] NAGC, *Annual Report and Accounts of the National Association for Gifted Children, 1971–2*, p. 3.

[82] NAGC, 'Practical Support from the Inner Location Education Authority', *Looking to their Future: The News Letter of the National Association for Gifted Children*, June 1976, p. 1.

but no one wants to as they would all much rather play "catch".[83] For this child, the Saturday club meant that he was able to meet an 'older boy', who 'discusses with me everything I would like to know about the wealth of Great Britain, the world monetary system, and political parties and what they stand for.'[84]

In his testimony, the thirteen-year-old boy likewise emphasised that this Club furnished him with a level of intellectual engagement that he had missed at school and home. He stated that when starting education at the age of five, he had already completed the relevant reading and 'found school very uninteresting'. Unlike the ten-year-old boy, who was able to socialise with his classmates, the thirteen-year-old found it 'difficult' to mix socially as 'there was little I could share with them'.[85] This statement reflected a vision of friendship, echoed above, as shaped by the exchange of knowledge and information, but also, potentially, adult ideas that giftedness would be socially excluding. This boy 'found solace only in reading' and was frequently 'bored and restless'.[86] When he met a psychologist, who 'explained to me that I was "gifted"', his life changed.[87] For the next two years, he explained, he felt 'timid and withdrawn', though academically he continued to perform well. Aged nine he joined the Saturday Club and was able to socialise with peers and to develop special interests in computers, photography, and philosophy. The boy stated that these things gave him 'something to work at and be proud of', as well as a peer group with whom he could identify and socialise.[88]

These testimonies presented the label 'gifted' as a gateway to emotional and social transformation via the leisure pursuits of the National Association. For children, this label was given by psychologists and by voluntary associations, rather than by themselves or by families. In the second testimony, while knowing that he was ahead at school, the child did not *feel* gifted until formally diagnosed by a psychologist. Indeed, he felt socially excluded from his peer groups. On being assigned this label, the children reported personal and emotional change: from being 'timid' and 'withdrawn', 'bored' and 'restless', to finding intellectual satisfaction, notably shaped around visions of world affairs and niche pursuits.

While curated, this sense of enjoyment and positivity also emerged from testimonies collected by the National Association after their summer courses and published in newsletters. Reflecting on the children's critique of food on the courses, and on their length and content, the newsletters reported that overall children had enjoyed opportunities to meet others; that they would rate such courses 'well over eight' out of ten; and that they had called for courses to be

---

[83] Bodleian Library, Per 264505 e. 4, NAGC, *Journal of the Gifted Child*, Autumn 1979, 'Saturday Club', p. 46.
[84] Ibid.   [85] Ibid., p. 50.   [86] Ibid.   [87] Ibid., p. 51.   [88] Ibid.

repeated in following years.[89] Indeed, the Association provided spaces for children and parents alike to reflect on, and to critique, their schemes and their limitations, hoping to spark debate and improve their provision. The Easter 1982 edition of the magazine *Dialogue*, directed at children aged twelve to seventeen 'or thereabouts', for example, contained a page of children's letters about the residential courses.[90] One child asked why the residential courses were called 'Explorations'.[91] In response, the editor emphasised that the idea of 'courses' had been 'mis-leading', because 'Residential Explorations' were 'NOT like school'. While they offered 'skills and knowledge', they provided 'a great deal more'.[92] Neither, the respondent wrote, were the courses 'holidays', given that 'they are no rest cure and most participants end up enthralled but exhausted'.[93] While admitting that the term sounded 'contrived', the National Association representative argued that this was only 'because you're not yet used to it and, being a brand new word, we're still not fluent in using it'.[94] This response was accompanied by another, directed at a child disappointed that there was only one 'non-academic' holiday for the over-sixteens. The National Association again defended their courses, emphasising that they had a high degree of practical *and* intellectual involvement.[95]

While defending their courses, the National Association volunteers also invited children to critique their nature, titles, and contents. The children's magazines frequently invited more children to write in, asking: 'What sort of Explorations would you like? Tell us.'[96] All children who participated in Explorer courses in 1980 were asked to fill in a comment form. The results—reported in the organisation's November 1980 newsletter—offered critique as well as praise, and the newsletter indeed emphasised that: 'One Explorer's paradise was another Explorer's torture chamber'.[97] While noting that this was 'a little bit exaggerated', the newsletter found 'direct contradictions' in the children's feedback. Children's comments for example described food as delicious but also foul, and noted that there

---

[89] Peter Fry, 'The Fourth Annual Explorers' Computer Course', *Looking to their Future: The News Letter of the National Association for Gifted Children*, November 1977, p. 15; Ron Brewer and Anna Comino-James, 'Solving the problem of problem solving', *Looking to their Future: The News Letter of the National Association for Gifted Children*, November 1978, p. 16; A. E. Preston, 'Giant molecules course', *Looking to their Future: The News Letter of the National Association for Gifted Children*, November 1978, p. 17; 'Back-up Service: Extract from an Educational Psychologist's report during 1977', *Looking to their Future: The News Letter of the National Association for Gifted Children*, November 1977, p. 16. Evidence from North American experiments with gifted education likewise found that children supported 'identifying' the gifted, because this label enabled them to access new services, construct new peer networks, and pursue interests beyond their formal school curricula (Bodleian Library, Per 264505 e. 4, NAGC, *Journal of the Gifted Child*, Autumn 1979, 'Helping a gifted child with mathematics', Yael Naim Dowker and Clifford Hugh Dowker, pp. 59–60).
[90] NAGC, Dialogue, Easter 1982, 'Last words—first', p. 3.
[91] Ibid. [92] Ibid. [93] Ibid. [94] Ibid. [95] Ibid. [96] Ibid.
[97] NAGC, 'Residential Courses 1980 or what Explorers had to say', *Looking to their Future: The News Letter of the National Association for Gifted Children*, November 1980, p. 10.

were too many and too few outings planned.[98] While the Association's overall analysis was that 'the general feeling about the courses was good, and in most cases VERY good', the newsletter also featured critical responses from the children. Children provided direct feedback such as, 'Change the cook', or reflected that they had enjoyed a course because 'I felt I could do without my parents.'[99] The rise of social surveys, as traced by Mike Savage, was used by voluntary groups here, and provided a space for children to curate and experiment with a new sense of self, and to disrupt organisational and familial narratives and hierarchies.[100] While these children's magazines faced 'unknowable mediation', and were curated by adults, children did respond to and challenge the National Association's work, and the magazines provide valuable insight into their lives.[101]

Overall, being labelled as 'gifted' gave children access to new opportunities through the voluntary sector: in this case, the opportunity to engage in correspondence and debate with interested adults, to reshape the provision of leisure activities, and to have their words published within specialist magazines, constructing a virtual network of gifted youth. Such spaces for children's feedback demonstrated the unique agency of the gifted child. Their opinions were *more* sought out, *more* respected, and *more* widely disseminated than those of children not labelled in this way.

Gifted Children

While many gifted young people thus participated enthusiastically in the new leisure spaces available to them in the 1970s and 1980s, these children were still conceptualised very clearly *as children*. While the children had unique spaces in which to air their opinions, they were nonetheless constrained by adult provision and ongoing structural hierarchies: able to be disruptive and critical, but within the clear understanding that they were youthful, and thus, perhaps, non-threatening purveyors of critique.[102]

The Association frequently published testimony from the adult organisers of voluntary groups, which emphasised how young participants were still being framed by adult ideas of childlikeness. For example, the November 1977 newsletter contained a detailed account of a residential course held in the Highlands that discussed 'one lad' who had, 'for safety's sake', had to be 'severely reprimanded

---

[98] Ibid.   [99] Ibid.
[100] Mike Savage, *Identities and Social Change in Britain: The Politics of Method* (Oxford: OUP, 2012).
[101] Siân Pooley, 'Children's writing and the popular press in England 1876–1914', *History Workshop Journal*, 80 (1) (2015), p. 81.
[102] See also: Laura Tisdall, 'State of the field: the modern history of childhood', *History*, 107 (378) (2022), p. 8.

half-way through the week'.[103] The child was able to access new physical and outdoor pursuits in the Highlands because of his label 'gifted', but his intellect did not supersede safety considerations—he was still conceptualised firmly as a child, in need of protection and discipline by adults. Indeed, the boy's childlikeness was further emphasised as the author stated that he was 'really reluctant and in tears saying goodbye' at the end of the course; his emotional state at odds with his previous bravery and intellectual maturity.[104]

Accounts of residential courses emphasised the ways in which the children were encouraged to remain fundamentally deferential towards adults, and to recognise rules and appropriate child-like emotional regimes. The organiser of the South Wales course stated that part of the purpose of these courses was to enable children to fail within 'the protective environment of school and home'; something that gifted youth may not otherwise do.[105] Further accounts suggested that children labelled gifted must be provided with 'as many opportunities as possible', but also that the Association worked 'on a tight budget' and that children's requests must be 'REASONABLE', as they were 'NOT trying to provide the equivalent of a five star hotel'.[106] Because of their gifts, children were permitted to attend, and to critically discuss, new leisure activities, but these discussions had to remain within the boundaries shaped by their age, framed by ideas of 'reasonable' and rational child behaviours.[107]

There was a constant process of mediation between children and adults within this voluntary group. Young people influenced the adults through how they wrote about these courses, which they chose to participate in, and how they described and reviewed them afterwards. Notably then, we must recognise that at times the gifted participants framed themselves with reference to age; this was not solely an adult construct. Significantly, young people writing to Association newsletter typically included their precise age besides their stories, letters, or poetry (for example, 'age 9¾').[108] Accounts from parent organisers also suggest the ways in which young participants expected their interactions with one another to be framed by age. Describing a South Wales course over six weeks, for six-to-ten year olds, organised in May 1977, one parent wrote that the guests 'had not played with other Explorers before', and hence 'were not used to competition. They were used to winning. And they did not much like the new experience of being

[103] 'The Week at Ardtrostan', *Looking to their Future: The News Letter of the National Association for Gifted Children*, November 1977, p. 13.
[104] Ibid.
[105] 'Country Holidays for Young Explorers', *Looking to their Future: The News Letter of the National Association for Gifted Children*, May 1977, p. 5.
[106] NAGC, 'Residential Courses 1980 or what Explorers had to say', *Looking to their Future: The News Letter of the National Association for Gifted Children*, November 1980, p. 10.
[107] For a fascinating account of the concept of being 'unreasonable', and manifesto in this area, see: Kirsty Sedgman, *On Being Unreasonable: Why Being Bad Can Be a Force for Good* (London: Faber, 2024).
[108] NAGC, 'Residential Courses 1980 or what Explorers had to say', *Looking to their Future: The News Letter of the National Association for Gifted Children*, November 1980, p. 10.

beaten.'[109] Indeed, a 'sturdy nine-year-old', she reported, 'took it very hard that he could be beaten at target shooting by a weedy seven-year-old'.[110] Meanwhile, the 'Mastermind' competition winner 'was not even seven' and the camp proved 'a real struggle for a ten-year-old, used to the masculine environment of preparatory school where he shone at everything, to accept that a mere girl was better at making a camp fire than he was'.[111] This account was written by an adult, but may also have reflected how young people's interest in age, and age hierarchies, enabled and reinforced adult ideas of 'childlikeness'.

Notably, this testimony discussed younger Explorers than those at the Moberly club. The children on this summer course were aged between six and nine, while those at the Moberly club were aged ten to thirteen. This leaves open the suggestion that gifted children may have initially struggled to negotiate their new identities, while still at such a young age, facing conflict with one another when expected hierarchies of age were subverted. Potentially, in later years, these gifted youth developed in confidence, and in the ability to appreciate fellow Explorers as peers, rather than competitors.

Clearly then, ideas about age and childlikeness continued to frame the actions of the young participants within the National Association, even if they were seen as, at times, intellectually equal, or superior, to adults. More broadly also, educational conferences in the 1970s would emphasise that gifted children were still children, needed peers their own age, or, indeed, 'their teddybears'.[112] Clementine Beauvais has argued that the early-twentieth century saw child psychologists fixate on distinct categories in relation to giftedness, in part as an interesting intellectual puzzle.[113] These testimonies, from the late 1970s, demonstrate that parents and voluntary leaders again engaged with such debates, not merely as a puzzle but actively looking to rationalise how their children behaved. However, it also suggests that interest in age may have been further strengthened by the analysis and lived experience of the young themselves.

Rejecting Giftedness?

It is difficult to trace children's acceptance of giftedness. It is even more difficult to uncover cases where children rejected, ignored, or denied this label.[114] By their

---

[109] 'Country Holidays for Young Explorers', *Looking to their Future: The News Letter of the National Association for Gifted Children*, May 1977, p. 5.

[110] Ibid.   [111] Ibid.

[112] Institute of Education, London, SCC/555/1152/049, Gifted Pupils—Identification and Provision—Policy and Finance, 1979–1983, Provision for Gifted Children, DES Invitation Conference N522, 19–23 November 1979, Conference Report, p. 6.

[113] Clementine Beauvais, 'Ages and ages: the multiplication of children's "ages" in early twentieth-century child psychology', *History of Education*, 45 (3) (2016), pp. 304–318.

[114] For an interesting meditation on the nature of 'denial' in history more broadly, see: Catherine Hall and Daniel Pick, 'Feature: denial in history', *History Workshop Journal*, 84 (2017), pp. 1–23.

nature, these kinds of encounter were fleeting and unlikely to be recorded, since those creating documents about giftedness were typically invested in promoting gifted education.[115] Nonetheless, some archival traces of children's rejection of this label exist, demonstrating that while many young people enjoyed and actively participated within giftedness organisations, many also did not accept themselves as gifted, and were not comfortable with this label nor with intelligence testing more broadly. While professionals were interested in noting cases of childhood rejection of this term, this section focuses on how young people themselves explained this.[116]

National Association materials enable us to see children's accounts of why they rejected the label 'gifted'. In the National Association's *Explorers Bulletin* newsletter of summer 1979, a group of 'ninth and tenth graders' in a 'Mentally Gifted Programme' in Alhambra, California, wrote a composite letter to address British children, entitled 'What's it like then?'[117] Challenging the label as arbitrary, and questioning the psychological systems that underpinned it, the letter stated, '[t]hink of the position I have been put in since first grade, just because I passed a silly test of describing pictures.'[118] Further, the group of students wrote, 'Ever since then I am expected to always be straight A or on top. You say, "Here, do this, you are supposed to be smart".'[119] Indeed, the authors wrote that they were always 'push[ed] harder' by teachers because they were in the gifted programme.[120] Rather than acting in this way, the authors would like those reading—adults of a 'generation...far removed from mine'—to 'recognize my wishes and help me', and to '[u]nderstand me a little more.'[121] They noted that they would like to own books, in addition to using the library, and that they 'see myself as a person, but not as a child'; indeed, they wrote, 'I do not think I have ever really thought of myself as a child.'[122] Criticising parental and psychological pressures, the letter stated that adults should 'not expect me to live up to *your* expectations', and 'I wish you would stop pulling the child psychology bit.'[123] The letter closed by rejecting the label, and stressing that gifted children were all different, but nonetheless all required respect as humans.[124] The collective authors thus rejected the labels 'child' and 'gifted', instead asking to be analysed as 'human'.

This letter shows that while young people may have enthusiastically participated within giftedness programmes, recognising the new opportunities they

---

[115] See also: Sarah Mills, 'Cultural-historical geographies of the archive: fragments, objects and ghosts', *Geography Compass*, 7 (10) (2013), pp. 701–713.

[116] Ann F. Isaacs, 'Role expectancy and its effect on performance and achievement among gifted students', *The High School Journal*, 48 (2) (1964), p. 106; Peter J. Congdon, *Spot the Gifted Child: A Guide for Parents and Teachers* (Solihull: Gifted Children's Information Centre, 1978), p. 4; Bodleian Library, Per 264505 e. 4, NAGC, *Journal of the Gifted Child*, Autumn 1979, 'The highly gifted child', Phyllis Wallbank, p. 72; Bodleian Library, Per 264505 e. 4, NAHC, *Journal of the Gifted Child*, Autumn 1979, 'Helping a gifted child with mathematics', Yael Naim Dowker and Clifford Hugh Dowker, p. 54.

[117] NAGC, *Explorers Unlimited Newsletter*, Summer 1979, 'What's it like then?', p. 1.
[118] Ibid.   [119] Ibid.   [120] Ibid.   [121] Ibid.
[122] Ibid.   [123] Ibid.   [124] Ibid.

offered for leisure and socialisation, they could simultaneously have a critical relationship with the label 'gifted'. For these young people, being labelled 'gifted' had given access to new educational programmes provided in their state, and the opportunities to write to British children in a related group. But, with this came the challenges of increased expectations from peers and teachers, and potentially being seen *only* through the lens of a label rather than as complex individuals.[125] This testimony had popular resonance with British readers of the *Explorers Unlimited* newsletter. Indeed, in the next Bulletin, published in Autumn 1979, the newsletter's editor stated that this was '[o]bviously a topic Explorers feel very strongly about, judging by the letters I've had in.'[126] Of the letters published in response, one thirteen-year-old author wrote that, 'I felt just like that towards my parents—I presume it [the original letter] is aimed at parents.'[127] Another contributor, aged twelve, stated similarly that he agreed that 'we are given a label.'[128] For this child also, their friends said that they should get better marks at school, 'but I remind them that I also get harder work.'[129] Subsequent letters continued to ask why peers could not accept children who were different.[130] While these children thus felt relatively empowered to question and to correct their peers in this space, and indeed to challenge the National Association itself, they also said that their daily lives were damaged by the label gifted. These letters therefore—and the suggestion of further unpublished ones besides—show how gifted children lived with this label. Suggesting the terse environment of these debates, and the pressures on those labelled as 'gifted', the newsletter editor stated that she had anonymised the letters, 'just in case the authors get into difficulties for making their views known.'[131] Again, featured children were empowered as their testimonies became visible through this forum, but also adults assumed that they needed to be protected, in this case with enforced anonymity.

Youth-authored poetry sent to the National Association further reveals how young people at times enthusiastically participated in voluntary giftedness spaces—writing to their magazines—but were cynical about the construction of 'giftedness'. Many young authors writing to the National Association playfully mocked ideas of measurement, categorisation, and IQ testing, for example, which

---

[125] In terms of understanding the flexibility of labels, particularly in a psychological setting, I have long been influenced by Ian Hacking, for example: Ian Hacking, 'Making Up People', in Heller, Sosna, and Wellbery (eds), *Reconstructing Individualism: Autonomy, Individuality, and the Self in Western Thought* (Stanford: Stanford University Press, 1986), pp. 222–236; Ian Hacking, 'Kinds of people: moving targets', *Proceedings of the British Academy*, 151 (2007), pp. 285–318; O. J. Madsen, J. Servan, and S. A. Øyen, '"I am a philosopher of the particular case": An interview with the 2009 Holberg prizewinner Ian Hacking', *History of the Human Sciences*, 26 (3) (2013). A useful reflection on historicising Ian Hacking's theories is: Chris Millard, 'Concepts, Diagnosis and the History of Medicine: Historicising Ian Hacking and Munchausen Syndrome', *Social History of Medicine*, 30 (3) (2017), pp. 567–589.
[126] NAGC archives, Bletchley, *Explorers Unlimited Newsletter*, Summer 1979, 'What's it like then?', p. 1.
[127] Ibid.   [128] Ibid.   [129] Ibid.   [130] Ibid.   [131] Ibid.

could frame psychological and public perceptions of giftedness. In a 1985 edition of *Questors Ho!*, a nine-year-old wrote a poem entitled 'Measurement'. The poem stated: 'There's centimetres, / Inches, / Feet and metres, / Pounds, / Grams, / Pints and litres.'[132] The child wrote, 'Oh! I really wish I / knew / The different betwwen [sic]/centigrade and feet, / I used to think I was five / ounces deep! / Now I reckon I'm nine stone tall, / I think I'm right, / But I'm not sure at all!' [133] This playful poem questioned all measurements and their relation to ideas of self. The child used various measurements to interpret her own size and depth, and fundamentally challenged whether these misunderstandings mattered.

Such poetry was part of young people playing with a broad range of social norms, beyond ideas of giftedness alone. Poetry by National Association members often used themes of death and destruction, with little respect for the social systems adults had created. For example, one poem by an eleven-year-old boy, published in the March 1981 edition of the *Explorers Unlimited Newsletter*, discussed a fire that would 'waltz' around a church, 'Warning of triumph to flames and death to men', until 'The flames remove their masks, / Underneath charred wood and smoke.'[134] Also in this edition, a ten-year-old contributor wrote a poem from the perspective of a fox, stating that: 'Oh I wish I was away far from this horrible place / This pathetic and stupid zoo.'[135] A poem on spiders by an eleven-year-old considered this 'peaceful' creature who then 'slyly' killed flies, and a poem on bats described a creature that could, if entering your house, be cooked to 'have bat soup.'[136] Another poem discussed anxious experiences of London Underground travel, portraying carriages as 'huge, grinning, gaping mouths / Waiting to swallow me up, into their long snakelike stomachs.' The author felt disempowered, ending her poem with the statement that while she repeatedly iterated, 'I'll never go on a tube again', she knew: 'I'm wrong, there's always a next time.'[137] This statement left it unclear as to why the author returned to the underground system; whether due to their own need to travel, or to adult enforcement of a schedule.

These poems deployed a range of styles, themes, and messages, but notably all suggested broad interests in subverting traditional power relations, for example between animals and humans, humans and nature, adults and children. The poems spoke to the anxieties of many child contributors, and to the interest of the magazine curators in enabling children to express such concerns in creative ways. The poems did not explicitly reject the idea of giftedness, but nonetheless revealed more about the experiences of being gifted. The poems showed that

---

[132] NAGC, *Questors Ho!*, 1985, 'Measurement', p. 9. [133] Ibid.
[134] NAGC, *Explorers Unlimited Newsletter*, March 1981, 'The Great Fire', p. 22.
[135] NAGC, *Explorers Unlimited Newsletter*, March 1981, 'The Fox', p. 23.
[136] NAGC, *Explorers Unlimited Newsletter*, March 1981, 'Catch a Bat', p. 24; NAGC, *Explorers Unlimited Newsletter*, March 1981, 'The Spider', p. 24.
[137] NAGC, *Explorers Unlimited Newsletter*, March 1981, 'The Tube Train', p. 22.

intelligent children looked to articulate their experiences in creative ways, using voluntary fora to share their critique with professionals, parents, and other children across the world. The children's poems paradoxically demonstrated both the ways in which being labelled as gifted enabled children new access to new communities—across Britain, Australia, and North America—and yet also constrained their daily lives. Children challenged the label of gifted—its utility, arbitrariness, and relationship to educational and familial expectations—but also relied on new peer groups and new spaces for 'the gifted' in which to air their critiques.

These poems represent a rich addition to professional narratives of this time, and further explain the range of factors that dissuaded children from harnessing the identity 'gifted' without question. Beyond sympathetic voluntary spaces, however, children's critical thinking was not always taken seriously. Notably, in tabloid coverage and media the gifted young's engagement with intelligence testing or categories could be put 'on display' for interested adults, and contributed to a prevailing vision of gifted children as uniquely disruptive, perceptive, and critical.[138] A *Daily Express* article of 1971, for example, emphasised that 'some gifted youngsters can be quite rude to adults trying to test how bright they are'. Even in response to the authority figure of a 'Cambridge don', indeed, one 'lively 10-year-old', when asked, 'What uses can you think of for a tin of boot polish?', replied, 'Smear it over the faces of people who ask silly questions!'[139] Even in psychological research from this period, young people's rejection of ideas of giftedness were often explained, for example, as simply looking to 'spite his parents', being 'unaware of his own unique abilities', or having already accepted a school's evaluation of them.[140] In all of these accounts, the child's rejection of the term was not a rational, thoughtful choice, but something to be overcome, pushing the child towards the 'right' way of thinking. Underlying this, in psychological discourse, was concern about the significant psychological costs if gifted children could not 'realise their true selves' and reach their full 'potential'.[141]

Young people looked to resist and renegotiate the identity of giftedness, as well as accepting and enthusiastically participating in giftedness spaces such as at the National Association. Young people's reasons for questioning ideas of giftedness were complex—reflecting perceived pressure from adults and peers, a broader

---

[138] See also: Rosiemarie Garland-Thomson, 'The politics of staring: visual rhetorics of disability in popular photography', in Sharon Snyder, Brenda Jo Brueggemann, and Rosemarie Garland-Thomson (eds), *Disability Studies: Enabling the Humanities* (New York: Modern Language Association of America, 2002), pp. 56–75; Stuart Murray, 'Autism and the contemporary sentimental: fiction and the narrative fascination of the present', *Literature and Medicine*, 25 (1) (2006), p. 29.

[139] 'Two in every 100—the children who behave like adults', *Daily Express*, 25 March 1971, p. 6.

[140] Isaacs, 'Role Expectancy', p. 106; Congdon, *Spot the Gifted Child*, p. 4; Bodleian Library, Per 264505 e. 4, NAGC, *Journal of the Gifted Child*, Autumn 1979, 'The Highly Gifted Child', Phyllis Wallbank, p. 72; Bodleian Library, Per 264505 e. 4, NAGC, *Journal of the Gifted Child*, Autumn 1979, 'Helping a gifted child with mathematics', Yael Naim Dowker and Clifford Hugh Dowker, p. 54.

[141] NAGC, 'Annual General Meeting', *Newsletter*, May 1969, p. 3.

sense of dissatisfaction or need to challenge the world and all norms, or uneasiness with measurement and comparison.

'She's a nice person but': Gifted Children on Their Teachers

Regardless of how young people engaged with the term 'gifted' and with 'giftedness' spaces, encountering this term fundamentally reshaped their lives. Most significantly, young people's writings show that ideas of giftedness reshaped, often quite negatively, their engagement with teachers, while at times improving relationships with their peers. We have reasonably rich archival evidence describing gifted children's relationships within schools, with teachers and peers, because the editors of children's magazines, published through the National Association, were interested in asking them their opinion on 'subjects, teachers, discipline, uniforms, timetables, homework, and so on and so on', assuming that school life was something that all children could discuss together.[142] Notably, children rarely discussed the structure and organisation of schooling—comprehensives, grammars, special schools for gifted children, etc. Rather, and perhaps following the Association framing above, they focused instead on the key routines and relationships that structured their daily lives, whatever the setting.

Overall, young people labelled gifted had great variety in their encounters with education. Such variety was captured in the National Association newsletter of Autumn 1971, when two children from the Wolverhampton branch were orally recorded discussing this topic.[143] The first child was '11 plus', a boy called 'J'. He stated that he went to school aged four and 'was permitted to work on my own from books and allowed to go as far as I liked. I enjoyed this and being so far ahead of the other children'.[144] Primary school was a good experience, though he noted that his preferred subjects 'depends on the teacher and if he/she like me or not'. The second interviewee was 'B' who was '12 plus' and female. She noted that she first went to school 'very apprehensive about the work I was going to do' but was subsequently 'disappointed' because the work was 'not hard'. She stated that 'I became flippant and enjoyed saying things and asking questions which made the other children laugh and the teacher cross'. Again, the student emphasised that her education depended on her relationships with specific teachers, and that, 'I liked all the teachers except the last one and we did not get on at all. She's a nice person but she kept on about me not being worthy of the honors [sic] I got and I got sick of it.'[145]

---

[142] NAGC, Explorers Unlimited, Spring 1977, 'So what ABOUT school?', p. 2. For a related account, albeit 10–15 years earlier, see the essay collection Edward Blishen, *The School That I'd Like* (London: Penguin Education, 1967).

[143] NAGC, Newsletter, Autumn 1971, 'Wolverhampton', p. 8.

[144] Ibid.   [145] Ibid.

While these children's accounts were different, key themes emerged within young people's writings when describing how they related to teachers. First, newsletters showed that many children labelled as gifted subsequently felt empowered and entitled to make judgements about teachers and their capacities, identifying whether they knew 'how to teach' and were properly utilising their skills.[146] Second, and relatedly, many gifted children felt that their teachers were particularly cruel and strict to them, because they were seen as gifted.[147] Of course, it is not only gifted children who have judged their teachers.[148] Nonetheless, it is worth exploring how children considered 'gifted', in particular, may have been brought in to conflict and tension with teachers. Broader historical research about teachers' attitudes, for example by Tisdall, shows that in post-war England and Wales, gifted children—and especially gifted working-class children—were 'explicitly penalised'; they were 'stereotyped as "cocky"', and their success was undermined by developmental claims that their accelerated academic development was abnormal.[149] Philip Kirby argues that dyslexic children—also labelled in education—often faced hostility from teachers, meeting 'sceptical and unhelpful…authority figures' in their educational journeys.[150] Archivally, we see frequent traces of teachers struggling with gifted children, finding it difficult and confusing given a broader lack of support in this area—or even reporting being 'afraid of being out-manoeuvred'.[151]

Academic interviews with adults, recalling childhood experiences, further our understanding of tensions between gifted children and their teachers, and show how such experiences were compounded for gifted children who also had a disability. In a 1998 interview study, subsequently published in *Gifted Education International*, adults who were gifted and Deaf described childhood experiences where teachers were unable to sign to them or even forbade them from signing to one another, and also found that 'teachers expected less of Deaf students' and that

---

[146] Bodleian Library, Per 264505 e. 4, National Association for Gifted Children, *Journal of the Gifted Child*, Autumn 1979, 'Helping a gifted child with mathematics', Yael Naim Dowker and Clifford Hugh Dowker, p. 60.

[147] NAGC, Explorers Unlimited, Newsletter Summer 1981, 'Simon starts school', p. 28.

[148] On this, await publication of the paper by Laura Carter, 'Managing the mayhem: pupil–teacher relations in English and Welsh comprehensive schools, 1960s–1980s', as presented to University of Oxford Centre for the History of Childhood, 20 November 2023.

[149] As cited in Laura Tisdall, *A Progressive Education? How Childhood Changed in mid-twentieth-century* (Manchester: Manchester University Press, 2020), p. 196.

[150] Philip Kirby, 'Gift from the gods? Dyslexia, popular culture and the ethics of representation', *Disability & Society*, 34 (10) (2019), p. 11.

[151] When recruiting, the Brentwood project leaders found many college students reluctant to be involved with teaching the children, 'on the grounds that they felt that they lacked the quickness of mind necessary to deal with quick-witted children': S. A. Bridges, 'The pilot scheme' in S. A. Bridges (ed.), *Gifted Children and the Brentwood Experiment* (London: Sir Isaac Pitman & Sons Ltd, 1969), p. 2; NAGC, *Looking to their future: The News Letter of the National Association for Gifted Children*, May 1977, 'At work in Bulgaria', no page reference; Institute of Education, London, SCC/555/1152/049, Gifted Pupils—Identification and Provision—Policy and Finance, 1979–1983, Provision for Gifted Children, DES Invitation Conference N522, 19–23 November 1979, Conference Report, p. 2.

they lacked role models.[152] Many students interviewed felt that their educational experience was fraught with contingency, and that they relied on individual teachers who were sympathetic and could assist them.

Of course, however, for other gifted young people individual teachers fundamentally improved their experiences of schools, even if teachers as a group were seen in a negative light. In an undated *Explorers Unlimited* magazine, an anonymous 11-year-old poet composed a 28-line poem entitled 'The Wall', which described how: 'They laughed at me and called me names / They wouldn't let me join their games'. Teachers were no better than peers, and the poem stated that: 'Teachers told me I was rude, / Bumptious, overbearing, shrewd, / Some of the things they said were crude.' Eventually 'then came Sir, / A jovial, beaming, kindly man' who helped the boy, 'took my hand', and enabled him to now 'laugh with them, / Not in any unkind way, and 'understand'.[153]

As suggested in this poem, membership of a giftedness organisation, and this identity, often invited children to negatively reassess their peer relationships. The two children from Wolverhampton, discussing education in the Autumn 1971 newsletter, both reflected at length on the loneliness and isolation they felt from peers, because they were gifted.[154] The boy, 'J', said that in primary school, 'although I had friends in the early days, I did not form close friendships. In fact, I was "solitary" but I was satisfied about always being top and I invented a "Fly Family" like Superman and I played games with this family instead of other children.'[155] When the interviewer asked him if he would have preferred being at school with other children of the same intelligence, he said 'I suppose I would because then I could have the same level of conversation about shared work and interests, but it would have meant I was not always top and I would not have liked that'—an experience he noted he was now having at secondary school.[156] 'B', the girl, by contrast stated that, 'I was hero worshipped at school and I hated it but I liked to invite school friends to tea then I got so bored with them that I asked for them to be taken home again.'[157] Again at secondary school the girl felt that 'I can have loads of friends if I want to but I think I'm becoming a "lone wolf" and I like it.'[158]

Both of these children *felt* and lived with the assumption of their own high intelligence—an assumption buoyed by membership of the National Association and attendance of its weekend clubs. This new sense of self fundamentally changed their peer relationships in school. Both children were able to have friendships with peers, or to imagine them, but in part due to their self-perception of extreme intelligence they chose to focus instead on themselves or on imaginary

---

[152] Wilma Vialle and John Paterson, 'Deafening silence: the educational experience of gifted deaf people', *Gifted Education International*, 13, pp. 14–15.
[153] NAGC, *Explorers Unlimited*, Undated newsletter, 'The Wall', p. 1.
[154] NAGC, Newsletter, Autumn 1971, 'Wolverhampton', p. 8.
[155] Ibid. [156] Ibid. [157] Ibid. [158] Ibid.

friendships, finding peers boring or a competitive threat. While ideas of giftedness were created to agitate for extra educational or leisure provision, then, they also shaped children's social lives on a daily level beyond the spaces of voluntary organisations. Young people recognised that their peer relationships were among some of the most important. One twelve-year-old wrote to the *Explorers Unlimited* newsletter in 1980 that it was 'vital', as 'we all need other children'.[159] It mattered, then, if children's peer relationships were changed by encounters with giftedness: these were significant in structuring their lives.

Thus, children's daily experience of school—shaped by their teachers and peers—were fundamentally changed by the idea that they were gifted, and by the provision of voluntary spaces in which they could exchange their views, as emerged in the 1970s and 1980s. This was emphasised by young people themselves, and encouraged by the editors of children's magazines, seeing gifted youth as particularly useful analysts of how teachers were working and how educational policy was functioning in practice.

Conclusion

This chapter has explored how new voluntary spaces in the 1970s and 1980s, notably organised by the National Association, enabled young people whose families identified them as 'gifted' to socialise with new peers. The National Association endeavoured to involve all young people, and to ensure that these weren't dominated by middle-class families, although this was never entirely successful. Young people's writings show that many relished weekend and holiday clubs accessed through the Association. Others still felt conflicted about the identity of 'gifted', even if they enjoyed their new leisure pursuits. Young people were empowered by these voluntary organisations to share writings with new communities: children in Britain and abroad identified as 'gifted' and adults interested in their thoughts. Ideas of childlikeness continued to frame their testimonies and their lived experiences of residential courses.

The Association, as we saw in Chapter Two, focused on providing and facilitating new educational, leisure, and support spaces for young people. These were a significant driver of parental membership—parents emphasised that they joined the National Association so that both themselves and their children could meet others 'like them', and form social networks of solidarity. The Association wrote that many parents joined them 'to air their anxieties', and that they were, 'above all, a caring organization'.[160] Notably, this positions the National Association

---

[159] NAGC, *Explorers Unlimited*, August 1980, 'School in vital', p. 1.
[160] Institute of Education, London, SCC/1030/1037/1037/608, 'National Association of Gifted Children–Proposal to Make a Film', 1978–1979, 'Profile: The National Association for Gifted Children', 12 March 1978, p. 1.

outside histories of formal education. Advocates for gifted education in the 1970s tended to criticise extra-curricular and voluntary provision, believing that the gifted child must be managed within the school, and that these brief, fleeting encounters would not particularly benefit their education: for Lord Rusholme they were 'uneconomic and ineffective, even when they are not actually harmful'.[161] Parents at the National Association, meanwhile, were rarely interested in publicly lobbying for significant educational change, but rather chose to make their emotions and experiences visible, in the quest of sympathy and companionship.

The Association typically sought to make leisure clubs for all young people, rather than to identify or privilege 'elites of the future'. This kind of voluntary work had significant successes in the 1970s and 1980s in particular yet, at the same time, as the next chapter will show, these debates also saw psychologists entwined with eugenics and racial science seeking to use ideas of 'the gifted child' for their own purposes, and to police strict definitions of which families were likely to be gifted, and how this should be measured and assessed; quite the opposite of the inclusive attempts of the National Association. Cultural interest in ideas of giftedness, which was high in the 1970s and 1980s, meant that this term could bring young people together, and get funding directed at their leisure time, but also that it would be appropriated in quests for national economic and political success. Young people, as ever, had a critical response to such developments.

'Gifted Children' in Britain and the World: Elitism and Equality since 1945. Jennifer Crane, Oxford University Press.
© Jennifer Crane 2025. DOI: 10.1093/9780198928881.003.0004

---

[161] Borthwick Institute for Archives, York, JAM/2/1/1, Scripts, Speeches and Lectures, 'The Education of the Gifted Child', Lord James of Rusholme, 1970s, p. 9.

Making Future Leaders: Psychology, Giftedness, and Legacies of Eugenics, 1970–1989

> I complete my own existence knowing that my potential may or may not be great, I feel I can offer nothing of great importance to the world…I have no power, no money, no influence and little experience. I have, however, a mind, and this I feel I can offer to the world.
> *Bodleian Library, Per 264505 e. 4, National Association for Gifted Children, Journal of the Gifted Child, Autumn 1979, 'Saturday Club', p. 50.*

This testimony was written by a thirteen-year-old boy who attended a Saturday Club in Moberly, London, run by the National Association for Gifted Children, and who spoke to their journal in Autumn 1979. This boy clearly recognised, felt, and lived with the idea that, because he had been labelled 'gifted', he must in some sense provide future leadership to, in his words, 'the world'. While feeling the weight of significant expectations, the boy also feared that he acted from a position of relative powerlessness. Indeed, he stated that he could offer 'nothing of great importance', and reflected on his lack of power, money, influence, and experience. The boy felt that his only significant resource was 'a mind'.

This chapter explores the varied arenas in which the idea that gifted children could and should be elites of the future gained significance in the 1970s and 1980s. First, it analyses how psychologists interested in eugenics, particularly Cyril Burt, advocated this. This was no marginal work of psychology; rather, Burt influenced the structure of Britain's education system. Second, the chapter shows how the conservative tabloid press engaged with this idea, reiterating ideas that elites of the future were born, not made, and the vision that they must be urgently identified. Conservative tabloids used this idea to criticise the comprehensive education system and a range of other contemporary equalities movements. Third, the chapter shows how the National Association engaged with ideas of elites of the future in these decades. It argues that making elites of the future was not a primary aim of the National Association, which continued—as shown in Chapter Three—to focus instead on the welfare of and provision for gifted children and their families, and to seek to identify all gifted children, regardless of race, ethnicity, and class. Nonetheless, ideas of elites, leadership, and futures were at times present in newsletters and activities organised by this voluntary group. Finally, the chapter considers how young people labelled as 'gifted' engaged with these ideas. It shows that some felt responsibility for national futures, while others rejected the concept. Young people's vision of 'the world' was affected by contemporary stereotypes around race, ethnicity, and the 'other' in these decades.

Overall, this chapter shows how ideas of gifted children as elites of the future were powerful across multiple spaces with highly different aims. These were powerful yet flexible ideas that could suit the aims and agendas of many, and no one group clearly defined in this period what gifted children should do in 'the future', nor how they should be trained (as Chapter Five shows, such ideas were much more clearly defined by the late 1990s and 2000s under New Labour and in its National Academy for Gifted and Talented Youth). Further, this present chapter also shows the complex ways in which legacies of eugenicist thought, from the late nineteenth and early twentieth centuries, interacted with debates about giftedness in the late twentieth century. While voluntary organisations and young people sought to avoid these associations, and to use giftedness as a movement for equality, identifying all those who needed support, elements of tabloid reporting and psychological debate continued to draw on older ideas of the gifted as an 'elite', inheriting innate intelligence. At times, also, tabloid and psychological rhetoric also focused on reproduction, positioning gifted children as 'national stock' who were at risk of being 'wasted'.[1] Following Alison Bashford, this chapter therefore traces distinct, but relevant, afterlives of eugenics after 1945, 'pursuing a more strictly historical process of showing connections over time'.[2] Rubahanna Amannah Choudhury, relatedly, has powerfully shown how 'the legacy of eugenic concepts was felt by marginalised groups in Britain' into the 1960s and 1970s.[3] This chapter continues this analysis, and emphasises also that the gifted young themselves were often critical of such psychological and social measurements, or of any vision of their 'elite' future roles.

---

[1] On the longer term nature of these concerns, see Mathew Thomson, *The Problem of Mental Deficiency: Eugenics, Democracy, and Social Policy in Britain, c. 1870–1959* (Oxford: OUP, 1998); Adrian Wooldridge, *Measuring the Mind: Education and Psychology in England, c. 1860–1990* (Cambridge: CUP, 1994); Alison Bashford and Philippa Levine (eds), *The Oxford Handbook of the History of Eugenics* (Oxford: OUP, 2010); Pauline Mazumdar, *Eugenics Human Genetics and Human Failings: The Eugenics Society, its Source and its Critics in Britain* (London: Routledge, 1992).
[2] Alison Bashford, 'Epilogue: where did eugenics go?', in Bashford and Levine (eds), *The Oxford Handbook of the History of Eugenics*, p. 540.
[3] Rubahanna Amannah Choudhury, 'The forgotten children: The Association of Parents of Backward Children and the Legacy of Eugenics in Britain, 1946–1960', Thesis submitted for the Degree of Doctor of Philosophy at Oxford Brookes University, December 2015 <https://radar.brookes.ac.uk/radar/file/26b8d017-0527-4006-8029-0426ea259b75/1/choudhury2015forgottenRADAR.pdf> (26 March 2024), p. 282.

Psychology, Eugenics, and Giftedness

In the 1970s and 1980s influential psychologists, notably Cyril Burt, believed in, and subsequently sought to analyse and measure, the inherited intelligence of gifted children. These theories—connecting intelligence, genetics and, at times, race and class—were controversial and critiqued, yet they were also echoed in factions of the tabloid press.

Born in 1883, Cyril Burt had had an early interest in eugenics, psychology, and intelligence. Following his undergraduate studies in 'Greats' at the University of Oxford (1902–1906), in 1907 one of his lecturers, the psychologist William McDougall, encouraged him to become involved in an anthropometric survey of Britons proposed by Francis Galton, consulting on how to standardise psychological tests.[4] He continued this work in 1909, analysing the performance of school children in testing, and writing a paper that argued that children in private preparatory schools performed better in such tests than those in state elementary schools, because of their innate superiority.[5] Burt was subsequently appointed as a lecturer in psychology at the University of Liverpool. Following the *Mental Deficiency Act* of 1913, which stated that 'defective children' should be transferred to specialist schools, Burt designed such tests as a psychologist for the London County Council.[6]

The eugenicist movement was prominent amongst intellectuals in the 1930s, when Burt's views were developing; and in general 'an extraordinarily protean idea, assuming markedly different forms in different locations and among different constituencies' across the world from the late nineteenth to mid-twentieth centuries.[7] Burt was involved in the Eugenics Society, chairing their Pauper Pedigree Project which, historian Pauline M. H. Mazumdar writes, 'was designed to show that the pauper class was a closed, inbreeding group of interrelated families, and that pauperism could be traced to a heritable biological defect of temperament, showing itself in moral imbecility, feeble-mindedness, nervousness, and criminality.'[8] Burt's work had significant influence over social policy

---

[4] Pauline M. H. Mazumdar, 'Burt, Sir Cyril Lodowic', *Oxford Dictionary of National Biography*, 23 September 2004. For discussion of McDougall, see: 'the era's most influential British psychologist but now a largely forgotten figure', in Mathew Thomson, *Psychological Subjects: Identity, Culture, and Health in Twentieth-Century Britain* (Oxford: OUP, 2007), ch. 3: Reframing the discipline. On the relationship between Burt's work and that of Galton, see: Wooldridge, *Measuring the Mind*, pp. 74–78.

[5] Mazumdar, 'Burt, Sir Cyril Lodowic', *ODNB*.

[6] Mazumdar, 'Burt, Sir Cyril Lodowic', *ODNB*; Gillian Sutherland and Stephen Sharp, '"The Fust Official Psychologist in the Wurrld": Aspects of the professionalisation of psychology in early twentieth century Britain', *History of Science*, 18 (1980), pp. 181–208; Wooldridge, *Measuring the Mind*, pp. 80–88. For further discussion of the context of this Act, see: *The Problem of Mental Deficiency: Eugenics, Democracy and Social Policy in Britain, c. 1870–1959* (Oxford: OUP, 1998), Introduction.

[7] See Philippa Levine, 'Is comparative history possible?', *History and Theory*, 53 (2014), p. 345; Alison Bashford and Philippa Levine (eds), *The Oxford Handbook of the History of Eugenics* (Oxford: OUP, 2010).

[8] Mazumdar, 'Burt, Sir Cyril Lodowic', *ODNB*.

discussions throughout the twentieth century; for Adrian Wooldridge, indeed, he was 'undoubtedly the most important' of a group of psychologists looking to apply psychological theory to education; he 'alone combined success' in 'moving easily between the worlds of scientific research, educational administration, teacher training and popular journalism'.[9]

Burt was interested in 'gifted' children, who scored highly in IQ tests, as well as in those who did not test well. He wrote a significant number of unpublished papers and notes about these young people from the 1930s until the 1970s, which have been stored at the University of Liverpool archives. Some of these papers were also brought together in a full book, *The Gifted Child*, published in 1975 after Burt's death from cancer in 1971.[10] The volume was collated by Charlotte Banks, a lecturer in psychology at University College London who published research papers with Burt in the 1940s and 1950s.[11] These works were cautious about the validity of IQ tests as a sole measure, but nonetheless emphasised the significance of genetic inheritance for creating gifted children.[12] Typically, for Burt, the gifted child would be 'the son of a gifted father'. In addition to this hereditarian thinking, Burt noted the significance of environment, also, writing that this child would likely have also 'received from his earliest years an exceptionally erudite tuition from a learned relative at home'.[13] Burt was also fascinated by what he called 'innate but normal variation'—cases where young people, despite no 'organic disease nor environmental limitations', had low IQ.[14]

Echoing rhetoric encountered throughout this book, Burt argued that gifted children had been 'unduly neglected' compared to 'the dull, the backward, the neurotic, the delinquent'.[15] Further, he stated that they had a critical role to play in developing the world, stating, '[b]y way of warning' that 'time and again in this history of civilization, nations have declined sometimes temporarily, sometimes permanently, in power, prestige, and the well-being of their humbler members' if their political, military, and economic leaders were insufficiently 'gifted'.[16] Burt was concerned that gifted children would not be identified because, into the 1960s and 1970s, 'psychologists, sociologists, educationists and teachers' adhered to 'egalitarian doctrines'.[17] In an unpublished paper, again, he estimated that about 3,000 students at school in Britain had IQs of 150 or over, far more than the normal distribution would suggest, and about 300 with IQs of 175 or over.

---

[9] Wooldridge, *Measuring the Mind*, p. 73.
[10] Cyril Burt, *The Gifted Child* (New York: Hodder & Stoughton, 1975).
[11] I. C. McManus, Richard Rawles, James Moore, and Matthew Freegard, 'Science in the making: right hand, left hand: A BBC television programme broadcast in 1953', *Laterality*, 15 (1), pp. 136–165.
[12] Liverpool University Special Collections and Archives (hereafter LUSCA), D191/20/5/7, Papers of Cyril Burt, *The Gifted Child*, no date, p. 2.
[13] Burt, *The Gifted Child*, p. 12.   [14] Ibid., p. 15.   [15] Ibid., p. vii.
[16] LUSCA, D191/20/5/8, Papers of Cyril Burt, 'What are we doing for the highly gifted?', 15 November 1967, p. 8.
[17] Burt, *The Gifted Child*, p. 9.

He believed that about half were unrecognised and about three-quarters failed to get adequate education or training.[18]

The kind of arguments that Burt was making, connecting giftedness to questions of genetics and 'national stock' were being taken up in another form by 'Britain's best-known psychologist of the era', Hans Eysenck.[19] Eysenck had been brought up in Germany by his grandmother, before fleeing to England in the 1930s, as he had 'openly detested Nazism from the beginning'.[20] He studied psychology at University College, London, from 1935, receiving teaching from Cyril Burt, before going on to research and teach in areas of personality and individual difference at the Maudsley Hospital Clinic and Institute of Psychiatry.[21] From the 1950s and 1960s he became, Mathew Thomson has written, an 'almost constant presence through appearances in the press, radio, and television' as well as through his popular essay collections published by Penguin.[22] By the 1980s, he was making controversial statements about smoking, crime, astrology, and extrasensory perception.[23] From his significant platform, in 1980 he also addressed contemporary debates about intelligence, not only drawing attention to genetics, but also explicitly comparing how he believed intelligence would vary by race. He wrote, for example, that there was 'no doubt' that IQ differences were associated with race, and that, for example, '[s]ocio-economic status, or better education, can hardly account for the superiority of Chinese and Japanese, or the equality of Eskimos with whites; neither can the fatuous argument that IQ tests are made by white, middle-class psychologists to favour white middle-class children.'[24]

These psychologists then tied together intelligence and genetic inheritance and, at times, race and class. The views of Burt and Eysenck were relatively prominent and well-known, but far from uncontroversial in the mid-to-late twentieth century. As early as the mid-1950s, sociologists and social psychologists questioned the fairness of the 11+ selection process, and its failure to 'dispose of the problem of equality of educational opportunity'.[25] Responding to these debates in the *British Journal of Statistical Psychology* in 1961, Burt emphasised that recent 'uncompromising criticisms' were wrong to blame intelligence testing for making

---

[18] LUSCA, D191/20/5/8, Papers of Cyril Burt, 'What are we doing for the highly gifted?', 15 November 1967, p. 8.
[19] Thomson, *Psychological Subjects*, p. 258.
[20] Graham Richards, 'Eysenck, Hans Jurgen', ODNB, 23 September 2004.   [21] Ibid.
[22] Thomson, *Psychological Subjects*, p. 258.   [23] Richards, 'Eysenck, Hans Jurgen', ODNB.
[24] Hans Eysenck and Steven Rose, 'Race, intelligence and education', *New Community*, 7 (2) (1979), p. 280.
[25] J. E. Floud, A. H. Halsey, and F. M. Martin, *Social Class and Educational Opportunity* (London: William Heinemann Ltd., 1956), as cited in Peter Mandler, *The Crisis of the Meritocracy: Britain's Transition to Mass Education since the Second World War* (Oxford: OUP, 2020), p. 57. See also: Flann Campbell, *Eleven-Plus: The Grammar School in a Changing Society* (London: Watts, 1956); J. E. Floud and A. H. Halsey, 'Intelligence tests, social class and selection for secondary schools', *The British Journal of Sociology*, 8 (1) (1957), pp. 33–39; Michael Carter, *Home, School and Work: A Study of the Education and Employment of Young People in Britain* (Oxford: Pergamon, 1962); J. W. B. Douglas, *The Home & the School* (London: MacGibbon & Kee, 1964).

grammar schools an 'undisputed preserve of the middle class', with the son of a non-manual worker three times more likely to enter a grammar school than a working-class boy.[26] For Burt, 'the shortcomings of the present methods of selection have, I fancy, been much exaggerated'.[27] This debate continued to rage in the 1970s, with advocates of school selection arguing that they were misrepresented: that selection did not rely on testing in a single day, that there could be reassessment, and indeed that, 'so far as those tests appear inadequate, their faults usually arise from attempts to make them fairer as between children from different cultural backgrounds'.[28]

In the 1970s, also, Burt was being criticised directly in reanalysis by Leon Kamin, a psychologist at Princeton; Oliver Gillie, a medical correspondent for the *Sunday Times*; and former biographer Leslie Hearnshaw, accusing him of falsifying research data, and even inventing twins and research assistants, though these claims themselves were further challenged in the 1980s and 1990s.[29] Eysenck was also prominently challenged, by Steven Rose, a biologist, in the 1970s and 1980s, notably in a significant pamphlet for the National Union of Teachers, on *Race, Intelligence, and Education*.[30] Rose argued that the idea of a general intelligence factor had been 'discarded by most modern psychologists working on cognition as virtually useless', and that Eysenck's work was thus 'as fallacious and outdated as phrenology'.[31] For Rose, the reasons for differences in IQ must 'be sought in discrepant cultures, languages and social experiences within xenophobic societies'.[32] Significant critique also emerged from educational sociology in America in the 1980s and 1990s, where giftedness programmes were more common than in Britain, building on contexts discussed in Chapter One. Researchers argued that children who were minoritised ethnic, from a minority culture, or spoke English as a second language, as well as those who were poor or female, were less likely to be identified as 'gifted' by achievement or IQ testing or teacher recommendations, because of the vague definition of 'giftedness'; misuses of testing; and because tests were normed for white, middle-class boys, although

---

[26] First quote is, LUSCA, D191/32/15, Papers of Cyril Burt, 'The gifted child', *The British Journal of Statistical Psychology*, November 1961, p. 132; second quote is Floud, Halsey, and Martin, *Social Class and Educational Opportunity*, p. 143, as cited in LUSCA, D191/32/15, Papers of Cyril Burt, 'The gifted child', *The British Journal of Statistical Psychology*, November 1961, p. 132.

[27] Ibid., p. 136.

[28] Borthwick Institute for Archives, York, JAM/2/1/1, Scripts, Speeches and Lectures, 'The Education of the Gifted Child', Lord James of Rusholme, 1970s, p. 4.

[29] Leon J. Kamin, *The Science and Politics of I.Q.* (Abingdon: Lawrence Erlbaum Associates, 1974); L. S. Hearnshaw, *Cyril Burt, Psychologist* (London: Hodder Arnold, 1979). Subsequent psychologists and sociologists at the turn of the 1990s sought to rehabilitate Burt's work: see Mazumdar, 'Burt, Sir Cyril Lodowic', *ODNB*; the changing debates around this are charted in Adrian Wooldridge, *Measuring the Mind*, ch. 13.

[30] National Union of Teachers, *Race Education, Intelligence: A Teacher's Guide to the Facts and the Issues* (NUT, 1978), p. 3.

[31] Eysenck and Rose, 'Race, intelligence and education', p. 281.   [32] Ibid., p. 282.

psychologists disagreed on whether to abandon, or merely reshape, intelligence testing as a result.[33]

While ideas about intelligence testing and genetic inheritance were then highly controversial, testing continued to have significant influence in the lives of young people in Britain into the 1960s, 1970s, and 1980s. Most significantly, as Rob Waters has shown, Black children were disproportionately identified as educationally subnormal in this period, because of the biases within IQ testing, and thus were over-represented in special needs education.[34] These debates also formed an intellectual background for broader ideas, particularly in conservative tabloid media, over the 1970s and 1980s, about how gifted children were part of 'national stock', necessary to provide British leadership within the broader world. This also formed the contexts against which voluntary organisations working in the name of the 'gifted child' carefully framed their work, looking to support all children with high intelligence and to evade any controversial or historically eugenicist associations of the term 'gifted'.

Tabloid Media and National Futures

Interest in giftedness, genetics, and, at times, also race flourished within parts of psychology, and was occasionally present at times in factions of the conservative tabloid press in the 1970s and 1980s. More commonly, however, such press focused on the idea of gifted children as necessary to reverse Britain's perceived imperial decline. David Edgerton's significant work has challenged whether anxieties about decline had a firm basis in economic reality.[35] Nonetheless, tabloid debates both sought to confront a perception of British 'decline', and also to critique a series of changing equalities measures instated in the 1960s and 1970s. Such debates foreshadowed and influenced the rise of popular individualism and the electoral success of Margaret Thatcher. Notably, these debates revealed a lack of priority on childhood wellbeing and familial autonomy, and again framed debates about what it meant to be a 'gifted child'.

---

[33] For example E. Susanne Richert, 'Identification of gifted children in the United States: The need for pluralistic assessment', *Roeper Review*, 8 (2) (1985), pp. 68–72; E. Susanne Richert, 'Rampant problems and promising practices in the identification of disadvantaged gifted students', *Gifted Child Quarterly*, 31 (4) (1987), pp. 149–154; Donna Y. Ford, 'The underrepresentation of minority students in gifted education: Problems and promises in recruitment and retention', *The Journal of Special Education*, 32(1) (1998), pp. 4–14; J. John Harris and Donna Y. Ford, 'Hope deferred again: minority students underrepresented in gifted programs', *Education and Urban Society*, 31 (2) (1999), pp. 225–237.

[34] Rob Waters, *Thinking Black: Britain, 1964–1985* (University of California Press, 2019), p. 130.

[35] David Edgerton, *The Rise and Fall of the British Nation: A Twentieth-Century History* (London: Allen Lane, 2018). See also David Edgerton, *England and the Aeroplane: Militarism, Modernity and Machines* (London: Penguin, 2013); David Edgerton, *Warfare State: Britain, 1920–1970* (Cambridge: CUP, 2005).

Displaying how factions of psychology were brought into tabloid media at this time, in the *Daily Mail* on 13 August 1975, the Education Correspondent provided a highly positive write-up of Burt's *Gifted Child* book, referring to the author as, 'Britain's leading expert on children's intelligence'.[36] The article used Burt's book to make broader critique of the comprehensive school movement, which emerged in the 1960s. This book had now, the article stated, showed that 'comprehensive schools are wasting the talents of our brightest children because staff "teach down" to the dunces'.[37] By contrast, the *Mail* emphasised, if gifted children were sent to specialist schools they could learn twice as fast and then be able to take 'the subjects they needed' such as higher mathematics and nuclear physics.[38] This analysis, the *Mail* stated, 'calls into question the Government's plans to phase out the 174 direct grant grammar schools, which cater for the brightest children'.[39] The frameworks offered by Burt were then redirected towards the newspaper's broader discontent with the education system and comprehensive movement. By the 1990s, newspaper coverage was also rehabilitating Lewis Terman; an American psychologist who began the largest ever longitudinal study of gifted children in 1921, but one premised around ideas of the 'essential nature of great man' and intellectual precocity as 'pathological' and biological.[40]

Again, showing longer legacies of eugenicist thought in the late twentieth century, tabloid coverage also fixated on genetic inheritance, suggesting that gifted children had their genes 'in the right place'.[41] Metaphors of the young gifted as animals, in need of training and breeding, were common: young people were a 'new breed' and should be 'trained like a potential Derby winner—groomed, as it were, for stardom'.[42] Tabloids also framed their work in terms of 'waste', echoing

---

[36] 'When bright pupils are just a nuisance', *Daily Mail*, 13 August 1975, p. 12.
[37] Ibid.   [38] Ibid.   [39] Ibid.
[40] The limited contemporary reporting around Terman's work in the British press included: E. M. Goodman, 'Testing brains', *Daily Telegraph*, 9 August 1919; 'The Intelligence Quotient: measuring brain power', *The Manchester Guardian*, 10 April 1931, p. 6. In the 1970s and 1980s, it was discussed as controversial work. See for example: Alan Ryan, 'The psychometric disaster', *The Sunday Times*, 6 June 1982; By the 1990s and 2000s, his work was being discussed as interesting, with the concerns about eugenics no longer a strong feature of news coverage. See: James Le Fanu, 'Honesty is the best policy for a long life', *Sunday Telegraph*, 16 April 1995; George Gordon, 'Earning a long life', *Daily Mail*, 31 August 1995; Victoria McKee, 'Rich gifts with a high price', *The Times*, 18 April 1990; Sarah Vine, 'Today's little darlings…or tomorrow's little monsters?', *The Times*, 25 November 2008. On the connections between Terman's work and eugenics: Lewis Terman, *Genetic Studies of Genius: Volume 1*, Preface. Terman's interest in eugenics was demonstrated by his memberships of the Human Betterment Foundation, the American Eugenics Society, and the Eugenics Research Association. This is a legacy with which members of the University of Stanford continue to grapple. See for example: Ben Maldonado, 'Eugenics on the Farm: Lewis Terman', *The Stanford Daily*, 6 November 2019 <https://www.stanforddaily.com/2019/11/06/eugenics-on-the-farm-lewis-terman/> (14 September 2021); 'The Vexing Legacy of Lewis Terman', *Stanford Magazine*, July/August 2000 <https://stanfordmag.org/contents/the-vexing-legacy-of-lewis-terman> (14 September 2021). See also: Alexandra Minna Stern, *Eugenic Nation: Faults and Frontiers of Better Breeding in Modern America* (California: University of California Press, 2015).
[41] June Southworth, 'What becomes of child prodigies?', *Daily Mail*, 2 December 1995, p. 3.
[42] Lynda Lee-Potter, 'Our son, the new captain of Eton!', *Daily Mail*, 26 July 1980, p. 7; Elizabeth Farrant, 'Be bright…', *Daily Mail*, 3 June 1971, p. 21.

tropes used in the 1890s.[43] An article in the *Daily Mail* in March 1976, 'Brain power just going to waste!', for example, stated that Britain was 'not only wasting and stunting' the abilities of gifted children, but 'also causing suffering to them and to their parents'.[44] In this vision, the 'waste' of gifted children, and their 'brain power' was situated emphasised, as was their potential as 'our most precious national asset'.[45]

A particular trope of tabloid coverage was fixation on gifted youth from working-class backgrounds, demonstrating how newspapers positioned this as 'unexpected'. In July 1980, for example, a *Daily Mail* article interviewed two proud parents. The headlines stated: 'Father sells spare parts for cars, mother was a bank clerk, yet…Our son, the new captain of Eton!'[46] The eighteen-year-old had gained this position having joined Eton on a scholarship scheme years earlier. His predecessors, the article stated, by contrast were 'privileged sons of aristocrats and the wealthy sons of famous families, inheritors of great estates and destined for Eton before they were born'.[47] Yet, this child, they stated, lived only 'in a small remote cottage overlooking the flat Lincolnshire fields'.[48] Again, through this genetic lens, media coverage explicitly argued that anyone could produce a gifted child—'genius' could 'crash into the most humble home' and it was a 'genetic lottery'.[49]

At the same time, these tabloids also expressed surprise and even concern when giftedness was not concentrated within affluent families. Reading such coverage, it seems that the journalists, rather than the interviewees, were significant in positioning connections between class and intelligence. Indeed, the father of the new Eton captain was 'opening a bottle of champagne' to celebrate this news, while the mother stated confidently that '[i]f you force me to pin a label on us…then, yes, we're working class, of course we are. But I've never felt out of place or ill at ease at Eton.'[50] This type of coverage echoed 1930s sentiment where, Peter Mandler has argued, working-class children who reached grammar school

---

[43] Peter Mandler, *Crisis of the Meritocracy*, p. 19; Thomson, *The Problem of Mental Deficiency*; Wooldridge, *Measuring the Mind*; Bashford and Levine, *The Oxford Handbook of the History of Eugenics*; Mazumdar, *Eugenics Human Genetics and Human Failings*.
[44] 'Brain power just going to waste!', *Daily Mail*, 16 March 1976, p. 11.
[45] Nick Wood, 'Is your child a high flier?', *Daily Express*, 11 February 1986, p. 13.
[46] Lee-Potter, 'Our son, the new captain of Eton!', p. 7.   [47] Ibid.   [48] Ibid.
[49] 'Watch out, genius at work – and one's born every week', *Daily Express*, 20 August 1981, p. 9.
[50] Lee-Potter, 'Our son, the new captain of Eton!', p. 7. This idea was reiterated by an article in a National Association newsletter: written by a father who had grown up homeless, when his child was identified as 'gifted', and supported to a fee-paying school, he wrote he was 'so proud of our son, at a posh school, in a smart uniform'; and also that although he would drop the boy on the bus or in 'my big lorry', not 'some smart car', 'not once' did other parents 'look down on us as we thought they would', 'everyone was so kind' (Institute of Education, London, SA/5/1, Articles about Handwriting, 1983–1989, *Looking to their Future: The Newsletter of the National Association for Gifted Children*, Spring 1985, 'Do Dreams Come True?', p. 9.)

became 'visible and paraded', due to pride of their families, local authorities, and the labour movement more broadly.[51]

While popular tabloid press looked to highlight cases of success amongst working-class students, and emphasise that 'anyone' could be gifted, a different picture emerged in liberationist press. *Race Today*, for example, was launched in 1969 by the think-tank the Institute of Race Relations, and then later published by a collective, Race Today, as a leading outlet for discussing issues affecting Black communities in Britain and beyond. In 1975, the magazine described the case of an eleven-year-old boy, who had been assessed in the final grade of primary school as extremely gifted, receiving the highest possible grades. Despite this, the magazine wrote, his parents were home-schooling him, as he had been refused entry to the local grammar school following an interview with the headteacher. Describing a long history of tensions between this child's parents and the school, the magazine stated that the parents continued to engage in a 'long battle with the authorities' to redress this case. Overall, the paper noted that the urgency of this issue was compounded as the quality between grammar and comprehensive schools was stark across much of London. *Race Today* contended that a pupil with his qualifications '(especially if the pupil is white) would find no difficulty in finding a grammar school place....Alas not...—young, gifted and black.'[52] In a subsequent issue of this paper, a representative of the Inner London Education Authority replied to challenge this claim: arguing race was not relevant here; that the Authority would stop selecting pupils by ability in 1977; and that the Authority never made these decisions.[53] Regardless of the specificities of this case, it nonetheless shows how cases highlighted by the tabloid press—notably of white working-class boys making it to Eton—obscured broader debate about systematic issues of privilege, and particularly of race, in British schools.[54] The popular press

---

[51] Mandler, *Crisis of the Meritocracy*, p. 27.
[52] 'Young Gifted and Black', *Race Today*, April 1975, p. 77.
[53] 'I.L.E.A. Correction', *Race Today*, June 1975, p. 122.
[54] As contemporary materials from the National Union of Teachers and National Association of School Masters show, racist and sexist cultural assumptions pervaded school environments more broadly from the 1960s to the 1980s. Sources discussing racism in classrooms in this period include: MRC, 937/3/14/1, Universities & Left Review, no.5, Autumn 1958. 'The habit of violence'; MRC, 601/R/24/49, Marina Maxwell, 'Violence in the toilets: The experience of a black teacher in Brent schools', [1969]; MRC, MSS.639/11/43/5, 'National Union of Teachers Memorandum of Evidence submitted to Commonwealth Immigrants Advisory Council', 1963; MRC, NUT/6/7/Ra/4, National Union of Teachers, The N. U. T. View on the Education of Immigrants, 1967. Sources discussing sexism in classrooms in this period include: MRC, NSH/5/5/80, National Association of Schoolmasters, Men teachers for junior schools, 1950, pp. 3, 5–6. This argument was reiterated by the Association in MRC, NSH/5/5/77, National Association of Schoolmasters, Sex as a fundamental factor in education, 1950. Co-education was also questioned by the Association of Assistant Headmistresses into the 1960s, see: MRC, AAM/P/3/20, Association of Assistant Headmistresses, 'Conference on women and girls in co-educational schools', 1968. Examples of attempts to combat these stereotypes are: MRC, EOC/2/7/9, Equal Opportunities Commission, 'Ending sex-stereotyping in schools: A sourcebook for school-based teacher workshops', 1981; MRC, EOC/2/7/19, 'Letters to a thirteen year old—from members of the YWCA girl apprentice courses 1983–84, 1985; MRC, NUT/6/7/G/9, 'Towards equality for girls and boys: guidelines on countering sexism in schools', [c1989]. See also: MRC,

chose which 'exceptional' narratives to share—in the 1970s and 1980s, those of white, working-class boys, by the late 1990s and 2000s, also tales of children from Asian families displaying high academic achievement and acting as 'model minorities'.[55] In doing so, newspaper coverage positioned achievement beyond the white middle classes as shocking and unusual, yet also as demonstrative of a fundamental system of fairness and equality in education.

Beyond these examples, focused on individuals, the tabloid press in the 1970s and 1980s also looked more broadly, to make vague, ill-defined claims that gifted children must shape Britain's 'national futures'. Throughout the 1970s, right-wing tabloid press emphasised that gifted children were critical for forging 'our future'.[56] Children were presented by the *Daily Mail* as the 'most important asset that Britain possesses', and 'our greatest hidden asset', 'the guardians of Britain's future', and a 'huge, untapped source of Britain's future prosperity'.[57] One woman, from Cumbria, writing to the *Mail* in 1977, complimented enrichment centres for gifted children set up in Devon. This woman's letter did not focus on the benefits to the children themselves, but rather on the 'future prosperity and security' of the British nation.[58]

Tabloids highlighted a broad range of fields to which gifted children could contribute—they could be 'scientists, writers, administrators, generals and politicians', and contribute to 'the fields of science, medicine, engineering, law, music, etc.'[59] Newspapers described the prestigious citizens which children could grow up to be—'potential Einsteins'—without analysing whether the thinkers to whom the children were being compared had themselves been identified as gifted children.[60] The assertion that gifted children were a national asset was entwined with concerns about British national decline and insignificance. In 1973, the *Daily Express* warned that the country 'is not so rich in natural resources that it can

---

MSS.639/11/65/6, National Union of Teachers, 'An enquiry into the education of pupils between the ages of 13 and 16 of average or less than average ability', May 1962. See also Laura Tisdall, *A Progressive Education? How Childhood Changed in Mid-twentieth-century* (Manchester: Manchester University Press, 2020) on the able-bodied, white, male model of the 'ideal' school student.

[55] For examples of such coverage please see: Jane Kelly, 'Brightest Family in Britain', *Daily Mail*, 16 October 1998; Fran Abrams, 'A Touch of Class', *Sunday Telegraph*, 3 November 1991. For discussion of the 'model minority' trope, please see: Madeline Y. Hsu, *The Good Immigrants: How the Yellow Peril Became the Model Minority* (Princeton: Princeton University Press, 2015); Alice Bradbury, 'From model minorities to disposable models: the de-legitimisation of educational success through discourses of authenticity', *Discourse: Studies in the Cultural Politics of Education*, 34 (4) (2013), pp. 548–561.

[56] Ian Smith, 'Treated like a freak for being clever', *Daily Mail*, 28 November 1978, pp. 6–7.

[57] K. D. Barritt and E. Price, 'Come on, Britain, use your brains', *Daily Mail*, 20 April 1979, p. 36; June Southworth, 'Everything we all need to know about gifted children', *Daily Mail*, 18 August 1979, pp. 6–7; Smith, 'Treated like a freak for being clever'.

[58] 'Letters', *Daily Mail*, 15 June 1977, p. 27.

[59] Smith, 'Treated like a freak for being clever'; Barritt and Price, 'Come on, Britain, use your brains', p. 36.

[60] Smith, 'Treated like a freak for being clever'; Christopher White, 'At last, those bright children get a chance to shine', *Daily Mail*, 9 June 1977, p. 9.

afford to let slip its greatest wealth—brainpower'.[61] The economic framing of this rhetoric, with gifted children as an 'asset', 'resource', or economic unit, recurred in 1970s economic crises, and is a long-standing type of rhetoric in moments of concern about 'national efficiency'.[62]

Rhetoric did not focus on children's happiness or well-being, but rather on what they could achieve, and at times their destructive potential. In 1974, the *Daily Mirror* declared dramatically that gifted children were either 'tomorrow's business leaders, teachers, artists, scientists, musicians. Or tomorrow's dropouts, delinquents and potential suicides. The difference often depends on whether parents and teachers recognise these "super kids"—and treat them accordingly'.[63] While Louise Jackson has argued that the trope of deviant youth and delinquency was 'a motif for the defence of an older imagined social order' in the 1960s, discussion of gifted youth, particularly by the 1970s, reflected such fears and, simultaneously, hopes about national futures and possibilities.[64]

Indeed, these debates revealed conservative insecurities about Britain's capacity and future in the world. British conservative press in the 1960s and 1970s spoke admiringly of other school systems and their treatment of the gifted. As early as 1966, an article in *The Times* contrasted the 'special schools' for gifted children in America and Russia with how the British 'authorities' feared the social segregation of 'egghead communities'.[65] By the late 1970s and 1980s, comparisons in British newspapers began to operate more broadly, and to position British education against a range of emerging economies, with little consideration of the broader political contexts. In 1978, writing for the *Mail*, Christopher Rowlands discussed Claire, a gifted eleven-year-old who was 'a victim of the State system' in Britain.[66] For Rowland, British education was not 'geared to cope' with Claire's talents, but '[i]f she lived in Russia, China, Cuba or East Germany, she would be treated as someone very special'.[67] Relatedly, in an article about Singapore entitled, 'Full of eastern promise' for the *Mail* in 1989, journalist Graham Turner expressed admiration for a system 'based on the survival of the most able'.[68] He discussed competitive exams whereby children were separated aged nine into a 'fast stream, a slow stream and what amounts to a "no" stream'.[69] Here, Turner wrote wistfully, 'there are no patronising "progressives" leading their pupils down the primrose path of educational unreality, very few mixed ability classes in

---

[61] Peter Chambers, 'What happens to IQ kids who are too bright for the teachers?' *Daily Express*, 17 April 1973, p. 11.
[62] Mandler, *Crisis of the Meritocracy*, p. 19.
[63] Richard Sear, 'Superkids', *Daily Mirror*, 19 November 1974, p. 7.
[64] Jackson, '"The coffee club menace"', p. 289.
[65] 'New body aims to get help for the gifted child', *The Times*, 18 June 1966, p. 10.
[66] Christopher Rowlands, 'Why gifted Claire is a misfit', *Daily Mail*, 9 August 1978, p. 6.
[67] Ibid. There is a whole file of press clippings from British press interested in selection and education in the USSR at: Institute of Education, London, SIM/3/3, Press Cuttings—Newspaper Articles.
[68] Graham Turner, 'Full of eastern promise', *Daily Mail*, 23 June 1989, p. 32.   [69] Ibid.

secondary schools, no peace studies, no pamphlets explaining that it can be fun to have homosexual parents'.[70] However, the article cautioned that there was also 'plenty to criticise' in a system that 'curtails childhood ...pursues success ruthlessly and is distinctly unsentimental about failure'.[71]

Ideas of seeking out gifted children in Britain as national leaders, drawing on a range of comparative international environments, have long-standing precedents but must also be situated within the cultures of New Right tabloid politics. More broadly, these tabloids often used such debates to critique comprehensive education, women's movements, and LGBTQ+ education. The conservative press argued that a burning and 'new' interest in equality, typified by the social movements of a decade before and by advocates of free speech and liberalism, were damaging the progress of gifted youth. Articles published in the *Daily Mail* criticised Britain's 'equality-obsessed society': a system 'geared to the ideal of equality at all costs' and pursuing 'dreary egalitarianism'.[72] Another *Mail* article published in 1971 was entitled, 'How to help these bright boys along'. Analysing the plight of gifted children—carelessly identified as 'boys'—Dobbin stated that, '[w]e must not neglect our high fliers because we have become obsessed by equality'.[73] For *Mail* columnists, the pursuit of equality was so powerful that parents of gifted children refused to have their photos taken or names published, 'as if having a rare intelligence were some kind of social stigma'.[74]

Definitions of 'equality' in these debates were fuzzy and porous, but broadly used to critique 'several modern trends'.[75] Schools were often the focus of such reporting. A *Mail* article in 1973 argued that 'bright pupils fail' due to 'anti-intellectualism in schools', low expectations from parents and teachers, and shifts towards group work and peer-led marking.[76] According to this article by the paper's education correspondent, a recent report found that 'some teachers' were 'biased' against giving extra help to the gifted, feeling it would 'conflict with their notions of "equality"'.[77] In a *Mail* article from 1978, this critique was expanded to challenge the 'State education machine': both teachers and the governmental and educational systems underpinning their work were endangering the nation's future.[78] Schools were not the only target of conservative critique around equality, however, and the *Mail* also pinned the blame for failures in gifted education on the Women's Liberation Movement. In a 1981 article, 'Mother and Superwoman', the *Mail* argued that a woman could not have a 'perfectly planned, gifted child', concentrating 'wholly' on its development', while also being 'Superwoman'. Thus,

---

[70] Ibid.   [71] Ibid.
[72] Ray Massey and Ray Honeyford, 'A dream of genius', *Daily Mail*, 16 April 1991, p. 32; Rowlands, 'Why gifted Claire is a misfit', p. 6; Smith, 'Treated like a freak for being clever'.
[73] Jane Dobbin, 'How to help these bright boys along', *Daily Mail*, 31 May 1971, p. 10.
[74] Smith, 'Treated like a freak for being clever'.
[75] Max Wilkinson, 'Why bright pupils fail', *Daily Mail*, 20 September 1973, p. 21.
[76] Wilkinson, 'Why bright pupils fail', p. 21.   [77] Ibid.
[78] Rowlands, 'Why gifted Claire is a misfit', p. 6.

the article pronounced, '[c]hild-centred education is in direct conflict with Women's Lib.'[79] Equality was a proxy through which to question not only the treatment of gifted children in schools, but new social norms and structures. As Laura Tisdall has argued, any shifts towards 'progressive' or 'child-centred' education faced a 'backlash' from conservative commentators and original supporters.[80] Conservative commentators were able to mobilise ideas of giftedness as part of their critique.

This tabloid critique had clear connections to broader agendas of New Right politics. There was also a level of media pushback against these ideas, particularly that the gifted child was *only* valuable because of their potential contributions to Britain's future. Writing in 1979, an education correspondent for *The Sunday Times* stated that the 'real justification' for treating gifted children differently was 'not that our future national prosperity depends on their brains'. This proposition, the journalist stated, was not only 'extremely doubtful' but also 'Philistine'.[81] Nonetheless, they still recognised that gifted children were seen as a national resource and, indeed, offered their own vision of the children's purpose: to 'inspire others'.[82]

Even so, conservative tabloid visions that gifted children must be identified, and potentially even segregated from families and peers to begin to restore Britain's global fortunes, were highly significant. These newspapers were highly critical of what they framed as 'egalitarianism' or 'equality', and associated ideas of selection with 'natural difference'. Such ideas were also echoed beyond newspapers, for example, by prominent advocates of selective education. Lord James of Rusholme, for example, discussed in Chapter Two, argued in a speech during the 1970s that, '[t]he increasingly egalitarian temper of our kind of society resents and resists any frank acceptance of differences in human endowment.'[83] Purported support for the gifted, then, could justify critique of 'equality', particularly if mobilised in defence of an imagined national future.

The National Association for Gifted Children and Britain's Elites of the Future

The National Association related to these debates about equality, elitism, and national futures in complex ways. The Association framed its establishment, as

---

[79] 'Mother and Superwoman', *Daily Mail*, 10 September 1981, p. 12.
[80] Tisdall, *A Progressive Education?*, ch. 7.
[81] Bodleian Library, Per 264505 e.49, NAGC, *Journal of the Gifted Child*, Autumn 1979, 'Comprehensive Schools and the Gifted Child', pp. 43–44.
[82] Ibid.
[83] Borthwick Institute for Archives, York, JAM/2/1/1, Scripts, Speeches and Lectures, 'The Education of the Gifted Child', Lord James of Rusholme, 1970s, p. 5.

discussed in Chapters Two and Three, to aide families living with complex issues of child mental wellbeing and care. The Association emphasised frequently that IQ tests were arbitrary, and also undertook measures to reach out to families from a diverse range of backgrounds, as discussed. Nonetheless, the Association did at times reflect broader interests in gifted children as holding promising futures, of course, with various activities offering related suggestions to their child members.

The Association communicated with psychologists who believed that the gifted could be identified from a very young age, and that they must be mobilised into leadership roles. Notably, for example, in 1977, Ronald Illingworth, a famous paediatrician, lectured at the National Association conference in Burton Manor, Cheshire. For Illingworth, it was worth trying to assess a child's potential, because 'We have to remember that the future of a country depends on the quality of its children.'[84] Illingworth had assessed 850 babies for a local authority for potential adoption, 230 of which were followed up to school age. When assessed at six weeks or six months, he had graded them as average, superior, above average, below average, and inferior. When assessed again by educational psychologists, who did not know of this grading, aged six or seven and using 'the standard tests', the scores had correlated with those he made earlier.[85] He found that specific measures were more important predictors than others—age of sitting and walking had been the 'least important', while 'alertness, interest in his surroundings, curiosity, concentration, determination, responsiveness, and the glint in his eyes, and the quality of his vocalisations' had been most important.[86]

However, the Association had no intention of using psychological testing to identify all gifted children. Indeed, the National Association's internal publications and engagement with families alike emphasised the significant limits of psychological testing. In the March 1979 edition of the organisation's newsletter *Looking to their Future*, for example, there was an article by the Senior Educational Psychologist for North Gwent.[87] He emphasised that an IQ of 140 was, of course, 'not a magic dividing line between intellectual excellence and the dross of mediocrity', but rather 'simply a convenient reference point.'[88] He stated that the limitations of this research were at times forgotten, but that,

> Having bestowed an I.Q. of 195 on an 8 year old prodigal a psychologist cannot gaze into his crystal ball and see a 'First in Greats' inexorably rising from the clearing mists.... our powers of prediction are not that certain.[89]

---

[84] NAGC, *Looking to their Future*, November 1977, 'Predicting potential and helping the child to achieve it', R. S. Illingworth, p. 1.
[85] Ibid.   [86] Ibid.
[87] NAGC archives, *Looking to their Future*, March 1979, 'Gifted Children: Psychologist's Eye View', p. 15.
[88] Ibid.   [89] Ibid.

Instead, he urged readers to view intelligence 'as a repertoire of abilities rather than an amount of something to which a person is limited', and to use 'flexible rather than standardised testing procedures'.[90] An assumption that the gifted existed as a group, and could be identified, remained here, but this article still complicated any assumed path that a 'gifted' child must 'rise' to academic or national success.

Furthermore, typically the Association's practical advice for parents and supporters did not focus on these tests. This was made clear in a publication by the Education Committee of the National Association, for example, published in November 1989 and entitled *Help with Bright Children*.[91] Pragmatically, this publication emphasised that intelligence tests 'can be useful' and were 'the best single predictor of academic achievement that we have'.[92] Nonetheless, the publication stated, 'they are not particularly good predictors, nor are they very accurate measures of intellectual ability'.[93] This was because, the report stated, their results were shaped by 'time of day, mood, anxiety level, physical conditions, tiredness and so on'.[94] Such factors of mood, rather than cultural differences, were the key focus for this report in showing how these tests were arbitrary, although the report did acknowledge that 'learning conditions' as well as 'intelligence' determined achievement and also that, for some students, 'cultural background may not enable him to make the required responses'.[95] Therefore, the report did not advise testing children under school age and advised caution when assessing results from children in the early years of primary school.[96]

This type of engagement with IQ tests was echoed in handbooks by other voluntary groups in this period: Peter Congdon, for example, founder of the Gifted Children's Information Centre in Solihull, acknowledged in 1978 that these tests 'may be unsuitable for a child who comes from a markedly different cultural background', while also suggesting that they were the 'best measure of potential which we have at present'.[97] Writing for the journal of the National Association in 1979, Congdon described how all children in North Warwickshire were being screened for IQ between the ages of 8 and 9.[98] The county's plans were developed in collaboration with experts from the National Association, Her Majesty's Inspectorate of the Department of Education and Science, and the University of Warwick.[99] Tests were administered by a local educational psychologist, to each

---

[90] Ibid.
[91] The Education Committee of the NAGC, *Help with Bright Children* (London: National Association for Gifted Children, 1989).
[92] Ibid., p. 16.   [93] Ibid.   [94] Ibid.
[95] Ibid., pp. 16 and 19.   [96] Ibid., p. 16.
[97] Peter J. Congdon, *Helping Children of High Intelligence: A Handbook for Parents* (Solihull: Gifted Children's Information Centre, 1978).
[98] Peter J. Congdon, 'How North Warwickshire identifies gifted children', *Journal of the Gifted Child*, Autumn 1979, p. 68.
[99] Ibid., p. 67.

child teachers identified as 'potentially gifted'.[100] Final lists were made in dialogue between teacher scores and IQ testing, and then parents were contacted to work with teachers, the educational psychologist, a senior psychiatric social worker, and a liaison officer.[101] This was a local experiment but highly significant for those affected. Congdon acknowledged that '[t]he very act of identification has resulted in a change of attitude on the part of both parents and teachers. As one teacher put it when considering a particular child, "I began to see him in a new light".[102]

The National Association did occasionally mention the significance of the gifted for leadership or the future of the nation in its press statements.[103] Nonetheless, its broader aims were not framed around identifying future leaders, but rather helping all families and young people struggling with high intelligence. The Association argued frequently that such work was significant for creating an equal society, rather than identifying an elite. Association newsletters from the 1970s and 1980s are full of articles discussing how teachers wrongly assumed that gifted education was 'incompatible' with the 'philosophy' of a comprehensive school, or misunderstanding that 'social pressure towards equality of opportunity' had to mean one form of education for all.[104] A 1977 National Association newsletter bemoaned 'notions of elitism that bedevil this subject', and argued that the organisation 'could not stress too often that we are not concerned with privilege or preferential treatment but with meeting the educational needs of ALL pupils including the gifted'.[105] The Association continued to argue into the 1980s that curriculum development for gifted children would help 'the whole education system in Great Britain'.[106] These arguments were, to an extent, heard in broader policy work. In a pamphlet of 1970, for example, the Stop the Eleven Plus campaign group emphasised that 'research shows that comprehensive schools do not "hold back" the bright child and that these children, by their presence, markedly raise the standards of the remainder and hence of our community as a whole'.[107] The National Association, then, like many other campaign groups of this moment,

---

[100] Ibid. [101] Ibid. [102] Ibid.

[103] '"Miracle" view of gifted children criticized', *The Times*, 9 November 1970, p. 2.; Linton Mitchell, 'Where are all the missing Children of Gold?', *Reading Evening Post*, 21 July 1975, p. 6.

[104] NAGC, *Looking to their Future*, November 1977, 'The gifted child in the community', p. 5; NAGC, Newsletters, May 1969, p. 4. The Association wrote that gifted children 'should not be treated as members of an Elite but they *are* "different" and need all our understanding and help to learn to live with their "differentness" so that they can develop their gifts and play their part as valuable members of society'. NAGC, *Looking to their Future*, November 1977, 'The gifted child in the community', pp. 7–8.

[105] NAGC, *Looking to their Future*, November 1977, 'The gifted child in the community', pp. 7–8.

[106] NAGC, The National Association for Gifted Children, *Annual Report 1981*, 'Message from the President', p. 3. This idea remained in later decades: New Labour, in the *Excellence in Schools* white paper, explicitly argued that 'The pursuit of excellence was too often equated with elitism' (*Excellence in Schools*, July 1997, Cm 3681 http://www.educationengland.org.uk/documents/wp1997/excellence-in-schools.html (17 November 2020).)

[107] MRC, *Stop the eleven plus*, campaign pamphlet, 1970 https://mrc-catalogue.warwick.ac.uk/records/CST/4/6/5/49 (25 November 2020).

was broadly in favour of gifted children being taught in comprehensive schools, rather than grammar schools or specialist institutions, believing also that it was to their social and educational benefit.

The National Association's specific activities, however, across a broad range of voluntary branches and volunteers, did at times suggest the influence of ideas of futures, leadership, and elites. Central magazines for child-members suggested this, for example by offering significant information about global events (such as the Space Race), or showing youth clubs observing rocket launches, space agencies sending information to schools, and reviews of books about 'Tomorrow's World'.[108] At times Association newsletters asked young members to think of themselves as helping others across the world, if not leading them. In its Spring 1979 Bulletin, the Association asked children to reflect on the idea that 'THE YOUNG PEOPLE OF THIS COUNTRY HAVE A GREAT DEAL TO OFFER TO HELP THOSE LESS FORTUNATE THAN THEMSELVES—BOTH WITH IDEAS AND DIRECT HELP'.[109] The magazine asked children to undertake projects on key themes, such as war ('One day a "small" war could grow into the nightmare of total devastation by nuclear weapons. What can we do to begin to lessen the risks and start building a lasting peace?');[110] hunger ('How can we achieve a sense of unity in the world when some of us have so much and others lack the basic necessities?');[111] and freedom ('All over the world the basic human rights are being denied because of race, colour or belief. In Britain, freedom is being eroded. What can we do to turn the tide?')[112]

In looking to equip children for global roles, the Association's Bristol and Isle of Wight Saturday Clubs taught children Esperanto, a language created for international use. One teacher in Bristol, Mrs C. C. Preston, told the Association's April 1978 newsletter that, 'in taking up Esperanto one takes up a key to world understanding and to world harmony'.[113] Association magazines also advertised 'Project Trident'; a 'year between scheme' enabling young people who left school at eighteen to participate in voluntary service, work away from home, and take 'challenging Outward Bound courses, Brathay expeditions or Ocean Youth Club sailing cruises'.[114] The purpose of these experiences were to show students, before they entered university or established careers, 'how and where they fit in the wider community and what it means to be trusted, respected, needed by and important to other people'.[115] Demonstrating the significance of this work, the Association also sought to establish its own small 'in between' scheme, describing

---

[108] NAGC archives, Bletchley (hereafter NAGC), Dialogue, Easter 1982, 'Youth club rockets into space', p. 11; NAGC, *Explorers Unlimited Bulletin*, Autumn 1979, 'Tomorrow's World', p. 8.
[109] NAGC, *Explorers Unlimited Bulletin*, Spring 1979, 'Help your fellow man?', p. 1.
[110] Ibid.   [111] Ibid.   [112] Ibid.
[113] NAGC, Mrs C. C. Preston, 'The Esperanto Class', *Looking to their Future*, April 1978, p. 8; NAGC, 'Goings on in Northern Ireland, *Looking to their Future*, November 1980, p. 12.
[114] NAGC, *Dialogue*, Easter 1982, 'Project Trident: Year between scheme', p. 6.   [115] Ibid.

the work of its first participant in 1982.[116] Further positioning its members as global citizens, the Association helped children to identify and communicate with-pen pals from America and Australia, looking to develop conversations that 'might eventually spread all over our beautiful little world'.[117]

The Association, therefore, was interested at times in engaging its youth membership as responsible global citizens. Yet the Association was not necessarily pushing the vision of the young as elites of the future, as present in the tabloid press or influential psychology. Susannah Wright, studying the League of Nations Union in the interwar period, explores how this 'large and prominent' group had branches in many schools, and pushed a 'liberal-internationalist version of "world citizenship" that accommodated existing loyalties to nation and empire as well as loyalty to the wider international sphere'.[118] The National Association, by contrast, was a space were these ideas may have been lived out and contested, but focused primarily on ideas of social struggle and psychological burden for the gifted.

Young People Engage with Leadership in 'the World'

Archival evidence demonstrates that some gifted children understood and recognised the national and global expectations placed on their futures in the 1970s and 1980s, but also that many revised and renegotiated them. Many of the gifted young enjoyed thinking about global affairs and their potentially exciting role in the future, and many had great awareness of warfare. Yet, for others, this was a burden and they focused more on ideas of individual happiness and wellbeing as a priority.

The magazines of the National Association display children's stories, poetry, letters, and opinion pieces. These diverse forms of writing show that child members positioned their lives in a global context, and that awareness of world events shaped their thinking and frames of reference. For example, first, in a 1982 edition of the magazine *Dialogue*, aimed at children aged twelve to seventeen, one sixteen-year-old criticised the nuclear deterrence defence system as 'farcical', given that 'many non-aligned countries have developed or could develop weapons of massive death potential', and that neither side would be engaging with similar premises.[119] Second, in a 1979 edition of *Explorers Unlimited*, aimed at children aged five to twelve, a child who recorded their age as '13 or 14' wrote a short horror story, in which a fortune-teller predicted that a man would live for

[116] Ibid.   [117] NAGC, *Dialogue*, Easter 1982, 'Last words—first', p. 3.
[118] Susannah Wright, 'Creating liberal-internationalist world citizens: League of Nations Union junior branches in English secondary schools, 1919–1939', *Paedagogica Historica*, 56 (3) (2020), pp. 321–340.
[119] NAGC, *Dialogue*, Easter 1982, 'Political Forum', p. 9.

only three more days. Feeling that this was superstitious and unlikely, the man in question 'was taking no chances anyway', and on the third night after this encounter unplugged his various electronic items from the mains, turned off his gas supply, and closed all his windows. When he heard a plane fly overhead, he thought, '[p]erhaps it was Russian. It might be carrying a bomb, an atomic bomb. There might be another war'.[120] Writers to the magazines, hence, showed how children identified as gifted were influenced by contemporary debates around the Cold War and the legacies of World War Two.[121] It shows also that these influences shaped their political discussions and their fiction. Adults chose to display these particular testimonies within the magazines, but children did write these letters and stories. More children subsequently read these publications, and thus ideas about war and a changing global order continued to be woven into their daily lives.

Troublingly, some students also reflected casual racist cultural stereotypes of the time, reiterating them as small details in their stories and letters. This was visible for example in one child's casual use of a racially derogatory term in a poem, as a nickname for their dog.[122] Another wrote a poem about an imagined old woman, living near Glasgow. It stated that she lived in line with many stereotypes of the aged: she kept a cat, suffered with 'rhumatics', ate chocolate-covered digestive biscuits, and read Mills and Boon. As part of this poem containing casually racist language, her 'yellowy bulky cooker door' was compared to another racial slur.[123] One review of a joke book highlighted the joke 'What is sandpaper? An Irishman's map of the desert.'[124] Again building on contemporary national stereotypes, other book reviews discussed a 'tearaway sister who arrives from Ireland declaring she has run away and has come to live with them', for example.[125] A review of a book (*Timewarps* by John Gribbin) stated that it used 'oriental religions, with their unfamiliar views of time', to inform its narrative.[126]

Engagement with fiction hence reflected the stereotypes that these children and young people lived among, and these affected how they viewed themselves in relation to 'the world'. Yet engagement with certain books could also provide a bridge to empathy and was, as one child wrote, a window through which they could see 'how life may be for some people'.[127] This was visible in reviews in particular of fiction about Northern Ireland; a close neighbour, living under the Troubles during this period. In 1982, a thirteen-year-old's review of *The Twelfth Day of July*, for example, stated that 'this story brings home the facts about the

---

[120] NAGC, *Explorers Unlimited*, Autumn 1979, 'Pantophobia: Fear of everything', p. 14.
[121] NAGC, *Explorers Unlimited*, Summer 1979, 'Father Allan', p. 9.
[122] NAGC, *Explorers Unlimited*, December 1971, 'Dennis the Dachsund', p. 6.
[123] NAGC, *Dialogue*, Easter 1982, 'Not far from Hampden', p. 7.
[124] NAGC, *Explorers Unlimited*, March 1981, 'More Crazy Jokes', p. 13.
[125] NAGC, *Dialogue*, Christmas 1981, 'Hostages to Fortune', p. 7.
[126] NAGC, *Explorers Unlimited*, Summer 1979, 'Timewarps', p. 4.
[127] NAGC, *Explorers Unlimited*, n.d, 'The Street That Disappeared', n.p.

differences felt between Protestant and Catholic people in Belfast'.[128] Explorers also reviewed books about, for example, youthful attempts to help 'an illegan [sic] Kenyan immigrant' to evade authorities and find his uncle.[129] Another collection of short stories, *Long Journey Home* by Julius Lester, was said to 'give[s] a vivid insight into black American history', showing 'the hardships, cruelty, and prejudice encountered by slaves and ex-slaves before and after liberation'.[130] The fourteen-year-old reviewer wrote that this was a 'delightful and well written book with six stories—a joy for anyone who likes good short stories or who is keenly interested in American history'.[131] These books were then entertaining for the readers, and presenting detached imagined worlds, while also 'about real people and real problems' with plots that were 'not altogether improbable'.[132]

In part, the gifted young in these magazines expressed ideas of British and particularly English superiority, in addition to these stereotypes, reiterating ideas in the tabloid press. This manifested in multiple ways. Having read one account of the foundation of 'civilisation', and reviewed it, one sixteen-year-old author wrote into the November 1980 issue of the *Explorers Bulletin* to state that, '[t]he biggest problem that England faces at the moment is that the population is too large. Many feel they have no share in the government of the state and that it is them against the state.'[133] Another reviewer questioned whether 'the loss of separate identity seems to be the price we have to pay for world peace'.[134] For these students 'England' was under threat in this moment. For other students writing in, 'developing countries' required assistance from elite British children. While those in what student-authors called 'developing countries' were described as undernourished and unable to access healthcare or educational services, gifted readers in Britain were urged to issue 'new commitment from every single one of us'. Indeed, the Explorers organisation urged, individuals or groups of school-aged children must provide art, written work, painting, photography, dance. These media, from such apparently powerful authors, were presented as part of broader efforts to alleviate the huge issues of technological and wealth inequality, war, natural disasters, and restricted freedoms.[135]

There is also evidence from young people's writings that other British children felt pressured to contribute to the nation's future, without a clear understanding of how or why they should do this. In 1979, a headteacher from Devon sent the Association a poem written by a gifted boy aged eight. The child's parents had moved house so that he could attend this school at four years of age. Echoing the

---

[128] NAGC, 'Bookworms', *Dialogue*, Easter 1982, p. 12.
[129] NAGC, 'The Runaway Summer', *Gallimaufry*, Easter 1982, p. 14.
[130] NAGC, 'Long Journey Home', *Explorers Unlimited*, Summer 1979, p. 14. [131] Ibid.
[132] NAGC, 'The Runaway Summer', *Gallimaufry*, Easter 1982, p. 14.
[133] NAGC, 'Community spirit?', *Explorers Bulletin*, November 1980, p. 28.
[134] NAGC, 'Or separate identities?', *Explorers Bulletin*, November 1980, p. 29.
[135] NAGC, 'Help your fellow man?', *Explorers Unlimited*, Spring 1979, p. 1.

thirteen-year-old discussed above, the eight-year-old child suggested that he viewed himself primarily—even solely—as a 'mind'. Visiting a local manor house, the boy wrote, '[m]y mind arrived before my body.... My mind flew away like a leaf in the wind'.[136] The child closed the poem by reflecting on his 'two lives': one 'rushed and physical', the other 'quiet and peaceful / Allowing time for my mind to grow'.[137] This assertion demonstrated the boy's concern about his own mental development, and his present sense of stress or anxiety.

Children labelled as gifted thus at times acutely felt and criticised the expectations placed upon them. Other children, however, rejected or ignored these expectations entirely—and adult-led publications were also equally keen to chart children's alternative ambitions. A ten-year-old, also identified as gifted, told the National Association newsletter of 1979 that he had reshaped grandiose visions of his national role. This child would 'like to become a barrister and a Member of Parliament as I find law and politics fascinating and I love talking'.[138] While aiming for powerful positions in this testimony, the child couched his future in terms of what he would 'like' to do, rather than what he felt obliged to do. While his preferred imagined future—in that moment—was pursuing law or politics, potentially productive pathways for a gifted child, he stated that he would pursue these routes because he found them 'fascinating' and 'love[d] talking'.[139] Again, this testimony was chosen and presented by a voluntary organisation, but nonetheless provided space in which the child could renegotiate and determine their visions of their own futures, aside from national and global agendas.

These magazines are complex spaces. While, as Wright has shown, voluntary organisations had long used 'education, intellectual exchange, and youth movement activity' to spread internationalist norms, children also pushed back against these concepts.[140] Particularly by the individualist years of the 1970s, 1980s, and 1990s, newspapers and even adult-curated child magazines were interested in presenting children's rejection of their broader global roles, and this must be read in conversation with changing ideas of childhood precocity as well as in line with cultural imaginations of Britain's declining global place. Young people identified as gifted drew on prevalent stereotypes about the wider world, and British military victory and moral leadership, which shaped their ideas of themselves as 'elites of the future'. However, these children also engaged thoughtfully with contemporary fictional and non-fictional accounts about life in other countries, thinking carefully about how life must be for the young across the world. These

---

[136] Bodleian Library, Per 264505 e. 4, NAGC, *Journal of the Gifted Child*, Autumn 1979, 'The Highly Gifted Child', Phyllis Wallbank, p. 71.
[137] Ibid., p. 70.
[138] Bodleian Library, Per 264505 e. 4, NAGC, *Journal of the Gifted Child*, Autumn 1979, 'Saturday Club', p. 46.
[139] Ibid., p. 46. [140] Wright, 'Creating liberal-internationalist world citizens'.

young people also, at times, ignored or rejected ideas of a global role entirely, thinking primarily instead in terms of individual fulfilment.

Conclusion

Chapter Three traced how the National Association looked to recruit young people who could benefit from being identified and supported as 'gifted'. It analysed also how the organisation created specialist voluntary spaces for the gifted young, and described how the gifted young received and reshaped these in the 1970s and 1980s. These spaces saw free play, structured and led by young people themselves, that focused on a distinct constellation of interests around rural life, science, ancient history, and logic puzzles. Chapter Four has shown how the ideas of gifted children also had great significance beyond these specific voluntary spaces in the 1970s and 1980s. Indeed, psychologist Cyril Burt also published significant amounts of research in the mid-to-late twentieth century positioning the gifted child within debates about genetic inheritance and intelligence, where connections were being made more broadly by racial scientists in this period. Tabloid press also casually used language around the genetics of the gifted young, and expressed surprise when gifted children came from working-class backgrounds. Conservative newspapers also expressed anxiety about Britain's place in the world, in part to build popular support against egalitarian or equalities, left-wing policies, and this strengthened notions of popular individualism. Eugenics, then, often considered to have 'swept the world' primarily from the late nineteenth to mid-twentieth century, also had a longer-lasting legacy.[141] As Bashford argues, later manifestations are not the same as nineteenth- and early twentieth-century eugenics, but, nonetheless, we have analytical insight to gain from asking, 'Where did eugenics go?' after 1945.[142] In this examination, we see that strands of eugenicist thought continued to swirl around the gifted young, in the late twentieth century: factions of psychology and media continued to represent intelligence as innate, and as gifted more to some children than others. A focus on population growth and change, central to early twentieth-century eugenics, had largely dissipated in these late twentieth-century debates, though ideas of 'national stock' were occasionally still present. Eugenic ideas then continued to operate, in part.

---

[141] Bashford and Levine (eds), *The Oxford Handbook of the History of Eugenics*, quote from abstract, chapters throughout discuss case studies to make this point.
[142] Bashford, 'Epilogue: where did eugenics go?', p. 540. See also: Rubahanna Amannah Choudhury, 'The forgotten children: The Association of Parents of Backward Children and the Legacy of Eugenics in Britain, 1946–1960', Thesis submitted for the Degree of Doctor of Philosophy at Oxford Brookes University, December 2015 <https://radar.brookes.ac.uk/radar/file/26b8d017-0527-4006-8029-0426ea259b75/1/choudhury2015forgottenRADAR.pdf> (26 March 2024).

The ideas of the gifted child discussed in Chapters Three and Four may seem difficult to reconcile. On the one hand, the gifted child was likely to be born from privilege, a form of 'national stock', which must be identified and mobilised to national advantage. On the other, anyone could be intellectually gifted, and these children were often desperate figures in need of help and support, who could only flourish within specific voluntary environments. While seemingly disparate, these ideas must be analysed in conjunction. Notably, the National Association had to conduct its voluntary support work against the background of these psychological and tabloid ideas. Further, young people, as we have seen, were influenced by broader debates about Britain's place in the world and also by visions of future elites. Whether they looked to reshape or repeat these ideas, young people were aware of, and influenced by, stereotypes of Britishness, Englishness, nationhood and otherhood, which also shaped tabloid print. As such, these young people operated within a distinct form of 'waithood'; while told that they were 'future elites', they consistently thought carefully and in doing so 'destabilise[d] privilege' and 're-imagine[d] spatialised power relations'.[143]

Notably, all those interested in gifted children by the 1970s and 1980s were framing their arguments around equality, elitism, and leadership. Yet various actors had hugely varying relationships with these fuzzy concepts—from Burt and the tabloids' purported anxiety that 'egalitarianism' was preventing the gifted from fulfilling their leadership destinies, to the National Association's argument that the gifted were not 'elite' but rather must be helped as part of an equal state. The gifted child was, in the 1970s and 1980s, a key symbol of this cleavage in society, and these 'elites of the future' would potentially reshape it.

'Gifted Children' in Britain and the World: Elitism and Equality since 1945. Jennifer Crane, Oxford University Press.
© Jennifer Crane 2025. DOI: 10.1093/9780198928881.003.0005

---

[143] On waithood, see: Tatek Abebe, 'Lost futures? Educated youth precarity and protests in the Oromia region, Ethiopia', *Children's Geographies*, 18 (6) (2020), pp. 584–600; Alinda M. Honwana, *The Time of Youth: Work, Social Change, and Politics in Africa* (London: Kumarian Press, 2012). The quote in this sentence is taken from: Janine Wiles, 'Health geographies 1: Unlearning privilege', *Progress in Human Geography*, 46 (1) (2021), p. 220.

Industrial and Industrious Future Elites, 1990–2010

> 'We are the National Academy for Gifted and Talented Youth, or the "boffs", the "geeks", the "bright ones", the ones "who can look after themselves", and for the first time the Government has set up a scheme to support and stretch the top five per cent of England's youth.'
>
> *Modern Records Centre, UWA/PUB/DEP/29/5, Aspire (magazine) for gifted and talented youth, 2002–2007, December 2002, 'Summer School 2002—a student's view', p. 8.*

The quote above is from one of the first participants on the New Labour-funded National Academy for Gifted and Talented Youth summer school, which started work in 2001. This participant emphasised the uniqueness of the opportunity available to them—this was indeed 'the first time' that the British government had funded such a scheme or tried to make a national programme of gifted education. The quote also shows how young people referred to themselves in this context, seeing themselves as outliers or being classified as such by peers.

This chapter argues that interest in the gifted child fully entered national policies, for the first time, in the 1990s and 2000s. While previously this interest was primarily confined—with significant effects—to local experiments and voluntary action, it featured in the educational and social policies of both John Major's Conservative and Tony Blair's New Labour governments. Throughout this period, interest in identifying elites of the future was signified by policies around streaming, specialisation, parent 'choice', testing, and standards. At the same time, the language of 'aspiration', a form of equality putting the responsibility onto individuals, became very powerful, as Jon Lawrence has argued.[1] In these policies, all young people were positioned as equally able to 'aspire' to being elites of the future, to recognise a broad variety of 'gifts', and achieve their potential in the job market. The frameworks of equality and elitism were increasingly measured, ranked, and compared in this decade through policy interest in the gifted child.

Tensions between equality and elitism had significant effects on young people's experiences of schools, their expectations for their careers, and their visions of

---

[1] Jon Lawrence, *Me, Me, Me? The Search for Community in Post-war England* (Cambridge: CUP, 2019), p. 208.

their own ability. The chapter argues that many happily received the vision of themselves as elites of the future, and that ideas of childhood 'agency' must account for enthusiastic acceptance of psychological and educational labels, as well as resistance.[2] Nonetheless, the chapter also shows that new official, commercial giftedness schemes of the 1990s and 2000s less commonly traced young people's resistance to this idea, and critique of it, contributing to a dissipation in the 1970s and 1980s voluntary vision of the gifted young as uniquely disruptive subjects. Given the different sources available for this chapter compared to earlier ones—the more structured, formal magazines of corporate-sponsored, government-organised summer schools, rather than the free-form publications of the National Association—we must read against the grain and carefully trace young people's engagement in this period.

The chapter first analyses the policies of John Major, with focus on a case study of National Records of Achievement, which looked to encourage all young people to document their own 'gifts'. It demonstrates, also, that adults speaking in the 2010s and 2020s had strong memories of the power of these documents. Second, the chapter explores New Labour policy, paying particular attention to the National Academy for Gifted and Talented Youth, which aimed to identify gifted young people and train them as scientific and industrial elites of the future. Third, the chapter attempts to read against the grain of National Academy publications, looking to unearth how young people experienced and felt in this space.[3] It shows that many young people experienced these schools as a highly positive space, in which they could build new peer relationships and learn new things; many also embraced the ideas of their own elite status and future leadership roles. Fourth and finally, the chapter explores the responses of 'gifted child alumni': adults identified as 'gifted' in the 1970s and 1980s and then had, by the 1990s and 2000s, grown up. These adults responded to the national interest in giftedness in the tabloid press, through the voluntary groups they used to work with, and in online parenting fora. Their responses were typically critical of the idea that gifted young

---

[2] Susan A. Miller, 'Assent as agency in the early years of the children of the American Revolution', *Journal of the History of Childhood and Youth*, 9 (1) (2016), pp. 48–65; Tatek Abebe, 'Reconceptualising children's agency as continuum and interdependence', *Social Sciences*, 8 (3) (2019), pp. 1–16.

[3] Reading these archives, 'against the grain', is conducted with reference to research about practices of archiving, for example: Merle Patchett, 'Archiving', *Transactions of the Institute of British Geographers*, 44 (2019), pp. 650–653; Andrew Flinn, 'Archival activism: independent and community-led archives, radical public history and the heritage professions', *Interactions: UCLA Journal of Education and Information Studies*, 7 (2) (2011); Tim Cresswell, 'Value, gleaning and the archive at Maxwell Street, Chicago', *Transactions of the Institute of British Geographers*, 37 (1) (2012), pp. 164–176; Sarah Mills, 'Cultural-historical geographies of the archive: fragments, objects and ghosts', *Geography Compass*, 7 (10) (2013), pp. 709–710; Mela Dávila-Freire, 'Reading the archive against the grain: Power relations, affective affinities and subjectivity in the documenta Archive', *Art Libraries Journal*, 45 (3) (2020), pp. 94–99; Kate Boyer, 'Feminist geography in the archive: practice and method', WGSG, *Geography and Gender Reconsidered*, August 2004, pp. 169–174; Maria Fannin and Julie MacLeavy, 'Feminism, resistance and the archive', in Sarah M. Hughes (ed.) *Critical Geographies of Resistance* (Cheltenham: Edward Elgar, 2023), pp. 26–40.

people should be identified, and tended to suggest that the gifted would live mundane, normal lives, rather than 'rule the world'. Yet these responses were not recognised in national policy. Rather, the gifted child, as a construct, had been successfully remade for a new age. Memories of the 1990s and 2000s have then been remade again in the 2010s and 2020s, and thrive in the lively discussions of online communities. Analysing these gives a further glimpse into how political schemes around giftedness were received and changed on an everyday and cultural level, and also shows how conceptions that this book traced in the 1970s and 1980s remained powerful for decades to come.

Overall, this chapter shows the flexibility of ideas about the gifted child. Identifying gifted young people could be the answer to fears of industrial and British decline raised by the conservative press discussed in Chapter Four. For the New Labour administrations, equally, identifying gifted young people could form part of agendas around social mobility, inner city rejuvenation, and education for all. A gifted child could be a future political, industrial, or economic leader. The idea of 'gifts', it was thought, could also be presented to all young people, encouraging them to identify and document their own talents, and to become productive workers. Throughout this book, we see that there is little inherently 'elitist' or 'equal' about any concept of 'the gifted child'. Nonetheless, the ways in which ideas of giftedness have been applied, and grasped by a series of political and voluntary leaders, has had significant impact on young people's lives, and shifted alongside an uneasy balance between equality and elitism in modern Britain.

Documenting 'Aspiration'

Conservative Prime Minister John Major came to power at the turn of the 1990s, on 28 November 1990, following the resignation of Margaret Thatcher. For historians Peter Dorey and Derek Gillard, John Major's education policies were 'a clear example of inheritance in public policy':[4] In comparison to Thatcher's, Major's policies were 'equally committed to selection and elitism; equally determined to continue diminishing the role of the local authorities, and equally confrontational in its attitude to the teaching profession'.[5] Selection was maintained in Major's continuation of grant-maintained schools, advocacy of school specialism and parent 'choice', continuing measures towards compulsory student testing (avidly opposed by teachers), and introduction of 'standards' through league

---

[4] Peter Dorey, 'The 3 Rs—Reform, Reproach and Rancour: Education Policies under John Major', in Peter Dorey (ed.), *The Major Premiership* (London: Palgrave Macmillan, 1999), pp. 146–164.
[5] Derek Gillard, 'John Major: more of the same', *Education in England: A History*, May 2018 <http://www.educationengland.org.uk/history/chapter16.html> (20 September 2021).

tables and the creation of the school inspectorate, Ofsted, as well as in rhetorical calls to bring back streaming and 'old-fashioned teaching methods' in primary schools.[6]

While allowing these selective measures, Professor of Education Clyde Chitty argues that Major simultaneously held 'a more traditional Conservative belief in the self-evident values of a meritocratic society'.[7] This was manifested in his desire for schools to offer different specialisms, and for parents to choose schools based on information about league tables and pupil performance, as well as the 'continued blurring of the boundaries between the private and state sectors'.[8] Major also emphasised 'One Nation Conservativism', particularly before the 1997 election. In speeches, he positioned these dual commitments—to 'competition' and 'meritocracy'—as compatible, and indeed as reflecting his own humble upbringing in Brixton, his comprehensive education and few formal qualifications, all of which had given him (the *Daily Mail* diligently reported) 'a compelling insight into the aspirations of ordinary families'.[9]

The specific phrase 'gifted child' was rare in Major's speeches and the construction of his vision. He did use this term in speeches directed to Young Conservatives, think-tanks, and Conservative women, yet, in doing so, Major's emphasis was on his intention to promote learning for *both* '[g]ifted children and those with learning disabilities'.[10] If anything, he emphasised how his policies would benefit all children, but 'perhaps most importantly, the less gifted and the deprived', and 'not just the most gifted'.[11] Nonetheless, his administration's work in developing testing in schools positioned children as more or less academically able from the age of school entrance, in ways that would shape their experiences throughout their education. Building external pressures in this area, an internal memo sent around the Department of Education and Science in January 1991 stressed that 'provision

---

[6] Ibid; see also Robin Alexander, Jim Rose, and Chris Woodhead, *Curriculum Organisation and Classroom Practice in Primary Schools: A Discussion Paper* (London: Department of Education and Science, 1992).
[7] Clyde Chitty, *Education Policy in Britain* (2nd edition, Basingstoke: Palgrave Macmillan, 2009), p. 55, as cited in Gillard, 'John Major: more of the same'.
[8] Chitty, *Education Policy in Britain*, 2009), p. 55, as cited in Gillard, 'John Major: more of the same'.
[9] Andrew Sparrow, 'Major: My vision of a chance for all', *Daily Mail*, 21 March 1996.
[10] 'Mr Major's Speech to the Conservative Party Women's Conference—4 June 1993', John Major Archive <Mr Major's Speech to the Conservative Party Women's Conference—4 June 1993—The Rt. Hon. Sir John Major KG CH (johnmajorarchive.org.uk)> (16 September 2021); 'Mr Major's Speech to Young Conservatives Conference—9 February 1991', John Major Archive <Mr Major's Speech to Young Conservatives Conference—9 February 1991—The Rt. Hon. Sir John Major KG CH (johnmajorarchive.org.uk)> (16 September 2021).
[11] 'Mr Major's Speech to the Adam Smith Institute—16 June 1992', John Major Archive <Mr Major's Speech to the Adam Smith Institute—16 June 1992—The Rt. Hon. Sir John Major KG CH (johnmajorarchive.org.uk)> (16 September 2021); 'Mr Major's Speech to Young Conservatives Conference—9 February 1991', John Major Archive <Mr Major's Speech to Young Conservatives Conference—9 February 1991—The Rt. Hon. Sir John Major KG CH (johnmajorarchive.org.uk)> (16 September 2021).

for gifted children... is an emerging issue of significance', and that a recent review had found that 'most teachers could not match different tasks and topics to individual ability, whether high or low!'[12] In August 1991, Mensa's Foundation for Gifted Children launched a scheme to allow any school to become a 'Mensa Foundation Chartered School', if they met standards accredited by Mensa. The group claimed to have eighty schools apply before the official launch, although the scheme was not broadly supported within internal discussions at the Department of Education and Science.[13] A 1992 review by Her Majesty's Inspectors focused specifically on the education of 'very able' children in maintained schools, finding them 'often insufficiently challenged by the work they are set', and in 1994 the newly created Ofsted included giftedness as a category for equal opportunities guidelines, alongside ethnicity, gender, and social circumstance.[14] Major's governments also sought out giftedness in elite sport from 1996, in part funded by the new National Lottery.[15]

Under John Major's Education Ministers, while being increasingly tested and measured, young people were also given more opportunities to document their own diffuse 'gifts', and to mobilise these towards long-term 'aspirations'. A key symbol of such thinking was the National Record of Achievement system. Ideas about creating such a record had circulated from the 1960s, as local authorities offered equivalents, particularly 'as accreditation for lower achievers'.[16] Through the 1970s and 1980s, alongside consumer rights movements, Parliament debated whether such a document could help all learners manage their own learning and plan their future and be tied to 'an agenda that was set by the presumed needs of industry'.[17] The first national system was launched in February 1991, by Conservative Employment Secretary Michael Howard. The choice of Minister here—Employment rather than Education—demonstrating the scheme's planned connections to the labour market. Initially, 20,000 folders were sent to schools: heavy, maroon objects with clear plastic sleeves to hold certificates, school reports

---

[12] National Archives, Kew, ED 183/331, 'Provision for gifted children: correspondence with MENSA', 1990–1991, 'Mensa Accreditation of Independent Schools', 23 January 1991, p. 1.

[13] See fascinating discussions in a lengthy file: National Archives, Kew, ED 183/331, 'Provision for gifted children: correspondence with MENSA', 1990–1991.

[14] Her Majesty's Inspectorate, *The Education of Very Able Children in Maintained Schools* (London: Department of Education and Science, 1992); NAGC Newsletter, Winter 1995, 'The New Framework for Inspections', p. 2.

[15] Neil King, *Sport Policy and Governance: Local Perspectives* (Oxford: Butterworth-Heinemann, 2009), p. 59; Mick Green and Barrie Houlihan, *Elite Sport Development: Policy Learning and Political Priorities* (Abingdon: Routledge, 2005), pp. 54–59. David Cowan is currently conducting fascinating research about the inception of the National Lottery from 1994 and its relationships to popular views of religion (as yet unpublished).

[16] Elizabeth Ann Hodgson, 'The National Record of Achievement: Just another Initiative or a Useful Tool for the Future?' PhD thesis submitted to the University of London, 1997, p. 26; Christopher Rhodes, James Avis, and Hugh Somervell, 'Records of achievement, higher education and work: passport or passenger?' *Research in Post-Compulsory Education*, 4(3) (1999), p. 322.

[17] Rhodes et al., 'Records of achievement', p. 322.

and personal statements.[18] Ministers stated that these records were a 'record of life, a passport to progress', a 'super curriculum vitae', to be 'constantly updated throughout their working lives'.[19]

Showing the significance of this thinking, Ministers planned to make these records compulsory in 1993. Although this did not happen, by 1996 over 80 per cent of schools in England and Wales used these for Year 11 students.[20] Policy research from the same year suggested that the records may need refining to recognise more types of skills and gifts, and that they would have relatively little impact on the career choices of women and individuals from poorer communities.[21] Their use continued into the subsequent New Labour administration, and were officially phased out as a national requirement from 2006, although they were relaunched in Scotland in 2007 and many local versions continued in England. While their time was thus brief, National Records of Achievement symbolised an important new strand of thinking about the potential of all young people, and the role of government in encouraging and accessing this.

Notably, these Records revealed the entwined assumptions that *all* young people had gifts and talents; that documenting these would raise young people's aspirations; and that these gifts and talents *must* be used to increase access to employment and industry. Announcing the scheme in December 1991, Michael Howard MP stated that they would 'encourage everyone to fulfil their potential, to make the most of our abilities, to make the greatest possible contribution to our national economy'.[22] These records were thus a critical part of forging a dynamic and economically valuable Britain in the 1990s: they would be part of a 'skills revolution which will ensure that the United Kingdom makes the most of its competitive advantages and faces with confidence the fierce international competition that will characterise the rest of the decade'.[23] Notably, they would work within a broader system of 'training credits, opportunities in open learning, improved information and advice services, career development loans and the tax incentives announced in the last Budget'.[24] These records emerged, and were used, as the Department of Education grappled with questions of whether to strengthen state provision in education or the alternative of the independent

---

[18] 'Taking a leaf out of This Is Your Life', *Daily Mail*, 28 February 1991.   [19] Ibid.

[20] *The Dearing Review: Review of Qualifications for 16–19 year olds* (Hayes: SCAA Publications, 1996), p. 41.

[21] Ibid., p. 44; National Archives, SH 1/179, 'Equal Opportunities Commission: Meeting Thursday 14 July 1994', pp. 9, 11; Institute for Employment Studies, 'Report summary: Employers' Use of the National Record of Achievement', Institute for Employment Studies website, <https://www.employment-studies.co.uk/report-summaries/report-summary-employers%E2%80%99-use-national-record-achievement> (20 January 2021).

[22] Michael Howard, 'Marking a milestone on the road to a skills revolution in Britain', *The Times*, 18 December 1991.

[23] Ibid.   [24] Ibid.

sector (and, in 1993, as it faced teachers' unions boycotting national testing).[25] They were an attempt to demonstrate that all state education equipped young people with 'skills' and to broaden out visions of educational attainment beyond formal tests. They also represented Major's broader attempts to slow the pace of inequality, and the retrenchment policies that had contributed to Thatcher's downfall. Major spoke more affectionally about the welfare state, and retreated on issues such as cuts to Child Benefit, while also remaining fundamentally committed to ideas of competition, audit, and inspection.[26]

Significant evidence suggests that these Records shaped school experiences for young people. First, academic studies from this period found that teachers and students felt these records could 'make a perceptible difference to achievement, progression and participation levels in their schools and colleges' and 'foster empowerment in the labour market'.[27] Second, local newspaper coverage shows how young people incorporated these records into the rituals of school life. End-of-school leaving events were frequently framed as a 'National Record of Achievement ceremony' by individual schools at this time, marked also by the hiring of 'exotic cars', dancing, music, and appearances from local celebrities.[28] Again, the presentation ceremonies and newspaper coverage revealed assumptions that documenting gifts in this way would contribute to individual and national economic success. The *Grimsby Evening Telegraph* in 1999, for example, reported on how local figures from business told young people at one school that 'future employers would pay a great deal of attention to attendance and punctuality', as noted in these Records.[29]

A third and final source of evidence for the power of these Records comes from retrospective memories on the community chat forum Reddit.[30] Here, users

---

[25] Peter Scott, 'Education Policy', in Dennis Kavanagh and Anthony Seldon (eds), *The Major Effect* (London: Macmillan, 1994), pp. 342, 343–344.

[26] Discussed in Paul Pierson, 'The New Politics of the Welfare State', *World Politics*, 48 (2) (1996), pp. 143–179, p. 163; Robert M. Page, 'The Conservative Party and the welfare state since 1945', in Hugh Bochel (ed.), *The Conservative Party and Social Policy* (Bristol: Policy Press, 2011), p. 34.

[27] Hodgson, 'The National Record of Achievement', p. 10; Rhodes et al., 'Records of achievement', p. 328.

[28] 'Start Your Engines', *The Globe and Mail*, 1 August 2013; 'Robert Blake leavers' tribute', *Bridgwater Mercury*, 18 July 2009; 'School celebrates a record year', *East Kent Mercury*, 9 June 2011; 'Pupils go platinum', *East Kent Mercury*, 28 January 2010; 'Boxing legend helps pupils celebrate their achievements', *Sheffield Star*, 2 June 2008; Karen Morrison, 'The fast and the studious', *The Sun*, 19 July 2013.

[29] 'Students scoop achievement awards', *Grimsby Evening Telegraph*, 9 June 1999.

[30] Research with the internet is increasingly popular. During the pandemic, in particular, multiple scholars turned to the internet and internet fora as a source which they could access, despite lockdowns. This chapter briefly engages with digital materials—notably from Netmums, Mumsnet, and Reddit—likewise, for multiple reasons. First, much of this book was also written during lockdowns, from 2020 to 2021, or post-lockdowns but while 'shielding' due to pregnancy. Second, this book consulted these pages because they throw light on 'everyday' discussions of giftedness, conducted in spaces beyond policy, and show the ongoing cultural memories around the kinds of debates earlier chapters traced to the 1970s and 1980s. The websites used in this book were all publicly accessible, and indeed many users are aware that these chat threads are viewed by those beyond their immediate

writing in the 2010s and 2020s stated that many had kept these folders, feeling unable to throw them away, yet not knowing why. Even those who had lost them a long time ago, or 'threw mine out the other day' recognised the name of the folder, and many had it 'safely stored away' or still 'came across it' while tidying. For some, the folders continued to occupy a space in their domestic lives: they were repurposed as mouse mats or used to keep sheets of choir music, with new labels stuck over historic logos. Such threads, recurring throughout the 2010s and inviting 20–200 comments, emphasised that users had expected these records to be highly significant. Users stated, for example, that careers professionals at school made them seem critical, as if they would be requested at interview. Many students recognised the connections between these folders and ideas of 'gifts', and still relied on these to build a notion of self-identity and worth. Contributors wrote, for example, that because they were a 'gifted student' they had 'slightly-too-good-to-be-true' materials stored and thus that the document made them appear a 'fraud'. Discussions suggested that the folders were used, as intended, to capture a range of gifts and talents, and contributors described how their folders contained swimming certificates, amateur radio licences, or chief scout's awards, as well as academic documents.

These Records hence marked an attempt in education policy to motivate all young people to actively document their own 'gifts' and 'achievements', offering a counter-narrative to moves towards segregating by academic ability only, through testing and streaming, occurring at the same time. The Records were designed to 'empower' young people to be economically productive within a well-functioning national economy, and to shape all young people into future workers. A diffuse range of evidence shows that these economic expectations, as well as ideas about the significance of cataloguing and documenting skills, pervaded the minds of

---

digital communities—participants on mums' fora, for example, often address imagined audiences, and are aware of the huge media interest in their debates. I note, also, that participants discussing gifted children and National Records of Achievement are likely not particularly vulnerable and that the points they shared, furthermore, on these pages were brief and did not leave identifiable information. Nonetheless, I adopted the following procedure when reading and writing about the quotes used above to discuss these internet sites: I do not mention any usernames, did not save or store the threads of discussion from internet anywhere, ensure quotations are very short, and do not link specific threads in this chapter. These decisions were taken having read the following articles and their reflections on best practice in academic research with social media, as an emergent field: Nicholas Norman Adams, '"Scraping" Reddit posts for academic research? Addressing some blurred lines of consent in growing internet-based research trend during the time of Covid-19', *International Journal for Social Research Methodology*, 27 (1), pp. 47–62; Casey Fiesler, Michael Zimmer, Nicholas Proferes, Sarah Gilbert, and Nathan Jones, 'Remember the human: A systematic review of ethical considerations in Reddit research', *Proceedings of the ACM on Human-Computer Interaction*, 8 (5) (2024), pp. 1–33; Clive Seale, Jonathan Charteris-Black, Aidan MacFarlane, and Ann McPherson, 'Interviews and Internet Forums: A Comparison of Two Sources of Qualitative Data', *Qualitative Health Research*, 20 (5) (2010), pp. 595–606; Riley Botelle and Chris Willott, 'Birth, attitudes and placentophagy: a thematic discourse analysis of discussions on UK parenting forums', *BMC Pregnancy and Childbirth*, 20 (2020), pp. 1–10; Gareth Millward, 'A history with web archives, not a history of web archives: A history of the British measles-mumps-rubella vaccine crisis, 1998–2004', in N. Brügger, N and I. Milligan (eds) *SAGE Handbook of Web History* (Sage: Thousand Oaks, 2018), pp. 464–478.

young people from school and into their later lives. This was a framework in which ideas of 'giftedness' were not explicit. Nonetheless, young people were trained to think about their own 'gifts', document them, and mobilise them for economic benefit.

Identifying 'Gifted and Talented'

New Labour, led by Tony Blair, won the general election of 1 May 1997. Central planks of its policy platform included more funding for schools in deprived areas, free nursery provision for young children at Sure Start centres, Educational Maintenance Allowances for students on low incomes to stay in education after 16, and expanding places in higher education. These measures emphasised equality of opportunity and the raising of standards for all, framed in the political language of 'social cohesion, stakeholding, community, social exclusion and inclusion'.[31] As Ruth Levitas has argued, what precisely this language meant was not always clear.[32] Educational researchers have further questioned the extent to which this agenda was successful, arguing that it also continued to enable racial and ethnic inequalities, brought more testing, centralised control of teachers, and a hierarchical academic-vocational divide.[33] More broadly, historians and policy theorists have argued that New Labour's first term was relatively cautious, continuing or responding to the policies of Margaret Thatcher and Major, rather than a radical new vision.[34] Certainly, moves towards selection in schools continued under New Labour, and schools could set entrance tests, and select by faith (or sometimes aptitude). Grammar schools were also able to increase their intake, and the practice of parents moving house to gain their children entry to 'good schools' carried on.[35]

External pressure in this area continued to build: Ofsted commissioned a study, published in 1998, on how best to identify and educate the gifted, while the House

---

[31] Ruth Levitas, *The Inclusive Society? Social Exclusion and New Labour* (Basingstoke: Palgrave, 2005), p. 2.
[32] Ibid.
[33] Sally Tomlinson, 'New Labour and education', *Children & Society*, 17 (3) (2006), pp. 195–204; Sally Tomlinson, 'Race, ethnicity and education under New Labour', *Oxford Review of Education*, 31 (21) (2005), pp. 153–171.
[34] James E. Cronin, *New Labour's Pasts: The Labour Party and its Discontents* (Abingdon: Routledge, 2004); Richard Heffernan, *New Labour and Thatcherism: Political Change in Britain* (Basingstoke: Palgrave Macmillan, 2000); Colin Hay, *The Political Economy of New Labour: Labouring under False Pretences?* (Manchester: MUP, 1999). Interestingly, this collection discusses 'just how much the present Labour government [of 2006] owes to the efforts and history of the wider movement since 1900'—quote in Glen O'Hara and Helen Parr, 'Conclusions: Harold Wilson's 1964 Governments and the heritage of "New" Labour', *Contemporary British History*, 20 (3) (2006), pp. 477–489. For a broader special issue, see: Glen O'Hara and Helen Parr (eds), 'The Wilson Governments 1964–90 Reconsidered', *Contemporary British History*, 20 (3) (2006).
[35] Tomlinson, 'Race, ethnicity and education under New Labour', pp. 159–160.

of Commons Education and Employment Committee ran a similar inquiry.[36] Demonstrating an interest in hyper-selection, though underpinned by visions of equalities, under New Labour giftedness became explicitly incorporated into educational policy for the first time. The New Labour government's white paper *Excellence in Schools* (1997) called for 'every school and LEA to plan how it will help gifted children', and the creation of 'an atmosphere in which to excel is not only acceptable but desirable'.[37] Labour's 2001 manifesto, the first main party manifesto to mention this issue since 1945, reaffirmed the party's commitment to 'extend provision for gifted children as we nurture children's special talents'.[38] In particular, these special talents would be nurtured through higher education, and in 1999 Blair set a target for 50 per cent of young adults to go to university in the 2000s.[39]

In part, New Labour's policy in this area continued the Major interest in identifying the gifts of as many young people as possible, and tying these to ideas of future employability. The *Excellence in Cities* report, launched in 1999, aimed to 'combat urban disadvantage, and bring together schools, community and business influence to improve attainment'.[40] It had some ramifications for giftedness in that it expected 58 local authorities to identify 5–10 per cent of children as academically gifted or talented in art or sports, mainly in secondary schools. Authorities were given ring-fenced funding for this, which was primarily spent on enrichment and extra provision, with additional funding for specialist schools catering for specific 'gifts'.[41] Beyond this 5–10 per cent students, 25 per cent of schools were to operate as specialist schools and government select committees also debated whether some 30–40 per cent of children may have significant extra

[36] Education and Employment Committee, Highly Able Children, 1998–9, Volume 1: Report and Proceedings of the Committee; Joan Freeman, *Educating the Very Able: Current International Research* (London: OFSTED, 1998).
[37] *Excellence in schools*, July 1997, Cm 3681 http://www.educationengland.org.uk/documents/wp1997/excellence-in-schools.html (17 November 2020).
[38] '2001 Labour Party General Election Manifesto: Ambitions for Britain', Labour Party Manifestos <http://www.labour-party.org.uk/manifestos/2001/2001-labour-manifesto.shtml> (25 November 2020).
[39] This target was announced in Tony Blair's Leaders Speech, Bournemouth 1999, *British Political Speeches* <http://www.britishpoliticalspeech.org/speech-archive.htm?speech=205> (23 September 2021). Participation in higher education then increased from 8.4% in 1970, 19.3% in 1990, to 33% in 2000. It reached 50% in 2019 (Paul Bolton, 'Education: Historical statistics', *House of Commons Library*, 27 November 2012 <https://researchbriefings.files.parliament.uk/documents/SN04252/SN04252.pdf> (23 September 2021), p. 19; Sean Coughlan, 'The symbolic target of 50% at university reached', *BBC News*, 26 September 2019 <https://www.bbc.co.uk/news/education-49841620> (23 September 2021). For context on debates in higher education, see: debates in higher education are aptly discussed in: Josh Patel, 'Imagining the role of the student in society: ideas of British higher education policy and pedagogy 1957–1972', PhD thesis, University of Warwick (2021); Josh Patel, 'The Puzzle of Lionel Robbins: How a Neoliberal Economist Expanded Public University Education in 1960s Britain', *Twentieth Century British History*, 34 (2) (2023), pp. 220–245.
[40] Tomlinson, 'Race, ethnicity and education under New Labour', p. 158.
[41] See a comprehensive description of this work in Margaret Brady, 'An Exploration of the Impact of Gifted and Talented Policies on Inner City Schools in England: A Case Study', PhD thesis, Brunel University, March 2015, pp. 69–70; Education and Employment Committee, Highly Able Children, 1998–9, Volume 1: Report and Proceedings of the Committee, p. xix.

'gifts' that required extra support to be realised.[42] Reforms to the curriculum, teacher working, and teacher expectations around gifted education were also couched as improving opportunities for all children, and gifted children were framed as young and childlike, to be analysed alongside all children (not merely 'brains on legs').[43]

While the New Labour government sought to mark out a relatively large number of young people as gifted, and to offer gifted education within mainstream education, it also established a scheme that revived the 1970s and 1980s ideas of the gifted as elites of the future: the National Academy for Gifted and Talented Youth.[44] Established in 2002, this organisation sought to ensure that 'we as a country find our most able students'.[45] The organisation also sought to develop academic and professional knowledge about giftedness, create training and guidance for teachers, and support practitioner research projects.[46] It was closely linked to government, taking responsibility for creating the National Register for Gifted and Talented Learners, producing guidance for schools that was disseminated through the Department for Education, and working at the heart of a network of academies, universities, non-governmental organisations, and government agencies in this area.[47] However, in addition to a grant from the Department for Education and Skills (providing 85 per cent of its funding in 2006–07), it also received external funding from companies, universities, and charitable foundations.[48]

The organisation also worked directly with young people and families. The National Academy stated that their students were their 'heart', critical in 'shaping provision and informing the national policy debate about gifted issues'.[49] This was realised through the creation of a student council of 102 students on 9 regional boards, who held meetings, introduced new members to the Academy, answered questions on the organisation's online fora, and gathered students' ideas.[50] By 2007, youth membership of this organisation—those able to participate via its newsletter, online network, training days, events, and summer schools—numbered 152,000, encompassing students from 77 per cent of schools.[51] Young

---

[42] Education and Employment Committee, Highly Able Children, 1998–9, Volume 1: Report and Proceedings of the Committee, pp. ix, 15–22.

[43] Ibid., pp. vii, xix, 2.

[44] The intention to establish such an 'Academy for Gifted and Talented Youth' was outlined in the white paper *Schools Achieving Success* (Cm 5230, 2001) <https://assets.publishing.service.gov.uk/government/uploads/system/uploads/attachment_data/file/355105/Schools_Achieving_Success.pdf> (28 July 2021). This is discussed in: Modern Records Centre, UWA/PUB/DEP/29/2 Leaflet—on gifted and Talented youth—The National Academy at University of Warwick, p. 2.

[45] 'Providing for Gifted and Talented Youth', *University of Warwick podcasts*, <https://warwick.ac.uk/newsandevents/podcasts/media/?podcastItem=gifted.mp3> (1 October 2024).

[46] Modern Records Centre, UWA/PUB/DEP/29/3, Annual Report 2006–2007, 'Securing G&T education within national policy', p. 7.

[47] Ibid.   [48] Ibid., 'Financing the work of NAGTY', pp. 37–8.

[49] Ibid., 'Identifying and tracking the top 5%', p. 28.   [50] Ibid.

[51] Modern Records Centre, UWA/PUB/DEP/29/5, *Aspire* (magazine) for gifted and talented youth, 2002–2007, July 2007, 'Being a member, what does it mean?', p. 4; Modern Records Centre, UWA/PUB/DEP/29/3, Annual Report 2006–2007, p. 3.

people were identified between the ages of 11 and 19. Assessment to join looked broadly at test scores (Key Stage Levels, World Class Tests, CAT scores, or public exam grades); a letter from the student, describing how they would benefit from Academy membership and questions they would pose to an 'expert' in their field of interest; and recommendation from a teacher or a professional, or a marked piece of work.[52]

The National Academy frequently emphasised that these combined measures could help to overcome biases in IQ testing, discussed in this book's Introduction and Chapter Four, towards white, middle-class boys. The Academy positioned one of its key priorities as 'increasing social mobility for gifted and talented students from disadvantaged backgrounds'.[53] Its promotional materials and internal magazines featured photos of and testimonies from enthused participants across a range of racial groups, trying to curate an inclusive vision of giftedness. Seeking to foster economic inclusion, the organisation did not charge attendees at summer schools whose parents earned less than £17,500 a year, and provided a sliding scale bursary scheme whereby parents earning over £31,001 a year were the only ones to pay full fees (the average wage in 2005 was £23,900).[54] The organisation also ran a 'Goal' programme for disadvantaged students, which, by 2007, reached 450 students in 75 schools with 100 of those Goal students accepted for the summer school.[55] Students were identified by local authorities and G&T coordinators in schools, and then attended extra residential courses to help with motivation and goal-setting.[56]

By 2007, the organisation's student members—152,000 students—were reported to be 82.1 per cent white, 5.8 per cent did not disclose, 5.6 per cent Asian, 2.8 per cent Mixed, 1.7 per cent Black, 1.2 per cent Chinese, and 0.8 per cent Other. The students came from 91.6 per cent maintained schools, 8.36 per cent independent, and 0.04 per cent were home educated. They were 51.1 per cent female and 48.9 per cent male.[57] While 5.8 per cent did not disclose their ethnicity, on the surface these percentages appear to suggest a relatively representative sample of the population as a whole attended the National Academy—nonetheless, contemporary educational research still found that ethnic minoritised pupils faced 'continued

---

[52] Modern Records Centre, UWA/PUB/DEP/29/5, *Aspire* (magazine) for gifted and talented youth, 2002–2007, April 2003, 'Loc8or Lands', p. 8.
[53] Modern Records Centre, UWA/PUB/DEP/29/3, Annual Report 2006–2007, p. 3.
[54] Justin Parkinson, 'What is there for bright children?', *BBC News*, 14 July 2006 <BBC NEWS | Education | What is there for bright children?> (18 May 2021). On average wage figures see: 'Average wages in 2005', *Trade Union Council*, <https://www.tuc.org.uk/research-analysis/reports/average-wages-2005> (23 September 2021). The tensions within New Labour about means testing, and particularly between Frank Field and Gordon Brown, are discussed throughout Hugh Bochel and Andrew Defty, *Welfare Policy Under New Labour: Views from Inside Westminster* (Bristol, Policy Press, 2007).
[55] Modern Records Centre, UWA/PUB/DEP/29/3, Annual Report 2006–2007, p. 6.
[56] Ibid., 'Identifying and tracking the top 5%', p. 29.   [57] Ibid., pp. 25-26.

disadvantage and new forms of exclusion' in education.[58] An evaluation from the 2004 summer schools found that students saw 'class and ethnic differences' in the Academy, and believed this was 'a benefit'. The evaluators wrote of 'a sense that the commonality of purpose enabled the students to form friendships that benefited from the differing backgrounds of other students', while for many, 'this was their first experience mixing within such a diverse group'.[59] Including children from relatively diverse socioeconomic and ethnic backgrounds was thus presented as socially just, yet this would also, the Academy's first leader Deborah Eyre stated, improve the workforce, encouraging the disadvantaged to raise their 'aspiration' and 'self-esteem', and to later 'make good' and 'excel'.[60] Indeed, the Academy's 2007 annual report included an infographic positioning its goals as both 'social justice' and 'optimisation of human capital'.[61]

The Academy replicated the long-standing ideas that children identified as 'gifted' were, in some way, special and unique, and also that they could—and indeed must—play a unique role in forging the future of the nation. Events organised by the National Academy, in collaboration with museums, heritage attractions, and universities, considered 'modern careers'—veterinary medicine, particle physics, chemistry, maternal and child health, radio, film production, crime scene investigating, and social marketing. Events also included 'modern skills': presentation skills, reading the media, language events, and understanding social divides. These were organised alongside events less clearly tied to economic potential, such as learning about Leonardo Da Vinci, photographing marine life, and writing horror stories.[62] As ever, the constellation of interests for the gifted young was complex, baffling, and unpredictable.

Nonetheless, the National Academy was also in part interested in identifying and shaping students who could be future economic, scientific, and technological leaders. It quickly developed significant commercial links, benefiting from industry interest in 'corporate responsibility' and growing links between the public and private sectors in this period. In 2003, the National Academy was awarded a quarter of a million pounds by the Goldman Sachs Foundation, as part of the

---

[58] Quote is Tomlinson, 'Race, ethnicity and education under New Labour', p. 167. In the 2001 census, nearly 8% of the UK population identified as from an ethnic minority. The majority of these respondents were 'British citizens, settled minorities originally from the Caribbean, Africa, India, Pakistan, Bangladesh, Hong Kong, China, and Cyprus'. These citizens typically lived in Britain's largest cities or in small towns in the north of England that had had significant employment in the 1970s in textiles. (Office for National Statistics, 2003, as cited in Tomlinson, 'New Labour and education'; Tomlinson, 'Race, ethnicity and education under New Labour', pp. 155, 159, 162.)

[59] Modern Records Centre, UWA/PUB/DEP/29/6 Evaluation of the Summer School 2004, p. 90. Notably, this was a justification also often used for grammar schools.

[60] 'Providing for Gifted and Talented Youth', *University of Warwick podcasts*, <https://warwick.ac.uk/newsandevents/podcasts/media/?podcastItem=gifted.mp3> (1 October 2024).

[61] Modern Records Centre, UWA/PUB/DEP/29/3, Annual Report 2006–2007, p. 4.

[62] Modern Records Centre, UWA/PUB/DEP/29/5, *Aspire* (magazine) for gifted and talented youth, 2002–2007, April 2006, 'Forthcoming Events', pp. 8–9.

foundation's interest in 'Developing High-Potential Youth'. In their statement for the Academy magazine, Goldman Sachs stated that '[d]eveloping well-prepared leaders for tomorrow is a driving goal of the Foundation. We are pleased to be working with the Academy to help develop leaders of the future.'[63] A commercial link with Caterpillar Inc, 'the world's largest maker of construction equipment, diesel engines and power systems' followed in July 2003, as part of the organisation's 'corporate social responsibilities'.[64]

The idea that young people were future economic and corporate leaders was disseminated to attendees through, for example, the Academy's relationship with the Gifted Entrepreneurs Programme. Here, young people in schools were encouraged to act as business leaders, and to prepare themselves for these roles, designing small business projects in groups. Involvement required significant commitment: six months of 'training, planning, strategizing and good old fashioned hard-work' by the student finalists.[65] The Academy framed this reshaping of student's leisure time as within 'the government's clear agenda on enterprise training'.[66]

The scientific and technological potential of young people was also emphasised in the Academy. In magazines directed at students, readers were asked, for example, 'would you consider future employment in a nuclear-based power industry?'[67] They were told also about 'a national shortage of young people studying as Electrical Engineers'.[68] To an extent, youth readers were framed as empowered to make their own decisions, yet they were also told that 'power is definitely worth bearing in mind when the time comes to consider your career!'; about 'the exciting and rewarding career opportunities in the science world'; and that a degree in 'physics or another science' could 'open a number of doors in the labour market'.[69] Students were frequently advised to 'boost your employability' through 'transferable skills and work experience', and presented with role models of undergraduates studying scientific subjects.[70] The aspirations of readers were not only their own, but a 'key part of the UK economy with the potential to make a real difference to the world'.[71] Tabloid newspapers since the 1970s and 1980s, as traced in Chapter Four, had long offered these visions. Yet, by the 1990s and 2000s, government programmes and rhetoric were also making the commercial needs of Britain, as defined by industry, central to shaping the provision of gifted education and young people's social lives. Under New Labour, gifted young people were both the key to Britain's industrial and scientific futures, and yet also

---

[63] Ibid., April 2003, 'Academy Awarded £1/4 Million to Young Entrepreneurs', p. 3.
[64] Ibid., July 2003, 'Sponsorship will help disadvantaged', p. 3.
[65] Ibid., July 2005, 'Gifted Entrepreneurs Programme', p. 5.
[66] Ibid.   [67] Ibid., April 2006, 'Welcome to Aspire 11', p. 1.
[68] Ibid., 'Does working with electricity spark your interest?', p. 2.
[69] Ibid., 'Scientific Futures', p. 10.   [70] Ibid., 'A Physics Case Study', p. 11.
[71] Ibid., 'Does working with electricity spark your interest?', p. 2.

finding them was a mechanism through which to promote social mobility and equal life chances for all.

Experiencing the National Academy

We can gain some idea of how young people experienced the National Academy, and particularly its summer schools, through its annual reports, professional evaluations, and its magazine, *Aspire*. Distributed to student members, parents, and interested professionals, *Aspire* was very different from the kinds of youth magazines studied in Chapters Three and Four, the informal sources curated by the National Association for Gifted Children in the 1970s and 1980s. While children's letters, poetry, drawings, and discussions were central to magazines of the National Association, they were side-lined in *Aspire*. This magazine served a broader audience and was run by a more staffed, funded, and professionalised organisation, highly aware of its links and responsibilities to government, industry, and charities. *Aspire* not only focused on young people's voices, but also gave significant space to commercial sponsors, the writings of adult editors and participants, and promotional material. While recognising the curation involved in these sources, they nonetheless give an insight into the opportunities offered to young people by the National Academy, and their responses to these, whether via the organisation itself or professional academic evaluators.

Overall, it appears that young people typically engaged very positively with the National Academy. In 2004, the programme commissioned an evaluation of its summer school programmes from the independent Centre for Educational Development, Appraisal, and Research (CEDAR) at the University of Warwick. By this point, the Academy ran seven summer schools hosted by the universities of Durham, Exeter, Lancaster, Warwick, York, Imperial College London and Christchurch College Canterbury. They catered for over 1,000 children in two-to-three-week residential courses. The CEDAR evaluation conducted 48 interviews with small groups of students and received an additional 968 survey responses from students (a 96 per cent response rate).[72] These survey responses were anonymous, and the interviews were with academics who were not engaged with the Academy.

Typically in this evaluation, students praised the provision, social aspects, logistics, and organisation of these courses. Over 99 per cent of student respondents regarded it as a positive experience, citing 'improved confidence, having made stronger friendships, improved social skills, improved academic performance

---

[72] Modern Records Centre, UWA/PUB/DEP/29/6 Evaluation of the Summer School 2004, pp. 4–5.

in school and a greater sense of academic and personal independence'.[73] The report was open in documenting the criticism from the minority of students, who suggested that the label 'gifted and talented' was 'problematic', and that students could have had more time to themselves during the courses.[74] Three students—out of the 968 survey responses—stated that the summer school had a negative effect: it 'hasn't helped me'; 'made me more depressed'; 'I have become rude and lazy'.[75]

Overall, the primary benefits described by young people were peer contact and social opportunities. Of the 968 student respondents, 90 per cent rated the 'social and leisure aspects' of the summer school as 'very good' or 'good', and 93 per cent stated that socialising with 'like-minded peers' at the summer school was 'greatly' or 'somewhat' important.[76] This comes through clearly in the detailed accounts provided in *Aspire*. Reviewing the first summer course of the National Academy, one student wrote that they initially felt apprehensive, 'it dawned on me that three weeks of my summer holidays were going to be torn away from me'.[77] Yet, by the end of the course, she was 'filled with sorrow at the thought of returning home and leaving my new best friends'.[78] The report emphasised that the social time was the most important for forging friendships, and that this student had participated in a range of activities including robot building, discos, and Olympics. Echoing assumptions from the 1970s and 1980s, the student emphasised that '[t]here was a general feeling that we could be ourselves and still be accepted; we all had something in common.' She went on, '[i]t's not that I don't like school; I do. I fit in and I get good marks. But the fact that I try makes me stand out'.[79] Other student attendees similarly emphasised the power of 'making new friends and meeting new people of the same age with similar abilities on Academy courses, earnestly writing that 'friendship is probably the greatest thing that you will ever learn'.[80] For one attendee, such friendships were made across class, ethnic, racial, and regional differences, and they wrote about keeping in touch with new friends 'from all four corners of the British Isles from Belfast to York and from Newcastle to the Isle of Wight'.[81] The author wrote that, '[i]t was fascinating to listen to these different dialects and meet people from all over the country'.[82] The social side was framed in very liberationist terms, with further quotes in *Aspire* discussing how the peer cultures of the National Academy produced a 'huge family', made students 'less isolated', created 'new friends', and

---

[73] Ibid., p. 158.   [74] Ibid., p. 90.   [75] Ibid., p. 156.   [76] Ibid., p. 90.
[77] Modern Records Centre, UWA/PUB/DEP/29/5, *Aspire* (magazine) for gifted and talented youth, 2002–2007, December 2002, 'Summer School 2002—a student's view', p. 8.
[78] Ibid.   [79] Ibid.
[80] Ibid., 'My meta-cognitive thinking skills week', p. 11; ibid., July 2005, 'Villiers Park Report', p. 14.
[81] Ibid.   [82] Ibid.

meant that 'I have accepted and learned to love my intelligence level...[and] who I am'.[83]

In part, then, young people engaged with the National Academy for personal and social benefit. Yet, many also accepted the ideas of themselves as elites of the future with enthusiasm. Indeed, young people talked about themselves as future leaders of 'the world', 'the economic', and 'politics', and were enthused by these mixed ideas. In terms of their global role, the *Aspire* magazine of July 2003 featured a student letter arguing that:

> ...there is still a vast amount of oppression and inequality throughout the world. Having accepted ourselves as the brightest among the younger generation, we should acknowledge that we are set to inherit the world and it is practically our duty to make it the best place possible.[84]

The letter echoed older ideas of the responsibility and potential of gifted youth, but now as a humanitarian imperative.[85] Constructing a community of those reading, the letter argued, 'We have the power to change the world. Isn't it time we used it?'[86] In April 2006, another student wrote in again to emphasise the responsibility of the gifted to save the world. This time concerned about climate change, the thirteen-year-old student argued that, '[i]f we don't make any attempt to change the world who will?...It's time for change and YOU have the power.'[87] Certain Academy activities—such as encouraging young people to raise money for Street Child Africa and to write about Live Aid—furthered these ideas.[88] In these constructions, gifted young Britons were 'purposeful' and 'activist', while the imagined young people of the broader 'world' were not fully described or conceptualised.[89]

The Academy's young people also recognised assumptions of themselves as future economic leaders in Britain. Indeed, there are some traces of young people resisting these ideas. In the April 2003 edition of *Aspire*, for example, one young person wrote about her skill in maths, one of the most popular university subjects

---

[83] Ibid., July 2007, 'Being a member, what does it mean?', p. 4.
[84] Ibid., July 2003, 'Students letters and comments', p. 10.
[85] These ideas are further explored in the next chapter. For a fascinating account of earlier ideas of international friendship and child diplomats, see Matthias Neumann, 'Children diplomacy during the late Cold War: Samantha Smith's visit of the "Evil Empire"', *History*, 104 (36) (2019), pp. 275–308.
[86] Modern Records Centre, UWA/PUB/DEP/29/5, *Aspire* (magazine) for gifted and talented youth, 2002–2007, Summer Edition 3—July 2003, 'Students letters and comments', p. 10.
[87] Ibid., April 2006, 'Global Warming—The Tipping Point', p. 13.
[88] Ibid., July 2007, 'Get your own copy of The Greatest Gift!', p. 3; ibid., July 2005, 'Chatham House Announces Writing Competition', p. 16.
[89] Tamara Myers, 'Local Action and Global Imagining: Youth, International Development, and the Walkathon Phenomenon in Sixties' and Seventies' Canada', *Diplomatic History*, 38 (2) (2014), p. 288.

for Academy alumni.[90] She stated that, '[o]ne teacher told me that the big bucks is [sic] in corporate financing.'[91] Despite being 'brilliant at maths, so I'm told', and having originally applied to do work experience at Canary Wharf, the student had nonetheless decided that this path would be a 'wasteful life'.[92] From assisting at a special needs school, she learnt that, '[t]he most rewarding profession in life is one where you put faith into other people, so that they believe in themselves and have the will power to do better.'[93] She stated,

> I personally believe that you may be the most intelligent person in the world and yet achieve nothing of significance. I'd encourage you to try and be the most admirable person instead, gaining all the knowledge you can and using what you know for the benefit of others.[94]

Not all young participants then accepted the idea that they were future economic or scientific leaders, nor that their primary contribution to the world should be raising capital. The Academy was happy to engage with these ideas in part, reprinting them in its magazine *Aspire*; it was not solely engaged in creating elites of the future, and remained interested in the dissonant gifted self, as traced in Chapter Three.

The young people of the Academy also recognised a vision of themselves as future national political elites and, as far as we can tell from *Aspire* magazine, seemed to accept these ideas positively. In 2007, a small group of National Academy students was brought to conduct policy research over three days with a range of Government departments, ending their course with a visit to Number 10 Downing Street. Discussing this in *Aspire*, a student from Derbyshire stated that, 'I thought politicians were really evil, but they listened to our ideas and it was great to see where everything happens—I can't believe they let us in!'[95] Again, the Academy were happy to encourage young people to engage critically with existing institutions. Inviting participants to an information day at Windsor Castle, for example, in April 2006, the Academy encouraged attendees with 'strong opinions on the role of the monarchy in modern society' as well as those who 'would like to find out more about the history of the Royal family and Windsor Castle.'[96]

---

[90] Modern Records Centre, UWA/PUB/DEP/29/5, *Aspire* (magazine) for gifted and talented youth, 2002–2007, April 2003, 'Give a Child a Life', p. 11. On the University subject choices of Academy alumni, see Modern Records Centre, UWA/PUB/DEP/29/3, Annual Report 2006–2007, 'Identifying and tracking the top 5%', p. 26. The most popular University subject choices were medicine and mathematics, in line with the focus above on science, but followed by English, history, and law.
[91] Modern Records Centre, UWA/PUB/DEP/29/5, *Aspire* (magazine) for gifted and talented youth, 2002–2007, April 2003, 'Give a Child a Life', p. 11.
[92] Ibid.   [93] Ibid.   [94] Ibid.
[95] Ibid., July 2007, 'Goal Programme scores again!', p. 3.
[96] Ibid., April 2006, 'Focus on Experts in Action', p. 4.

Students were there to learn about the British monarchy, and to be brought into this central historic institution of power, but also the advert suggested awareness that students would not necessarily do so from a neutral position. The Academy offered opportunities that invited young people to think of themselves as global, economic, and political elites, but also invited critical engagement with these concepts.

While we can see critical engagement from young people with the Academy, even in the Academy's own publications, it is also notable that the visibility of young people's responses has faded in these sources, in comparison with the National Association magazines of the 1970s and 1980s. In part, this reflected the different structures of these spaces, shaped by informal voluntary and professionalised commercial imperatives. The fading of visible dissent, however, may have also reflected the fact that Academy students were given significant new opportunities to socialise with others on these programmes, and also to enter famous institutions and engage with new courses. Many of the gifted young relished these opportunities, and enthusiastically accepted the ideas of themselves as gifted, distinct, and special.

Gifted Child Alumni

Ideas of the gifted child became more prominent in national life in the 1990s and 2000s. Yet, this idea had, as the book shows, emerged first in the 1970s and 1980s, so by the turn of the twenty-first century, there were significant numbers of 'gifted children alumni': those who had been identified in the 1970s and 1980s and then in later decades could comment on these debates as adults. The commentary of gifted child alumni was not sought out consciously by policy-makers, who were interested in reconstructing ideas about giftedness for their own purposes. Yet, the voices of gifted child alumni did become audible in diffuse spaces—through the national tabloid press, particularly sensationalist coverage from American publications; through writing to the National Association for Gifted Children about historic engagements with this group; and through discussions on popular online parenting fora. Three ideas competed: that being a gifted child had had little impact; that it had destroyed lives; and that it had provided new educational and leisure opportunities.

The idea that being a gifted child had destroyed one's confidence was most prominently advocated by sensationalist American press, although this dramatic coverage also found its way to Britain. This becomes visible through the coverage around Doron Blake. Doron—Greek for 'gift'—was the second child born from the Repository of Germinal Choice, informally called the Nobel Prize sperm bank, which was founded in America in 1971 by a eugenicist, Robert Graham, hoping to distribute the sperm of Nobel Prize winners across the nation.

As donations were made anonymously, it is unclear whose sperm was in this bank, but we know that 240 children were born using donations. Blake was born in August 1982, and his mother told media that she had opted for 'Red No. 28's' sperm, guided by the information that the donor taught science at a university, had won prizes for performances in classic music, liked swimming, and suffered from haemorrhoids.[97] Blake's mother spoke to several journalists throughout his childhood, who duly reported on his extraordinary intellect, his fascination with computers, and interest in building complex toys, such as 'something resembling a lunar-landing module'.[98] When Blake turned 18 in 2001, he began to lead media profiles and documentaries—granting so many interviews, in fact, that *Slate* magazine labelled him 'the Nobel sperm bank quote machine', 'filled with the boredom of 1,000 repetitions'.[99] Blake's interviews, with *Slate* and others, first reiterated common narratives of giftedness, seen throughout this book: as a newborn baby he 'could mark time to classical music with his hands; by kindergarten, he was reading *Hamlet* and learning algebra'.[100] Echoing other children's statements, Blake told *Slate* that while his IQ was very high, around 180, 'I wouldn't finish the test. I was so bored with it.'[101]

In addition to repeating common tropes about gifted children, Blake also used media attention to critique the idea of the gifted, in two key ways. First, Blake repeatedly argued that the term 'gifted' distorted public understandings of which human attributes were valuable.[102] Blake emphasised that his IQ did not make him 'good' and that '[t]he thing I like best about myself is not that I'm smart but that I care about people and try to make other people's lives better.'[103] Second, Blake argued that the label 'gifted' was no route to life satisfaction—his IQ did not make him 'happy'.[104] British tabloids and television were also interested in Doron Blake, and his journey from 'perfect baby' to 'noisy, blond-haired boy, who had his mother wrapped around his grubby fingers' and finally adult critic of 'the new master breed'.[105] More broadly, from the 1980s and particularly in the 1990s and

---

[97] 'David Plotz, 'The Nobel Sperm Bank Celebrity', Slate, 16 March 2001 <https://slate.com/human-interest/2001/03/the-nobel-sperm-bank-celebrity.html> (27 October 2020).

[98] Katharine Lowry, 'The Designer Babies Are Growing Up: At Home With the First Children of the "Genius" Sperm Bank', *Los Angeles Times*, 1 November 1987 https://www.latimes.com/archives/la-xpm-1987-11-01-tm-17535-story.html> (27 October 2020); Ann Walmsley, 'The "genius" babies', *Macleans*, 2 September 1985 https://archive.macleans.ca/article/1985/9/2/the-genius-babies (27 October 2020).

[99] Plotz, 'The Nobel Sperm Bank Celebrity'. [100] Ibid. [101] Ibid.

[102] On interested media coverage, see also: 'The Genius Sperm Bank', *BBC Science and Nature* <http://www.bbc.co.uk/sn/tvradio/programmes/horizon/broadband/tx/spermbank/doron/index_textonly.shtml> (5 August 2019).

[103] Plotz, 'The Nobel Sperm Bank Celebrity'. [104] Ibid.

[105] Tabloid coverage of Blake continued from the 1980s until the 2000s. See, for example, 'Is this little boy a perfect baby?', *Daily Mirror*, 17 August 1983, pp. 8–9; Heidi Kingstone, 'Superbabe...or just another little boy?', *Daily Mail*, 18 September 1986; Sarah Chalmers, 'The New Master Breed?', *Daily Mail*, 10 February 2001. Television programmes featuring Blake included 'The Visit', aired on BBC 1 in 1985.There was some interest in broadsheet newspapers in this case also, but using Blake to discuss issues such as sperm donation, rather than offering the pages of detailed coverage in the

2000s, British tabloids were interested in asking, 'What becomes of child prodigies?', sharing their life stories through lengthy interviews and narratives.[106] A particular interest of tabloids was asking gifted child alumni to provide critical commentary on current gifted youth.[107] These gifted adults, however, echoing Blake, typically argued that 'there is more to life than studying', and warned newspapers that, 'being gifted does not make you a person more likely to succeed', and that genes were 'pot luck' and relatively meaningless.[108]

The National Association also gave significant space to gifted child alumni, from the 1980s but escalating in the 1990s and 2000s. By the 1990s, the Association was asking whether the term 'gifted' put off future members, and whether it sounded 'embarrassing'.[109] In this period it also sought to consciously counteract what it perceived as media focus on 'the sensational stories' and the tragic cases of giftedness lost, rather than on 'those who have slipped quietly into society and are living happily ever after'.[110] The Spring 1991 edition of *Looking to their Future*, for example, featured letters that responded to the question of 'how former gifted children have progressed as they have grown-up to become young adults'.[111]

In this edition, one mother wrote a lengthy letter that first discussed what she perceived as early signs of her son's giftedness: walking when aged one, recognising pictures in books by eighteen months, and his first word being 'Hoover', which his mother felt was 'the first indication of his interest in engineering'.[112] The family was advised to join the National Association by the boy's teacher when he was ten, and helped to run a local Saturday club, while the child also participated in a residential course in Wales (the type described in Chapter Three).[113] Praising the voluntary sector as an alternative site of care, his mother wrote that this 'proved to be a very worthwhile and maturing experience for him'.[114] Ultimately, this child studied at the University of Cambridge. His mother reflected that he 'was always very good company and we missed him very much when he left home'.[115]

Other stories provided in *Looking to their Future* likewise emphasised the benefits of voluntary sector provision, and the positive effects of being labelled 'gifted' at a young age. Both stories were provided by a mother, who simultaneously reflected on her own experiences growing up without being recognised as gifted,

---

tabloids. See for example Desmond Christy, 'You mean I get paid for this?', *Guardian*, 26 August 1998, p. 19.

[106] June Southworth, 'What becomes of child prodigies?', *Daily Mail*, 2 December 1995, p. 3; Susan Clark, 'How gifted children can wither under the hot-house pressures', *Sunday Telegraph*, 19 July 1992; Stuart Wavell, 'Prodigies: a suitable case for treatment', *Sunday Times*, 21 May 1995.

[107] 'Being gifted is no ticket to top', *Daily Mail*, 10 December 1981, p. 3.

[108] Ibid.; Southworth, 'What becomes of child prodigies?'.

[109] NAGC archives, Bletchley, 'A new name?', *NAGC Newsletter*, Summer 1995, p. 7.

[110] NAGC archives, Bletchley, 'The Progress of Gifted Children', *Headquarters Newsletter*, February 1982, p. 5.

[111] NAGC archives, Bletchley, 'Letters to the Editor: What are they doing now?', *Looking to their Future*, Spring 1991, p. 12.

[112] Ibid.   [113] Ibid., p. 13.   [114] Ibid.   [115] Ibid.

and the experiences of her son, who did receive this label. The mother felt that she had 'slipped through the net, so to speak, of education'.[116] She was 'keen to learn but not what they were teaching at school' and exhibited signs of giftedness such as high creativity—making calendars, earrings, and a clay model—and trying to teach herself German, the Greek alphabet, and to memorise poems and Shakespeare plays.[117] Nonetheless, she failed the 11+ and attended a secondary modern, suspecting in hindsight that she may have been subject to exam tampering, after 'an ex-governor of one of the local schools [said] that it was policy at the time to doctor the pass figures in order to keep clever children'.[118]

The author subsequently had issues at home and at school, and left with few qualifications, before starting an unrewarding career in banking, a field she had little interest in.[119] When she had children, she focused on them, and quickly noticed that her eldest son was gifted: not speaking until he was two but then quickly forming full sentences, for example.[120] The National Association had this child tested by an educational psychologist, who pronounced that he was gifted and dyslexic, and recommended a school where he excelled.[121] Closing her letter, the mother stated that her children 'have profited by my frustrations and experiences', and that she would continue to 'look forward to' receiving the Association's newsletters, which she found 'very interesting'.[122] In all three of these stories, therefore, gifted child alumni emphasised the utility of the label 'gifted' over the life course, the potential damage to the family and the individual if the 'diagnosis' was not made, and the value of the voluntary sector for diagnosis and support.

Gifted child alumni also talked to one another within online parenting fora, which became highly popular, particularly for mothers, from the popularisation of the internet in the mid-1990s, discussing pregnancy and parenting through message boards, 'expert comment', advertising, and product guides.[123] In the UK, Mumsnet and Netmums became the most popular sites, and by the 2010s attracted millions of views monthly, tens of thousands of posts, and influenced electoral debate. While initially dominated by white, middle-class mothers, research shows that the audience for these sites has become more diverse, including in particular 'lone parents and those with lower levels of education and income'. Mumsnet typically catered for users with a household income over the national average, and Netmums for families with lower incomes.[124] In these websites, 'giftedness' was particularly controversial, ending in 'slanging matches', yet also of sufficient interest to generate distinct sub-messaging boards and conversations that continued

---

[116] Ibid., p. 14.   [117] Ibid.   [118] Ibid.   [119] Ibid.
[120] Ibid.   [121] Ibid.   [122] Ibid., p. 15.
[123] Deborah Lupton, Sarah Pederson, and Gareth M. Thomas, 'Parenting and Digital Media: From the Early Web to Contemporary Digital Society', *Sociology Compass*, 10 (8) (2016), pp. 730–731.
[124] Ibid.; Sarah Pederson and Janet Smithson, 'Mothers with attitude—How the Mumsnet parenting forum offers space for new forms of femininity to emerge online', *Women's Studies International Forum*, 38 (2013), p. 101.

in real life and on other online platforms.[125] Gifted child alumni were particularly prominent in these spaces. Mothers stated, for example, that as a child they were given this label, 'gifted', and put in special classes or even that they were a young member of Mensa.

Parental views of experiences of gifted education in the 1970s and 1980s, from the 1990s and 2000s, were mixed, ranging from statements that extra classes were 'brilliant', 'challenging', 'stimulating', or that they were '"singled" out' or bullied. Some contributing mothers had attended National Association or parallel such leisure groups, charted in Chapter Three. Again, their experiences and views varied. Some mothers stated that they had found that the group was full of 'pushy parents' and that the gifted children had 'formed a clique' or 'dominated everything'. Others described the group as 'brilliant', because of the constellation of activities described in Chapter Three—blending athletic and intellectual pursuits—or because, again as charted in this previous chapter, the groups felt as if they were organised and run by children themselves.

We can then not only look at children as 'being' and 'becoming', in relation to the present and future; both important lenses in contemporary childhood studies.[126] Indeed, we can also think about being as 'been'; looking at how adult memories of childhood shape contemporary opinions and debate. Significantly, for the mothers studied here, childhood experiences had shaped their view of current provision. Notably, some argued that catering for the gifted was part of creating an equal Britain, as, 'society doesn't want to celebrate these children' otherwise, and that state schools could not adequately provide for them. For others, however, the very term was 'elitist', and IQ tests did not correlate with school performance or personal worth. Parents became highly significant as drivers of educational policy in the mid-to-late twentieth century, particularly through their influence on local schools and education authorities.[127] In debates about the gifted, also, government select committees interviewed headteachers, educational researchers, and voluntary organisation representatives who consistently emphasised that parents wanted to shape gifted provision, and that their voices should be incorporated into how schools were managed and run.[128]

---

[125] See footnote 30 for a fuller discussion of the use of internet archives in this chapter.

[126] Emma Uprichard, 'Children as "Being and Becomings": children, childhood and temporality', *Children & Society*, 22 (4) (2008), pp. 303–313. Useful discussion of the 'Being' and 'Becoming' distinction in contemporary scholarship in: Sarah L. Holloway, Louise Holt, and Sarah Mills, 'Questions of agency: capacity, subjectivity, spatiality and temporality', *Progress in Human Geography*, 43 (3) (2018), pp. 467–470.

[127] Peter Mandler, *The Crisis of the Meritocracy? Britain's Transition to Mass Education since the Second World War* (Oxford: OUP, 2020).

[128] Education and Employment Committee, Highly Able Children, 1998–9, Volume 1: Report and Proceedings of the Committee, pp. xix, xlvi, 10, 15, 16, 59. See also Hilary Radnor, Valsa Koshy, and Alexis Taylor, 'Gifts, talents and meritocracy', *Journal of Educational Policy*, 22 (3) (2007), p. 283; Valsa Koshy and Catrin Pinheiro-Torres, 'Are we being de-gifted Miss? Primary school gifted and

Despite concurrent moves towards public consultation and public–patient involvement in state and welfare in this period, the voices of gifted alumni and parents of gifted children were rare in the policy documents of John Major and Tony Blair. 'Gifted child alumni' had become visible in tabloids, voluntary organisations, and online in the 1990s and 2000s. They felt that they had significant comments on national debates in this area. Yet, national policy-makers wished to make the vision of the gifted child anew. Despite the view of many alumni, the gifted child was to be the solution to inner city decline, child loneliness, industrial productivity, equality, and elitism alike.

Conclusion

Multiple visions of giftedness co-existed in the 1990s and 2000s. First, the long-standing idea that gifted children were a potential source for political, economic, and world future elites; second, the idea that all young people had 'gifts' that must be identified, documented, and mobilised to the benefit of science and industry. In part, these distinct visions reflected the distinct range of historical definitions of 'elitism' and 'equality' in relation to giftedness. Yet, giftedness debates were also distinct to the contexts of the 1990s and 2000s. Private involvement in government contracting and the expansion of global commercial businesses reshaped gifted provision. New commercial partnerships for gifted organisations drove the increased focus on the gifted as 'future workers', as well as 'leaders'.

While gifted young people in Britain were expected to save local industries, globally they were still expected to perform remarkable feats, preventing wars and restoring or creating countries' economic futures (as Chapter Six further explores through analysis of transnational organisations). Also specific to the 1990s and 2000s, efforts in gifted education took on a particular congratulatory tone, contributing to building nationhood and national pride domestically.[129] Further, many of those involved in giftedness debates in the 1990s and 2000s were critically aware of the time at which they were writing and saw it as a potential turning point. These decades were seen as an opportunity to enable all young people to fulfil their potential, a new moment for Britain to re-imagine its place in the world, and a series of technological opportunities for a new workplace, and particularly for youth.[130]

---

talented co-ordinators' responses to the Gifted and Talented Policy in England', *British Educational Research Journal*, 39 (2013), p. 961.

[129] Kevin O'Sullivan, 'History and humanitarianism: a conversation', *Past & Present*, 241 (1) (2018), e6.

[130] Education and Employment Committee, Highly Able Children, 1998–9, Volume 1: Report and Proceedings of the Committee, p. vi. My thinking on the 1990s as a turning point was informed by participation in Helen McCarthy and David Geiringer's workshop, 'Rethinking Britain in the 1990s:

This chapter has also traced how young people themselves felt about these changes, notably how young people experienced and remembered the National Records of Achievement and the National Academy for Gifted and Talented Youth. The chapter argues that the spaces for young people to resist and critique the label 'gifted', dissipated somewhat in the 1990s and 2000s. While the press became more interested in discussing 'gifted youth gone bad', voluntary organisations, such as the National Association, which had previously provided rich spaces for complex critical cultures of writing, faded. In their place, organisations such as the National Academy were less focused on mapping the dissonant, disruptive terrain of the young gifted mind. Nonetheless, effective theories of agency must take seriously young people's enthusiastic consent to and rejection of psychological and educational labels.[131] These organisations were also, because of their funding, able to offer more significant opportunities for the young gifted participants to enjoy, and the social space was important for many.

Finally, this chapter has also engaged with memories from this period, and with ideas of how gifted child alumni, and alumni of the National Records of Achievement scheme, remembered and reconstructed their childhoods as adults. The chapter demonstrates that we must engage with rich new sources available because of the specific technologies of this time: notably internet fora, which were significant spaces in which people negotiated their lives and identities as parents, students, and individuals, and created new social identities and formations.[132] Analysis of Reddit subverted assumptions from the professional literature, showing that the National Record of Achievement, despite dismissal by researchers, remained significant in shaping people's identities and memories as they aged. Considering Netmums and Mumsnet, likewise, showed that parents assessing giftedness were perhaps more affected by their own childhood memories than the contemporary context, which perpetuated concepts from the 1970s and 1980s. Ideas of giftedness moved most powerfully into national policy in the 1990s and 2000s. Yet, even as Blair tried to offer these ideas anew, their reception, particularly among parents and gifted child alumni, was fundamentally shaped by the historic debates traced in this book.

'Gifted Children' in Britain and the World: Elitism and Equality since 1945. Jennifer Crane, Oxford University Press.
© Jennifer Crane 2025. DOI: 10.1093/9780198928881.003.0006

Towards a new research agenda', which is partially documented here: 'When was the nineties', *Past and Present* website <https://pastandpresent.org.uk/when-was-the-nineties/> (22 March 2024).
[131] Miller, 'Assent as agency'; Abebe, 'Reconceptualising children's agency'.
[132] See also Millward, 'A history with web archives, not a history of web archives', pp. 464–478.

Gifted Children Saving 'Europe' and 'the World', 1975–2000

> Superior?
> Maybe, but maybe only in other's eyes.
> Able? Yes to a point.
> Not perfect, never perfect.
> Sometimes overrated, overworked.
>
> *An extract from 'Being Gifted', by Kate, Grade 10 student, Toronto, Canada, as cited in 'Children's Corner', World Gifted: Newsletter of the World Council for Gifted and Talented Children, 8 (1) (March 1987), p. 13.*

The poem, 'Being Gifted', was written by a girl of 15 or 16, from Canada, and published in the newsletter of the World Council for Gifted and Talented Children in March 1987. The World Council had been established over a decade earlier in 1975, following the first World Conference on giftedness held in London and led by representatives of the British National Association for Gifted Children. In this poem, Kate recognised the entwined psychological, educational, and popular language of 'giftedness', 'ability', 'perfection', 'talent', and 'superiority', and its power. At the same time, Kate was not fully convinced by ideas of giftedness. She argued that these abilities were constructed externally by society, and indeed that gifted children were sometimes both 'overrated' and 'overworked', or indeed negatively affected by this label, and thus led to being 'overconfident'.

Through the World Council, Kate's words were disseminated beyond Canada towards interested professionals, parents, and other young people across the globe. This chapter studies how two transnational voluntary organisations—the World Council for Gifted Children (founded in 1975) and the European Council for High Ability (founded in 1988)—constructed gifted young people, 'Europe', and 'the world' in the late twentieth century. It demonstrates that both of these organisations had high hopes that such young people, because of their special talents, could forge special global connections across borders, and that these connections could be used for a variety of contemporary aims: to prevent warfare, promote cultural ties across Europe, and fuel international development. At the same time, the chapter also demonstrates that lofty rhetoric from these groups, calling for these children to shape 'a better world and our common future', did not always shape broader practical work with the young themselves.[1] The 'Children's Corner', indeed, was a rare feature in the World Council newsletter, and these organisations did not have the resources or logistical capabilities to conduct transnational work that directly involved young people.

This case study can significantly develop our understandings of 'cultural internationalism': activities, particularly in the voluntary sector, undertaken 'to link countries and peoples through the exchange of ideas and persons, through scholarly cooperation, or through efforts at facilitating cross-national understanding'.[2] At present, historians and geographers emphasise the significance of the interwar, post-war, and Cold War moments for making children 'international diplomats', connecting cultures through state- and voluntary-organised friendship societies and exchange programmes.[3] Tamara Myers and Richard Ivan Jobs situate the 1960s, 1970s, and 1980s as particularly significant, as young people's 'activist subjectivit[ies]' themselves shaped global exchanges, for example through youth travel and youth-led voluntary action.[4] Matthias Neumann and Sean Guillory highlight the same period through case studies of how the Soviet Union promoted youth exchanges to showcase and demonstrate their cultural superiority to parts of both America and Africa.[5]

Cultural internationalism into the 1990s and early 2000s has been studied less.[6] Existing accounts often assume that 'efforts to use children exclusively as pawns',

---

[1] Herman W. van Boxtel, 'Final Report', in Franz J. Mönks, Michael W. Katzko, and Herman W. Van Boxtel (eds), *Education of the Gifted in Europe: Theoretical and Research Issues, Report of the Educational Research Workshop held in Nijmegen (The Netherlands), 23–26 July 1991* (Netherlands: Swets & Zeitlinger B. V., 1992), p. 27; European Council for High Ability news, volume 8, number 2, 2 September 1994, as cited in 'The History of ECHA', European Council for High Ability website, <https://www.echa.info/history-25-years/content/2-about-echa> (18 July 2019).

[2] Akira Iriyre, *Cultural Internationalism and World Order* (Baltimore: John Hopkins University Press, 1997), p. 3.

[3] See Mischa Honeck and Gabriel Rosenberg, 'Transnational generations: organizing youth in the Cold War', *Diplomatic History*, 38 (2) (2014), p. 234; Matthias Neumann, 'Children diplomacy during the late Cold War: Samantha Smith's visit of the "Evil Empire"', *History*, 104 (360), (2019), pp. 277–278; Sara Fieldston, 'Little cold warriors: child sponsorship and international affairs', *Diplomatic History*, 38 (2) (2014), pp. 240–250; Christina Norwig, 'A first European generation? the myth of youth and European integration in the fifties', *Diplomatic History*, 38 (2) (2014), pp. 251–260; Marcia Chatelain, 'International sisterhood: Cold War girl scouts encounter the world', *Diplomatic History*, 38 (2) (2014), pp. 261–270; Sean Guillory, 'Culture clash in the Socialist paradise: Soviet patronage and African students' urbanity in the Soviet Union, 1960–1965', *Diplomatic History*, 38 (2) (2014), pp. 271–281; Tamara Myers, 'Local action and global imagining: youth, international development, and the Walkathon Phenomenon in sixties' and seventies' Canada', *Diplomatic History*, 38 (2) (2014), pp. 282–293; Sarah Mills, 'Geographies of youth work, volunteering and employment: the Jewish Lads Brigade and Club in post-war Manchester', *Transactions of the Institute of British Geographers*, 40 (4) (2015), pp. 523–535.

[4] Myers, 'Local action and global imagining', p. 283; Richard Ivan Jobs, *Backpack Ambassadors: How Youth Travel Integrated Europe* (Chicago: University of Chicago Press, 2017), ch. 3: Youth movements.

[5] Neumann, 'Children diplomacy during the late Cold War', pp. 277–278; Guillory, 'Culture clash in the Socialist paradise'.

[6] Although recent geographical work is exploring these debates in the present: Matthew C. Benwell and Peter Hopkins, *Children, Young People and Critical Geopolitics* (London: Routledge, 2017); Moses Okech, Matt Baillie Smith, Bianca Fadel, and Sarah Mills, 'The reproduction of inequality through volunteering by young refugees in Uganda', *Voluntas: International Journal of Voluntary and*

such as in state-programmes in this area, were 'passing into the history of another time' from the end of the Cold War.[7] Yet, this case study shows that such ideas of the potential of the young did not diminish after this period. Rather, they simply became more targeted. The 1990s saw significant work undertaken by the World Council and European Council. In this decade, both made use of new technologies of communication, travel, and printing to more closely connect professionals interested in this area from across the world, more fully, quickly, and easily than ever before. The development of new technologies in this period, then, was critical in enabling smaller groups, with specific interests, to flourish and expand. Yet, at the same time, these technologies were still not sufficient to enable the organisations to run their own significant youth programmes in depth—the European and World Council members, from different countries, had unequal access to resources, and still often struggled to find funds to provide their newsletters and regular meetings; their resources did not extend to providing consistent child-centred programmes as well.

In this context, we can see the 1990s as a period when the child continued to play a significant role in developing cultural internationalism. Ideas from the post-war and Cold War periods remained—that young people would fuel reconciliation, economic development, and disseminate specific cultural values. Yet transnational voluntary organisations, rather than national governments or national voluntary organisations, were the critical generators of these ideas. Young people themselves became involved, primarily, symbolically. Chapter Five argued, with regards to the British context, that the 1990s and 2000s are a more difficult period in which to trace the feelings and opinions of the young, because national programmes that catered to them—such as the National Academy for Gifted and Talented Youth—became professionalised and were less interested in recording children's views than 1970s and 1980s organisations such as Britain's National Association for Gifted Children. In this chapter, this argument is extended, and again the 1990s seem to be a moment in which children's own contributions and voices were somewhat lost in giftedness debates.

This chapter first examines the inception of the World Council for Gifted Children at a 1975 conference in London, organised by key figures from the National Association, Henry Collis and Felicity Ann Sieghart. It demonstrates that initially the organisation, due to its strong British connections, framed its work around arguments about the gifted as both 'elite' and 'equal'. Second, the chapter explores the later years of the World Council in to the late twentieth

---

Nonprofit Organisations, first view 15 February 2024; Craig Jeffrey, 'Geographies of children and youth II', *Progress in Human Geography*, 36 (2) (2012), pp. 245–253; Matt Baillie Smith, Sarah Mills, Moses Okech, and Bianca Fadel, 'Uneven geographies of youth volunteering in Uganda: Multiscalar discourses and practices', *Geoforum*, 134 (2022), pp. 30–39.

[7] Paula S. Fass, 'Intersecting agendas: children in history and diplomacy', *Diplomatic History*, 38 (2) (2014), p. 298.

century. It demonstrates that this organisation became more global from the mid-1970s, and explores the logistical issues that shaped its work. Third, the chapter considers what 'World' this Council looked to represent, describing the tensions the Council framed between 'developed' and 'developing' nations. Fourth, the chapter discusses the European Council for High Ability, founded in 1988. Britons were less central in the foundation of this organisation, though British psychologist Joan Freeman played a key role. Sadly, this organisation has left fewer archival traces than the World Council, but nonetheless the chapter shows the hierarchies it created between 'East' and 'West' Europe, and how they related to issues of resource and logistics. Fifth and finally, the chapter asks where young people sat within these transnational organisations. There are few indications of young people's voices—such as Kate's poem—in material from the European or World Council. The chapter reads available material closely, to suggest that young people played a primarily performative and symbolic role in these groups.

Overall, the chapter demonstrates that ideas of giftedness were not only important in Britain but also across parts of the world more broadly. British campaigners, who had been mobilising in Britain in the 1970s and 1980s—notably Freeman, Sieghart, and Collis—were significant within transnational voluntary organisations, where they worked closely with campaigners from across the globe. This chapter also shows the power of transnational voluntary networks, including relatively small groups with specific causes, to spread ideas. The chapter helps us to think through the distinctiveness of the British case study. Concerns about 'equality' and 'elitism' that were central to framing British debates, were present in the European and World Councils, but were not their primary concerns. Rather, these groups were more concerned with negotiating what exactly 'Europe' and 'the world' were, and how gifted young people could improve these configurations. British voluntary action was significant in framing early global interest in giftedness— from the 1970s and 1980s—but faded in prominence thereafter. From this point, transnational organisers used very broad visions of 'the gifted' and their purposes to unite international partners. Underlying these debates were significant disagreements, notably about the role of children, the number of young people being referred to as 'gifted', the appropriateness of special schools, and the gifted as political, artistic, or cultural leaders. Reading newsletters from these organisations, work by and interviews with their founders, alongside contemporary academic and media discussions, demonstrates that, as ever, the idea of 'the gifted child' was both powerful and flexible enough to accommodate a broad range of political interests and agendas.

Founding the World Council

The World Council for Gifted Children was founded in 1975, after Henry Collis organised the first World Conference on Gifted Children in London, in his role as Director of Britain's National Association. Collis took a strange path to this position. As a boy, later press coverage of Collis reported, he was 'unable to manage more than one solitary percentage mark in his geometry test in the Common Entrance examination', which he 'now openly boasts' was 'a charity mark'.[8] He was also, apparently, 'quite untalented in games, somewhat gauche and even slightly gawky', and thus 'could not have been a worse candidate for the traditional British public school'.[9] Nonetheless, Collis attended Clifton College Preparatory School, a public school in Bristol. Later, he studied at the University of Cambridge, where he 'scraped a Pass'.[10] Framing this narrative of success despite ineptitude, Collis told the *Daily Telegraph* in 1981 that, '[i]n those days marks were not everything.'[11] He became an English teacher, teaching for five years before World War Two, when he fought. He then became Headteacher of the Eastbourne College Prep School, an independent school, and later Colet Court, a preparatory school for the prestigious St Paul's, London.[12]

Collis told the *Daily Telegraph* that his interest in gifted children came from his time as a Headteacher. He recalled that he was sent a boy who had won a scholarship and arrived with the note, '[h]e is frustrated, disruptive and an isolate [sic]. In fact, he is a pain in the neck and may not do well on paper in case he is accepted and has to work too hard, but for heaven's sake take him—he is brilliant.'[13] Collis stated that at Colet Court each year the school admitted six 'exceptionally able boys' on a means test, paying low or no fees. He stated that, '[s]ome were lazy; some were self-centred and most were unable to accept failure. Most of them got Oxbridge awards on leaving St Paul's.'[14] In 1974, he took early retirement and became director of the National Association, taking over from Margaret Branch (see Chapter Two).

Collis worked closely in this role with the Chairman of the National Association, Felicity Ann Sieghart (1927–2019). Sieghart had taken a very different path to her role from Collis—there was no 'typical' voluntary leader in this period. Sieghart had a highly privileged childhood, granddaughter of a Member of Parliament and raised in the countryside near Bishops Stortford by a wealthy metals trader. Her childhood was, her obituary in *The Times* stated, 'surrounded by maids, cooks, butlers, gardeners and chauffeurs'.[15] In World War Two, she missed two years of school due to her parents' concern about rationed petrol. She then attended Hertfordshire and Essex Girls' High School, and studied history at Oxford University from 1944.[16] Sieghart was not able to enjoy a significant professional career after this, however, aside from brief positions in filing and

---

[8] John Izbicki, 'Teaching the gifted child', *Daily Telegraph*, 17 August 1981.
[9] Ibid. [10] Ibid. [11] Ibid.
[12] Ibid. [13] Ibid. [14] Ibid.
[15] 'Felicity Ann Sieghart obituary', *The Times*, 11 June 2019 <https://www.thetimes.co.uk/article/felicity-ann-sieghart-obituary-lngt6fnsv> (12 October 2021).
[16] Ibid.

administration at Chatham House and the British School in Rome. Her time was instead dominated by marriage and family. In 1953 she married John Ward, who was a sisal planter in Mozambique, and Sieghart went there to live with him. Demonstrating her capacity for learning, she learnt Portuguese and Swahili, in addition to already being proficient in French, German, Italian, and Latin. She later divorced Ward and married Paul Sieghart, a barrister and human rights campaigner, and they had two children. Her obituary reported that her interest in giftedness came from raising these children, using the Socratic method to debate politics at the dinner table, as well as from her own childhood talents.[17] She became involved with the National Association during this period.[18]

Early leaders of the National Association, hence, brought very different forms of expertise to their roles: psychological, media, educational, and parental. However, Collis and Sieghart shared an interest in making this organisation global, and in looking to 'unite the educators of the gifted around the world, who were already convening at national levels'.[19] Subsequently, they organised the World Conference event at the Royal College of Surgeons in Lincoln's Inn. The event's flyer stated its intention to mark the 'beginning' of 'international co-operation', 'contacts', and 'friendship'.[20] Collis stated that, 'nothing quite like it had ever been staged before'.[21]

From its foundation, the World Council was global, and yet also grounded in British voluntary and professional circles. Over 500 delegates attended its first Conference, from 53 countries, including, as highlighted by newspaper coverage, the USA, New Zealand, Israel, Czechoslovakia, Poland, Thailand, and Mexico.[22] Yet British speakers remained central at this event. The honorary President of the National Association, Sir George Porter—the Director of the Royal Institution, London, and winner of the Nobel Prize for Chemistry in 1967—wrote a motivational letter to all delegates, welcoming them, and emphasising that thanks 'in large part to the work of the' National Association, people now understood that 'in every generation there are far too many children whose great potential will never become realised to the full because we fail to identify them early enough'.[23] The conference's opening speeches were given by the Deputy Lord Mayor of Westminster, Councillor Donald du Parc Braham; Sir Rodney Smith, President of the Royal College of Surgeons; John Hudson, the Acting Permanent Secretary

---

[17] Ibid.   [18] Ibid.
[19] 'History', World Council for Gifted and Talented Children website <https://world-gifted.org/about-wcgtc/history/> (12 October 2021).
[20] NAGC archives, Bletchley, 'From the President of the National Association for Gifted Children (UK)', *World Conference on Gifted Children Flyer*, 1975, p. 3.
[21] Izbicki, 'Teaching the gifted child'.
[22] 'World conference on gifted children', *Guardian*, 7 January 1975, p. 19; 'Needs of gifted children to be discussed', *The Times*, 15 May 1975, p. 20.
[23] Joy Gibson and Prue Chennells (eds), *Gifted Children: Looking to their Future* (Essex: The Anchor Press, 1976), p. i.

at the Department for Education and Science; and Collis himself. Many key figures from British histories of giftedness spoke during the Conference, such as Lord Rusholme, who spoke on behalf of the National Association in the first House of Parliament debate in this area, and the Headmaster of the innovative Yehudi Menuhin School (both discussed in Chapter Two).[24]

The conference's aims emphasised global intentions but were significantly shaped by distinctly British anxieties and concerns. The aims were:

TO FOCUS world attention on gifted children and their valuable potential contribution to the benefit of mankind.

TO EXPLORE the nature of their talents and resultant problems in childhood and adolescence.

TO CREATE a 'climate' of acceptance of gifted children, not as a privileged elite, but as an invaluable global asset.

TO ASSEMBLE, for an exchange of ideas and experiences, people from all over the world influential in the fields of medicine, education, psychology and sociology.

TO PERSUADE the governments of the world to recognise gifted children as a category for special attention in normal educational programmes.

TO ESTABLISH means for a continuing world-wide exchange of ideas, experiences, teaching and teacher-training techniques in respect of gifted children.[25]

These aims positioned gifted children as able to benefit all of 'mankind' and an 'invaluable global asset'. The Conference and Council looked to unite relevant experts from 'all over the world' to discuss these talented youth, organising a 'world-wide exchange of ideas' to influence 'governments of the world'. This framing was in keeping was Tehila Sasson's analysis of the 1970s as a 'breakthrough' moment in thinking globally about human rights, when an international community 'began to advocate for global justice beyond national borders' for the first time.[26] At the same time, the World Council's aims were also shaped by British concerns—notably, ensuring that gifted children were not seen as a 'privileged elite'.

These concerns were echoed in the event's opening speeches. The Deputy Lord Mayor of Westminster, for example, emphasised that, 'I personally deplore the ever-increasing pressures by society to produce egalitarianism compulsorily in all aspects of life, especially in the educational field'. Echoing debates seen throughout this book in Britain, he further stated that, '[i]n education, for instance, they appear to have fallen into the trap of believing that equality of

---

[24] 'Conference Programme', World Conference on Gifted Children <https://www.world-gifted.org/wp-content/uploads/2018/02/1975-London-Conference-Information.pdf> (12 October 2021).
[25] Gibson and Chennells (eds), *Gifted Children*, p. ii.
[26] Tehila Sasson, 'Milking the Third World: Humanitarianism, Capitalism, and the Moral Economy of the Nestlé Boycott', *American Historical Review*, 121 (4) (2016), p. 1198.

opportunity should imply equality of achievement.'[27] Facets of the British press also gave critical coverage to this early conference, again using ideas of 'equality' and 'elitism' as framing devices. Weeks later, John Hatch, writing for the *Guardian*, stated that the event showed that schools should devote their energies to, 'preparing the masses of children to recognise and meet their responsibilities, rather than coaching an elite to concentrate still more influence in fewer hands'.[28]

Beyond ideas of 'elitism', other facets of British debate seen throughout this book framed the first World Conference. Ideas that these gifted young people could be 'leaders of tomorrow—in the sciences, the arts, the learned professions and commerce', or alternatively 'drop-outs or delinquents, all the more dangerous on account of their high level of individual ability' were common in opening speeches, for example.[29] These notions of the future also informed a subsequent book, looking to summarise this event, *Gifted Children: Looking to their Future* (1976). When offering 'a representative selection of the questions asked, either after the individual papers or in the general question period', this book listed questions about how to train student teachers, inform fathers as well as mothers about their responsibilities to gifted youth, recognise giftedness in preschool children, encourage creativity, and to build relationships. Several questions focused on the future.[30] One asked, 'whether truly to educate the gifted child, and therefore perhaps produce future social critics and revolutionaries; or to indoctrinate them as upholders of conventional morality and tools for preserving the status quo'.[31] Another, when discussing relationships, couched this in terms of how to 'get on better terms with the 50% who have to support us'.[32]

Closing the World Conference in 1975, Sieghart emphasised that the gifted young were 'enormously important…because it is to their generation that we, their parents and their teachers, will have to hand over our world in a very few years—far sooner than many of us perhaps realise.'[33] She argued also that, 'I now feel convinced that this conference will mark the beginning of a series of world conferences, of world-wide trans-national professional and lay concern for gifted children, their problems, their future, and what we can do about them.'[34] One delegate recalled in 2017 that this happened as Harold Lyon, Director of the Office of Gifted and Talented in America, 'enthusiastically carried a plastic globe around the hall in which participants could deposit funds, and 150 contributed to become members of the proposed organization'.[35] The subsequent World Council that was established had strong roots in British voluntary action, but also began

[27] Gibson and Chennells (eds), *Gifted Children*, p. 1.
[28] John Hatch, 'Tomorrow's world', *Guardian*, 2 December 1975, p. 20.
[29] Gibson and Chennells (eds), *Gifted Children*, pp. i, 5.
[30] Gibson and Chennells (eds), *Gifted Children*, pp. 216–228.
[31] Ibid., p. 216.   [32] Ibid., p. 221.   [33] Ibid., p. 374.   [34] Ibid., p. 376.
[35] Dorothy A. Sisk, 'History of the World Council for Gifted and Talented Children', World Council for Gifted and Talented Children website <https://www.world-gifted.org/wp-content/uploads/2018/01/WCGTC-History.pdf> (12 October 2021), p. 1.

to encompass far broader, and more intriguing, visions of 'the world' in subsequent years. The initial bold claims about the gifted and their purposes would continue to expand, and to conceal a broad range of agendas and preferences for specific policy measures and systems.

Gifted Children Save 'the World'!

The World Council for Gifted and Talented Children grew in size and reach significantly from its 1975 foundation event. Its membership and leadership began to encompass figures from across the world. Institutional materials continued to present a hopeful vision of a collaborative, co-operative, organisation, although reading against the grain shows that significant hierarchies remained within this organisation.[36] Members from low-income countries faced significant logistical challenges to being actively involved, and the organisation struggled to generate significant income, given the national focus of many funding schemes. Almost immediately after its foundation event in London, the World Council's leadership moved beyond Britain. The organisation was formally established as a non-profit organisation and registered in Delaware in 1976.[37] Its first representatives were leaders from policy, education, and research around giftedness in Britain, America, and Israel: Dan Bitan, Henry Collis, Dorothy Sisk, Elizabeth Neuman, and Alexis Du Pont DeBie.[38] At this time, America and Israel were seen, by educators interested in giftedness, as the 'world leader in gifted/talented education' and as 'lead[ing] the world in level of commitment to gifted/talented education'.[39]

---

[36] Reading these archives, 'against the grain', is conducted with reference to research about practices of archiving, for example: Merle Patchett, 'Archiving', *Transactions of the Institute of British Geographers*, 44 (2019), pp. 650–653; Andrew Flinn, 'Archival activism: independent and community-led archives, radical public history and the heritage professions', *Interactions: UCLA Journal of Education and Information Studies*, 7 (2) (2011); Tim Cresswell, 'Value, gleaning and the archive at Maxwell Street, Chicago', *Transactions of the Institute of British Geographers*, 37 (1) (2012), pp. 164–176; Sarah Mills, 'Cultural-historical geographies of the archive: fragments, objects and ghosts', *Geography Compass*, 7 (10) (2013), pp. 709–710; Mela Dávila-Freire, 'Reading the archive against the grain: Power relations, affective affinities and subjectivity in the documenta Archive', *Art Libraries Journal*, 45 (3) (2020), pp. 94–99; Kate Boyer, 'Feminist geography in the archive: practice and method', WGSG, *Geography and Gender Reconsidered*, August 2004, pp. 169–174; Maria Fannin and Julie MacLeavy, 'Feminism, resistance and the archive', in Sarah M. Hughes (ed.) *Critical Geographies of Resistance* (Cheltenham: Edward Elgar, 2023), pp. 26–40.
[37] Sisk, 'History of the World Council for Gifted and Talented Children', p. 2.
[38] Ibid. Israel had had an active giftedness programme run by its government since 1976, managed by the Department for Gifted Children under the Ministry of Education and Culture (see Blanka Burg, 'Gifted Education in Israel', *Roeper Review*, 14 (4) (1992), pp. 217–221).
[39] Quotes are from Bruce M. Mitchell and William G. Williams, 'Education of the Gifted and Talented in the World Community', *The Phi Delta Kappan*, 68 (10) (1987), p. 532. Israel for example, by the late 1970s, had a 'Department for Gifted Children' within the Ministry of Education, and also the Jerusalem Foundation for the Gifted Child, a supplementary institute set up in 1971 to take around 300 children between kindergarten age and 14 from ordinary schools for extra post-school education (Maurice Rosenbaum, 'Freeing the gifted child—so that wisdom keeps pace with technology', *Daily Telegraph*, 6 July 1979).

From here, the organisation's leadership expanded to include members from across the world. By 1977, the Executive still had leading members from America, the UK, and Israel, but it was chaired by a psychologist from Iran, Dr Iraj Broomand, who was the National Director of Gifted Programs in Iran from 1975 to 1979 (until the Iranian Revolution).[40] Broomand was joined by members from Australia, Venezuela, and Bulgaria. This mix of low- and high-income countries on the organisation's management committee continued in the 1980s and 1990s.[41] The organisation also had a global membership. Its biannual conferences, for example, which attracted between 700 and 1,200 members and delegates, were held across the globe: in Jerusalem in 1979; Montreal in 1981; Manila in 1983; Hamburg in 1985; Utah in 1987; Sydney in 1989; Nijmegen in the Netherlands in 1991; Toronto in 1993; Hong Kong in 1995; and Seattle in 1997.[42] Conferences were organised, with the support of the transnational Executive, by national leaders in gifted education. Consequently, this list is also typically one of areas where giftedness programmes were more established, and where, consequently, national organising committees could facilitate, plan, and host these events—even funding the costs upfront and reclaiming them later via conference registration fees.[43]

While the Council then maintained a global presence, this was challenging. During his tenure as President, in June 1981, Collis wrote for the World Council's newsletter, *World Gifted*, that this organisation could be 'an impecunious international body', which could 'very easily lack cohesion and even credibility'.[44] As Collis wrote, the organisation already had members in thirty-two countries, with vastly different systems, priorities, and issues to navigate. The Council's newsletter—founded in April 1980—was an attempt to ameliorate this. It collated information about research projects in progress, new books, new projects, and forthcoming conferences, and it was distributed to all organisation members,

---

[40] Broomand subsequently moved to America and stated in an interview of 1982 that the Shah's regime had qualified the former giftedness programme as 'anti-revolutionary' due to its international links—it had had contracts with the United States, England, and France to man a physical centre and train staff ('Gifted Child Today meets with...Dr and Mrs Iraj Broomand', *Gifted Child Today*, 1 September 1982, p.56.)

[41] 'Executive Committee History', *World Council for Gifted and Talented Children* <https://world-gifted.org/about-wcgtc/history/executive-committee-history/> (13 October 2021).

[42] Sisk, 'History of the World Council for Gifted and Talented Children', p. 3. Descriptions of these conferences are available in the World Council's newsletters: 'Montreal Conference Draws 1200', *World Gifted*, 1983, 2 (3), p. 1; 'World conference on gifted and talented children', *World Gifted*, 1985, 6 (2), p. 1; 'Manila, 1983', *World Gifted*, 1983, 2 (3), p. 8; 'Hamburg conference', *World Gifted*, 1984, 5 (1), p. 1; 'President's message', *World Gifted*, 1986, 7 (1), p. 1; 'Message from the President', *World Gifted*, 1988, 9 (2), p. 1. A full list of conferences is available on the Council's website: 'World Conference Proceedings', World Council for Gifted and Talented Children website, https://world-gifted.org/publications/world-conference-proceedings/ 19 July 2019).

[43] Several of these countries are discussed in Mitchell and Williams, 'Education of the Gifted and Talented', pp. 531–534. The process of organising these conferences is further explained in 'Bids Solicited for 1987 Conference', *World Gifted: Newsletter of the World Council for Gifted and Talented Children*, May 1983, Volume 4, Number 2, p. 2.

[44] Henry Collis, 'Where Now?', *World Gifted: Newsletter of the World Council for Gifted and Talented Children*, June 1981, Volume 2, Number 2, p. 1.

initially by post and later online. Beyond this virtual contact, in-person Council meetings were limited, due to the cost of air fares, and not everyone could attend the biannual conference.[45] The organisation primarily raised central funds via a membership fee ($40 for two years membership from 1985, $75 for two years membership from 1994, $95 from 1999), which covered one permanent member of staff to compile the newsletter; edit the organisation's journal, *Gifted International*; answer queries; represent the World Council at relevant national meetings; and liaise between members.[46] The organisation needed approximately 1,000 members to be financially viable.[47] The World Council's functioning was also reliant on significant efforts by leading members. Harry Passow, a Professor of Education at the Teachers College, Columbia, for example, produced and edited the newsletter at the Teachers College, propping up the organisation's own 'very slender means'.[48]

Beyond this administrative centre, the World Council sought to establish a nationally-based Assembly of Delegates, where all countries involved would be represented by national co-ordinators, who could actively build networks in their own countries.[49] This required significant effort. World Council newsletters emphasised the 'devoted work', and 'arduous' and 'dogged' efforts of Committee members.[50] When recruiting new Committee members, they also sternly warned of the need for those who could '*engage actively in the work of the committee*, shaping that work and contributing to it, and not just passively receiving mail from the committee'.[51] The July 1993 newsletter stated that, 'the time for honorary positions is long past. The WCGTC requires a working Executive Committee.'[52]

Hierarchies between member countries were ingrained in the organisation and function of this small voluntary group. Notably, World Council publications discussed the significance 'break[ing] down' what it called 'barriers of language, custom and tradition'.[53] Yet, in part because of its foundation in America, but also reflecting the key active members of the World Council, the organisation's newsletter was published in English, which was also the key language of

---

[45] Ibid.
[46] 'Report from the Secretariat: Tasks and Functions of the Executive Administrator', *World Gifted: Newsletter of the World Council for Gifted and Talented Children*, April 1990, Volume 11, Number 1, p. 4; 'Application for Membership', *World Gifted: Newsletter of the World Council for Gifted and Talented Children*, April 1990, Volume 11, Number 1, p. 12; 'Application for Membership', *World Gifted: Newsletter of the World Council for Gifted and Talented Children*, August 1985, Volume 6, Number 2, p. 7; 'Membership Application', *World Gifted: Newsletter of the World Council for Gifted and Talented Children*, Fall 1998, Volume 17, Number 3, p. 16; 'World Council for Gifted and Talented Children: membership application', *World Gifted: Newsletter of the World Council for Gifted and Talented Children*, Winter 1999, Volume 18, Number 1, p. 16.
[47] 'The Secretariat's First Four Years', *World Gifted: Newsletter of the World Council for Gifted and Talented Children*, October 1983, Volume 4, Number 3, p. 2.
[48] Collis, 'Where Now?', p. 1.   [49] Ibid.
[50] Ibid.; Henry Collis, 'From the Chairman of the World Council', *World Gifted*, March 1981, 2 (1), p. 1; 'Funding concerns and efforts', *World Gifted*, September 1980, 1 (2), p. 5.
[51] 'World Council Committees', *World Gifted*, March 1987, Volume 8, Number 1, p. 2.
[52] 'Mönks Resigns from WCGTC Executive Committee', *World Gifted*, 13 (2), July 1993, p. 1.
[53] 'From the Secretariat', *World Gifted*, June 1984, 5 (2), p. 2.

conferences.[54] The World Council did make efforts to reach beyond English-speaking participants, but these were often reliant on the work of non-Anglophone members. For example, the Council sought interpreters for conferences, and for volunteers to translate introductory materials for parents and teachers, 'so we can send these resources around the world to anyone seeking assistance'.[55]

Furthermore, the countries involved and national co-ordinators had vastly different scales of resources available. One of the early American founders of this organisation, Alexis Du Pont DeBie, was a member of the Du Pont dynasty, and able to provide the services of his family lawyer while the organising committee drafted their application to become a non-profit organisation.[56] American organisers remained central to maintaining the organisation's core: while founded at Columbia Teachers College, from 1983 to 1990 the Secretariat relocated to the University of South Florida, under the management of Dr Dorothy Sisk, a professor there, who had also directed America's Office of Gifted/Talented Education, founded by the U.S. Office of Education in 1972.[57] With the support of a doctoral student, Hilda Rosselli, and institutional resources such as office space, the expenses for the newsletter and the organisation's journal were met by the College of Education's Gifted Program.[58]

Other leading figures in this organisation, from lower-income or less stable countries, could not afford this level of involvement, and did not have these institutional resources from universities or the state. The World Council's President from 1977 to 1979, for example, Broomand, felt that he had 'practically no resources' available while establishing the first giftedness programme in Iran, which was an independent body supported by the Prime Minister's Office, establishing schools for the gifted and a new research centre. When contemplating the resources available to him, Broomand later noted that American campaigners were 'not faced with that problem'.[59] Showing the political realities of such work also, Broomand's efforts in Iran came to a rapid end in 1979 during the Iranian Revolution. His work was deemed 'anti-revolutionary', because his research centres had international links with the USA, England, and France, and because his schools mixed genders and made the gifted 'special'.[60] Broomand stepped down from his role at the World Council, although he later moved to America and continued to pursue this line of work. The World Council's fifth World Conference in Manila was also organised in difficult national circumstances in 1983, as the dictatorship of Ferdinand Marcos underwent economic failure and

---

[54] '7th World Conference on Gifted and Talented Children', *World Gifted*, April 1986, p. 7.
[55] Ibid.; 'Resources, contact persons and translators needed', *World Gifted*, January 1994, 14 (1), p. 3; 'Creata created in Cape Town', *World Gifted*, May 1983, 4 (2), p. 6; 'Announcing a new magazine for gifted educators', *World Gifted*, Spring 1994, 14 (2), p. 6.
[56] Sisk, 'History of the World Council for Gifted and Talented Children', p. 2.
[57] Mitchell and Williams, 'Education of the gifted and talented', p. 532.
[58] Sisk, 'History of the World Council for Gifted and Talented Children', pp. 8–9.
[59] 'Gifted Child Today meets with..', p. 57.   [60] Ibid., pp. 56–57.

civil unrest. The World Council's newsletter of 1983 commended the key organisers of this conference, notably Dr Aurora Roldan, for managing this 'adventurous undertaking of high risk'.[61]

As a result of strained resources, language barriers, and national interests, the submission of manuscripts to this organisation's journal, and the attendees at conferences, were dominated by Global North members although a range of countries were represented at the Council.[62] The World Council sought to overcome this in various ways. In the 1970s and 1980s, it looked to facilitate cheap accommodation for conferences—'such as in a university residence hall, ministry guest house, or with a local family'—or to 'subsidize attendance for members from developing countries'.[63] Into the 1990s, however, the Council had high hopes that new technologies would make global contact easier for all. The World Council's newsletter of 1990 stated optimistically that technology had left the globe 'very small—only an arm's length or telefax away'.[64] Yet, organisers also recognised inequalities of access, and conducted a survey of members in 1994 asking about their familiarity with, and access to, telephones, fax machines, computers, modems, and the internet.[65] Even institutional sources, it seems, revealed how the term 'gifted' could bring international interest, yet primarily when vaguely defined.

Geographic Imaginaries

What vision of 'the world' did the Council work with? Notably, the Council repeatedly made a distinction between the 'developing' and 'developed' world: fuzzy categories that encompassed a range of nation-states. At times, the Council in part denied the significance of these categories, presenting a vision of global citizenship within which all young people belonged to the same world as 'humans'. Typically, however, Council publications and events suggested that the 'developing' world needed help from the 'developed', while also suggesting that 'developing' countries were typically more innovative in gifted education, and offered models to emulate.

The idea that gifted children were special world citizens was common in World Council rhetoric, although less often visible in the organisation's events or programmes. Speaking in 1977, for example, Sieghart stated that:

> Children are children and gifts are gifts the world over....the debt which the gifted individual owes to his country, and the *obligations* which I see every

---

[61] 'The Secretariat's First Four Years', *World Gifted*, October 1983, 4 (3), p. 1.
[62] 'Important numbers to note', *World Gifted*, Fall 1994, 14 (3), p. 3.
[63] 'Delegates Propose Action', *World Gifted*, Winter 1998, 17 (1), p. 1.
[64] 'Canada: Toronto', *World Gifted*, September 1990, 11 (2), p. 2.
[65] 'WCGTC Communications and Information Technology Survey', *World Gifted*, Fall 1994, 14 (3), p. 11.

country as having towards its members—gifted or not—do not depend on climate, economics, or (most important or [sic] all) political ideologies. They are part of the incidence of being *human*.[66]

These ideas were sometimes echoed in *Gifted Child Quarterly*, the publication of the American Association for Gifted Children: an article in 1975, for example, complimented the 'international orientation' of Japanese students, and 'their interest in the world beyond their boundaries'. Overall, it urged: 'Let's prepare our gifted to share their ideas with the world.'[67] In these interpretive accounts, the role of the gifted transcended ideology and circumstance. Giftedness was a fundamental part of 'being human', and must thus be shared and supported throughout the world. It was this very idea, of being 'human', that one decade later Kate, the Canadian teenager quoted at the start of this chapter, would challenge.[68]

While this rhetoric was significant at the World Council—and in its national counterparts—ideas about the 'developing' and 'developed' world, and about which needed to learn from the other, were more key in this organisation's historic writings. From the World Council's earliest work, leaders suggested that the educators in the 'developing' world needed training in managing the gifted. Collis, for example, wrote to *The Times* about 'a matter of considerable anxiety' to the World Council, that '[a]s the developing world gradually raises educational standards, more and more of its 1,300 million children will be seen to have a learning capacity far superior to the average. Unless their needs are taken seriously, there can only be unhappiness leading to aggressive disruption.'[69] This, he stated, would be one of the 'major topics' of discussion at the fourth conference of the Council, held in 1981 in Montreal.[70]

The World Council also took action around this rhetoric, primarily in terms of training led by interested individuals. The organisation's Spring 1997 newsletter stated that the Secretary of the World Council's Executive Committee, Dr David George, a former teacher in England, had 'visited several developing countries to give courses on the education of gifted and talented children'.[71] The framing of 'developing' countries here was broad—George had visited Croatia, Slovenia, India, and Turkey, where he had given a course for teachers, about how to identify gifted children early on, and participated in a school lecture tour.[72]

---

[66] Felicity Sieghart, 'Opening of the Second World Conference', *Looking to their Future*, November 1977, p. 4.
[67] 'The most academically talented students in the world', *Gifted Child Quarterly*, 19 (3), September 1975, p. 188.
[68] 'Children's Corner', *World Gifted*, March 1987, 8 (1), p. 13.
[69] Henry Collis, 'When being bright can be a mixed blessing', *The Times*, 9 September 1980, p. 10.
[70] Ibid.
[71] 'Support for developing countries', *World Gifted*, Spring 1997, 16 (1), p. 5.   [72] Ibid.

Richer countries in the World Council also looked to learn from poorer ones—or at times to draw on their resources or 'human capital' to enhance their own national economies. From the World Council's inception in 1975, it sought to learn from the Communist regimes of Eastern Europe. Led by the Soviet Union, many countries of Eastern Europe in this period had special schools for students in the visual and performing arts, languages, and athletics, and pioneer organisations for enrichment outside of school.[73] Ignoring the broader human rights abuses of the Soviet Union system, giftedness campaigners saw these as providing potentially positive models to analyse and copy. In 1977, for example, Collis visited Bulgaria to learn more about the country's work in giftedness. He was enthusiastically hosted by the country's Communist Party. Collis wrote in May 1977 that the country had, because of central planning, been able to develop a 'far-reaching plan' for identifying and nurturing gifted youth, and was also planning logistical and financial support for voluntary action and residential courses.[74] This interest was significant, revealing the porous and broad definition of 'giftedness' that the World Council operated with. While speaking enthusiastically about these schemes in general, British leaders such as Collis, having represented the National Association, were against the foundation of special schools, as in Soviet systems. Furthermore, much framing in the British context, at least, as we have seen throughout this book, focused on the creation of political leaders, rather than cultural or artistic ones as trained here. Notably, a range of countries and political systems could be accommodated within the World Council's analysis and comparison, but primarily on a theoretical and rhetorical level; in terms of establishing policy details, these comparisons would be less clear.

From the 1980s, the World Council became interested in what it conceptualised as 'developing' or 'Third World Countries' and their models of giftedness.[75] In particular, the Council was interested in countries of the African continent and also many in Asia and South and Central America. The National Association newsletter in Britain, reflecting on the World Council conference of 1983 in Manila, argued that:

> There is no doubt that Third World Countries view such programmes as indispensable in helping them to overcome their economic, social and political problems. In contrast, many of our more developed societies have taken an ambivalent attitude towards the subject.[76]

---

[73] Mitchell and Williams, 'Education of the gifted and talented', p. 533.
[74] Henry Collis, 'At work in Bulgaria', *Looking to their Future*, May 1977, pp. 9–10. Also discussed in: 'Gleanings from Triennial Children's Banner of Peace Assembly', *World Gifted*, March 1983, 4 (1), p. 5.
[75] On the emergence of the term 'Third World', and its politics, in the late 1960s, see: Patrick Bresnihan and Naomi Millner, *All We Want is the Earth: Land, Labour, and Movements Beyond Environmentalism* (Bristol: Bristol University Press, 2023), ch. 3.
[76] NAGC archives, Bletchley, 'Coming of age', *Looking to their Future*, June 1984, p. 1.

This idea was in part supported by some representatives from these countries identified. At the 1981 conference, the World Council newsletter stated that one delegate from Nigeria, Dr Coker, discussed how gifted education 'intersects with a commitment to universal education after centuries of elitism in a colonial era, with objectives in the area of multi-culturalism, and with goals of national unity, economic strength and technological development'. Furthermore, Dr Coker argued, gifted children were 'essential as an instrument of development in the Third World'.[77] Nigeria, one of the most populous countries in West Africa, established an innovative programme for the gifted young, through a National Policy on Education. This was supported by a series of democratic and military governments between 1977 and 1986, following the independence of Nigeria from British colonial rule in 1960. In 1987, the country founded a special Academy for Gifted Children, which brought together children who had been identified in previous involved 'magnet schools'; a second such school was established in 1993, focusing particularly on children who could be 'future technicians and engineers'.[78]

In 1992, representatives from Britain's National Association visited Nigeria to learn more about its schemes. They found that the school's Principal 'held our attention as he described his country's scheme, in operation now for five years, to provide for the able and talented' by identifying the top 0.5 per cent via national tests taken at age 11, and then educated specifically 'to become leaders in their society'.[79] Presenting this model as 'rational', the National Association stated that, '[w]e envied him his clear and confident goals', while '[h]e found our situation "confusing", which is probably a polite way of putting it.'[80]

Nigerian programmes faced public criticism as wasteful, for example, given the lack of resources for other schools, but nonetheless they were significant as many African nations more broadly in this period looked to invest in youth, because they 'symbolized the future' and because of the hope that young professionals educated abroad would 'facilitate the modernization of their countries'.[81] Despite this broader shift, however, very few African countries other than Nigeria had specific special programmes for the gifted.[82] A survey of members of

---

[77] 'Presentations feature conference', *World Gifted*, 1981, 2 (3), p. 4.

[78] Ibrahim A. Kolo, 'Reflections on the development of gifted education in Nigeria', *Roeper Review*, 19 (2) (1996), pp. 79–81.

[79] NAGC archives, Bletchley, 'Classroom Learning & Teaching, *Looking to their Future*, Autumn 1992, p. 7.

[80] Ibid.

[81] Guillory, 'Culture clash in the Socialist paradise', p. 271. See also: Tatek Abebe, *African Futures and Childhood Studies in Africa* (CODESRIA Books, 2022).

[82] Speaking at the World Council Conference, Henry Coker, a senior lecturer at Lagos University, 'explain[ed] how developing countries are trying to reconcile "democratisation" of education and the teaching of gifted children', for example (as reported by Izbicki, 'Teaching the gifted child'). While noting that few African countries had special programmes for the gifted, Mitchell and Williams note that two respondents to their survey sought more resources in this area: a respondent from Ghana had called for the nation to have more educational psychologists, to develop standards to identify the gifted young and to train them, while a respondent from Kenya noted that the government funded

ministries of education and World Council members, conducted between 1984 and 1985, concluded that, '[i]n general, the developing nations have had concerns more pressing than the education of gifted and talented young people.'[83]

Overall, certain countries identified as 'developing' by the World Council had participants who were interested in hosting World Council members, and in subverting established global hierarchies by presenting their innovative work in this field. This was the case in Bulgaria and Nigeria, and also South Korea, Taiwan, and the Philippines, which all offered, from the 1980s, government-led national funding for special schools, while also running classes for the gifted, teacher training, and active parent groups.[84] Many World Council members wished to learn from this engagement. At times, however, these debates seemed not only to 'learn from' other countries, but also actively to recruit young people to migrate to wealthier areas. In the June 1984 newsletter, for example, the President of the World Council, James J. Gallagher, described this in explicit human capital terms. He wrote that what he called 'industrialized nations' were concerned about running out of petroleum, but that, by contrast, 'our human resources, an important part of which would be the gifted and talented children, may be even more important to us, and what is more, they are renewable generation after generation'.[85] Gallagher argued that 'outstanding abilities appear in every ethnic and racial group', but that 'world-wide', 'outstanding ability may well go to waste and may be uncultivated'.[86] Women and girls, in particular, he argued were 'the largest total untapped source of ability in the world'.[87] Gallagher stated that only in the 'Western World' had there recently been recognition of this, describing a lack of sustained focus, seen throughout this book, on gender as related to giftedness.[88] The idea of richer countries benefiting from identifying the gifted in poorer countries was echoed again in a World Council newsletter of 1990, which suggested that the organisation might benefit from a 'brain drain' from Hong Kong, providing 'oriental language' skills amongst the workforce.[89]

Related ideas were also framed by Broomand in humanitarian terms. By 1990, Broomand was living in America, a member of a School District Board of Education in Los Angeles, and Director of a school for emotionally disturbed students. He continued to attend international events organised by the World Council and European Council for High Ability. Speaking to the *Los Angeles Times*, having given a keynote address to the European Council for High Ability in 1990, he stated that, '[w]e have millions of refugees in north Africa, South Africa, the Middle East, Latin America and southeast Asia who are very educated.' His suggestion was that these individuals could become teachers in wealthier nations,

---

national boarding schools, which acted as centres of excellence for students older than 13 years of age (Mitchell and Williams, 'Education of the Gifted and Talented', p. 533.)

[83] Mitchell and Williams, 'Education of the gifted and talented', p. 533.   [84] Ibid., p. 534.
[85] 'President's Message', *World Gifted*, June 1984, 5 (2), p. 1.   [86] Ibid., pp. 1–2.
[87] Ibid., p. 2.   [88] Ibid.   [89] 'Canada: Toronto', p. 2.

'giving them some pay and dignity'.[90] In debates, therefore, about the talented workforce of Hong Kong, and skilled international migration, leading figures in the World Council focused on gifted adults, rather than children. In part this shows that, by the 1990s broader cultural and political interest in human capital and adult migration had pervaded campaign groups designed to focus on the gifted young. Yet, this dissonant focus—between gifted young and gifted adults— again also spoke to the challenges of clearly defining the purpose and uses of an organisation as broad as the World Council.

By the mid-2000s, academic and research debate, which reached into the World Council, began to challenge the power imbalances within these ideas of 'the world'. In this decade, more broadly, journals interested in giftedness began to publish research that engaged explicitly with the ideas of biases in national systems—around 'model minorities', for example, and biases towards white children in IQ testing.[91] Such journals also began to engage more with ideas of how to assess intelligence differently across the globe, overcoming a predominance of studies from Europe and North America.[92] In 2012, these debates came to a head in *Gifted and Talented International*, the journal of the World Council. Roland S. Persson, of the School of Education and Communication, Jönköping University, Sweden, published an article arguing that giftedness research had a 'problem' with cultural bias, that giftedness itself was presented as a scientific fact but in fact represented American and European models which, because of a broader demand to export forms of education for profit, such as university learning, were then pushed onto Africa and Asia.[93] Several authors responded to these points. Typically, they agreed, stating that the piece had 'thrown down the gauntlet' and that it was 'timely, fascinating, important and powerful'. Don Ambrose, of the College of Liberal Arts, Education, and Sciences at Rider University, Lawrenceville, positioned this critique more broadly within an economic critique of the neoclassical economic theory, focusing on the free market as beneficial globally.[94] For Ambrose, the widespread nature of neoclassical economic assumptions in American culture,

---

[90] Sharon D. Smith, 'Europeans impress trustee board member brings education ideas home', *Los Angeles Daily News*, 8 November 1990.

[91] K. Yang, 'Southeast Asian American children: not the "model minority"', *The Future of Children*, 14 (2) (2004), pp. 127–133; Shane N. Phillipson and Maria McCann, (eds), *Conceptions of Giftedness: Sociocultural Perspectives* (Mahwah, NJ: Lawrence Erlbaum, 2004).

[92] Robert J. Sternberg, Catherine Nokes, P. Wenzel Geissler, Ruth Prince, Frederick Okatcha, Donald A. Bundy, and Elena L. Grigorenko, 'The relationship between academic and practical intelligence: a case study in Kenya', *Intelligence*, 29 (5) (2001), pp. 401–418; Phillipson and McCann (eds), *Conceptions of Giftedness*.

[93] Roland S. Persson, 'Cultural variation and dominance in a globalised knowledge-economy: towards a culture-sensitive research paradigm in the science of giftedness', *Gifted and Talented International*, 27 (1) (2012), pp. 15–48.

[94] Don Ambrose, 'Revealing additional dimensions of globalisation and cultural hegemony: a response to Roland S. Persson's call for cultural sensitivity in gifted studies', *Gifted and Talented International*, 27 (1) (2012), p. 100.

encourages us to assume that we can identify, select, and educate the gifted to prepare them for their rightful places in a true meritocracy with the most creative and talented individuals rising to the top of a hierarchical power and reward structure.[95]

While subsequent responses to the piece also queried or problematised specifics around this research, overall they did suggest a feeling that the relationships between 'giftedness' and 'the world' had not been adequately explored. While the World Council sought to unite as many countries as possible, this research suggested, it had not always been clear on how to address issues of power between participating delegates and, as such, the assumptions were often that, for example, English would be the default language of a conference, or that British and American research would structure debate. These issues of hierarchy are littered across histories of humanitarianism and aid from this period. The 'geographic imaginaries' of the World Council, then, had long caused tensions and challenges between delegates, and yet became visibly controversial only from the 1990s and 2000s.[96] These academic tensions were barely visible in earlier institutional newsletters, but, reading against the grain, and examining issues such as language and technology, we see that they were likely inflecting debate below the sheen of institutional representations.

Gifted Children Can Save Europe!

The European Council for High Ability was founded in 1988. It sought to mobilise gifted youth to ease tensions between East and West Europe, while simultaneously hoping to learn from former state-sponsored Communist educational systems. In many ways, then, its history held clear parallels with the World Council for Gifted and Talented Children: it was significantly influenced by British founders from its inception, and faced logistical issues and constraints for richer and poorer attendees, as well as the challenges of transnational global activism. Yet, this organisation was also distinct. Notably, its configuration of 'Europe' was very powerful, and looked to use the gifted young to further empower and construct an idea of a united Europe, amidst the decline of state-sponsored Communism. The European Council still faced a very diverse continent, but was able to function slightly more easily within this smaller configuration. Nonetheless, its definition of the gifted and their purposes remained intentionally vague—in part to unite its members, and in part to bolster its self-image as an organisation grounded in research and questioning, rather than policy recommendations.

---

[95] Ibid., p. 100.   [96] Honeck and Rosenberg, 'Transnational generations', p. 238.

A critical founding figure in the European Council was the British psychologist Joan Freeman (1935–2023). Freeman was born in England, but spent time as an evacuee in rural Canada during World War Two. She recalled in an oral history interview of 2017 having an early interest in ideas of giftedness. She claims to have felt during that experience that giftedness was unlikely to become visible when the majority of children left school early to 'work the land, tend the animals and spread the gospel of Jesus'.[97] She also felt aware, from an early age, that young boys would not want to see young girls as 'gifted' in the classroom.[98] When she returned to post-war England in 1946, Freeman passed the 11-plus examination and attended a girls' grammar school.[99] She was then in a minority of Britons, and particularly of British women, to study at university, and received a degree in psychology from the University of Manchester.[100] Her interest in gifted children was furthered when working post-graduation as a teacher, and she then moved to the field of research, appointed as Senior Lecturer in psychology at the Lancaster University Teacher Training campus for mature students.[101] Her primary research interest was developing 'high-level potential'.[102]

Freeman moved into voluntary action when she was commissioned by the head of Britain's National Association, Margaret Branch, to examine the group's 4,500 child members in 1974.[103] This work led Freeman to start a more focused study of 210 gifted children and their parents from 1976. A third of Freeman's sample were children whose parents identified them as gifted through the National Association, which did not have a formal admission test. These children were each matched with one control child with comparable intelligence (according to psychological testing), and a second at random, all from the same school.[104] In addition to working with the Association, Freeman stated later that she had identified research subjects 'in places as different as the governor's office in a women's open prison, a brewery laboratory, the back of a taxi and the head's office in a school'.[105] Freeman visited these people when their children were aged between 5 and 14, and then ten years later, ultimately tracing their lives and outcomes for 35 years.[106] Eighty-one per cent of the sample returned for the second stage of the study, alone or with parents.[107]

---

[97] Taisir Subhi Yamin, 'Interview: Joan Freeman', *International Journal for Talent Development and Creativity*, 6 (1) (2018), p. 203.
[98] Ibid, p. 204.   [99] Ibid.
[100] Ibid. See also 'Briefing paper: Grammar Schools', *Secondary Education and Social Change project*, January 2018 <https://sesc.hist.cam.ac.uk/wp-content/uploads/2018/01/Briefing-paper-Grammar-Schools.pdf> (2 September 2021). Another interview with Freeman is available in Mojca Jurilevic, '"Gifted lives": an interview with Professor Joan Freeman', *Horizons of Psychology*, 20 (3) (2011), pp. 139–144.
[101] Subhi Yamin, 'Interview: Joan Freeman', p. 205.   [102] Ibid.
[103] A key summary of this research can be found in Joan Freeman, *Gifted Lives: What Happens when Gifted Children Grow up* (Abingdon: Routledge, 2010).
[104] Victoria McKee, 'Genius: a gift or hard graft?', *The Times*, 10 September 1991.
[105] Ibid.   [106] Ibid.   [107] Ibid.

Freeman drew many conclusions from this work. She felt that there were many 'negative myths about the gifted' in Britain. She identified in particular the ideas that they would have 'fragile morality and emotions', and that they were 'have-it-alls', not needing or deserving extra psychological or educational attention.[108] These ideas were also critical to how the National Association framed its early work, as discussed in Chapter Two.[109] She emphasised 'the invidious effect of social class in this country', citing the case of a boy, whose father was a lathe-turner, who had achieved highly at Manchester Grammar School, and then turned to 'digging ditches' rather than university, believing '[i]t's not for me. It's for them monied boys'.[110] She also argued for the significance of home environment and parental engagement in determining giftedness.[111] While Freeman, then, had significant research expertise, newspaper coverage of her work often emphasised that she was a former gifted child and a parent: 'the mother of four children, at least two of whom, she maintains, are gifted'.[112]

Freeman thus had a significant role in the field of giftedness research, and a place in British campaigning in this area. Yet her role in founding the European Council for High Ability in the late 1980s was inflected by chance. In 1986, she later recalled, she spoke with Pieter Span, a professor of psychology in the Department of Educational Research at the University of Utrecht, who told her about his idea of a 'European alliance' in this area, and proposed that she could become President because of the significance of her research.[113] Freeman started this campaigning work alongside leading educationalists in this area from West and East Europe: Klaus Urban and Harald Wagner (West and East Germany), Candido Genovard (Spain), Eva Gefferth (Hungary), Andrzej Sekowski (Poland), and Pieter Span (Netherlands). This membership had points of overlap with the World Council. Klaus Urban, a professor in special education psychology, sat on the World Council Executive Committee from 1979 until 1987, and again from 1995 to 2005.[114]

The founding secretary of the group, Span, later recalled when sending a proposal for this group to a range of European agencies that, 'some respondents objected', arguing that, 'Europe was not yet ready for such an association'.[115] Others felt that there should be more of a link with the World Council.[116] The organisation's initial aims, Span recalled, were to co-operate with the World

---

[108] Subhi Yamin, 'Interview: Joan Freeman', p. 206.
[109] Oliver Pritchett. 'The loneliness of the too-gifted child', *Guardian*, 20 March 1966; 'Serious lack of facilities for creative children', *Guardian*, 21 March 1966, p. 2; 'New body aims to get help for the gifted child', *The Times*, 18 June 1966.
[110] McKee, 'Genius: a gift or hard graft?'   [111] Ibid.   [112] Ibid.
[113] Subhi Yamin, 'Interview: Joan Freeman', p. 207.
[114] 'Executive Committee History', *World Council for Gifted and Talented Children* <https://world-gifted.org/about-wcgtc/history/executive-committee-history/> (15 October 2021).
[115] 'History 25 Years', European Council for High Ability <https://www.echa.info/history-25-years> (12 May 2021).
[116] Ibid.

Council and national associations, publish scientific research and a newsletter, organise conferences, and found divisions for research and education.[117] Yet, these organisations did not always have an easy relationship. Freeman later stated that when announcing the European Council to the World Council, '[i]t was not at all well received' and '[a]ngry words were exchanged'. She felt that her group was pressured to become a 'branch' of the World Council.[118] While aiming to cooperate from the inception of the European Council, in 2014 Span reflected that this aim was 'not realized'.[119] The European Council instead developed a distinct identity, focused on what 'Europe' was, and what it could be. It quickly expanded to organise annual conferences, which alternated in location between East and West Europe.[120] It also published a quarterly newsletter and peer reviewed journal (the *European Journal for High Ability*, later *High Ability Studies*), and organised a Diploma qualification.[121] In 1994, the European Council recognised the group as one of its advisory bodies, demonstrating its reach and signalling its links to ideas of a unified Europe.[122] The European Council frequently emphasised that there were distinct 'European' issues that gifted young people could solve. The first newsletter of the European Council, published in December 1987, stated that this organisation 'heralds the start of a Continental movement which is going to grow and grow'.[123] Various issues of the organisation's journal emphasised that supporting and nurturing talent was 'a crucial problem in Europe'.[124] Freeman later argued that, while the American and Soviet approaches focused on 'measurable achievement whether for personal satisfaction or the glory of the nation', the 'European approach' would be different, more focused on 'the *processes* of learning and thinking than the *outcomes*'.[125]

The idea of developing a 'European' approach to giftedness moved beyond the Council itself, in part because of its successful advocacy and connections to European integrators. In 1992, this idea was reiterated by Michael Vorbeck from the Council of Europe's Educational Research Team. Speaking to the European Council's Third conference, on 'Competence and Responsibility', he stated that the Council of Europe would promote research and education for the gifted

[117] 'Pieter Span (founding secretary of ECHA, 1987–1990)', European Council for High Ability <https://www.echa.info/history-25-years/pieter-span-founding-secretary-of-echa-1987-1990> (15 October 2021).
[118] Joan Freeman, 'ECHA: The Early Years', unpublished paper of 17 September 2014.
[119] 'Pieter Span (founding secretary of ECHA, 1987–1990)'. Editorials in the World Council newsletter did frequently pay tribute to leading members of the European Council, and refer to effective joint working (for example, 'President's Message', *World Gifted*, January 1994, 14 (1), p. 4.
[120] 'History 25 Years'. [121] Ibid. [122] Ibid.
[123] 'Welcome to ECHA', ECHA News, December 1987, Volume 1 Number 1, p. 1.
[124] Manfred von Ardenne, 'Facilitating the development of talents', *European Journal of High Ability*, 1 (2) (1991), pp. 127–135.
[125] Freeman, 'ECHA: The Early Years'; Subhi Yamin, 'Interview: Joan Freeman', p. 207.

under a model of the 'homo europaeus'.[126] All of these publications hence positioned the gifted children of Europe as somehow distinct, emphasising the possibilities and potential of unifying Europe, and making the young central in this. Yet discussion of divides between East and West of Europe remained critical for these organisations. The idea that gifted children could ease East–West tensions was significant in the foundation of the European Council. The group's founding narratives reiterated the need to speak with 'professionals behind the (then) "iron curtain"'.[127] In 1991, the Council for Cultural Cooperation of the Council of Europe brought together voluntary organisations, researchers, and policy-makers analysing giftedness at a conference in Nijmegen, the Netherlands—the only European centre for the study of the gifted.[128] Subsequent publications for this event were framed around the idea that gifted children could foster 'East–West cooperation', and that all nations must therefore learn to better identify, manage, and develop their gifted young.[129] Describing the event, Kurt A. Heller, a psychologist from Germany, wrote that,

> The opportunities of a united Germany and its integration into the European and non-European international community will only be successful if the mental resources of our young people can be successfully motivated.[130]

In this formulation, gifted children could use their 'mental resources' to heal the divisions of the Cold War—between and across countries—acting as 'agents of future promise'.[131]

Yet, while looking to mobilise European children to heal East–West divides, and to promote a 'European' sense of identity and movement, these organisations also emphasised national differences and, at times, sought to valorise, or at least learn from, the perceivedly more efficient approach of Eastern European members, in line with World Council interest in the Soviet Union in the 1970s. Leading

---

[126] 'Opening speeches', in Kurt A. Heller and Ernst A. Hany (eds), *Competence and Responsibility: The Third European Conference of The European Council for High Ability held in Munich*, 11–14 October 1992, p. 2.

[127] 'History 25 Years'.

[128] Mönks et al., *Education of the Gifted in Europe*, Table of Contents. The assertion that this area 'boasts the continent's only centre for the study of the gifted' is in John O'Leary, 'New hope for Britain's brightest children', *The Times*, 5 August 1991.

[129] Ibid., p. 27, back cover.

[130] Kurt A. Heller, 'Giftedness research and education of the gifted and talented in Germany', in Mönks et al., *Education of the Gifted in Europe*, p. 76.

[131] 'Mental resources' of the gifted child are discussed in Heller, 'Giftedness research and education', p. 76. See also: Laura King, Vicky Crewe, and Lindsey Dodd, 'Children and notions of "the future"', *History & Policy*, 5 February 2015 <http://www.historyandpolicy.org/opinion-articles/articles/children-and-notions-of-the-future> (18 July 2019); Laura King, 'Future citizens: cultural and political conceptions of children in Britain, 1930s–1950s', *Twentieth Century British History*, 27 (3) (2016), pp. 389–411.

figures in the European Council suggested that there were 'strong inhibitions in the capitalist parts of Europe against the promotion of talent'.[132] This was echoed in a publication by the Council of Europe in 1994, which highlighted the 'almost complete absence' of research on giftedness in France and Switzerland.[133] By contrast, these organisations heralded the success of giftedness programmes in Eastern Europe. A 1991 article in the *European Journal of High Ability* discussed schools in the German Democratic Republic, where the 'fostering of gifts and talents' was 'an integral component of a system promoting the unity of general education and special provision for the highly able' and 'part of the process of recognizing and fostering gifts and talents in all areas of human activity'.[134] Joan Freeman, writing for the World Council in 1990, argued that Eastern Europe had been 'more concerned with the practicalities of teaching and outcome, whereas the West has a more prolific output of theory'. She suggested, the 'thousands of bright young people seeking a better life' in 'Western Democracies' may thus bring 'world-class teaching expertise in subject areas such as top sports, gymnastics, singing, ballet, circus, and mathematics'.[135] Such exchanges, Freeman argued, would become easier with greater freedom of travel and education across the European Economic Community from 1992; again, the success of the gifted was a result of, and could further promote, European unity.[136]

To an extent, therefore, discussions of giftedness in these networks subverted the 'unevenness of power within international networks', as European organisations sought to use gifted children to 'heal' East–West divides, while also remaining interested by the potential of state-sponsored authoritarian education.[137] Yet hierarchies and unevenness of power remained. This becomes visible through a case study of the second conference of the European Council for High Ability, which has been well documented by contemporary publications and the retrospective analysis of participants. Held in 1990 in Budapest, in a hotel on the Danube, the event was designed to analyse 'High Ability in a Changing Europe'.[138] The conference hosted 171 contributors and 200–220 participants from 24 countries.[139] Those attending from Eastern countries were charged less.[140] The idea of the conference as a site for East–West encounters was reiterated frequently, for example in leaflets emphasising that this was a 'lovely meeting place for participants coming

---

[132] 'Trends for the coming decade for the gifted in Western Europe', *World Gifted*, September 1990, 11 (2), p. 8.
[133] van Boxtel, 'Final Report', pp. 26–27.
[134] Horst Drewelow, 'Fostering ability in the schools of the German Democratic Republic', *European Journal of High Ability*, 1 (2) (1991), pp. 136–143.
[135] 'Trends for the coming decade for the gifted in Western Europe', p. 8.   [136] Ibid., p. 9.
[137] Emily Baughan, 'History and humanitarianism: a conversation', *Past & Present*, 241 (1) (2018), e11.
[138] '2nd International ECHA Conference, Budapest', European Council for High Ability Website <https://www.echa.info/echa-conferences/2nd-international-echa-conference-budapest-25-28-oct-1990> (12 May 2021).
[139] Ibid.   [140] Ibid.

from the East and the West', with special 'setting, beauty and special atmosphere'.[141] Budapest, conference publicity stated, would offer both the 'warm hospitality of the people of that small country in the heart of Europe' and 'an uplifting scientific and social experience'.[142] In her opening address, Freeman noted that it was 'exciting to be living in Europe during this time of swift and positive change'.[143] She stated that 'we are even attempting to learn each other's languages—something that ECHA is taking a special interest in.'[144] Speeches at the event emphasised that the 'West and the East needed each others' expertises'.[145] In many ways then participants and delegates looked to learn from Eastern Europe, and positioned its young people as highly gifted, and its research as globally significant. Yet, conference materials also replicated hierarchies about 'Western values', emphasising what Hungary could learn from Western Europe. Conference materials also described the challenges of publishing and using currency at the time, and a local taxi strike in response to rising fuel prices, which blocked planned trips to rural schools.[146] Span recalled that the last night of the conference was 'overshadowed by alarming information about social unrest in the country'.[147]

This case study reflects the ways in which gifted young people were expected to solve a range of distinct, yet never fully defined, European problems of the 1990s. In this period, much of the European Council's primary work was framed around the idea that gifted children were key to managing the decline of Communism, or promoting Europe as a global leader. Notably, transnational global organisations could position the gifted young as saviours of 'the world' or of 'Europe'; this concept was significantly alluring across multiple diverse national case studies, and held multiple meanings. At the European Council, the concept, 'gifted child', played a significant role in buttressing ideas of the 'new Europe'; a vision that made it appealing beyond the organisation itself.

What Did This Mean for the Gifted Young?

These organisations positioned the gifted child as the potential saviour of 'Europe' and 'the world', which involved significant logistical challenges for adults. But what did this mean for children? Overall, young people were rarely directly involved in these organisations. Occasionally, their writings were featured in relevant publications—as with the poem by Kate that opened this chapter—or they performed at relevant conferences. The programmes—whether due to lack of resources, interest, or focus—did not provide active programmes for children themselves,

---

[141] Ibid.   [142] Ibid.   [143] Ibid.   [144] Ibid.
[145] Ibid. See also Rainer Ortleb, 'Federal support programs for gifted and talented young people in Germany: concepts and initiatives'; Heller and Hany (eds), *Competence and Responsibility*, p. 3.
[146] '2nd International ECHA Conference, Budapest'; 'History 25 Years'.
[147] 'Pieter Span (founding secretary of ECHA, 1987–1990)'.

and thus the gifted child discussed by these groups was at times somewhat abstract.

The hopes placed on gifted young people, in the rhetoric of the European and World Councils, were very high. World Council newsletters, for example, would frequently open with statements emphasising how the gifted young alone could ameliorate contemporary issues. The October 1982 newsletter spoke of 'widespread pessimism about the future, a sense that we are all on a runaway train going down a mountainside, and that no one knows how to stop it', as 'many children in the world go to bed hungry...the workings of our international economic system go awry...our ability to solve disputes among nations, each with legitimate grievances, remains feeble'.[148] The September 1990 edition emphasised how this organisation could, 'mobilize our own forces to influence the making of the New World Order'.[149] Gifted young people were—in ill-defined ways—responsible for creating 'a fulfilling and fruitful future for the planet and for humankind'.[150]

Yet these lofty aims seemed detached from the work the Council did to engage with the gifted young themselves. Gifted young people would sometimes perform or volunteer at European and World Councils conferences, but would rarely directly inform their work. In terms of volunteering, the second European Council conference in Budapest, for example, hired local 16- to 19-year-olds to form a 'Smile Brigade' as assistants, providing delegates with folders and paper and selling books and postcards.[151] In subsequent summaries of the event, these young people were framed as gifted. The Council placed testimonies from members about using their 'problem-solving activities' during the event on their website, finding it a 'good opportunity to practice our English', and their hopes that they would 'perhaps in the future' be 'participants of a congress as well'.[152] World Council conferences also featured fleeting attendance of the gifted young, through performance or display: young people's art was shown at the Montreal conference in 1981 and the Manila conference in 1983, for example, and the Hamburg conference of 1985 featured a chess competition between adult delegates and young chess players.[153]

The newsletter of the World Council also rarely (approximately one in every seven issues) featured a 'Children's Corner' of children's poetry and artwork, such as the poem written by Kate. This was a small part of the overall newsletter: a quarter of a page within the shorter six-page newsletters, or a full page within the longer fifteen-page newsletters, and usually featured up to three contributions. Little particular context was offered as to why, where, or how the young

---

[148] 'Our Need for Gifted/Talented Students', *World Gifted*, October 1982, 3 (2), p. 1.
[149] 'Letter from the President', *World Gifted*, September 1990, 11 (2), p. 1.
[150] 'A Message from the President', *World Gifted*, Winter 1999, 18 (1), p. 11.
[151] '2nd International ECHA Conference, Budapest'.   [152] Ibid.
[153] Sisk, 'History of the World Council for Gifted and Talented Children', pp. 7, 10; 'Cultural/Social Conference Events', *World Gifted*, November 1981, 2 (3), p. 5.

GIFTED CHILDREN SAVING 'EUROPE' AND 'THE WORLD', 1975–2000   183

people's poetry or artworks had been produced. Indeed, the poetry and artwork appears to have been more typically sent by voluntary organisations working with children than by children themselves. Further, the pieces collected in Children's Corner were somewhat random, with little clear overall meaning. Pieces included, for example, a drawing of a school by an eighteen-year-old girl, who was also deaf and mute and who lived in Deegu, Korea; and a poem about 'the Promised Land' by a young person, without age provided, from Manila.[154] It is unclear what the overall purpose of these pieces was. World Council language around the involvement of the gifted young suggested that young people's performances and writings were at times displayed to bolster adult-centric ideas of childhood precocity, as seen throughout this book. Describing the Third Asia-Pacific Conference on Giftedness in 1994, for example, the World Council newsletter stated that gifted and talented youth had 'entertained the conference participants' during a Farewell Dinner activity and alongside adult performers.[155] Young people's writings, when shared with the World Council, were also at times viewed in this manner, for example as, 'Pearls of wisdom from the mouths of babes', or 'items written by the children (*bless 'em*) themselves'.[156]

Since young people themselves did not directly feature heavily in these organisations, there is little evidence of how they related to these representations, or how they felt about performing at these conferences—whether it was seen as an honour and an exciting opportunity, an inconvenience, or something else. One small trace of young people's perspectives, however, was visible in World Council coverage of an International Youth Summit in Toronto, in 1993. Seventy-three students from fifteen countries were brought together by a global network of teachers to share their concerns about education.[157] Students met one another, had a learning styles workshop to think more about their personal needs, and shared concerns about education with educational leaders.[158] The subsequent report on this for the World Council, written by adult organisers of the Youth Summit, stated that young people, 'felt it was truly a conference to meet their needs and they were not "intellectual freaks" put on display to amaze adult audiences'.[159] While it is minimal and was transmitted through adults, this short sentence nonetheless suggested that factions of the gifted young were often reduced to 'cultural objects' in other contexts, having to perform or display their skills to adult audiences.[160] Kate's poem also referred to gifted young people as not only

---

[154] 'Children's Corner', *World Gifted*, April 1986, 7 (1), p. 9; 'WCGT's Childrens Corner', *World Gifted*, August 1987, 8 (2), p. 2.
[155] 'Asia-Pacific Conference', *World Gifted*, Fall 1994, 14 (3), p. 13.
[156] 'Pearls of Wisdom from the Mouths of Babes', *World Gifted*, May 1983, 4 (2), p. 5; 'New Zealand newsletter', *World Gifted*, March 1983, 4 (1), p. 7.
[157] 'Special Report on the International Youth Summit, Toronto, 1993', *World Gifted*, January 1994, 14 (1), p. 7.
[158] Ibid.   [159] Ibid.
[160] The concept of the 'child as cultural object' is in Myers, 'Local action and global imagining', p. 287.

'overrated' and 'overconfident' but 'overworked', potentially signifying similar ideas. Certainly, we can assume, as Mischa Honeck and Gabriel Rosenberg have argued, that young participants at Council events were 'complex players with their own agendas, interests, and desires'.[161]

The gifted young did have opportunities to exchange experiences with one another globally in the late twentieth century. The Youth Summit was repeated in subsequent years. From America, transnational organisations such as Gifted Children's Pen Pals International, active in the 1980s, had a membership of nearly 1,000 children aged between 4 and 18, 'in many parts of the world'.[162] A similar scheme, 'Letter Link', encouraged all students aged 10 to 17 to write 'in their own language about discoveries they have made about the world and community in which they live'. The need for children to translate these letters was intended to encourage them to, 'interact locally with other cultural groups'.[163] The European Union and Council of Europe also both sponsored programmes to promote youth travel in the 1980s and 1990s.[164] National schemes made efforts to connect young people globally—as traced in Chapter Four, Britain's National Association facilitated international pen-pal links, particularly between Britain and America, and this organisation also experimented in 1991 with sending a 'pioneer candidate' to Hungary, in a scheme designed to satisfy a Hungarian 'longing to be acknowledged by the West and to make friends'.[165] In 1994, the British Embassy in Budapest and UK Foreign Office sponsored an exchange of thirty-eight British and Hungarian children to enjoy 'an East European adventure'.[166] All of these schemes—and those documented by historians and geographers looking across the globe—sought to make young people themselves central in developing new global relationships.[167]

World Council leaders did occasionally suggest similar schemes in their newsletters.[168] However, in general the European and World Councils did not prioritise the organisation of exchange visits, pen-pal schemes or events for young people themselves. These were instead left to such national or state

---

[161] Honeck and Rosenberg, 'Transnational generations', p. 239.
[162] 'Opportunities for students', *World Gifted*, December 1985, 6 (3), p. 9.   [163] Ibid.
[164] Jobs, *Backpack Ambassadors*; Sinisa Horak and Sanda Weber, 'Youth tourism in Europe: problems and prospects', *Tourism Recreation Research*, 25 (3) (2000), pp. 37–44.
[165] NAGC, 'International exchanges & visits', *National Association Gossip Column*, 8, Summer 1991, n.p.
[166] NAGC Newsletter, Summer 1995, 'GIFT went Hungarian', p. 6.
[167] Honeck and Rosenberg, 'Transnational generations', p. 234; Neumann, 'Children diplomacy during the late Cold War', pp. 277–278; Fieldston, 'Little cold warriors', pp. 240–250; Norwig, 'A first European generation?'; Chatelain, 'International sisterhood'; Guillory, 'Culture clash in the Socialist paradise'; Myers, 'Local action and global imagining'; Benwell and Hopkins, *Children, Young People and Critical Geopolitics*; Okech, Baillie Smith, Fadel, and Mills, 'The reproduction of inequality; Jeffrey, 'Geographies of children and youth II'; Baillie Smith, Mills, Okech, and Fadel, 'Uneven geographies of youth volunteering'.
[168] Raised by Iraj Broomand in 'From the Secretariat', *World Gifted*, December 1985, 6 (3), p. 4.

programmes described above. In general, this meant that the European and World Councils occupied an uneasy space in relation to narratives of transnational child diplomacy and child activism in this period. National governments—particularly in the Soviet Union—were keen to foster international exchanges and to use 'child diplomats' to demonstrate the significance and benefits of their economic and cultural systems.[169] Younger adults themselves also relished the opportunities to act as 'backpack Ambassadors' and to travel Europe.[170] In the European and World Councils, however, working at the same time and for decades later, young people were at times powerfully symbolic, able to forge global alliances between 'developing' and 'developed' worlds, even though resources were not available to support this. This frames how we understand the rhetoric employed by these transnational organisations: it at times focused on a gifted child to attract and unite global membership, with the construction of this gifted child left purposefully abstract.

Conclusion

A survey of World Council members and individuals serving in ministries of education, conducted by American Professors of Education in 1984–85, concluded that

> virtually all nations—developed or developing, communist or capitalist—are philosophically committed to an egalitarian society. Many of these societies have moved only recently from educational systems serving privileged elites to comprehensive systems...policy-making decisions are influenced by the fear that education for the gifted and talented may be just another form of elitism and privilege.[171]

These ideas echoed the debates traced throughout this book: that everyone must be 'equal' in post-war societies, and that this was a new phenomenon, being met by voluntary arguments that the cries against 'elitism' or forming 'elites of the future' were damaging the prospects of the gifted young. These ideas were visible in this survey, in protests outside the Hamburg Conference of the World Council in 1986, and in opposition to gifted education from West German teachers' unions.[172]

---

[169] See Neumann, 'Children diplomacy during the late Cold War', pp. 277–278.
[170] Jobs, *Backpack Ambassadors*.
[171] Mitchell and Williams, 'Education of the gifted and talented', p. 534.
[172] Protests mentioned in Sisk, 'History of the World Council for Gifted and Talented Children', p. 10. The opposition of West German teachers' unions is mentioned in Mitchell and Williams, 'Education of the gifted and talented', p. 531.

Yet, these ideas did not frequently permeate the publications of the World and European Councils in the late twentieth century. These organisations, instead, tended to focus in this period on questions of what exactly 'Europe' and 'the World' were, how gifted children could assist these global imaginaries, and how diverse countries could be connected through complex transnational action. The primary source bases for this chapter were newsletters, voluntary publications, statements, and webpages curated by these organisations. While the organisations had diverse and changing memberships with distinct aims, the narratives presented were shaped by organisational cultures, constructed amidst the need for funding, prestige, and cohesion. In terms of the explanations provided by these documents, both the European and World Councils faced significant logistical challenges in terms of uniting 'Europe' and 'the World'—they faced the challenges of using communication technologies of post and expensive air travel, and, later, unequal access to digital communication. It was also the case at both organisations, but perhaps particularly at the World Council, that delegates and even leading members from different countries had significantly different levels of support from their employers and nationally-funded programmes.

These logistical challenges were certainly significant. They reflected and further perpetuated distinctions within these organisations between participating members from richer and poorer countries, framed by the World Council in the language of 'developed' and 'developing'. Yet the relationships between these countries were never clear-cut. At times, American and British participants at the World Council were desperate to learn from Bulgaria and Nigeria, for example. Global contact could bridge cultural divides and enhance learning, but could also reaffirm all participants' 'sense of cultural superiority', as Sean Guillory has described in the contact between young people in the Soviet Union and Africa in the 1960s.[173] Nonetheless, overall longstanding global hierarchies continued to inflect the work of these groups. It seems likely that this was frustrating for participants who faced greater challenges of access to Council materials and conferences due to language barriers, particularly when much leadership momentum came from the English-speaking world. While these frustrations were not often explicitly aired within institutional materials from these organisations, throughout we see glimpses of how these tensions may have undergirded Council interactions. Notably, these concerns were aired explicitly within the academic journal of the World Council in the 2000s, when researchers openly criticised underlying ideas of the Global South as an exporter of 'human capital'.

These transnational organisations should be situated amongst the range of other voluntary and state exchange programmes which, in the mid-to-late twentieth century, sought to harness 'the symbolic potential of youth...for

---

[173] Guillory, 'Culture clash in the Socialist paradise', p. 280.

reimagining the nation in a transnational context'.[174] Historical scholarship around this focuses in particular on the post-war and Cold War periods, yet this case study shows that the symbolic power of the young did not diminish in the 1990s. Rather, buoyed by new technologies that made contact easier (although not without challenges), interested individuals from across the world were able to hone in on more and more specific groups of the young in this period. Those interested in the 'gifted child' could make contact, and meet to discuss this cause, more easily than ever.

There was little direct focus on the experiences of young people themselves within these transnational debates. The reasons for this are not addressed in interviews with founders or institutional sources. This may have not been their purpose, or perhaps due to a lack of interest or a perception of being unable to deliver child-centred work with existing resources. We see glimpses of young people's irritation in some newsletters—notably in the adult report of 1993 that young people had previously felt like 'intellectual freaks' who were 'put on display to amaze adult audiences'.[175] Certainly, British young people traced throughout this book who were given the opportunities to discuss their views by the National Association frequently challenged abstract understandings of children's lives, and the lack of contact between adult policy-makers and young people. With few young people consistently and directly involved in meaningful work at these Councils, the 'gifted young' were left abstract and mysterious, able to fit any possible description, to offer any necessary skills, to solve any national or world ills.

The absence of contact with children themselves in these organisations also meant that, while interest in 'the child' as a symbolic figure remained in the 1990s, the 'activist subjectivity' of the 1960s and 1970s, where young people shaped international activism, was not so present in these groups.[176] Extending arguments from Chapter Five, this chapter suggests that the 1990s may be a particularly difficult decade in which to trace the perspectives of the young. In this decade, and beyond, their views were less recognised and sought by transnational organisations focused on global communication, and dismissed by highly professionalised, streamlined national programmes. As Jobs has stated, the post-Cold War era was 'bureaucratic, financial, and corporate'.[177] These broader shifts in how organisations were run, and how they were funded, meant that young

---

[174] Quote is from Myers, 'Local action and global imagining', p. 283. See also Honeck and Rosenberg, 'Transnational generations', p. 234; Neumann, 'Children diplomacy during the late Cold War', pp. 277–278; Fieldston, 'Little cold warriors', pp. 240–250; Norwig, 'A first European generation?'; Chatelain, 'International sisterhood'; Guillory, 'Culture clash in the Socialist paradise; Benwell and Hopkins, *Children, Young People and Critical Geopolitics*; Okech, Baillie Smith, Fadel, and Mills, 'The reproduction of inequality'; Jeffrey, 'Geographies of children and youth II'; Baillie Smith, Mills, Okech, and Fadel, 'Uneven geographies of youth volunteering'.
[175] 'Special Report on the International Youth Summit, Toronto, 1993', p. 7.
[176] Myers, 'Local action and global imagining', p. 283; Jobs, *Backpack Ambassadors*, ch. 3.
[177] Jobs, *Backpack Ambassadors*, p. 259.

people's voices were heard less often—organisations such as the National Association, indeed, which captured such rich children's writings in the 1970s and 1980s, were no longer as active.

This chapter enriches our understandings of cultural internationalism into the 1990s, and with regards to transnational action around a specific group of the young. Furthermore, it also enhances our understandings of late twentieth-century Britain. This book argues more broadly that the idea of the gifted child as an elite of the future had peaked in the 1970s and 1980s in a British context. In part, reduced interest in this area reflected recognition of the historic role of racial science and eugenics in identifying giftedness, notably through IQ tests, and also critique by young people themselves. And yet, such controversies did not entirely rule out visions of gifted young people as elites of the future in a global context. While, in the 1970s and 1980s, gifted young people in Britain were expected to save declining local industries, by the 1990s, a similar network of voluntary leaders argued that, while this may not work, gifted children could still unite post-communist Europe and promote international development efforts across the Global South. British voluntary leaders such as Collis, Sieghart, and Freeman found new outlets for their work in transnational organisations in these later years.

Analysis of these specific organisations also tells us more about the distinctiveness of British debates about giftedness. Notably, British campaigners and press coverage, discussing the European and World Council, constantly framed these organisations in terms of elitism and equality: whether or not the groups supported 'the segregation of a gifted elite' and whether giftedness was 'too elitist for politicians to support' internationally as well as in Britain.[178] Such newspaper coverage emphasised the distinctiveness of British debate in this area: whether by stating that British research in this 'lags well behind that of the leading nations in the field' or that it was 'somehow unBritish to concentrate on people who are different because they are brighter than the rest'.[179] Giftedness debates across the world were no less contentious than those in Britain. Across national and transnational organisations interested in this area, the gifted young were, potentially, agents able to offer immense benefits to economy, society, and politics, if identified and trained properly. Yet, in Britain, in particular, these benefits were to be interpreted through the lens of 'equal elites', and framed, by politicians, campaigners, and publics alike, in terms of whether Britain itself was an 'equal' or 'elitist' society; themes this book's conclusion will now address.

'Gifted Children' in Britain and the World: Elitism and Equality since 1945. Jennifer Crane, Oxford University Press.
© Jennifer Crane 2025. DOI: 10.1093/9780198928881.003.0007

---

[178] Rosenbaum, 'Freeing the gifted child'; O'Leary, 'New hope for Britain's brightest children'.
[179] O'Leary, 'New hope for Britain's brightest children'.

Conclusion

Privilege is ingrained in the earliest years. It is lived out in the choices that parents and carers make about their children's very first play dates, their weekend and evening activities, and the curation of their relationships and networks. Such privilege continues to shape children's economic lives and fortunes as they age into employees (or not) and later to wealthy or bankrupt elders. Politicians speaking over the timespan of this book—the mid-to-late twentieth century—have sought to proclaim that we now live in a 'meritocracy' or 'equal society', and have reformed education and welfare systems in pursuit of this goal. Yet such shifts have failed to overcome the cultural, social, and economic inequalities borne from the earliest days of childhood. Interventions have been too broad, too narrow, or too late.

Powerful new bodies of literature have examined how class is tied to academic and occupational achievement—notably recent work by Sam Friedman, Daniel Laurison, Aaron Reeves, and Eve Worth.[1] These works have challenged the idea of 'meritocracy', conclusively demonstrating through analysis of social surveys and in original life interviews that 'those who start out ahead are the ones most likely to succeed'.[2] Studies of 'leadership', likewise, have shown how fixed adult ideas of elites are, and the assumptions that leaders will be white and male, in particular.[3] One key contribution of this book has been to such literature, through

---

[1] Sam Friedman and Daniel Laurison, *The Class Ceiling: Why it Pays to be Privileged* (Bristol: Policy Press, 2020); Sam Friedman and Aaron Reeves, 'From aristocratic to ordinary: shifting modes of elite distinction', *American Sociological Review*, 85 (2) (2020), pp. 323–350; Eve Worth and Aaron Reeves, '"I am almost the middle-class white man, aren't I?": elite women, education and occupational trajectories in late twentieth-century Britain', *Contemporary British History*, 38 (1) (2024), pp. 71–94; Eve Worth, Aaron Reeves, and Sam Friedman, 'Is there an old girls' network? Girls' schools and recruitment to the British elite', *British Journal of Sociology of Education*, 44 (1) (2023), pp. 1–25.

[2] Friedman and Laurison, *The Class Ceiling*, p. 31.

[3] See Nichole M. Bauer, 'Emotional, sensitive, and unfit for office? gender stereotype activation and support female candidates', *Political Psychology*, 36 (6) (2014), pp. 691–708; Roosmarijn A. de Geus, John R. McAndrews, Peter John Loewen, et. al., 'Do voters judge the performance of female and male politicians differently? Experimental evidence from the United States and Australia', *Political Research Quarterly*, 74 (2) (2021), pp. 302–316. On management theory, see: H. Astin and C. Leland, 'Women of influence, women of vision: a cross generational study of leaders and social change' (Wiley, 1999); Kari Pöllänen, 'Northern European leadership in transition—a survey of the insurance industry', *Journal of General Management*, 32 (1) (2006), pp. 43–63. For management or business studies perspectives, with focus on efficacy, see for example: Ingeborg Tömmel and Amy Verdun, 'Political leadership in the European Union: an introduction', *Journal of European Integration*, 39 (2) (2017), pp. 103–112; M. Arslan, 'A cross-cultural comparison of achievement and power orientation as leadership dimensions in three European countries: Britain, Ireland and Turkey', *Business Ethics: A European Review*, 10 (4) (2001), pp. 340–345; M. Arslan, 'A cross-cultural comparison of Turkish

a new angle and disciplinary approach. The book has examined historically situated writings from children, parents, and community organisers, particularly those gathered together by the National Association for Gifted Children, National Academy for Gifted and Talented Youth, European Association for High Ability, and World Council for Gifted and Talented Children. In doing so, the book has traced 'grounded', everyday mechanisms and moments in which privilege has been lived and embodied in associational spaces, constructed as local, national, and global.[4] Notably, the book has shown that a variety of groups set up for 'gifted' children in the late twentieth century, founded in the name of 'equality', engaged typically white, middle-class families. These families were denoted as 'special', deserving of and receiving more resources than those provided by existing welfare states. Significantly, this work has also reflected on how children themselves engaged with these spaces. Through children's writings, it has shown that young people did not always seek out such privilege—they were often hugely critical of adult interest in finding 'the gifted' and of the associational spaces set up in their names. Nonetheless, the expressed 'agency' of the young was often simply incorporated into existing models of the gifted young, and interpreted as symbolic of their peculiarly lively and resistant minds.[5]

What does this mean for our present thinking about equality and elitism, and for our interpretation of the interplay between these categories? Certainly, there is a need to understand concepts of 'elites', 'equality', and indeed 'leaders' as dynamic and flexible—they have changed over time and space and, significantly, start to be ingrained in childhood and youth. Young people play a critical role in shaping how we visualise, understand, and accept 'leaders', and they vote for, accept, and become elites or leaders in subsequent years, embedding childhood

---

and British managers in terms of Protestant work ethic characteristics', *Business Ethics: A European Review*, 9 (1) (2000), pp. 13–19; S. Mukkamala and K. L. Suyemoto, 'Racialized sexism/sexualized racism: a multimethod study of intersectional experiences of discrimination for Asian American women', *Asian American Journal of Psychology*, 9 (1) (2018), pp. 32–46; Y. Cho, R. Ghosh, J. Y. Sun, and G. N. McLean (eds), *Current Perspectives on Asian Women in Leadership: A Cross-Cultural Analysis* (London: Palgrave, 2017); A. H. Eagly, C. Nater, D. I. Miller, M. Kaufmann, and S. Sczesny, 'Gender stereotypes have changed: A cross-temporal meta-analysis of U.S. public opinion polls from 1946 to 2018', *American Psychologist*, 75(3) (2020), pp. 301–315; Friedman and Laurison, *The Class Ceiling*, pp. 39–40.

[4] Craig Jeffrey, 'Geographies of children and youth II: Global youth agency', *Progress in Human Geography*, 36 (2) (2011), p. 249.

[5] Chris Millard, 'Using personal experience in the academic medical humanities: a genealogy', *Social Theory & Health*, 18 (2019), pp. 184–198; Mona Gleason, 'Avoiding the agency trap: caveats for historians of children, youth, and education', *History of Education*, 45 (4) (2016), pp. 446–459; Lynn M. Thomas, 'Historicising agency', *Gender & History*, 28 (2) (2016), pp. 324–339; Sarah L. Holloway, Louise Holt, and Sarah Mills, 'Questions of agency: Capacity, subjectivity, spatiality and temporality', *Progress in Human Geography*, 43 (3) (2018), pp. 458–477; Susan A. Miller, 'Assent as agency in the early years of the Children of the American Revolution', *Journal of the History of Childhood and Youth*, 9 (1) (2016), pp. 48–65; Tatek Abebe, 'Reconceptualising children's agency as continuum and interdependence', *Social Sciences*, 8 (3) (2019), pp. 1–16; Jeffrey, 'Geographies of children and youth II', pp. 245–253. See also the classic: Walter Johnson, 'On agency', *Journal of Social History*, 37 (1) (2003), pp. 113–124.

play, discussions, and understandings. Ideas of equality, likewise, were hugely flexible throughout this book, but again embedded in childhood. Young people saw when equality meant that the post-war welfare would provide them all with education for longer. Young people saw when equality meant that those labelled 'gifted' would receive extra provision, whether from families or schools, in the 1970s and 1980s. And young people saw when, in the late 1990s and early 2000s, equality would mean that the disadvantaged (by state-led criterion) would be invited warmly into giftedness schemes.

This text has traced the fuzzy and inconsistent manifestations of debates around gifted children as 'elites' or 'leaders' and as symbols of 'elitism' and 'equality'. While these terms were used inconsistently, they were used repeatedly, and thus have to be attended to. This analysis has helped to problematise, also, any idea of a clear shift from the 'equal' post-war welfare state, to the permissive legislation of the 1960s, rent asunder by the neoliberal divided society of the 1980s.[6] The welfare state was not 'universal', equally providing for everyone.[7] Even in the 1940s and 1950s, coinciding with rhetoric around the welfare state, equality, and universalism, local newspapers were awash with concern that the gifted young must be found and identified as 'elites', and supported to rule future societies. Voluntary groups capitalised on this interest and, as early as the 1950s and 1960s, fostered a new sense of 'popular individualism', telling the gifted young that they were special, and deserved special provision. This investigation hints towards the longstanding foundations on which Thatcherism would be constructed and emerge—not only as a powerful political force, but as something shaping culture and everyday life.[8] Subsequently, in the 1990s and 2000s, psychological and legal categories extended state management of 'the self', yet these were also resisted in

---

[6] See also: Emily Robinson, Camilla Schofield, Florence Sutcliffe-Braithwaite, and Natalie Thomlinson, 'Telling stories about post-war Britain: popular individualism and the "crisis" of the 1970s', *Twentieth Century British History*, 28 (2017), pp. 268–304; Jon Lawrence, *Me, Me, Me? The Search for Community in Post-war England* (Oxford: OUP, 2019); Florence Sutcliffe-Braithwaite, *Class, Politics, and the Decline of Deference in England, 1968–2000* (Oxford: OUP, 2018); Mathew Thomson, *Lost Freedom: The Landscape of the Child and the British Post-war Settlement* (Oxford: OUP, 2013); Amy Edwards, *Are We Rich Yet? The Rise of Mass Investment Culture in Contemporary Britain* (California: University of California Press, 2022); Alex Davies, Ben Jackson, and Florence Sutcliffe-Braithwaite (eds), *The Neoliberal Age? Britain since the 1970s* (London: IHR Press, 2021).

[7] See also: Daisy Payling, '"The people who write to us are the people who don't like us:" Public responses to the government Social Survey's Survey of Sickness, 1943–1952', *Journal of British Studies* 59 (2020), pp. 315–42; Gareth Millward, *Sick Note Britain: A History of the British Welfare State* (Oxford: OUP, 2022), ch. 2; Jane Lewis, 'Gender and the development of welfare regimes', *Journal of European Social Policy*, 2 (2) (1992): pp. 159–173; Helen McCarthy, *Double Lives: A History of Working Motherhood in Modern Britain* (London: Bloomsbury, 2020); Roberta Bivins, *Contagious Communities: Medicine, Migration, and the NHS in Post-War Britain* (Oxford: OUP, 2015); Caroline Rusterholz, *Responsible Pleasure: The Brook Advisory Centres and Youth Sexuality in Postwar Britain* (Oxford: OUP, 2024).

[8] Sutcliffe-Braithwaite, *Class, Politics, and the Decline of Deference*, pp. 4–8; Lawrence, *Me, Me, Me?*, p. 2; Robinson, Schofield, Sutcliffe-Braithwaite, and Thomlinson, 'Telling stories about post-war Britain', pp. 268–304.

complex and spatially distinct ways: for example, in this book, through and by children speaking and writing to one another in giftedness societies.[9]

Voluntary groups play a critical role here. Voluntary action did not decline in the post-war period, nor did it solely shift to becoming privatised or professionalised either.[10] Rather, lively voluntary action remained in messy, varied, dynamic groups, such as in the National Association's weekend and holiday clubs. The groups studied in this book were products of the 1970s and 1980s. In a moment of debate about the viability of the welfare state, they both supported and undermined welfare state provisions. They were often run by Eve Worth's 'welfare state generation', women who felt a need to 'give something back' to the state they felt bore them, but who also felt deeply concerned about its future.[11] Voluntary groups provided alternate networks for education and psychological testing, such that the patchwork provision of the welfare state was not further challenged for this absence. Yet in so doing, and in catering primarily for a middle-class demographic, they in part undermined any universalist ethos. These voluntary organisations created new networks and solidarities between parents, yet also empowered families to seek out individual paths to fulfilment and happiness, rather than to place themselves within systems of national or collective benefit. These organisations thus emerge as both conformist—enabling a welfare system to continue, even while it did not cater to all children—but also disruptive, as they sought to bring families together to challenge health and educational systems, and often encouraged children to embrace giftedness on their own terms. Notably, also, the organisers of these 1970s and 1980s groups shaped their demands in the experiential and emotional terms of these decades. While very different from second-wave feminism or gay liberation—with far more limited demands—the groups discussed

---

[9] On expanding psychological and legal categories, see: Bonnie Evans, *The Metamorphis of Autism: A History of Child Development in Britain* (Manchester: MUP, 2017), especially pp. 430–433; Millward, *Sick Note*, ch. 6. Significant further thinking about this decade will come from Helen McCarthy and David Geiringer's landmark 2020 workshop, 'Rethinking Britain in the 1990s: Towards a new research agenda', see: 'When was the nineties', *Past and Present* website <https://pastandpresent.org.uk/when-was-the-nineties/> (22 March 2024).

[10] Relevant debates: Frank Prochaska, *Christianity and Social Service in Modern Britain: The Disinherited Spirit* (Oxford: OUP, 2006), p. 97; Frank Prochaska, *The Voluntary Impulse: Philanthropy in Modern Britain* (London: Faber & Faber, 1988); Nick Crowson, Matthew Hilton, and James McKay (eds), *NGOs in Contemporary Britain: Non-state Actors in Society and Politics since 1945* (Basingstoke: Palgrave Macmillan, 2009) p. 3, 1–20; Matthew Hilton, James McKay, Nicholas Crowson, and Jean-François Mouhot, *The Politics of Expertise: How NGOs Shaped Modern Britain* (Oxford: OUP, 2013); Colin Rochester, George Campbell Gosling, Alison Penn, and Meta Zimmeck (eds), *Understanding the Roots of Voluntary Action: Historical Perspectives on Current Social Policy* (Brighton: Sussex Academic Press, 2011), p. 22; Pat Thane, 'Voluntary action in Britain since Beveridge', in Melanie Oppenheimer and Nicholas Deakin (eds), *Beveridge and Voluntary Action in Britain and the Wider British World* (Manchester: MUP, 2011), p. 123; Caitriona Beaumont, Eve Colpus, and Ruth Davidson (eds), *Histories of Welfare: Experiential Expertise, Action and Activism* (Basingstoke: Palgrave Macmillan, 2024).

[11] Eve Worth, *The Welfare State Generation: Women, Agency and Class in Britain since 1945* (London: Bloomsbury, 2021).

sought to represent raw emotion, suffering, and trauma when speaking to the press. These groups recast our thinking around 'activism' and 'resistance'; their work was not necessarily always 'constant, shared' or 'antagonistic', but rather 'inconsistent', 'personal, inventive and also sustained by care'.[12]

The book examines voluntary groups that rose in the 1990s and 2000s, as well as those primarily situated in the 1970s and 1980s. Thus, it shows the changing hopes placed on the gifted young, when conceptualised as elites or leaders of 'the future'. In the 1970s and 1980s, conservative critics, particularly tabloid newspapers, hoped to use these young people as economic resources; human capital to arrest national decline. In European voluntary circles in the same decades, and into the 1990s, it was hoped that gifted youth could represent liberal democratic values across the East—West divide, managing the decline of state-sponsored Communism. In global voluntary circles, centred on Britain, from the 1980s and into the 1990s, it was hoped that gifted young people would fuel international development: young people were positioned as able to set promising examples and also as capable of forging new solutions for change. In the late 1990s and 2000s, even as the popularity of the term, 'gifted', declined in general, businesses and government sought to motivate gifted youth to become involved in 'science', addressing a perceived skills crisis and creating new solutions for the production of energy and scarce resources. The different types of gifted youth identified thus revealed the shifting coalitions interested in creating 'the future' and 'elites', and the different priorities placed on various skills. This analysis shows changing ways in which campaigners in Britain conceived of and related to other parts of the world. In particular, campaigners shifted constantly in the late twentieth and early-twenty-first centuries between defining themselves as 'local', 'national', or 'global' players yet, throughout, they were convinced that voluntary organisations, even if run messily from one family's house, were able to solve the very biggest issues of their times.

Think of the Children

Using testimonies from children and young people was central to this book's methodology. It examines children's writings, poetry, letters, and drawings throughout, as critical sources. Fundamentally, one of its core arguments is perhaps simply that scholars must rally against this uncritical assumption that we cannot trace children's views—whether because of a perceived lack of historical

---

[12] Maria Fannin and Julie MacLeavy, 'Feminism, resistance and the archive', in Sarah M. Hughes (ed.), *Critical Geographies of Resistance* (Cheltenham: Edward Elgar, 2023), pp. 126–140; Paul Chatterton and Jenny Pickerill, 'Everyday activism and transitions towards post-capitalist worlds', *Transactions of the Institute of British Geographers*, 35 (4) (2010), pp. 475–490.

sources or because children are not 'an organized political constituency'.[13] The voices of the young should be no less central to our scholarship than those of 'the old'.[14] The voices of the young can illuminate our political and social histories and geographies, and destabilise our established chronologies, as above.[15] Furthermore, gifted young people have distinct social and spatial histories. From the 1960s and 1970s, declining from the late 1980s, they were told, they believed, and they argued that being in a distinct social group, 'gifted', meant that one required distinct social and educational spaces. Many of these children, also, keenly believed that they required specific spaces and supervision to reflect a niche constellation of interests—discussed in Chapter Three. These beliefs and this participation in voluntary spaces, this book shows, subsequently shaped how young people felt, and how they interacted with their families, communities, and in schools. The book shows that many young people happily received a vision of themselves as elites of the future, while others passionately challenged labels of 'giftedness' as unfair or plain silly. Ideas of 'waithood' and 'agency' must frame our thinking here, as we look to account for enthusiastic acceptance of psychological and educational labels, as well as resistance to them.[16] This book has explored a new strand of 'youth culture' important in the 1970s and 1980s. Beyond sex, drugs, and rock and roll, or deviant youth cultures, often the basis of existing

---

[13] Colin Heywood, 'On the margins or in the mainstream? the history of childhood in France', *Nottingham French Studies*, 59 (2) (2020), p. 135. The idea that children do not gain much historical attention because of their lack of political role is discussed by historian of childhood Harry Hendricks, interviewed in: Carmel Smith and Sheila Greene (eds), *Key Thinkers in Childhood Studies* (Bristol: Policy Press, 2015), p. 121. For further useful 'state of the field' discussions on geographies and histories of youth and childhood, see: Stuart C. Aitken, 'Children's Geographies: Tracing the Evolution and Involution of a Concept', *Geographical Review*, 108 (1) (2017), pp. 3–23; Sarah L. Holloway, 'Changing children's geographies', *Children's Geographies*, 12 (4) (2014), pp. 377–392; Darren P. Smith and Sarah Mills, 'The "youth-fullness" of youth geographies: "coming of age"?', *Children's Geographies*, 17 (1) (2019), pp. 1–8; Sarah Maza, 'The kids aren't all right: historians and the problem of childhood', *The American Historical Review*, 125 (4) (2020), pp. 1261–1285, and the responses to Maza's article: Steven Mintz, 'Children's history matters', *The American Historical Review*, 125 (4) (2020), pp. 1286–1292; Nara Milanich, 'Comment on Sarah Maza's "The kids aren't all right"', *The American Historical Review*, 125 (4) (2020), pp. 1293–1295; Robin P. Chapdelaine, 'Little voices: the importance and limitations of children's histories', *The American Historical Review*, 125 (4) (2020), pp. 1296–1299; Ishita Pande, 'Is the history of childhood ready for the world? a response to "The kids aren't all right"', *The American Historical Review*, 125 (4) (2020), pp. 1300–1305; Bengt Sandin, 'History of children and childhood—being and becoming, dependent and independent', *The American Historical Review*, 125 (4) (2020), pp. 1306–1316.

[14] 'Ewen Green lecture from Hester Barron (1998) 'Why schools matter to histories of interwar Britain', Youtube <https://www.youtube.com/watch?v=T6gl6kYmOOw> (3 April 2023). See also: Hester Barron, *The Social World of the School: Education and Community in Interwar London* (Manchester: MUP, 2022).

[15] Sian Pooley and Jonathan Taylor (eds), *Children's Experiences of Welfare in Modern Britain* (London: IHR Press, 2021).

[16] Millard, 'Using personal experience in the academic medical humanities'; Gleason, 'Avoiding the agency trap', pp. 446–459; Thomas, 'Historicising agency', pp. 324–339; Miller, 'Assent as agency', pp. 48–65; Abebe, 'Reconceptualising children's agency', pp. 1–16; Holloway, Holt, and Mills, 'Questions of agency', pp. 458–477; Jeffrey, 'Geographies of children and youth II'; Tatek Abebe, 'Lost futures? Educated youth precarity and protests in the Oromia region, Ethopia', *Children's Geographies*, 18 (6) (2020), pp. 584–600.

historiographies, thousands of lively subcultures of youth have flourished in modern Britain.[17] Those thought of as 'the gifted' were one of these. The gifted young were uniquely able, in the specific decades and specific sites traced here, to command, mobilise, and critique visions of 'the future', equality, and elitism.

Two reflections to close. The first is about the need to attend empathetically both to the experiences of suffering in our archives *and* to broader contexts of discrimination. Children labelled as 'gifted', as noted, often rejected this term. Again as noted, parents tended to couch their membership of giftedness organisations in terms of emotions like desperation and stress, even comparing themselves to the parents of disabled children, in terms of their struggles to provide adequate education and welfare provision to support their children in a declining welfare state. Encountering sources in this area—whether the quotes offered to newspapers by campaigners, or the letters written by individual parents to voluntary organisations—it is tempting to feel hugely sympathetic, picturing overwhelmed children who were bullied due to the label, 'gifted', and parents who were on the brink of separation from partners or friends due to the needs of their child. As Kate Boyer has written, using archives as a research method (rather than, or as well as, interviews or field trips) by no means mitigates the need to consider 'responsibilities to one's subjects and the potential violence of speaking for others'.[18] Sarah Mills, drawing on Carolyn Steedman, has emphasised that we may find 'moments of connection and familiarity' in our archives, while imaging our subjects' lives.[19]

At the same time, encountering our sources around giftedness we must also bear in mind that this concept was often intimately bound up with broader systems of structural discrimination. White, middle-class boys were disproportionately expected to be gifted, and labelled as such by psychologists, educators, and families alike. By the 1970s, tabloid newspapers interested in giftedness were excitedly referring to children's genetic make-up. In the same period, the writings

---

[17] For discussions of radical youth lives, see Celia Hughes, *Young Lives on the Left: Sixties Activism and the Liberation of the Self* (Manchester: MUP, 2015); Stanley Cohen, *Folk Devils and Moral Panics: The Creation of the Mods and Rockers* (London: Paladin, 1972); Bill Osgerby, 'The good, the bad and the ugly: postwar media representations of youth', in Adam Briggs and Paul Cobley (eds), *The Media: An Introduction* (Harlow: Longman, 1997); Angela Bartie, 'Moral panics and Glasgow gangs: exploring "the new wave of Glasgow hooliganism", 1965–1970', *Contemporary British History*, 24 (2010), pp. 385–406; Louise Jackson and Angela Bartie, *Policing Youth: Britain, 1945–1970* (Manchester: MUP, 2014). Acknowledging the variety in youth lives, see Michael Schofield, *The Sexual Behaviour of Young People* (London: Longmans, 1965); Michael Schofield, *The Sexual Behaviour of Young Adults* (London: Allen Lane, 1973); Pearl Jephcott, *Time of One's Own: Leisure and Young People* (Edinburgh: EUP, 1967); Jim Gledhill, 'White heat, guide blue: the Girl Guide movement in the 1960s', *Contemporary British History*, 27 (2013), pp. 65–84; Helena Mills, 'The experience and memory of youth in England c. 1960–c. 1969' (D.Phil. thesis, Oxford, 2016), https://ora.ox.ac.uk/objects/uuid:f0bdc321-b580-414d-a7ff-35d2c92e3ad4 (4 June 2021), pp. 2, 6.

[18] Kate Boyer, 'Feminist geography in the archive: practice and method', WGSG, *Geography and Gender Reconsidered*, August 2004, p. 170.

[19] Sarah Mills, 'Cultural-historical geographies of the archive: fragments, objects and ghosts', *Geography Compass*, 7 (10) (2013), p. 708.

of psychologists with eugenicist ties—such as Cyril Burt—shaped debates in popular newspapers. In the 1970s and subsequent years, children who were not white, middle-class, and male were often overlooked by teachers, parents, and voluntary organisations identifying 'the gifted'. The same set of ideas, scales, and norms that identified children as 'gifted' also identified others as 'subnormal' or 'ineducable'.[20]

This book then shows that labels such as 'gifted' have the power to uplift and collectively mobilise people on an individual and family level while, simultaneously, contributing to a system of damage within broader systems of structural discrimination. We must hold both of these things in our scholarship. Significantly, this book has shown that young people have been hugely capable of doing this, more so than adults. Young people—even those standing to benefit from the label 'gifted'—responded more critically to the power and discrimination embedded in this term than adults. Young people questioned IQ tests, for example, as 'silly' in the 1970s, decades before adult educational sociologists caught up. Mona Gleason and other historians of childhood urge us to read sources with 'empathic inference', thinking 'deeply and critically about how young people might have responded to any given situation in the past'.[21] From this perspective, then, studying how the gifted young acknowledged their privilege can help us to interrogate systems of power; young people, in this story, sometimes used the attention they received and their lived experiences to 'destabilise privilege and re-imagine spatialised power relations'.[22] This is not to romanticise the role of the young as uniquely able to understand or resist dynamics of power, but merely to draw attention to their writing as an additional source through which to interrogate how layers of power *work*.

The second reflection with which to close is about the nature of 'children's voices' over time. It may appear in this text that children's voices were most prominently heard in the 1970s and 1980s—when the National Association, as well as various schools and newspapers, actively sought out their poetry, drawings, and reflections on child and adult society alike. From the 1990s and 2000s, archival traces of those voices fade. Children's writings are less prominent in the newsletters of the National Academy for Gifted and Talented Youth, for example. Likewise, in the materials of the European Council for High Ability and World Council for

---

[20] Rob Waters, *Thinking Black: Britain, 1964–1985* (California: University of California Press, 2019), p. 130; Mathew Thomson, *Lost Freedom: The Landscape of the Child and the British Post-war Settlement* (Oxford: OUP, 2013), p. 199; Rubahanna Amannah Choudhury, 'The forgotten children: The Association of Parents of Backward Children and the Legacy of Eugenics in Britain, 1946–1960', thesis submitted for the Degree of Doctor of Philosophy at Oxford Brookes University, December 2015; Anne Borsay, 'Disabled Children and Special Education, 1944–1981', *History & Policy*, 26 November 2012 <https://www.historyandpolicy.org/docs/dfe-anne-borsay-text.pdf> (26 March 2024); Anne Borsay and Pamela Dale, (eds), Disabled Children: Contested Caring, 1850–1979 (Milton Abingdon: Routledge, 2016).
[21] Gleason, 'Avoiding the agency trap', p. 449.
[22] Janine Wiles, 'Health geographies 1: Unlearning privilege', *Progress in Human Geography*, 46 (1) (2021), pp. 220.

Gifted and Talented Children, operating in the late twentieth and early twenty-first centuries, the 'activist subjectivity' of children's writings from the 1960s and 1970s is not so present.[23] In part, this reflects a shift in the nature of the sources analysed: from consideration of local organisations that directly involved families to those run by teachers, professionals, and governments. Giftedness schemes, when run, were less likely to be local, disparate, and disordered, and more likely professionalised, streamlined, and bureaucratic.[24] At the same time, this examination also raises the question of whether rhetoric about the 'rise of children's voices' as a phenomenon of the 1990s is in tension with reality. The sources available changed because society changed. By the late twentieth and early twenty-first centuries, informal networks of giftedness groups were no longer so available, to encourage children's writings, and instead narratives around the 'gifted' were more often streamed through government initiatives looking to address inner city decline, educational inequality, and family demand alike. Children's voices became less centred in activism, despite broader interest in the experiential expertise of adults, because of increasing concerns about protecting children's mental health, and anxieties about the ethics of collecting and sharing their testimonies. In part, these anxieties came from the earlier testimonies of children—they had shared how systems of streaming and classification affected their mental wellbeing in previous decades, after all. Yet, also, children perhaps had fewer opportunities for self-expression and authorship on a daily level, and there was an uncomfortable assumption that adult rhetoric could now continue to capture and represent 'the child view'. Historians, geographers, sociologists, and other scholars must find the archival traces we can around childhood and youth, in addition to creating new interview, survey, and participatory research projects, to ensure that young people's voices are better centred and understood in our scholarship. Children have rich engagements and encounters with each other, families, schools, communities, voluntary groups, and states. Their perspectives contribute to overarching debates, and reshape everyday life. In the 1970s and 1980s in particular, gifted children were cast as symbols of equality and elitism. Children responded in varied ways: rejecting, accepting, or ignoring the adult invocations that they solve global tensions or declines in national productivity. Through and beyond this book's stories of optimism, hope, disappointment, and criticism, we can critically rethink invocations of equality and elitism in modern Britain and the world.

'Gifted Children' in Britain and the World: Elitism and Equality since 1945. Jennifer Crane, Oxford University Press.
© Jennifer Crane 2025. DOI: 10.1093/9780198928881.003.0008

---

[23] Tamara Myers, 'Local action and global imagining: youth, international development, and the Walkathon Phenomenon in sixties' and seventies' Canada', *Diplomatic History*, 38 (2) (2014), p. 283; Richard Ivan Jobs, *Backpack Ambassadors: How Youth Travel Integrated Europe* (Chicago: University of Chicago Press, 2017), ch. 3.

[24] Which Jobs describes as characteristic of the post-Cold War era itself ('bureaucratic, financial, and corporate'): Jobs, *Backpack Ambassadors*, p. 259.

Acknowledgements

The research which kick-started this book was generously funded by a Wellcome Research Fellowship, awarded in 2018, and entitled 'Constructing the "Gifted Child": Psychology, Family, and Identity in Britain since 1945' (212449/Z/18/Z). This fellowship supported me to have independent research time solely dedicated to this project, which was a huge privilege, and was also extended in time to replace two periods of research 'lost' to maternity leave—a great policy for EDI, thank you Wellcome. Thank you also to the Ludwig Fund, New College, Oxford, for further funding to extend particular aspects of this project.

This analysis relies primarily on archival sources, some catalogued, some not, some virtual, some physical. Key thanks go to Potential Plus, for granting me access to uncatalogued materials of the National Association for Gifted Children—thank you. I am hugely grateful also to the following archives, many of whom provided digital access to materials for research being conducted during the covid-19 pandemic (intended alphabetical order here): Bodleian Libraries, Archives, and Manuscripts, University of Oxford (and especially the Opie Archives, within this); Borthwick Institute for Archives, York; Cambridge University Archives; Institute of Education Archives, London; National Archives, London; Mass Observation Archives, Brighton; Modern Records Centre, Coventry; Special Collections and Archives, University of Liverpool Wellcome Collections, London. Materials from Mass Observation were reproduced with permission of Curtis Brown, London on behalf of the Trustees of the Mass Observation Archive © The Trustees of the Mass Observation Archive. I am thankful also to those who maintain and produce the digital archives of Parliamentary Papers, and local and national newspapers.

While formally starting in 2018, research for this project evolved over several years—the work substantially shifted as I shifted from the Universities of Warwick to Oxford to my wonderful academic home of University of Bristol, and I remain indebted and connected to wonderful scholars across these institutions and beyond:

- At the University of Warwick, huge thanks as ever to Mathew Thomson and Roberta Bivins, who remain key academic mentors of mine, as well as to Gareth Millward, a continued valued collaborator. Mathew and Roberta: all of my approach to my work started from the nurturing, experimental, supportive environment you have created and fostered, with wonderful colleagues such as Hilary Marland, at the Centre for the History of Medicine, thank you.

200 ACKNOWLEDGEMENTS

- From University of Oxford, I most sincerely thank Siân Pooley: your meticulous and innovative research, and your generous mentoring, remain hugely inspirational to me. Thank you for the care you put into your work, and thanks also to all members of Siân's research group, for your support in my work and life particularly during the restorative panicked online chat over pandemic lockdowns: Gillian Lamb, Elena Mary, Samantha McCormack, Jono Taylor, Helen Sunderland, Rachel O-Driscoll, thank you. Kathryn Gleadle, Christina de Bellaigue, and Catherine Sloan were fantastic inspirational colleagues. And Jono, thank you in particular for your research assistance paid for by the Ludwig Fund as well—you're brilliant.
- At University of Bristol, I substantially conceptualised, wrote up, rethought, and finalised this book, and then began to doubt its very premises and nature thanks to the sharp evaluative wisdom and alluring charisma of brilliant colleagues, so thanks for that. Colleagues at the School of Geographical Sciences have been so supportive of my work and attempts at life. Members of the Historical & Cultural Research group and Non-Representational Theory reading group, led by Merle Patchett and Joe Gerlach respectively, in particular, you have challenged and changed my thinking from now on— thank you—and thank you for persuading me to let the book go despite all that. The School of Geographical Sciences is full of inspiring thinkers and generous people, and I appreciate all insights and solidarities shared across departmental coffees, chance corridor encounters, and picket lines alike. I would also note here, as everywhere, that our School is held together by the wonderful Geography office staff, led inspirationally by Danielle Rubiano, thank you. Thank you also to Jess Farr-Cox, a brilliant scholar and editor at University of Bristol, for copyediting and proof-reading this work and compiling the index.

Thanks also to all the seminars where I presented this work, and I'm sorry for not listing them here, my brain has been fried by the pandemic and childcare but so much incredible feedback has been provided. Thank you also to the editorial team at Oxford University Press, my anonymous readers, and the fantastic copyeditor of this work. So many people gave kind but critical feedback on earlier versions and drafts and thoughts around this work—thank you Victoria Bates and Siân Pooley, for reading the whole thing, and Gareth Millward, Mathew Thomson, Laura Tisdall, Grace Huxford, Andrew Burchell, David Geiringer, Hannah Elizabeth, Catherine Sloan, Ed Atkins, and Naomi Millner, for reading parts of earlier drafts. Vickie Zhang, thank you so much for the wonderful inspiration for the cover, and thank you to the Design Team at OUP for designing this.

Earlier experiments with the ideas in this book were published in *Contemporary European History*, *Historical Journal*, and the forthcoming book edited by Caitriona Beaumont, Eve Colpus, and Ruth Davidson (eds), *Histories of Welfare: Experiential*

Expertise, Action and Activism (Palgrave)—thank you to all editors and reviewers of these articles for your wise feedback, and to relevant publishers and funding by Wellcome to publish these with open access licences.[1]

It's an acknowledgements' cliché to end with families, but I do want to end by sending the biggest thanks as ever to my family: to my partner, David, thank you for supporting me, particularly while writing up this book navigating a house move, job move, pregnancies, two young children. To my children, please keep purposefully and joyfully focused on play and life, rather than on categories such as 'gifted' (as you know, this is a boring grown up book with no pictures, I'm sorry).

---

[1] Full article references: Jennifer Crane, 'Britain and Europe's Gifted Children in the Quests for Democracy, Welfare and Productivity, 1970–1990', *Contemporary European History*, 32 (2) (2022), pp. 235–253; Jennifer Crane, 'Gifted Children, Youth Culture, and Popular Individualism in 1970s and 1980s Britain', *The Historical Journal*, 65 (2022), pp. 1418–1441 (both published under CC BY 4.0 license, permitting unrestricted re-use, distribution, reproduction, with proper citation and link to the license <https://creativecommons.org/licenses/by/4.0/>).

Select Bibliography

Aaron, Andrews, 'Dereliction, decay and the problem of de-industrialization in Britain, c. 1968–1977', *Urban History* 47 (2) (2019), pp. 236–256.

Abebe, Tatek, *African Futures and Childhood Studies in Africa* (Dakar, Senegal: CODESRIA Books, 2022).

Abebe, Tatek, 'Lost futures? Educated youth precarity and protests in the Oromia region, Ethopia', *Children's Geographies*, 18 (6) (2020), pp. 584–600.

Abebe, Tatek, 'Reconceptualising children's agency as continuum and interdependence', *Social Sciences*, 8 (3) (2019), pp. 1–16.

Agar, Jon, *Science in the Twentieth Century and Beyond* (London: Polity Press, 2013).

Aitken, Stuart C., 'Children's geographies: tracing the evolution and involution of a concept', *Geographical Review*, 108 (1) (2017), pp. 3–23.

Arslan, Mahmut, 'A cross-cultural comparison of achievement and power orientation as leadership dimensions in three European countries: Britain, Ireland and Turkey', *Business Ethics: A European Review*, 10 (4) (2001), pp. 340–345.

Arslan, Mahmut, 'A cross-cultural comparison of Turkish and British managers in terms of Protestant work ethic characteristics', *Business Ethics: A European Review*, 9 (1) (2000), pp. 13–19.

Astin, Helen and Leland, Carole, 'Women of Influence, Women of Vision: A Cross Generational Study of Leaders and Social Change' (San Fransico, USA: Jossey-Bass, 1999).

Baillie Smith, Matt, Mills, Sarah, Okech, Moses, and Fadel, Bianca, 'Uneven geographies of youth volunteering in Uganda: Multiscalar discourses and practices', *Geoforum*, 134 (2022), pp. 30–39.

Barke, J. Cohen, S., Cole, T., Henry, L., Hutchen, J., Latinwo-Olajide, V., McLellan, J., Pridgeon, E., and Whitmore, B., 'A history of survival: preserving and working with an archive of single parent activism', *Women's History Review*, 33 (1) (2024), pp. 117–130.

Barnett, Nicholas, *Britain's Cold War: Culture, Modernity and the Soviet Threat* (London: Bloomsbury, 2018).

Barnett, Nicholas, '"Russia wins space race: the British press and the Sputnik moment, 1957', *Media History*, 19 (2) (2013), pp. 182–195.

Barron, Hester, *The Social World of the School: Education and Community in Interwar London* (Manchester: MUP, 2022).

Barron, Hester, Ewen Green Lecture from Hester Barron on 'Why schools matter to histories of interwar Britain', <https://www.youtube.com/watch?v=T6gl6kYmOOw> (22 February 2023).

Bartie, Angela, 'Moral panics and Glasgow gangs: exploring "the new wave of Glasgow hooliganism", 1965–1970', *Contemporary British History*, 24 (2010), pp. 385–406.

Bashford Alison, and Levine, Philippa (eds), *The Oxford Handbook of the History of Eugenics* (Oxford: OUP, 2010).

Bauer, Nichole M., 'Emotional, sensitive, and unfit for office? gender stereotype activation and support female candidates', *Political Psychology*, 36 (6) (2014), pp. 691–708.

Beaumont, Catriona, Colpus, Eve, and Davidson, Ruth (eds), *Histories of Welfare: Experiential Expertise, Action and Activism* (Basingstoke: Palgrave Macmillan, 2024).

Beauvais, Clementine, 'Ages and ages: the multiplication of children's "ages" in early twentieth-century child psychology', *History of Education*, 45 (3) (2016), pp. 304–318.

Beauvais, Clémentine, 'Child giftedness as class weaponry: the case of Roald Dahl's Matilda', *Children's Literature Association Quarterly*, 40 (3) (2015), pp. 277–293.

Beers, Laura, *Red Ellen: The Life of Ellen Wilkinson, Socialist, Feminist, Internationalist* (Cambridge, MA: Harvard University Press, 2016).
Benwell, Matthew C. and Hopkins, Peter, *Children, Young People and Critical Geopolitics* (London: Routledge, 2017).
Bingham, Adrian, *Family Newspapers? Sex, Private Life, and the British Popular Press, 1918–1978* (Oxford: OUP, 2009).
Bivins, Roberta, *Contagious Communities: Medicine, Migration, and the NHS in Post-War Britain* (Oxford: OUP, 2015).
Bochel, Hugh and Defty, Andrew, *Welfare Policy under New Labour: Views from Inside Westminster* (Bristol: Policy Press, 2007).
Borsay, Anne and Dale, Pamela (eds), *Disabled Children: Contested Caring, 1850–1979* (Abingdon: Routledge, 2016).
Bos, M. Holman, J. Greenlee, Z. Oxley, and J. Lay, '100 years of suffrage and girls still struggle to find their "fit" in politics', *Political Science & Politics*, 53 (3) (2020), pp. 474–478.
Botelle, Riley and Willott, Chris, 'Birth, attitudes and placentophagy: a thematic discourse analysis of discussions on UK parenting forums', *BMC Pregnancy and Childbirth*, 20 (2020), pp. 1–10.
Boyer, Kate, 'Feminist geography in the archive: practice and method', WGSG, *Geography and Gender Reconsidered*, August 2004, pp. 169–174.
Boyle, Ryan, 'A red moon over the mall: the Sputnik panic and domestic America', *The Journal of American Culture*, 31 (4) (2008), pp. 373–382.
Bradbury, Alice, 'From model minorities to disposable models: the de-legitimisation of educational success through discourses of authenticity', *Discourse: Studies in the Cultural Politics of Education*, 34 (4) (2013), pp. 548–561.
Brady, Margaret, 'An Exploration of the Impact of Gifted and Talented Policies on Inner City Schools in England: A Case Study', PhD thesis, Brunel University, March 2015.
Bresnihan, Patrick and Millner, Naomi, *All We Want is the Earth: Land, Labour, and Movements Beyond Environmentalism* (Bristol: Bristol University Press, 2023).
Brzezinski, Michael, *Red Moon Rising: Sputnik and the Rivalries that Ignited the Space Age* (London: Bloomsbury, 2007).
Burchell, Andrew, 'At the margins of the medical? Educational psychology, child guidance and therapy in provincial England, c. 1945–74', *Social History of Medicine*, 34 (1) (2021), pp. 70–93.
Burchell, Andrew, 'Mass observing general practice', *People's History of the NHS project*, <https://peopleshistorynhs.org/mass-observing-general-practice/> (14 September 2021).
Cadbury, Deborah, *Space Race: The Battle to Rule the Heavens* (London: Harper, 2005).
Cameron, Harriet and Billington, Tom, 'The discursive construction of dyslexia by students in higher education as a moral and intellectual good', *Disability & Society*, 30 (8) (2015), pp. 1225–1240.
Campbell Gosling, George, Penn, Alison, and Zimmeck, Meta (eds), *Understanding the Roots of Voluntary Action: Historical Perspectives on Current Social Policy* (Brighton: Sussex Academic Press, 2011).
Chapdelaine, Robin P., 'Little voices: the importance and limitations of children's histories', *The American Historical Review*, 125 (4) (2020), pp. 1296–1299.
Chatelain, Marcia, 'International sisterhood: Cold War girl scouts encounter the world', *Diplomatic History*, 38 (2) (2014), pp. 261–270.
Chatterton, Paul and Pickerill, Jenny, 'Everyday activism and transitions towards post-capitalist worlds', *Transactions of the Institute of British Geographers*, 35 (4) (2010), pp. 475–490.
Cho, Yonjoo, Ghosh, Rajashi, Sun, Judy Y., and McLean, Gary N. (eds), *Current Perspectives on Asian Women in Leadership: A Cross-Cultural Analysis* (London: Palgrave, 2017).
Choudhury, Rubahanna Amannah, 'The forgotten children: The Association of Parents of Backward Children and the Legacy of Eugenics in Britain, 1946–1960', Thesis submitted for the Degree of Doctor of Philosophy at Oxford Brookes University, December 2015 <https://radar.brookes.ac.uk/radar/file/26b8d017-0527-4006-8029-0426ea259b75/1/choudhury 2015forgottenRADAR.pdf> (26 March 2024).

Clarke, Nick and Barnett, Clive, 'Archiving the COVID-19 pandemic in Mass Observation and Middletown', *History of the Human Sciences*, 36 (2) (2023), pp. 3–25.

Clarke, Nick and Moss, Jonathan, 'Popular imaginative geographies and Brexit: Evidence from Mass Observation', *Transactions of the Institute of British Geographers*, 46 (3) (2021), pp. 732–746.

Cohen, Deborah, *Family Secrets: The Things We Tried To Hide* (London: Penguin, 2014).

Cohen, Stanley, *Folk Devils and Moral Panics: The Creation of the Mods and Rockers* (London: Paladin, 1972).

Cook, Matt, '"Gay Times": identity, locality, memory and the Brixton squats in 1970s London', *Twentieth Century British History*, 24 (1) (2013), pp. 84–109.

Crane, Jennifer, *Child Protection in England, 1960–2000: Expertise, Experience, and Emotion* (Basingstoke: Palgrave, 2018).

Cresswell, Tim, 'Value, gleaning and the archive at Maxwell Street, Chicago', *Transactions of the Institute of British Geographers*, 37 (1) (2012), pp. 164–176.

Cronin, James E., *New Labour's Pasts: The Labour Party and its Discontents* (Abingdon: Routledge, 2004).

Crook, Sarah and Jeffries, Charlie (eds), *Resist, Organize, Build: Feminist and Queer Activism in Britain and the United States during the Long 1980s* (New York: SUNY Press, 2022).

Crook, Sarah, 'The Labour Party, feminism and Maureen Colquhoun's scandals in 1970s Britain', *Contemporary British History*, 34 (1) (2020), pp. 71–94.

Crossley, Michele and Crossley, Nick, '"Patient" voices, social movements and the habitus; how psychiatric survivors "speak out"', *Social Science and Medicine*, 52 (2001), pp. 1477–1489.

Crowson, Nick, Hilton, Matthew, and McKay, James (eds), *NGOs in Contemporary Britain: Non-state Actors in Society and Politics Since 1945* (Basingstoke: Palgrave Macmillan, 2009).

Davies, Alex, Freeman, James, and Pemberton, Hugh, '"Everyman a capitalist" or "free to choose"? Exploring the tensions within Thatcherite individualism', *Historical Journal*, 61 (2018), pp. 477–501.

Davies, Alex, Jackson, Ben, and Sutcliffe-Braithwaite, Florence (eds), *The Neoliberal Age? Britain since the 1970s* (London: IHR Press, 2021).

Davies, Jonathan, and Freeman, Mark, 'Education for citizenship: the Joseph Rowntree Charitable Trust and the educational settlement movement', *History of Education*, 32 (3) (2003), pp. 303–318.

Dávila-Freire, Mela, 'Reading the archive against the grain: Power relations, affective affinities and subjectivity in the documenta Archive', *Art Libraries Journal*, 45 (3) (2020), pp. 94–99.

Davis, Angela, *Pre-school Childcare in England, 1939–2010* (Manchester: MUP, 2015).

de Geus, Roosmarijn A., McAndrews, John R., Loewen, Peter John, et al., 'Do voters judge the performance of female and male politicians differently? Experimental evidence from the United States and Australia', *Political Research Quarterly*, 74 (2) 2021, pp. 302–316.

Delap, Lucy, 'Feminist bookshops, reading cultures and the Women's Liberation movement in Great Britain, c. 1974–2000', *History Workshop Journal*, 81 (1) (2016), pp. 171–196.

Delfino, Susanna, Graser, Marcus, Krabbendam, Hans, and Michelot, Vincent, 'Europeans writing American history: the comparative trope', *American Historical Review*, 119 (3) (2014), pp. 791–799.

Dickson, Paul, *Sputnik: The Shock of the Century* (New York: Berkley Books, 2001).

Dorey, Peter, 'The 3 Rs—Reform, Reproach and Rancour: Education Policies under John Major', in Peter Dorey (ed.), *The Major Premiership* (London: Palgrave Macmillan, 1999), pp. 146–164.

Durham, Martin, *Sex and Politics: The Family and Morality in the Thatcher Years* (Basingstoke: Palgrave Macmillan, 1991).

Durham, Martin, 'The Thatcher Government and "The Moral Right"', *Parliamentary Affairs*, 41 (1989), pp. 58–71.

Eades, Michael, 'Documenting disappearance: a day in the "research laboratory" of Iona and Peter Opie', *Performance Research: A Journal of the Performing Arts*, (24) (7) (2019), pp. 99–102.

Eagly, Alice H., Nater, Christa, Miller, David I., Kaufmann Michèle K., and Sczesny, Sabine, 'Gender stereotypes have changed: a cross-temporal meta-analysis of U.S. public opinion polls from 1946 to 2018', *American Psychologist*, 75(3) (2020), pp. 301–315.

Edgerton, David, *England and the Aeroplane: Militarism, Modernity and Machines* (London: Penguin, 2013).

Edgerton, David, *The Rise and Fall of the British Nation: A Twentieth-Century History* (London: Allen Lane, 2018).

Edgerton, David, *Warfare State: Britain, 1920–1970* (Cambridge: CUP, 2005).

Edgerton, David, 'The "White Heat" revisited: The British Government and technology in the 1960s', *Twentieth Century British History*, 7 (1) (1996), pp. 53–82.

Edwards, Amy, *Are We Rich Yet? The Rise of Mass Investment Culture in Contemporary Britain* (California: University of California Press, 2022).

Elizabeth, Hannah, 'Love carefully and without "over-bearing fears": the persuasive power of authenticity in late 1980s British AIDS education material for adolescents', *Social History of Medicine*, 34 (4) (2021), pp. 1317–1342.

Evans, Bonnie, *The Metamorphosis of Autism: A History of Child Development in Britain* (Manchester: MUP, 2017).

Fairless Nicholson, Jacob, 'From London to Grenada and back again: youth exchange geographies and the Grenadian Revolution, 1979–1983', *Antipode* (2020), pp. 708–728.

Fannin, Maria and MacLeavy, Julie, 'Feminism, resistance and the archive', in Sarah M. Hughes (ed.), *Critical Geographies of Resistance* (Cheltenham: Edward Elgar, 2023), pp. 26–40.

Fass, Paula S., 'Intersecting agendas: children in history and diplomacy', *Diplomatic History*, 38 (2) (2014), pp. 294–298.

Faulkner, Alison, 'User involvement in 21st century mental health services: "This is our century"', in Charlie Brooker and Julie Repper (eds), *Mental Health: From Policy to Practice* (London: Elsevier Health Sciences, 2009), pp. 14–26.

Fieldston, Sara, 'Little cold warriors: child sponsorship and international affairs', *Diplomatic History*, 38 (2) (2014), pp. 240–250.

Flinn, Andrew, 'Archival activism: independent and community-led archives, radical public history and the heritage professions', *Interactions: UCLA Journal of Education and Information Studies*, 7 (2) (2011).

Francis, Martin, 'Tears, tantrums, and bared teeth: the emotional economy of three Conservative Prime Ministers, 1951–1963', *Journal of British Studies*, 41 (2002), pp. 354–387.

Friedman, Sam and Laurison, Daniel, *The Class Ceiling: Why it Pays to be Privileged* (Bristol: Policy Press, 2020).

Friedman, Sam and Reeves, Aaron, 'From aristocratic to ordinary: shifting modes of elite distinction', *American Sociological Review*, 85 (2) (2020), pp. 323–350.

Gamble, Andrew, *The Free Economy and the Strong State: The Politics of Thatcherism* (Basingstoke: Palgrave Macmillan, 1994).

Garland-Thomson, Rosiemarie, 'The politics of staring: visual rhetorics of disability in popular photography', in Sharon Snyder, Brenda Jo Brueggemann, and Rosemarie Garland-Thomson (eds), *Disability Studies: Enabling the Humanities* (New York: Modern Language Association of America, 2002), pp. 56–75.

Gazeley, Ian and Langhamer, Claire, 'The meanings of happiness in Mass Observation's Bolton', *History Workshop Journal*, 75 (1) (2013), pp. 159–189.

Gleadle, Kathryn, *Borderline Citizens: Women, Gender and Political Culture in Britain, 1815–1867* (Oxford: OUP, 2009).

Gleadle, Kathryn, 'The Juvenile Enlightenment: British Children and youth during the French Revolution', *Past & Present*, 233 (1) (2016), pp. 143–184.

Gleason, Mona, 'Avoiding the agency trap: caveats for historians of children, youth, and education', *History of Education*, 45 (4) (2016), pp. 446–459.

Gledhill, Jim, 'White heat, guide blue: the Girl Guide movement in the 1960s', *Contemporary British History*, 27 (2013), pp. 65–84.

Green, Mick, and Houlihan, Barrie, *Elite Sport Development: Policy Learning and Political Priorities* (Abingdon: Routledge, 2005).

Gregory, Kirsten, 'Exceptional and destructive: the dangerous child and the atom bomb in postwar science fiction', in Monica Flegel and Christopher Parkes (eds), *Cruel Children in Popular Texts and Cultures* (London: Palgrave Macmillan, 2018), pp. 153–172.

Grissom, Jason A. and Reading, Christopher, 'Discretion and disproportionality: explaining the underrepresentation of high-achieving students of color in gifted programs', *AERA Open*, 2 (1) (2016).

Grossberg, Michael, 'Liberation and caretaking: Fighting over children's rights in postwar America', in Paula Fass and Michael Grossberg (eds), *Reinventing Childhood After World War II* (Philadelphia, PA: University of Pennsylvania Press, 2012).

Guillory, Sean, 'Culture clash in the Socialist paradise: Soviet patronage and African students' urbanity in the Soviet Union, 1960–1965', *Diplomatic History*, 38 (2) (2014), pp. 271–281.

Gurney, Peter, '"Intersex" and "Dirty Girls": mass-observation and working-class sexuality in England in the 1930s', *Journal of the History of Sexuality*, 8 (2) (1997), pp. 256–290.

Hacking, Ian, 'Kinds of people: moving targets', *Proceedings of the British Academy*, 151 (2007), pp. 285–318.

Hacking, Ian, 'Making up people', in Heller, Thomas C., Sosna, Morton, and Wellbery, David E., (eds), *Reconstructing Individualism: Autonomy, Individuality, and the Self in Western Thought* (Stanford: Stanford University Press, 1986), pp. 222–236.

Hall, Catherine and Pick, Daniel, 'Feature: denial in history', *History Workshop Journal*, 84 (2017), pp. 1–23.

Hay, Colin, *The Political Economy of New Labour: Labouring Under False Pretences?* (Manchester: MUP, 1999).

Heffernan, Richard, *New Labour and Thatcherism: Political Change in Britain* (Basingstoke: Palgrave Macmillan, 2000).

Hendrick, Harry, 'The Child as a social actor in historical sources: Problems of identification and interpretation', in Pia Christensen and Allison James (eds) *Research with Children: Perspectives and Practices* (London, 2008).

Heywood, Colin, 'On the Margins or in the Mainstream? The History of Childhood in France', *Nottingham French Studies*, 59 (2) (2020), p. 122–135.

Hilliard, Christopher, *To Exercise Our Talents: The Democratization of Writing in Britain* (Cambridge, MA: HUP, 2006).

Hilton, Matthew, 'Politics is ordinary: non-governmental organizations and political participation in contemporary Britain', *Twentieth Century British History*, 2 (2011), pp. 230–268.

Hilton, Matthew, Baughan, Emily, Davey, Eleanor, Everill, Browen, O'Sullivan, Kevin, and Sasson, Tehila, 'History and humanitarianism: a conversation', *Past & Present*, 241 (1) (2018), pp. e1–e38.

Hilton, Matthew, McKay, James, Crowson, Nicholas, and Mouhot, Jean-François, *The Politics of Expertise: How NGOs Shaped Modern Britain* (Oxford: OUP, 2013).

Hinton, James, 'The "Class" complex: mass-observation and cultural distinction in pre-war Britain', *Past & Present*, 199 (2008), pp. 207–236.

Hinton, James, *Nine Wartime Lives: Mass Observation and the Making of the Modern Self* (Oxford: OUP, 2010).

Hodgson, Elizabeth Ann, 'The National Record of Achievement: Just another Initiative or a Useful Tool for the Future?' PhD thesis submitted to the University of London, 1997.

Holland, Patricia and Franklin, Ieuan, 'Editorial introduction: opening doors: the BBC's Community Programme Unit 1973–2002', *History Workshop Journal*, 82 (1) (2016), pp. 213–234.

Holloway, Sarah L., 'Changing children's geographies', *Children's Geographies*, 12 (4) (2014), pp. 377–392.

Holloway, Sarah L. and Valentine, Gill (eds), *Children's Geographies: Playing, Living, Learning* (Milton Keynes: Routledge, 2000).

Holloway, Sarah L., Holt, Louise, and Mills, Sarah, 'Questions of agency: capacity, subjectivity, spatiality and temporality', *Progress in Human Geography*, 43 (3) (2018), pp. 45–477.

Honeck, Mischa and Rosenberg, Gabriel, 'Transnational generations: organizing youth in the Cold War', *Diplomatic History*, 38 (2) (2014), pp. 233–239.

Honwana, Alinda M., *The Time of Youth: Work, Social Change, and Politics in Africa* (London: Kumarian Press, 2012).

Horak, Sinisa, and Weber, Sanda, 'Youth tourism in Europe: problems and prospects', *Tourism Recreation Research*, 25 (3) (2000), pp. 37–44.

Hsu, Madeline Y. *The Good Immigrants: How the Yellow Peril Became the Model Minority* (Princeton: Princeton University Press, 2015).

Hughes, Celia, *Young Lives on the Left: Sixties Activism and the Liberation of the Self* (Manchester: MUP, 2015).

Humphries, Stephen, *Hooligans or Rebels?: An Oral History of Working-Class Childhood and Youth 1889–1939* (2nd edition, Oxford: John Wiley & Sons, 1997).

Iriyre, Akira, *Cultural Internationalism and World Order* (Baltimore: John Hopkins University Press, 1997).

Jackson, Louise and Bartie, Angela, *Policing youth: Britain, 1945–1970* (Manchester: MUP, 2014).

Jeffrey, Craig, 'Geographies of children and youth II: Global youth agency', *Progress in Human Geography*, 36 (2) (2011), pp. 245–253.

Jeffreys, Kevin, 'R. A. Butler, the Board of Education, and the 1944 Education Act', *History*, 69 (227) (1984), pp. 415–431.

Jobs, Richard Ivan, *Backpack Ambassadors: How Youth Travel Integrated Europe* (Chicago: University of Chicago Press, 2017).

Johnson, Walter, 'On Agency', *Journal of Social History*, 37 (1) (2003), pp. 113–124.

Jolly, Jennifer L., 'The National Defense Education Act, Current STEMP initiative, and the gifted', *Gifted Child Today*, 32 (2) (2009), pp. 50–53.

Jopson, Laura, Burn, Andrew, and Robinson, Jonathan, 'The Opie Recordings: what's left to be heard?', in Andrew Burn and Chris Richards (eds), *Children's Games in the New Media Age* (Basingstoke: Taylor Francis, 2014).

Kavanagh, Dennis and Seldon, Anthony (eds), *The Major Effect* (London: Macmillan, 1994).

Kendall, Jeremy and Knapp, Martin, 'A loose and baggy monster: boundaries, definitions and typologies', in Justin Davis Smith, Colin Rochester, and Rodney Hedley (eds), *An Introduction to the Voluntary Sector* (Abingdon: Routledge, 1994), pp. 65–94.

Kenny, Sarah, '"Basically you were either a mainstream sort of person or you went to the Leadmill and The Limit": understanding post-war British youth culture through oral history', in Kristine Moruzi, Nell Musgrove, and Carla Pascoe Leahy (eds), *Children's Voices from the Past: New Historical and Interdisciplinary Perspectives* (London, Palgrave Macmillan, 2019), pp. 233–259.

Kidd, Kenneth, 'The child, the scholar, and the children's literature archive', *The Lion and the Unicorn*, 35 (1) (2011), pp. 1–23.

Kilgannon, David, 'Public attention for private concerns: intellectual disability parents' organisations in the Republic of Ireland, 1955–1970', *Medical Humanities*, 46 (2020), pp. 483–491.

King, Laura, 'Future citizens: cultural and political conceptions of children in Britain, 1930s–1950s', *Twentieth Century British History*, 27 (3) (2016), pp. 389–411.

King, Neil, *Sport Policy and Governance: Local Perspectives* (Oxford: Butterworth-Heinemann, 2009).

Kirby, Philip, 'Gift from the gods? Dyslexia, popular culture and the ethics of representation', *Disability & Society*, 34 (10) (2019), pp. 1573–1594.

Kirby, Philip and Snowling, Margaret J., *Dyslexia: A History* (Montreal, Quebec: McGill-Queen's University Press, 2022).

Klarman, Michael J., *Brown v. Board of Education and the Civil Rights Movement* (Oxford: OUP, 2007).

Kocka, Jurgen, 'Comparison and beyond', *History and Theory*, 42 (1) (2003), pp. 39–44.

Kverndokk, Kyrre, 'Talking about your generation: "Our Children" as a trope in climate change discourse', *Ethnologia Europaea*, 50 (1) (2020), pp. 145–158.

Langhamer, Claire, 'An archive of feeling? Mass Observation and the mid-century moment', *Insights*, 9 (4) (2016), pp. 1–15.

Langhamer, Claire, *The English in Love: The Intimate Story of an Emotional Revolution* (Oxford: OUP, 2013).

Langhamer, Claire, 'Mass observing the atom bomb: the emotional politics of August 1945', *Contemporary British History*, 33 (2) (2019), pp. 208–225.
Lawrence, Jon, *Me, Me, Me? The Search for Community in Post-war England* (Oxford: OUP, 2019).
Lay, J., Holman, M., Bos, A., Greenlee, J., Oxley, Z., and Buffett, A., 'TIME for kids to learn gender stereotypes: analysis of gender and political leadership in a common social studies resource for children', *Politics & Gender*, (2019), pp. 1–22.
Lerner, Gerda, 'Placing women in history: a 1975 perspective', *Feminist Studies* 3 (1975), pp. 5–14.
Levine, Philippa, 'Is comparative history possible?', *History and Theory*, 53 (2014), pp. 331–347.
Levitas, Ruth, *The Inclusive Society? Social Exclusion and New Labour* (Basingstoke: Palgrave, 2005).
Lewis, Jane, 'Gender and the development of welfare regimes', *Journal of European Social Policy*, 2 (2) (1992), pp. 159–73.
Lorenz, Chris, 'Comparative historiography: problems and perspectives', *History and Theory*, 38 (1) (1999), pp. 25–39.
Lupton, Deborah, Pederson, Sarah, Thomas, Gareth M., 'Parenting and digital media: from the early web to contemporary digital society', *Sociology Compass*, 10 (8) (2016), pp. 730–743.
Marren, Brian, *We Shall Not Be Moved: How Liverpool's Working Class Fought Redundancies, Closures and Cuts in the Age of Thatcher* (Manchester: MUP, 2016).
McCarthy, Helen. *The British People and the League of Nations: Democracy, Citizenship and Internationalism, c. 1918–45* (Manchester: MUP, 2011).
McCarthy, Helen, *Double Lives: A History of Working Motherhood in Modern Britain* (London: Bloomsbury, 2020).
McCulloch, Gary, *Philosophers and Kings: Education for Leadership in Modern England* (Cambridge: CUP, 1991).
Madsen, O. J., Servan, J., and Øyen, S. A., '"I am a philosopher of the particular case": an interview with the 2009 Holberg prizewinner Ian Hacking', *History of the Human Sciences*, 26 (3) (2013).
Mahood, Linda, *Policing Gender, Class and Family: Britain, 1850–1940* (London: UCL Press, 1995).
Mandler, Peter, *The Crisis of the Meritocracy: Britain's Transition to Mass Education since the Second World War* (Oxford: OUP, 2020).
Maza, Sarah, 'The kids aren't all right: historians and the problem of childhood', *The American Historical Review*, 125 (4) (2020), pp. 1261–1285.
Mazumdar, Pauline, *Eugenics Human Genetics and Human Failings: The Eugenics Society, its Source and its Critics in Britain* (London: Routledge, 1992).
Milanich, Nara, 'Comment on Sarah Maza's "The kids aren't all right"', *The American Historical Review*, 125 (4) (2020), pp. 1293–1295.
Millard, Chris, 'Concepts, diagnosis and the history of medicine: historicising Ian Hacking and Munchausen Syndrome', *Social History of Medicine*, 30 (3) (2017), pp. 567–589.
Millard, Chris, 'Using personal experience in the academic medical humanities: a genealogy', *Social Theory & Health*, 18 (2019), pp. 184–198.
Miller, Susan A., 'Assent as agency in the early years of the children of the American Revolution', *Journal of the History of Childhood and Youth*, 9 (1) (2016), pp. 48–65.
Mills, Helena, 'The experience and memory of youth in England c. 1960–c. 1969' (unpublished D.Phil. thesis, Oxford, 2016).
Mills, Sarah, 'Cultural-historical geographies of the archive: fragments, objects and ghosts', *Geography Compass*, 7 (10) (2013), pp. 701–712.
Mills, Sarah, 'Geographies of youth work, volunteering and employment: the Jewish Lads Brigade and Club in post-war Manchester', *Transactions of the Institute of British Geographers*, 40 (4) (2015), pp. 523–535.
Mills, Sarah, '"An instruction in good citizenship": scouting and the historical geographies of citizenship education', *Transactions of the Institute of British Geographers*, 38 (1) (2013), pp. 120–134.

Mills, Sarah, *Mapping the Moral Geographies of Education: Character, Citizenship and Values* (Milton Keynes: Routledge, 2022).
Millward, Gareth, 'A history with web archives, not a history of web archives: A history of the British measles-mumps-rubella vaccine crisis, 1998–2004', in N. Brügger, and I. Milligan (eds), *SAGE Handbook of Web History* (Sage: Thousand Oaks, 2018), pp. 464–478.
Millward, Gareth, *Sick Note: A History of the British Welfare State* (Oxford: OUP, 2022).
Millward, Gareth, 'Social security policy and the early disability movement—expertise, disability, and the Government, 1965–77', *Twentieth Century British History*, 26 (2) (2015).
Minna Stern, Alexandra, *Eugenic Nation: Faults and Frontiers of Better Breeding in Modern America* (California: University of California Press, 2015).
Mintz, Steven, 'Children's history matters', *The American Historical Review*, 125 (4) (2020), pp. 1286–1292.
Mold, Alex, *Making the Patient-consumer: Patient Organisations and Health Consumerism in Britain* (Manchester: MUP, 2015).
Mold, Alex and Berridge, Virginia, *Voluntary Action and Illegal Drugs: Health and Society in Britain since the 1960s* (Basingstoke: Palgrave Macmillan, 2010).
Moores, Chris, 'Opposition to the Greenham Women's Peace Camps in 1980s Britain: RAGE against the obscene', *History Workshop Journal*, 78 (1) (2014), pp. 204–227.
Mukkamala, S. and Suyemoto, K. L., 'Racialized sexism/sexualized racism: A multimethod study of intersectional experiences of discrimination for Asian American women', *Asian American Journal of Psychology*, 9 (1) (2018), pp. 32–46.
Murray, Stuart, 'Autism and the contemporary sentimental: fiction and the narrative fascination of the present', *Literature and Medicine*, 25 (1) (2006).
Myers, Tamara, 'Local action and global imagining: youth, international development, and the Walkathon Phenomenon in sixties' and seventies' Canada', *Diplomatic History*, 38 (2) (2014), pp. 282–293.
Nelson. Claudia, *Precocious Children and Childish Adults: Age Inversion in Victorian Literature* (Baltimore, MD: John Hopkins University Press, 2012).
Neumann, Matthias, 'Children diplomacy during the late Cold War: Samantha Smith's visit of the "Evil Empire"', *History*, 104 (360) (2019), pp. 275–308.
Norwig, Christina, 'A first European generation? The myth of youth and European integration in the fifties', *Diplomatic History*, 38 (2) (2014), pp. 251–260.
O'Hara, Glen and Parr, Helen, 'Conclusions: Harold Wilson's 1964 governments and the heritage of "New" Labour', *Contemporary British History*, 20 (3) (2006), pp. 477–489.
O'Hara, Glen and Parr, Helen (eds), *The Wilson Governments 1964–90 Reconsidered* (London: Routledge, 2006).
Oakley, Giles with Lee-Wright, Peter, 'Opening Doors: the BBC's Community Programme Unit 1930–2002', *History Workshop Journal*, 82 (1) (2016), pp. 213–234.
Ogborn, Miles, *Global Lives: Britain and the World* (Cambridge: CUP, 2008).
Okech, Moses, Baillie Smith, Matt, Fadel, Bianca, and Mills, Sarah, 'The reproduction of inequality through volunteering by young refugees in Uganda', *Voluntas: International Journal of Voluntary and Nonprofit Organisations*, first view 15 February 2024.
Opie, Peter and Iona (eds), *The Lore and Language of Schoolchildren* (New York: New York Review of Books, 2001).
Oppenheimer, Melanie, and Deakin, Nicholas (eds), *Beveridge and Voluntary Action in Britain and the Wider British World* (Manchester: MUP, 2011).
Osgerby, Bill, 'The good, the bad and the ugly: postwar media representations of youth', in Adam Briggs and Paul Cobley (eds), *The Media: An Introduction* (Harlow: Longman, 1997).
Page, Robert M., 'The Conservative Party and the welfare state since 1945', in Hugh Bochel (ed.), *The Conservative Party and Social Policy* (Bristol: Policy Press, 2011), pp. 23–40.
Pande, Ishita, 'Is the history of childhood ready for the world? a response to "The kids aren't all right"', *The American Historical Review*, 125 (4) (2020), pp. 1300–1305.
Patchett, Merle, 'Archiving', *Transactions of the Institute of British Geographers*, 44 (2019), pp. 650–653.

Patel, Josh, 'Imagining the role of the student in society: ideas of British higher education policy and pedagogy 1957–1972', PhD thesis, University of Warwick (2021).
Patel, Josh, 'The puzzle of Lionel Robbins: how a neoliberal economist expanded public university education in 1960s Britain', *Twentieth Century British History*, 34 (2) (2023), pp. 220–245.
Patterson, James T., *Brown v. Board of Education: A Civil Rights Milestone and Its Troubled Legacy* (New York: OUP, 2001).
Payling, Daisy, '"The people who write to us are the people who don't like us:" Public responses to the government Social Survey's Survey of Sickness, 1943–1952', *Journal of British Studies* 59 (2020), pp. 315–42.
Pederson, Sarah and Smithson, Janet, 'Mothers with attitude—How the Mumsnet parenting forum offers space for new forms of femininity to emerge online', *Women's Studies International Forum*, 38 (2013), pp. 97–106.
Pestel, Friedemann, 'Educating against Revolution: French émigré schools and the challenge of the next generation', *European History Quarterly*, 47 (2) (2017), pp. 229–256.
Phillipson, Shane N. and McCann, Maria (eds), *Conceptions of Giftedness: Sociocultural Perspectives* (Mahwah, NJ: Lawrence Erlbaum, 2004).
Pick, Daniel, *Brainwashed: A New History of Thought Control* (London: Wellcome Collection, 2022).
Pierson, Paul, 'The new politics of the welfare state', *World Politics*, 48 (2) (1996), pp. 143–179.
Pöllänen, Kari, 'Northern European leadership in transition—a survey of the insurance industry', *Journal of General Management*, 32 (1) (2006), pp. 43–63.
Pollen, Annebella, 'Research methodology in Mass Observation past and present: "Scientifically, about as valuable as a chimpanzee's tea party at the zoo?"', *History Workshop Journal*, 75 (1) (2013), pp. 218–222.
Pooley, Siân, 'Children's writing and the popular press in England, 1876–1914', *History Workshop Journal*, 80 (2015), pp. 75–98.
Pooley, Siân and Pooley, Colin, '"Such a splendid tale": the late nineteenth-century world of a young female reader', *Cultural and Social History*, 2 (2005), pp. 329–351.
Pooley, Siân and Taylor, Jono, *Children's Experiences of Welfare in Modern Britain* (London: IHR, 2021).
Prochaska, Frank, *Christianity and Social Service in Modern Britain: The Disinherited Spirit* (Oxford: OUP, 2006).
Rhodes, Christopher, Avis, James, and Somervell, Hugh, 'Records of achievement, higher education and work: passport or passenger?' *Research in Post-Compulsory Education*, 4(3) (1999), pp. 321–330.
Richardson, Sarah, *The Political Worlds of Women: Gender and Politics in Nineteenth Century Britain* (New York: Routledge, 2013).
Robinson, Ann and Jolly, Jennifer (eds), *A Century of Contributions to Gifted Education: Illuminating Lives* (New York: Routledge, 2013).
Robinson, Emily, *The Language of Progressive Politics in Modern Britain* (Basingstoke: Palgrave Macmillan, 2017).
Robinson, Emily, Schofield, Camilla, Sutcliffe-Braithwaite, Florence, and Thomlinson, Natalie, 'Telling stories about post-war Britain: popular individualism and the "crisis" of the 1970s', *Twentieth Century British History*, 28 (2017), pp. 268–304.
Rochester, Colin, Campbell Gosling, George, Penn, Alison, and Zimmeck, Meta (eds), *Understanding the Roots of Voluntary Action: Historical Perspectives on Current Social Policy* (Brighton: Sussex Academic Press, 2011).
Rowbotham, Sheila, *Hidden from History* (London: Pluto Press, 1990).
Rusterholz, Caroline, *Responsible Pleasure: The Brook Advisory Centres and Youth Sexuality in Postwar Britain* (Oxford: OUP, 2024).
Sandin, Bengt, 'History of children and childhood—being and becoming, dependent and independent', *The American Historical Review*, 125 (4) (2020), pp. 1306–1316.
Sasson, Tehila, Vernon, James, Ogborn, Miles, Satia, Priya, and Hall, Catherine, 'Britain and the world: a new field?', *Journal of British Studies*, 57 (2018), pp. 677–708.

Sasson, Tehila, 'Milking the Third World: humanitarianism, capitalism, and the moral economy of the Nestlé boycott', *American Historical Review*, 121 (4) (2016), pp. 1196–1224.

Savage, Mike, *Identities and Social Change in Britain: The Politics of Method* (Oxford: OUP, 2012).

Sedgman, Kirsty, *On Being Unreasonable: Why Being Bad Can Be a Force for Good* (London: Faber, 2024).

Severs, George J., *Radical Acts: HIV/AIDS Activism in Late Twentieth-Century England* (London: Bloomsbury, 2024).

Sewell, Claire, '"If one member of the family is disabled the family as a whole is disabled": Thalidomide Children and the Emergency of the Family Carer in Britain, c. 1957–1978', *Family & Community History*, 18 (1) (2015), pp. 37–52.

Sheridan, Dorothy, 'Writing to the archive: Mass Observation as autobiography', *Sociology*, 27 (1) (1993), pp. 27–40.

Shuttleworth, Sally, *The Mind of the Child: Child Development in Literature, Science, and Medicine, 1840–1900* (Oxford: OUP, 2010).

Simon, Brian, 'The 1944 Education Act: a Conservative measure?', *History of Education*, 15 (1) (1986), pp. 31–43.

Sloan, Catherine. 'Family, community, and sociability' in Heather Ellis (ed.), *A Cultural History of Education in the Age of Empire (1800–1920)* (London: Bloomsbury, 2023).

Sloan, Catherine, '"Periodicals of an objectionable character": peers and periodicals at Croydon Friends' School, 1826–1875', *Victorian Periodicals Review*, 50 (2017), pp. 769–786.

Smith, Carmel, and Greene, Sheila, (eds), *Key Thinkers in Childhood Studies* (Bristol: Policy Press, 2015).

Smith, Darren P., and Mills, Sarah, 'The "youth-fullness" of youth geographies: "coming of age"?', *Children's Geographies*, 17 (1) (2019), pp. 1–8.

Smith, Matthew, 'The hyperactive state: ADHD in historical perspective', in Ewen Speed, Joanna Moncrieff, and Mark Rapley (eds), *De-Medicalizing Misery II: Society, Politics and the Mental Health Industry* (Basingstoke: Palgrave Macmillan, 2014), pp. 89–104.

Somerville, Jennifer, 'The New Right and family politics', *Economy and Society*, 21 (1992), pp. 93–128.

Staats, Hans, '"Tag…You're It": Cold War comics and the performance of boyhood and criminality', in Monica Flegel and Christopher Parkes (eds), *Cruel Children in Popular Texts and Cultures* (London: Palgrave Macmillan, 2018), pp. 173–191.

Stargardt, Nicholas, 'German childhoods: the making of a historiography', *German History*, 16 (1) (1998), pp. 1–15.

Steedman, Carolyn, 'State-sponsored Autobiography', in B. E. Conekin, F. Mort, and C. Waters (eds), *Moments of Modernity? Reconstructing Britain, 1945–64* (London: River Oram Press, 1999).

Summerfield, Penny, 'Mass-Observation: social research or social movement?', *Journal of Contemporary History*, 20, 1985, pp. 439–452.

Sutcliffe-Braithwaite, Florence, *Class, Politics, and the Decline of Deference in England, 1968–2000* (Oxford: OUP, 2018).

Sutherland, Gillian *Ability, Merit and Measurement: Mental Testing and English Education, 1880–1940* (Oxford: OUP, 1984).

Sutherland, Gillian, and Sharp, Stephen, '"The Fust Official Psychologist in the Wurrld": Aspects of the professionalisation of psychology in early twentieth century Britain', *History of Science*, 18 (1980), pp. 181–208.

Tait, Lynda, and Lester, Helen, 'Encouraging user involvement in mental health services', *Advances in Psychiatric Treatment*, 11 (2005), pp. 168–175.

Thane, Pat, 'Family life and "normality" in postwar British culture', in Richard Bessel and Dirk Schumann (eds), *Life After Death. Approaches to a Cultural and Social History of Europe during the 1940s and 1950s* (Cambridge, 2003), pp. 193–210.

Thane, Pat, *Unequal Britain: Equalities in Britain since 1954* (London: Continuum, 2010).

Thane, Pat and Evans, Tanya, *Sinners? Scroungers? Saints?: Unmarried Motherhood in Twentieth-Century England* (Oxford: OUP, 2012).

Thomas, Lynn M., 'Historicising agency', *Gender & History*, 28 (2) (2016), pp. 324–339.
Thomlinson, Natalie, "Race and discomposure in oral histories with white feminist activists," *Oral History*, 42 (1) (2014), pp. 84–94.
Thomlinson, Natalie, *Race, Ethnicity, and the Women's Movement in England, 1968–1993* (Basingstoke: Palgrave, 2016).
Thomson, Mathew, *Lost Freedom: The Landscape of the Child and the British Post-war Settlement* (Oxford: OUP, 2013).
Thomson, Mathew, *The Problem of Mental Deficiency: Eugenics, Democracy, and Social Policy in Britain, c. 1870–1959* (Oxford: OUP, 1998).
Thomson, Mathew, *Psychological Subjects: Identity, Culture, and Health in Twentieth-Century Britain* (Oxford: OUP, 2006).
Tisdall, Laura, *A Progressive Education? How Childhood Changed in Mid-twentieth-century* (Manchester: MUP, 2020).
Tisdall, Laura, 'State of the Field: the modern history of childhood', *History*, 107 (378) (2022), pp. 949–964.
Tisdall, Laura, '"That was what life in Bridgeburn had made her": reading the autobiographies of children in institutional care in England, 1918-1946', *Twentieth Century British History*, 24 (2013), pp. 351–75.
Titmuss, R. M., *Problems of Social Policy* (London: Ministry of Health, 1950).
Tomlinson, Sally, 'New Labour and education', *Children & Society*, 17 (3) (2006), pp. 195–204.
Tomlinson, Sally, 'Race, ethnicity and education under New Labour', *Oxford Review of Education*, 31 (21) (2005), pp. 153–171.
Tömmel, Ingeborg and Verdun, Amy, 'Political leadership in the European Union: an introduction', *Journal of European Integration*, 39 (2) (2017), pp. 103–112.
Twells, Alison, *The Civilising Mission and the English Middle Class, 1792–1850: The 'Heathen' at Home and Overseas* (Basingstoke: Palgrave, 2009).
Uprichard, Emma, 'Children as "Being and Becomings": children, childhood and temporality', *Children & Society*, 22 (4) (2008), pp. 303–313.
van Der Waal, Jeroen, de Koster, Willem, and van Oorschot, Wim, 'Three worlds of welfare chauvinism? How welfare regimes affect support for distributing welfare to immigrants in Europe', *Journal of Comparative Policy Analysis: Research and Practice*, 15 (2) (2013).
Walker, Anders, *The Ghost of Jim Crow: How Southern Moderates used Brown v. Board of Education to Stall the Civil Rights Movement* (Oxford: OUP, 2009).
Wallace, R. G., 'The aims and authorship of the 1944 Education Act', *History of Education*, 4 (1981), pp. 283–290.
Warner, Marina, 'Introductory', in Iona and Peter Opie (eds), *The Lore and Language of Schoolchildren* (New York: New York Review of Books, 2001).
Waters, Rob, *Thinking Black: Britain, 1964–1985* (California: University of California Press, 2019).
Wells, Karen, *Childhood in a Global Perspective* (Third edition, Cambridge: Polity, 2021).
Welshman, John, *Underclass. A History of the Excluded, 1880–2000* (London: Bloomsbury, 2006).
Werner, Michael and Zimmermann, Bénédicte, 'Beyond comparison: Histoire croisée and the challenge of reflexivity', *History and Theory*, 45 (1) (2006), pp. 30–50.
Wiles, Janine, 'Health geographies 1: Unlearning privilege', *Progress in Human Geography*, 46 (1) (2021), pp. 215–223.
Wooldridge, Adrian, *Measuring the Mind: Education and Psychology in England, c. 1860–1990* (Cambridge: CUP, 1994).
Worth, Eve, *The Welfare State Generation: Women, Agency and Class in Britain since 1945* (London: Bloomsbury, 2021).
Worth, Eve and Reeves, Aaron, '"I am almost the middle-class white man, aren't I?": elite women, education and occupational trajectories in late twentieth-century Britain', *Contemporary British History*, 38 (1) (2023), pp. 71-94.
Worth, Eve, Reeves, Aaron, and Friedman, Sam, 'Is there an old girls' network? Girls' schools and recruitment to the British elite', *British Journal of Sociology of Education*, 44 (1) (2023), pp. 1–25.

Wright, Susannah, 'Creating liberal-internationalist world citizens: League of Nations Union junior branches in English secondary schools, 1919–1939', *Paedagogica Historica*, 56 (3) (2020), pp. 321–340.

Yang, K., 'Southeast Asian American children: not the "model minority"', *The Future of Children*, 14 (2) (2004), pp. 127–133.

Yeandle, Peter, *Citizenship, Nation, Empire: The Politics of History Teaching in England, 1870–1930* (Manchester: MUP, 2015).

Index

Since the index has been created to work across multiple formats, indexed terms for which a page range is given (e.g., 52–53, 66–70, etc.) may occasionally appear only on some, but not all of the pages within the range.

Please note that, as many Deaf and neurodivergent people (including children) do not regard themselves as disabled, Deaf children and neurodivergent children each have their own headings, rather than being nested under 'children, disabled'. Similarly, comparisons made by parents of gifted children between their own parenting struggles and those of parents with disabled children can be found under 'parents, disabled children, gifted children compared to', because such parents often did not have a specific disability in mind, but were rather referring to a generic, monolithic imaginary.

Ambrose, Don 174–5
astrology 112

Banks, Charlotte 111
Bitan, Dan 165
Blair, Tony *see also* New Labour 32–3, 140–1
Blake, Doron 150–2
Brackenbury, Antony 75–6
Branch, Margaret 20–1, 53–5, 63–8, 176
    letters 56
    NAGC, fulltime work for 79–80
    resignation 67
Brentwood Experiment, the 32, 54–62, 65, 73, 76–7, 104 n.151
Bridges, Sydney A. 58–61
British decline (national and imperial) *see also* children, gifted, 'elites of the future' 114, 118–19, 129–31, 134
Broomand, Iraj 166, 168–9, 173–4
Bulgaria 171–3, 186
Burt, Cyril 32, 110–14, 130–1, 195–6
    The Gifted Child 111, 115
Butler, Nicolas Murray 48

CEDAR *see* universities, Warwick
census data 144 n.58
Child Benefit 137–8
children, Deaf 104–5, 182–3
children, disabled *see also* children, Deaf; children, neurodivergent
    campaigners and charities 7–8, 69–70
    children, disabled *see* parents, disabled children, gifted children compared to
    education of ('ineducable') 36–7, 69, 195–6
    learning disabilities 135–6
    Mental Deficiency Act (1913) 110

children, gifted
    adults *see* intelligence, 'gifted child alumni'
    book reviews 127–8
    'childlikeness' 96–8, 105–6
    climate change, attitudes to 17 n.61, 148
    competitiveness 97–9, 105–6
    definitions of *see also* intelligence; testing 5–9, 89–90, 113–14
    education of *see* education
    'elites of the future' 16–21
        economic and corporate 49, 111–12, 119, 128, 144–5, 148–9, 155, 163–4
        humanitarian (cultural internationalism, war, poverty) 51, 125–8, 148, 157–8, 163, 182
        political 1–3, 8–9, 13–14, 38–9, 42–3, 49–50, 108, 111–12, 118–19, 129, 148–50
        military 111–12, 118–19
        scientific, medical, technological 51, 61, 75, 118–19, 128, 144–6, 163–4
    female 2, 8–9, 33, 97–8, 173, 176
    friendship 16, 44–5, 79, 85–94, 105–6, 146–8
        penpals 79, 85, 125–6, 184–5
    gender (mixing, roles) 60, 72, 168–9
    intelligence, notions of *see also* intelligence 1, 4, 27–31, 43–4
    interests
        art 144
        chess 93, 182
        cooking 93
        economics 93–4
        geology (mineralogy, fossil-hunting) 93
        languages 50–1, 125–6, 144, 152–3, 161–2, 182
        law 118–19

children, gifted (*cont.*)
  literature and creative writing 93, 144, 150–3
  medicine (human, veterinary) 118–19, 144
  music 57–8, 71, 73–4, 93, 118–19, 150–1
  philosophy 93–4
  photography 93–4, 144
  politics 93–4
  science, technology, engineering and maths (STEM) 50–1, 93, 115, 125, 144–52
  isolation
    boredom 90 n.65, 94, 105, 150–1, 192–3
    bullying 154, 195
    loneliness (misery, social difference) 44–5, 48, 59–60, 79, 105, 128–9, 155, 161
  minoritized ethnic backgrounds *see also* intelligence, stereotypes and biases 2, 8–9, 33, 53 n.100, 72, 83
  National Association for Gifted Children *see* NAGC
  parents *see* parents
  poetry 44–6, 100–2, 105, 126–9, 157, 182–3
  play 31, 43–6, 60–1
  racism of 127
  rebellion and resistance
    active *see also* testing, IQ, objections to 28, 80–1, 98–103, 151–2, 189–95
    expectations ('elites of the future') 1–2, 98–103, 148–9
    label ('gifted') 1–2, 11–12, 98–103, 132–3
    passive 33–4, 98–103, 189–95
  stereotypes *see* intelligence, stereotypes and biases
  teachers, relationship with 103–6
  'wastage' 1, 38–9, 46–8, 64–7, 72, 109, 115–16
  working-class 2, 50–1, 72–4
    attempts to identify (failed) 46, 59, 82–4, 121–2, 143, 177
    Pauper Pedigree Project 110–11
    'unexpected' 116–17, 130
children, neurodivergent
  autism 14–16
  dyslexia 12 n.45, 104, 153
Churchill, Winston 36–7
Coker, Henry 172
Cold War, the 1–3, 158–9
  nuclear war, threat of 50–1, 126–7
  space race 50–1, 53–4
  Soviet Union *see* Soviet Union
Collis, Henry 79–80, 87–8, 159–63, 165–7, 170–1
Congdon, Peter 123–4
COVID-19 pandemic 138 n.30
Crawford, Agnes 83–4
crime *see* juvenile delinquency
Crosland, Anthony 70–1

du Parc Braham 162–4
DuPont DeBie, Alexis 165–8

Earl of Roseberry 36 n.3
education *see also* schools; teachers
  'demand' 16
  extracurricular (informal) *see* NAGC, activities
  funding 56, 61, 65–6
  higher *see* universities
  home schooling 7–8, 88–9, 117–18, 143–4
  Inspectors of (Ofsted) 79–80, 123–4, 134–6, 140–1
  mainstream *see* schools
  National Records of Achievement *see* New Labour, National Records of Achievement
  policy and policy documents
    Education Act (1944) 5 n.12, 7–8, 36–7, 46, 57–8, 66, 77
    Education Act (1981) 88–9
    Educational Maintenance Allowance 140
    Education (Handicapped Children) Act (1970) 7–8, 37 n.7
    Education (Scotland) Act (1945) 36–7, 58
    Excellence in Cities 141–2
    Excellence in Schools 140–1
    Plowden Report, the 70–1
  subjects and disciplines *see* children, gifted, interests
  testing *see* intelligence, testing
equality and elitism
  definitions of *see also* intelligence, testing 2–3, 35–7, 119–21, 164, 188
  equal opportunities 36–7, 131–3, 160, 185, 189–91
eugenics *see also* intelligence, stereotypes and biases 13–14, 42–3, 47–8
  nationalist ('good'/'national stock') 109–12, 130–1
  organisations 47 n.68, 110–11
  proponents of *see* Burt; Eysenck; Galton; Graham; Terman
  Repository of Germinal Choice 150–1
  sterilization 54
European Council for High Ability (ECHA) 14, 31–3, 173–4
  children, gifted, working with 157–8, 175, 182, 187, 196–7
  conferences 178–82
  establishment 159–60, 175–7
  'Europe', definitions of 177–81, 186
  publications
    European Journal for High Ability 177–80
    High Ability Studies 177–8

extrasensory perception 112
Eyre, Deborah 143–4
Eysenck, Hans 112–14

France 51–2, 179–80
Freeman, Joan 159–60, 176–81
Fryd, Judy 7–8

Gallagher, James J. 50–3, 173
Galton, Francis 110
George, David 170
German Democratic Republic 179–80
Ghana 172 n.81
Gifted Children's Information Centre 123–4
Gifted Entrepreneurs Programme 145
giftedness *see* children, gifted; intelligence
Gillie, Oliver 113–14
Gilroy, Beryl 6–7
Goldman Sachs Foundation 144–5
Graham, Robert 150–1

Hatch, John 163–4
Health and Cleanliness Council 42–3
Hearnshaw, Leslie 113–14
Hechinger, Fred M. 51
Heller, Kurt A. 178–9
homosexuality, conservative fears of 119–20
Hong Kong 173–4
Horizon 59–62, 66–7, 86–7
Howard MP, Michael 136–8
Hungary 180–1, 184

Illingworth, Ronald 122–3
Institute of Race Relations 117–18
intelligence *see also* stupidity
  assessing *see* testing
  children's attitudes to *see* children, gifted, intelligence, notions of
  'discovery' ('diagnosis', identification, 'rescue') *see also* intelligence, testing 41–2, 51, 82–3, 123–4, 133–4, 140–2, 153
  female ('animal cunning') 41, 43 n.47
  'gifted child alumni' (adults) *see also* Mensa, membership 40–1, 150–6
  'human' *see* eugenics
  stereotypes and biases 2–3, 6–9, 19–20, 32–3, 108–9, 113–14
    blondeness 49–50
    cruelty (emotional/psychological disturbance) 49–50, 63–4, 90 n.65, 173–4

maleness *see also* children, gifted, female 84–5, 111, 120, 189–90
middle-classness and affluence *see also* children, gifted, working-class 41, 43, 59, 84–5, 189–90
whiteness *see also* children, gifted, minoritized ethnic backgrounds 43, 43 n.47, 47–8, 53 n.100, 59, 84–5, 112–14, 117–18, 143, 189–90
International Youth Summit 183–4
Iran 166, 168–9
Isaacs, Ann 49, 51–2
Israel 165–6

Japan 170
Jung, Carl 63–4
juvenile delinquency 12, 65, 90 n.65, 112, 119, 163–4

Kamin, Leon 113–14
Kenya 172 n.81

League of Nations 126
Lord Aberdare 73–4
Lord Carrington 72–5
Lord Edward Boyle 70–2, 74
Lord James of Rusholme 71, 74–5, 106–7, 121, 162–3
Lord Kennet 74
Lyon, Harold 164–5

Major, John 32–3, 133–8
Mass Observation 31, 39–40
  Mass Observers 40–3, 85–6
  Resistance to Advertising 39–40
McDougall, William 110
Mensa 51–2
  establishment 54
  Foundation for Gifted Children 88–91, 135–6
  membership 54, 57, 153–4
'meritocracy' *see* testing
Morrison, Charles 71–2

National Academy for Gifted and Talented Youth 27, 32–3, 109, 133–4, 142–4
Aspire 132, 146–50
funding 142–5
leadership *see* Eyre, Deborah
membership 142–4
National Register for Gifted and Talented Learners 142
student council 142–3
summer schools 132, 146–8
surveys 146–8, 156

National Association for Gifted
    Children (NAGC)
  activities 26-7
    enrichment classes 59, 70-1, 83-4, 118
    Explorers Clubs ('Unlimited') 79-81, 92-6
    Moberly Saturday Club for Gifted
      Children 92-4, 98, 108
    Project Trident 125-6
    residential camps 30, 32-4, 65-6, 84-98,
      105-6, 125-6, 152, 192-3
  Annual Reports 93
  archives 9-10, 20-1
  disability, attitude to see parents, disabled
    children, gifted children compared to
  establishment 32, 56-7, 63-8, 75-6, 121-2
  fees 82
  founder see Branch, Margaret
  government grants 20-1, 79-80
  House of Lords, support for 70-5
  In with a Head Start 86-7
  IQ testing see intelligence, testing
  leadership see also Branch; Collis 83, 157
  parents, membership of see also parents 3-4,
    11-12, 40-1, 65-6, 80-1, 85-91, 154, 192-3
  publications
    Dialogue 94-5, 126-7
    Explorers Bulletin (Unlimited) 99-101,
      105-6, 126-7
    Gallimaufry 1, 79
    Help with Bright Children 5, 91, 123
    Journal of the Gifted Child 108
    newsletter (Looking to their Future) 83-4,
      96-7, 103-5, 122-9, 152-3
    Questors Ho! 100-1
National Health Service (NHS) 36-7
National Lottery 135-6
Netherlands 178-9
neoliberalism see also Thatcher 3, 14-16, 191-2
New Labour see also Blair 2, 13-14, 109,
    137, 140-1
  Educational Maintenance Allowance 140
  National Academy for Gifted and Talented
    Youth see National Academy for Gifted
    and Talented Youth
  league tables 134-5
  National Records of Achievement 19-20,
    32-3, 133-4, 136-40, 156
Newman, Elizabeth 165
newspapers and periodicals
  Aberdeen Press and Journal 58
  Aspire see National Academy for Gifted and
    Talented Youth, Aspire
  Birmingham Daily Post 38-9
  British Journal of Statistical Psychology 112-13
  Coventry Evening Telegraph 37-8
  Daily Express 82-3, 86-7, 118-19
  Daily Mail 86-7, 115-21, 135
  Daily Mirror 86-7, 119
  Daily Telegraph 67, 87-8, 160-1
  ECHA publications see ECHA, publications
  Evening Post 82-3
  Gifted Child Today 52-3
  Gifted Child Quarterly see USA, AAGC,
    Gifted Child Quarterly
  Gifted Education International 104-5
  Grimsby Evening Telegraph 138
  Guardian 63-7, 83-4, 163-4
  Los Angeles Times 173-4
  Manchester Guardian 38-9
  NAGC publications see NAGC, publications
  New York Times 48, 51
  Race Today 117-18
  Slate 150-1
  Southwark News 63
  Stapleford & Sandiacre News 37-8
  Sunday Times 89-91, 113-14, 121
  Surrey Advertiser 37-8
  Times Literary Supplement 6-7
  Times 38-9, 56, 59-67, 82-3, 88, 119-20,
    161-2, 170
  World Council for Gifted and Talented
    Children publications see WCGT,
    publications
Nigeria 172-3, 186
Nobel Prize, winners of 150-1, 162

Onyeama, Dillibe 6-7
Opie Archive, the 31, 43-6

Pardoe, John 72
parents
  'choice' 132-5
  disabled children, gifted children compared to
    ('handicap of brilliance') 25-6, 56-7,
    64-6, 68-70, 77, 87-8, 111-12, 195
  internet fora 138 n.30, 153-4, 156
  isolation (jealousy, stigma) 66-7, 85-7, 120,
    153-4, 195
  marriage, impact upon 25-6
  NAGC, membership of see NAGC, parents,
    membership of
  single parents 24-5
  sperm donation 150-1
  'traditional' (heteronormative, two-parent)
    25-6, 119-20, 164
  welfare state, perceptions of see welfare state
Passow, Harry 166-7
Patten MP, John 89-90

Persson, Roland S. 174
Philippines 168-9, 173, 182-3
Plato 67, 75
Porter, Sir George 162
Potential Plus 10-11

Reddit 138-9
Robb, George 65
Roldan, Aurora 168-9
Rose, Steven 113-14
Rowlands, Christopher 119-20
Ruegg, Camilla 63-4

schools *see also* parents, 'choice'
   Acocks Green Junior School (West Midlands) 45-6
   American *see* United States of America
   Assisted Places 90-1
   Brentwood College of Education 58-60
   Colet Court 160-1
   Columbia Teachers College 168
   comprehensive 21, 62, 65-6, 115, 124-5
   Eastbourne College Prep School 160-1
   elementary 110
   Hertfordshire and Essex Girls' High School 161-2
   home schooling *see* education, home schooling
   Eton 71-2, 116-17
   Gifted Children in Middle and Comprehensive Secondary Schools 79-80
   grammar
      admissions *see also* testing, 11+ 5-6, 32, 64-5, 71, 112-13, 140
      failures of 21, 37-9, 62, 115-18
      parental preference for 24-5, 140
   grant-maintained 134-5, 143-4
   Independent Schools Association 62
   Kirkcaldy High School (Fife) 35, 45-6
   league tables 134-5
   Manchester Grammar 71, 177
   private (independent) 5-6, 41-2, 88-91, 110, 143-4
   Sale County Grammar School for Boys 44-6
   Sandroyd 73
   secondary modern 5-6, 152-3
   selective 2-3, 58, 65, 74, 112-13, 134-5
   Singaporean 119-20
   Soviet *see also* Soviet Union 51, 119-20, 171
   special needs 6-7, 110, 114
   teachers *see* teachers
   Westminster School 59-60
   Winchester 71

Yehudi Menuhin School (Surrey) 58-61, 73-6, 162-3
Sieghart, Felicity Ann 159-62, 164-5, 169-70
Sisk, Dorothy 165, 168
smoking 112
social democracy *see also* neoliberalism 3, 46-7, 74
South Korea 173, 182-3
Soviet Union, the 50-1, 126-7, 157-8, 170, 179, 184-6
Span, Pieter 177-8
Stop the Eleven Plus 124-5
'stupidity'
   appearance ('lacking signs of intelligence') 42-3
   children's attitudes to ('saps', 'mugs') 35, 45-6
   notions of 39-40, 75, 122
   popular culture, banality of 41
Switzerland 179-80

Taiwan 173
teachers 6-7, 9-10, 53 n.100
   National Association of School Masters 117 n.54
   National Union of Teachers (NUT) 7 n.19, 57-8, 113-14, 117 n.54
   pupils *see* children, gifted, teachers, relationship with
   testing, objections to 137-8
Terman, Lewis 49, 115
   Genetic Study of Genius 47-8
testing 43-4, 114, 123
   11+ 5-6, 36-7, 58, 73, 112-13, 124-5, 152-3
   Stop the Eleven Plus 124-5
   fictional 49-50
   IQ tests
      biases of 5-6, 112-14, 123-4, 143, 174, 188
      'high' 47, 59, 61, 63-4, 111-12, 122, 150-1
      'low' 7-8
      objections to (arbitrariness, lack of correlation) 100-1, 121-2, 151-2, 154, 188, 196
   psychological *see also* eugenics 110, 122, 176
   scholarship exams 41-2
Thatcher, Margaret
   election 14-16, 23-4, 114
   neoliberalism *see* neoliberalism
   Thatcherism *see also* neoliberalism 83-4, 191-2
   resignation 134-5, 137-8
trans, intersex and non-binary people 63-4
Turner, Graham 119-20
twins 113-14

United Nations Relief and Rehabilitation
    Administration (UNRRA) 63–4
United States of America 46–54
  **American Association for Gifted Children
    (AAGC)** 49
  Gifted Child Quarterly 51–2, 170
  Gifted Children's Pen Pals
    International 184
  Civil Rights Movement, the 52–3
  National Defense Education
    Act (1958) 50–1
  Office of Gifted and Talented 164–5, 168
universities
  admissions, expansion of 140–1
  Cambridge 71–2, 152, 160–1
  Christ Church College Canterbury 146
  Durham 146
  Exeter 146
  Imperial College London 146
  Jönköping 174
  Lagos 172 n.81
  Lancaster 146, 176
  Liverpool 83–4, 110–11
  Manchester 176
  Open 88
  Oxford 71–2, 110, 161–2
  Princeton 113–14
  Rider 174
  South Florida 168
  Stanford 115 n.40
  University College London 111–12
  Utrecht 177
  Warwick 123–4, 146
  York 71, 146

Vorbeck, Michael 178–9

welfare state, the *see also* NHS
  affection for 137–8
  campaigning, use of 54–5
  failure, parents' perception of 14–20,
    85–6, 189–95
  universalism, limits of 3–4, 13–17, 69
  'welfare state generation', the 2, 27, 29 n.103
Williams, Philip 61–2, 88
Witty, Paul 49
Women's Liberation Movement 120–1
Working Party on Gifted Children 58–9
**World Council for Gifted and Talented
    Children**
  Assembly of Delegates 167
  children, gifted, working with 1–2, 14, 31,
    157–8, 187, 196–7
  conferences
    biannual 166, , 168–72, 185
    World Conference for Gifted Children 74,
      157, 160–2
  establishment 32–3, 157–65
  language barriers (English, dominance of)
    167–9, 175, 182, 186
  publications
    *Gifted Children: Looking to Their
      Future* 164
    *Gifted (and Talented)
      International* 166–7, 174
    newsletter (*World Gifted*) 58–9, 157–8,
      166–9, 171–2, 182–3
  membership 165–7
  'world', definitions of 169–75, 186